Christian Circulations

Christian Circulations

Global Christianity and the Local Church in Penang and Singapore, 1819–2000

Jean DeBernardi

NUS PRESS
SINGAPORE

Published by:

NUS Press
National University of Singapore
AS3-01-02, 3 Arts Link
Singapore 117569

Fax: (65) 6774-0652
E-mail: nusbooks@nus.edu.sg
Website: http://nuspress.nus.edu.sg

ISBN 978-981-325-109-0 (paper)

National Library Board, Singapore Cataloguing in Publication Data

Name (s): DeBernardi, Jean Elizabeth.
Title: Christian circulations: global Christianity and the local church in Penang and Singapore, 1819–2000 / Jean DeBernardi.
Description: Singapore: NUS Press, [2020] | Includes bibliographic references and index.
Identifiers: OCN 1119376164 | ISBN 978-981-32-5109-0 (paperback)
Subjects: LCSH: Brethren churches--Malaysia--Pulau Pinang (State)--History. | Brethren churches--Singapore--History. | Independent churches--Malaysia--Pulau Pinang (State)--History. | Independent churches--Singapore--History.
Classification: DDC 286.509595--dc23

Cover image: Teh Phai Lian and his family at the Burmah Road Gospel Hall, c. 1945. Photograph courtesy of Ch'ng Oon Hooi and Radiance Chuang.

Typeset by: Ogma Solutions Pvt Ltd
Printed by: Mainland Press Pte Ltd

Contents

List of Illustrations

Preface

In 1979, I employed as my Hokkien teacher and research assistant a Chinese Malaysian Christian. Over the next 18 months she assisted me in my doctoral research on Chinese popular religious culture but also introduced me into her family and church network. Ch'ng Oon Hooi's great-uncle had founded and led the Charismatic Church of Penang, which then met in a two-storey colonial bungalow on Northam Road, opposite a grand seaside mansion owned by Malay royalty. Her mother lived with her uncle and aunt, and Shirley (her English name), together with her younger sister and one brother, had grown up in this house church.

Shirley had attended the Methodist Girls' School and could translate with ease between English, Mandarin, and Hokkien. I guessed that she had developed her linguistic skills at their church services, which were bilingual in Mandarin and Hokkien, involving constant translation between the two languages. She could read the Bible in Chinese and was well versed in what Hokkien-speakers call deep Hokkien, the Southern Min reading pronunciation of Chinese characters. She had even learned Greek, at least enough to consult a Greek dictionary on her great-uncle's behalf when he researched and wrote tracts defending his interpretation of charisma.

Her sisters and brothers attended this small house church, and I sometimes joined them at their Sunday service and the family meal that their mother prepared afterwards. When a church member translated a book that Teh Phai Lian had written in the 1950s, Elder Teh invited me to contribute a preface. As a lapsed Catholic with reservations about Christianity, I was reluctant, but as I read *Ancient Chinese Stories with a Modern Message* I found the parallels that he drew between Chinese historical tales, the Bible, and *Pilgrim's Progress* to be fascinating. Although I do not list it on my curriculum vitae, I count that preface as my first professional publication.

As I was leaving Penang in 1981, my notebooks filled with details on spirit mediums and festivals, I regretted that I had not learned more about the Charismatic Church of Penang. In 1993 I conducted a research project funded by the Canada ASEAN Centre focusing on policies of multiculturalism/multiracialism in Singapore, Malaysia, and Thailand. In a region in which religious identity is often closely bound up with ethnic identity, I found the small minority of Christians to be an intriguing anomaly. I approached Shirley's uncle, Teh Chiew Oo, for his permission to study the church. He agreed, with the provision that I not write about their family, a request that I have sought to respect in this study.

In 1995 I conducted a pilot study for a broadly conceived research project on "Chinese Christian Syncretism in Singapore and Penang, Malaysia". My first attempt to obtain funding from the Social Science and Humanities Research Council of Canada failed in the face of a reviewer who suspected that I was an evangelical Christian using this research to promote a personal agenda. I reapplied, and in my revised proposal affirmed my commitment to secular humanism. This time I won research grants from SSHRC and the Wenner-Gren Foundation for Anthropological Research. In 2004 I accepted an invitation from Dr Lai Ah Eng to continue my research on Christianity, with funding from the Singapore Institute of Policy Studies, as part of a larger project on "Religious Diversity and Harmony in Singapore", which culminated in an intercultural dialogue, a 2005 conference, and an edited volume (Lai 2005, 2008).

Between 1995 and 2004, I conducted formal interviews with Singaporean Christian leaders from a wide range of denominational and independent churches and parachurch groups, including Anglican, Assembly of God, Full Gospel Assembly, and Methodist churches; Bartley Christian Church; the Church of Singapore; the Wilkie Terrace Christian Assembly; the Asia Evangelistic Fellowship; the Bible Society of Singapore; Eagles Communications; Touch Community Services; and the Far East Broadcasting Corporation. I also attended missionary training courses, including a Mandarin course whose students comprised Singaporean doctors and nurses who planned to do medical missions in China, a night class on missions at the Church of Singapore, and classes at the Asia Crosscultural Training Institute at Bethesda Pasir Ris. I attended special events, including rallies at Singapore's Indoor Stadium, as well as regular Sunday services (see DeBernardi 1999, 2005, 2008a, 2008b, 2009a).

At church services and prayer meetings I heard remarkable stories of Christian outreach in China and elsewhere in Southeast Asia. The speakers usually agreed to be interviewed but were concerned that I maintain confidentiality. The topic is sensitive, especially when it concerns evangelical outreach in China, where local officials often tolerate Christians, but are sometimes called on to suppress their activities or even arrest members of unregistered house churches. Short-term mission trips of one or two weeks are common, and I was invited on trips to China, nearby islands in Indonesia, and Burma. With regret, I declined to join them, fearing that my presence with a group of Asian Christians might raise the suspicion that I was a missionary and put them at risk, especially in Indonesia, where widespread anti-Chinese and anti-Christian violence in 1997 had led many to flee their homes.

During a five-month period of ethnographic research in Singapore in 1999, I focused on the Brethren movement and churches that "came out of" the Brethren movement. On my arrival in Singapore, I sent a formal proposal to the Brethren Networking Fellowship in Singapore informing them of my research plans. While I waited for a response from them, I began my research with Bethesda Hall (Ang Mo Kio), which is regarded as the most conservative of the Singaporean assemblies and whose leadership had decided to remain independent of the network.

Members of the Brethren Networking Fellowship discussed my proposal at one of their meetings, but they took it for their information only (they are, after all, only a network of independent assemblies). After I heard informal confirmation that no one had objected to my plans, I visited assemblies and interviewed elders and full-time workers. I also conducted participant-observation research at many Brethren events, including regular Sunday services, a special service for female Philippine guest workers, Bible study classes, prayer meetings, baptisms, evangelistic outreach events, and Bible study meetings. In 1999, I attended the Brethren Missions Conference in Petaling Jaya, Malaysia, which gave me the opportunity to interact with a number of Brethren missionaries and evangelists.

When individuals move from one Christian denomination or network to another, both sides often chose to forget the other. Although the temporal range may be limited to 50 or so years, the method of oral history is one way to seek to recover the unwritten and largely forgotten past. In Singapore, Kuala Lumpur, Penang, and Taiping, I interviewed elders and church members on their memories of the 1963 and 1983 divisions that resulted in the founding of new independent churches, including the Charismatic Church of Penang, the Church of Singapore, and Full Gospel churches. I also interviewed Brethren elders who rejected the charismatic movement, including Dr Peter Wee, an elder at Bethesda Hall, and Harold Cooke, an elder at the Jalan Imbi Chapel in Kuala Lumpur.

On visits to Penang, I have continued to join my friends at events at the Charismatic Church of Penang. My former research assistant Ch'ng Oon Hooi became a full-time worker at the church, and her daughter, Radiance Chuang, who was an infant when her mother and I first started meeting for Hokkien tutorials in Ayer Itam, is now a college graduate and works at the church. I conducted formal interviews with members of the Charismatic Church of Penang (CCOP) and the Full Gospel Assembly, and Shirley shared copies of Teh Phai Lian's books and tracts with me.

I began the archival research for this study in 1999 at Bethesda Hall, which as the oldest assembly in Singapore, holds the original *Assembly Record Book* (1865–1934). I continued that historical research in Kuala Lumpur, where I was aided by Mr Harold Cooke of Kuala Lumpur, a Brethren elder whose extensive private collection of books, commemorative volumes, and personal files on the charismatic movement provided valuable resources for this study.

Between 2000 and 2006, I made three trips to England. In 2000, I visited the School of Oriental and African Studies Christian archives to consult the London Missionary Society archive. I also visited the Echoes of Service offices in Bath, where the staff generously allowed me to explore their library resources and correspondence files and to monopolize their photocopy machine for weeks. I discovered that their large archive of published missionary letters offered ongoing diaries of the activities and experiences of European and Asian Christians spanning decades and generations.

In 2004, Mr K.C. Ung of the Penang Burmah Road Gospel Hall allowed me to make photocopies of their early marriage records and he and Ooi Bok Kim took me to see the old Brethren Mission House on Farquhar Street. I guessed that it stood on the site where the London Missionary Society mission once stood, and realized that I had many questions about the almost 30-year period between the end of the London Missionary Society and the arrival of the first Brethren missionary. Seeking to answer those questions, I returned to England in 2005 to conduct an additional period of archival research at the School of Oriental and African Studies, the University of Manchester's John Rylands Christian Brethren collection (where most of the materials that I consulted at Echoes of Service have now been shifted), Müller House (Bristol), and Echoes of Service (Bath), where Joan Hookins helped me to explore their photographic archive. In 2006 I returned for a final period of research at the British Library, University of Birmingham, and Cambridge University's Bible Society Archive.

Acknowledgements

The Social Science Research Council of Canada and the Wenner-Gren Foundation for Anthropological Research provided funding for a research programme on "Chinese Christian Syncretism in Singapore and Penang, Malaysia" from 1997 to 2002. I conducted interviews with Christian leaders in Singapore in 2004 and 2005 as a researcher in a collaborative project on "Religious Diversity and Harmony in Singapore" with support from the Institute of Policy Studies in Singapore. At the University of Alberta, the Office of the Vice-President (Research) and the Faculty of Arts supported a 1995 pilot study for this programme of research and also archival research in England in 2005 and 2006. The ethnographic research was done with ethics approval from the Faculty of Arts at the University of Alberta.

Although most of this monograph has not been previously published, in my discussion of the Million Testament Fund, I draw on "Moses' Rod: The Bible as a Commodity in Southeast Asia and China" (2011). I summarize some of my conclusions in "The Brethren Movement and Evangelical Christianity in Singapore and Penang, Malaysia" (2015) and "Emplacing a Network Religion in a World in Motion: Evangelical Christianity and the Brethren Movement in Penang" (2017). I have presented earlier versions of sections of this monograph at a number of academic conferences and workshops, and thanks are due to organizers Daniel Bays, Wen-Chin Chang, Josh deWind, Neil Dickson, Jenna M. Gibbs, Rosalind Hackett, Julia Huang, Sünne Juterczenka, Lai Ah Eng, John Leavitt, Ivo Strecker, Eric Tagliacozzo, Robert Weller, and Manuel Vasquez, for including me in these events and for their helpful comments.

For assistance in archival research, I thank Graham Johnson and Jessica Smith (John Rylands Christian Brethren archive), Rosemary Mathew (Bible Society archive, Cambridge University), and the staffs of the Special Collections Reading Room at the School of Oriental and African Studies Library and of the University of Birmingham Special Collections Department. For his assistance in sorting out details concerning the independent missionaries of the mid-19th century, I am grateful to Gary Tiedemann.

Gordon Drever's and Dr Stephen Kent's special collections at the University of Alberta on new religious movements provided valuable resources as I sought to broaden my familiarity with the North American Pentecostalism of the 1950s and 1960s and Kong Duen Yee's New Testament Church. When I contacted the New Testament Church Grace of Jesus Christ Crusade in Taiwan to ask for help in this research, they mailed me copies of Kong Duen Yee's publications, including a compilation of letters she sent to the churches formed in Singapore and Malaysia after her crusade (Kong 1978a). Members also offered personal insights when I visited them at "Eden Homestead" on Mount Zion in Taiwan in 2008 (see DeBernardi 2009a). The University of Alberta's inter-library loan service gave me access to 20th-century Chinese Christian publications that gave new perspectives on the postwar schisms in Penang and Singapore. For this service, I thank both the library and the lending libraries that were willing to share these rare publications.

I also did research in digital archives of the Christian and Missionary Alliance (C&MA) and the Living Stream Ministry in Anaheim, California, which has extensively documented the history of Watchman Nee's local church movement. For information about issues of the *Shengjing Bao* held by the Christian and Missionary Alliance National Archives in Colorado Springs, I thank Managing Archivist Kristin Rollins.

Many individuals shared recollections, observations, information, manuscripts, and publications with me, including Prof. Freddie Boey, Michael Browne, Rev. Dr. Simon Chan, Dr. Ernest Chew, Radiance Wee Nuan Chuang, Elena Cooke, Harold Cooke, Dr. Violet James, Goh Ewe Kheng, Dr. Bobby Sng, C.S. Song, whom I interviewed in Berkeley when I was beginning this programme of research, Dr Peter Wee, Patrick Wee, and members of the Wilkie Terrace Christian Assembly and the Charismatic Church of Penang. I also have learned a great deal from Shirley (Ch'ng Oon Hooi) in casual conversations over the years. Although I draw on insights gained from these conversations, I regard these as personal confidences and have never recorded the details in my notes. But periodically I have taken out an audio recorder and asked her to tell me what exactly she wishes to put on record. I am grateful to her for her willingness to share her insider's perspective with me.

Klaus Fiedler, Tim Grass, Timothy Stunt, and Neil Summerton generously responded to emailed queries, and Neil Dickson offered detailed comments and valuable advice on the manuscript and tracked down sources on my behalf. I also thank Samuel Lee of Living Stream Ministry and Shu-chen Hsu Hsiung for helping me to better understand Charles Lee's background, and Rev. George Chu for sharing information about the history of *Steering* magazine. In 2019,

Pastor Lim Poh Teong at the Charismatic Church of Penang and librarian Chan Tock Seng (Lydia) allowed me to take inventory of the Chinese books in their library, most of which had belonged to their founder Teh Phai Lian, and Radiance Chuang and Shirley Ch'ng helped me locate and organize them.

In 2006 the Burmah Road Gospel Hall published on its website a paper I had written on the history of the Mission House in Penang (see DeBernardi 2017). Unexpectedly, I received emails from the descendants of many of the early missionaries, including Daniel Bausum, Jeff Gawthorne, James Hudson Taylor III, whom I later met in Hong Kong, Alexander Grant's descendants Ann Anderson and Hazel Andrews, who sent me copies of Lucy Lovitt's unpublished letters and poems (Lovitt 1904), and William Macdonald's descendant Carol Smith. Many of these individuals had done research on their family histories, which they generously shared.

As a lapsed Catholic and a non-Christian, I have had few advantages in my study of the Brethren movement. But one biographical detail sometimes opened doors for me. My mother's father was descended from Cornelius Waldo (1624–1700), who had emigrated from England to Ipswich, Massachusetts around 1647. Family tradition ascribes the origin of the Waldo family to Peter Waldo, the founder of the Waldensian movement in Lyons, France (Lincoln 1902: ii). When I mentioned this to the British Brethren elders in the Manvers Gospel Hall whom I visited in Bath, they joined together and made a gift to me of E.H. Broadbent's 1931 book *The Pilgrim Church: Tracing the Pathway of the Forgotten Saints from Pentecost to the Twentieth Century*, a gift that I greatly appreciate.

For permission to reprint illustrations from their magazines and archives, I thank Echoes of Service in Bath, England, now Echoes International. The "Map of India and Languages Spoken, 1822" is reprinted with permission of Center for Study of the Life and Work of William Carey, D.D. (1761–1834), William Carey University, 710 William Carey Parkway, Hattiesburg, Mississippi, 39401 USA. The lithograph of Karl Friedrich August ('Charles') Gützlaff, wearing Fujian dress by Richard James Lane, after George Chinnery, published 1835 was published under non-commercial academic licence from the National Portrait Gallery, London. The postcard portrait of Leland Wang is used courtesy of the Billy Graham Center Archives, Wheaton College, Illinois. The photograph of Leland Wang in Shanghai is from the FEBC International Archive, an online catalogue of digital images. Finally, I thank the Church Board of the Church of Singapore for consenting to reprint the diagram of their Charismatic Local Church network posted on their website, and to Jasmine Ho, Church Administrator, for arranging that consent.

Thanks are also due to the manuscript's reviewers, Murray Rubinstein and Jerry Dennerline, for their thoughtful detailed comments and recommendations, to Peter Schoppert and Paul Kratoska at the NUS Press for their patience while I revised a manuscript that I could not call done while the research was still leading me down new and unexpected paths, to Lena Qua and Wee Wong for their editorial work in preparing the manuscript for publication, and to Tan Li Kheng for preparing the map of Asia. Last but not least, I thank the staff of the Echoes of Service Office, who helped me access their library collection and correspondence files; Joan Hookins, who took time from her busy schedule to scan missionary postcards and illustrations for this manuscript; and John Aitken, the General Director of Echoes International for reviewing the manuscript and extending permission to use materials from their archival collection. The limitations of this study rest entirely with the author.

Map of Asia.This map identifies locations named in this monograph by both modern and older names.

Chronology

1706	Protestant mission established at the Danish East India Company colony at Tranquebar
1786	Captain Francis Light established George Town on Penang Island on behalf of the British East India Company (EIC)
1795	London Missionary Society (LMS) founded
1803–15	Napoleonic Wars
1804	British and Foreign Bible Society founded
1811	Thomas Stamford Raffles leads British invasion of Java, is appointed Lieutenant Governor of the Dutch East Indies
1813	Charter Act; British Crown asserts sovereignty over territories controlled by the British East India Company, opening them to Protestant missionaries
1814	Anglo-Dutch Treaty; Java returned to Netherlands; LMS sends missionaries to Batavia
1818	Anglo Chinese College launched, Malacca
1819	Raffles established a trading post on Singapore Island on behalf of the EIC; LMS missions launched in Penang and Singapore
1826	Straits Settlements formed (Penang, Singapore, and Malacca)
1834	Scriptural Knowledge Institution for Home and Abroad founded, Bristol
1834	Society for the Propagation of Female Education in China, India and the East (Female Education Society) founded
1839–42	First Opium War; Treaty of Nanking opens treaty ports to European residence
1850–64	Taiping Rebellion
1850	Chinese Evangelization Society founded
1856–60	Second Opium War; Treaty of Tientsin
1857	Worldwide commercial crisis sparks the Second Evangelical Awakening

1861–74	Larut Wars; Pangkor Treaty results in the creation of a British Residency in Perak
1865	China Inland Mission founded
1867	Straits Settlements (Penang, Malacca, Singapore, and Dindings) became a British Crown Colony reporting directly to London
1872–	*The Missionary Echo* commences publication; renamed *Echoes of Service* in 1885
1888	Christian and Missionary Alliance founded, Toronto
1900	Boxer Uprising
1911	Xinhai Revolution and the fall of the Qing dynasty
1912	Republic of China established with Sun Yatsen as the provisional first president
1913–62	*Shengjing Bao* (Chinese *Bible Magazine*) commenced publication
1927	Nanchang Uprising, and the start of the Chinese Civil War
1928	Chinese Foreign Missionary Union founded, Hong Kong
1931	Christian radio station XMHD launched in Shanghai
1934	Communists retreat and embark on the long march; the Guomindang launches the New Life Movement in Nanchang
1937–45	Second Sino-Japanese War
1941	Emmaus Bible School, Toronto founded
1941/42–45	Japanese Occupation of Penang and Singapore
1948	Far Eastern Broadcasting Company (FEBC) went on the air in Manila
1949	Communist revolution of 1949; Guomindang retreat to Taiwan
1957	Federation of Malaya gains independence
1963	Malaysia formed
1965	Singapore becomes an independent nation-state

Introduction

Christian Circulations

May the winds of Pentecost blow there and here.

Tan See Boo, 1872[1]

In the 1820s, a small group of Irish and British Christians separated from national churches and dissenting denominations, wanting to be known only as Christians. They sought to restore the practices of the primitive first-century church and saw evidence of the workings of the Holy Spirit in experiences that they described as Pentecostal. They called themselves undenominational evangelical Christians, and widely circulated people, texts, ideas, and donations, creating a religion that combined local churches with global networks.

Their first missionaries went to Penang in 1859 at the height of a revival that passed from North America to Britain to Asia. By the end of the 19th century, the Brethren movement had spread by migration to Canada, Australia, New Zealand, and the United States and supported missionaries in Europe, Africa, India, Asia, and the Americas. With no vestments, few ritual laws, no scripted liturgies or ordained ministers, the Brethren network soon included indigenous evangelists throughout the world.

In England and Ireland, support for the Brethren movement surged after mass revivals that emphasized tears and repentance. After reading about revival events in England and Ireland in *The Missionary Reporter*, Tamil evangelist John Christian Arulappan reported that his followers were having vivid dreams and confessing their sins with tears and trembling. George Müller published Arulappan's letter in his 1859–60 annual report, claiming that it showed "in what a striking way the Holy Spirit is now beginning to work in India also, as

[1] Tan See Boo, letter to William Macdonald, 15 October 1872, *ME* No. 15 (March 1873): 39.

well as in Ireland and other countries" (SKI 1860: 47).[2] In the same report, he announced that "a brother in the Lord and two sisters went out from our midst for missionary service, to labour in Penang, Straits of Malacca".[3]

In contemporary Singapore and Malaysia, Pentecostal megachurches dominate the Christian landscape, but the "big four" Protestant churches—Anglican, Methodist, Presbyterian, and Brethren—remain religions of heritage for many. Sixty Malaysian and nineteen Singaporean assemblies identify themselves as Christian Brethren,[4] and most trace their roots to the local churches whose history I write in Parts II and III of this monograph. After World War II, former Brethren elders founded new independent churches, from charismatic local churches and Pentecostal megachurches to exclusivist Brethren assemblies. This study is a transregional history of the Brethren movement and its emplacement in Singapore and Malaysia, but is also a history of discontinuous continuities that have shaped the modern field of religious practice.[5]

Contact with the Open Brethren helped spark what is now described as the first indigenous Pentecostal revival in India (Anderson 2013: 165; Dann 2004). But in the postcolonial era Brethren elders challenged the genuineness of charismatic practices like speaking in tongues and spiritual healing. They lost members to new Pentecostal churches, including some founded by their former elders. Although one Singapore Brethren assembly website describes their form of Christianity as "truly charismatic", many label them as conservative Bible fundamentalists, out of step with the 21st century.

---

[2] Perhaps anticipating skepticism, Müller mentioned that he had made a few "verbal alterations" in the 19 March 1860 letter before publishing it, but that it was otherwise "faithfully given" (SKI 1860: 47).

[3] The Scriptural Knowledge Institution gave them £285, which included the cost of Mr and Mrs Chapman's travel expenses (SKI 1860: 41, 63).

[4] Malaysia's assemblies are listed on this website: http://www.cbsm.com.my/index.php/assembly-directory. These include 6 on Penang Island and 1 in Butterworth, 6 in Perak, 13 in Selangor, and 6 in Kuala Lumpur (http://www.malaysian-brethren.org/). Singapore's are listed on an online registry of churches and Christian organizations in Singapore (http://www.directory.bible.org.sg/, accessed 1 September 2017). Eight Chinese-speaking assemblies in Singapore share space with the English assemblies but are otherwise autonomous (Tong 2014: 9).

[5] I borrow this term from Mary Mazur, who described the writing of history by early 20th-century Chinese historians in a time of rapid change, internal rebellion and division. She concludes that there was "discontinuity and yet continuity in this use of the past to inform the present cultural identity and create a national consciousness" (Mazur 2007: 109–10).

Because the Brethren have been eclipsed by the global growth of Pentecostalism, and because denominational Christians viewed them as sectarian, their historical impacts have been underestimated (Woodbridge 2019: 1–3). But in the 19th century, the Brethren took their radical movement beyond Britain's national boundaries, using technological advancements in print media, travel, and communications as tools to create a global parish. John Nelson Darby made repeated trips to the United States and Canada between 1862 and 1877, where he spread his theological system and influenced the development of fundamentalist Christianity (Akenson 2018). Starting in 1875, Open Brethren leader George Müller and his second wife embarked on 17 years of global travel, including a world tour from 1885–87, during which he lectured in Singapore, Penang, China, and Ceylon.

During the colonial period, Brethren missionaries and Chinese evangelists also travelled widely, visiting indigenous churches that existed independent of European missionaries or Protestant denominations. In Southeast Asia, most of these churches were formed by Chinese immigrants from Fujian Province and their descendants. But when historians ask how Christianity became indigenized in China, they rarely mention the Brethren or the independent Chinese churches of Java, Borneo, and Southern Thailand.

Global Christianity and the Local Church

Today more than half of the world's Christians live in Africa, Latin and Caribbean America, Asia, and the Pacific (Walls 2002: 1). As Lamin Sanneh observes, Christianity has emerged as a world religion even though the colonial order is no longer there to maintain it, and is "surging and prospering outside denominational structures" (Sanneh 2005: 3; 2008). Historians, anthropologists, and religious studies scholars have only just begun the project of documenting this cultural diversity and wide spectrum of creative innovations and experiments.[6]

Klaus Koschorke has proposed that historians must "place the various particular regional or confessional histories on an enlarged map of the global history of Christianity and to perceive them as part of a larger whole" (Koschorke 2014: 181; see also Beyer 2006). Although scholars of world Christianity may agree that this is a desirable goal, most have spent their lives gaining specialized

---

[6] Joel Robbins observes that anthropologists studying Melanesia have only recently focused attention on Pentecostal and Charismatic Christians, concluding that this is because Melanesians have themselves "impressed its importance on them" (Robbins 2004: 32).

expertise on the history of national and/or ethnolinguistic groups or specific Christian organizations. Encyclopedic studies of world Christianity remain committed to these boundaries, typically offering parallel histories of Protestant and Catholic missions in major world regions like South Asia, Southeast Asia, and East Asia, without exploring their interconnections.

Anthropologists also continue the well-respected tradition of doing intensive research on single ethno-linguistic groups in geographically remote locations.[7] If they do historical research, they tend to work within the archives of single missionary groups. Studies based on research in a single archive or community may not seek to write the larger story of global history of Christianity, but contribute pieces to that larger mosaic.[8]

In this monograph, I focus on Penang and Singapore, but this study is multisited, encompassing local, national, and trans-border relationships, including both social linkages and economic and political systems and events. In this I follow the theoretical recommendations of Ulf Hannerz, who proposed that the anthropologist of globalization connect particular fieldsites to a larger world by investigating four organizational frames for the circulation and production of culture: form of life, the state, the market, and movement (1996: 69).

I focus on the undenominational evangelical movement known as the Open Brethren movement and its role in the global expansion of evangelical Christianity. Although Christians in Singapore and Malaysia regard the Brethren as one of the 'big four' Protestant churches, few historians of world Christianity have written about the Brethren movement and its influence in Asia (but see Sng 2003: 77–80, 200–2; Woodbridge 2016, 2019).[9] When historians of Chinese

[7] Many anthropologists have collected and analyzed personal testimonies that reveal the experiential and personally transformative aspect of conversion, a topic closely related to revival (see, for example, Robbins 2004). Rarer are works like Kenneth Guest's *God in Chinatown: Religion and Survival in New York's Evolving Immigrant Community* (2003), a multisited study in which Guest traces the recent history of Christian migration from Fuzhou, Fujian Province, China to New York.

[8] In an innovative departure, Brian Stanley's world history of 20th-century Christianity explores 15 themes, each of which he investigates by comparing 2 case studies (Stanley 2018). Stanley's approach is not only geographically expansive, but also encompasses a wide range of Christian denominations, both Catholic and Protestant.

[9] Before my first visit to Echoes of Service, one prominent historian of Chinese Christianity advised me that my request for access was sure to be denied. This was not the case, but the transfer of archival materials to the Christian Brethren Archive at the University of Manchester has made these materials far more accessible to academic researchers (see Woodbridge 2019: 2).

Christianity do mention the Open Brethren, they typically misidentify them as followers of Darby and his premillennial dispensational theology, unaware that in 1848 the Brethren divided into two wings, one was led by Darby, the other followed the lead of Groves and Müller. Adding to the confusion, both were sometimes called Plymouth Brethren, and both claimed to continue the original movement.[10]

Darby developed the premillennial dispensational theology that scholars associate with the Plymouth Brethren, but the Open Brethren claim Anthony Norris Groves and George Müller as the founders of their missionary movement. As I discuss in Part I, Groves and Müller promoted the practice called living by faith, meaning that Christian workers rely on voluntary donation rather than the security of a fixed salary. They developed institutional means to support independent missionaries, publicizing their work in annual reports and magazines, and collecting and transmitting funds on their behalf.

Leaders of denominational missionary agencies questioned the qualifications, training, and supervision of independent faith missionaries like the Brethren, and many scholars describe them in similar terms. As recently as 2010, *The Handbook of Christianity in China* described the work of undenominational missionaries as loosely organized and ephemeral, claiming that in their focus on proselytism they paid little attention to building schools or medical facilities (Tiedemann 2010: 288). Other scholars have claimed that in China, faith missionaries closely adhered to their fundamentalist mission of diffusing the gospel and rejected the social gospel (Latourette 1929 [1967]: 386; Hirono 2008: 76–81).[11]

---

[10] Because one of their major meetings was in Plymouth, and because they called each other brothers and sisters, they were called Plymouth Brethren. Adding to the confusion, in China some called them "Christian Missions in Many Lands" (CMML), naming them with a phrase that the editors of *Echoes of Service* had added to their magazine's masthead between 1901 and 1928 (see, for example, Latourette 1929: 400; Marchant 1966: 38; Tiedemann 2009: 141–2; 2010: 287–8). They replaced it with the phrase "A Record of Labour in the Lord's Name" in 1928, perhaps to avoid confusion with an American Brethren group that adopted Christian Missions in Many Lands Ltd. as their registered name in 1921. I thank Graham Johnson at the John Rylands Christian Brethren Archive for identifying the likely source of the name.

[11] In his broadly comprehensive history of Christianity in China, Daniel Bays observed that faith missionaries who came to China in the early 20th century lacked institutional support or a salary, and that the attrition rate among them was high (Bays 2012: 105). Some naïve faith missionaries failed just as Bays has described. But he makes no mention of successful Open Brethren missions supported by Echoes of Service in Bath. For an analysis of the work of Open Brethren missionaries in Mongolia and Tibet, see Woodbridge 2019.

In China and Southeast Asia, denominational missions focused on building brick-and-board missions, measuring their success in the construction of schools and hospitals. The Open Brethren by contrast imitated the simplicity of the primitive first-century church. The editor of their magazine *Echoes of Service* W.E. Vine described the "Divine Plan of Missions" as a simple matter of forming local churches with "an entire absence of any institution or organization beyond the founding of churches". He observed that uniformity came about naturally without centralized control: "The seed sown produced plants similar to the parent plant but independent of it." He concluded that the simple methods of the first-century church were suitable in all nations and ages.[12]

In the cities and towns of the colonial Straits Settlements and Malay States, mosques, churches, temples, and monasteries jostled for attention on urban streets. Immigrants emplaced religious practices that helped them to maintain identity and cohesion and replicated material and temporal structures in new situations (DeBernardi 2004). Amid imperially-styled Chinese temples, Anglican churches with high steeples, polychromatic Hindu temples, and onion-domed mosques, the Open Brethren built plain one-storey bungalows with pitched roofs with little accommodation to indigenous architectural styles.

The Brethren recruited to their network charismatic revivalists who worked both collaboratively and independently as they sought open doors. With no centralized institutions or boards controlling them, they were free to follow what they described as the leadings of providence. Like the first-century evangelists, the Brethren workers travelled far and wide and described their experiences in letters that were widely shared. But they also took John Bunyan's 17th-century allegory *Pilgrim's Progress* as a model for the individual's quest for salvation.

The allegory recounts a dream in which the main character, Christian, travels from the City of Destruction to the Celestial City atop Mount Zion. Before reaching heaven, Christian faces many trials and opponents, but because he is saved he is able to persevere to the end (see Sharrock 1948). In an episode that was widely depicted visually and appreciated cross-culturally, he has only to meet face to face with the cross and the tomb on his spiritual journey, and the burden of sin that he has been carrying falls from his back. Presbyterians, Congregationalists, Baptists, the Dutch Reformed Church and its American

[12] "The Divine Plan of Missions Paper XIV The Relationship of Churches", W.E. Vine, *ES* No. 979 (July 1926): 147–8.

offshoot, the Reformed Church of America, shared some version of John Bunyan's Calvinist theology, as did the Brethren.[13]

The missionaries and indigenous evangelists wrote letters to the editors of Brethren magazines reporting on everyday activities, and describing adventurous travels and encounters with strangers in a world in motion. Each issue presented readers with a chorus of reports from Europe and Asia, Africa and South America, and the stories of individual workers in diverse locations unfolded issue after issue. In Parts II and III of this monograph, I have untangled the stories of a few individuals and refashioned them as biographical narratives.

The Brethren magazines were primarily a publication outlet for European Brethren, who used them to inspire interest and support for their work. But as I discuss in Chapter 7, a small but important set of letters were written in Chinese, translated, and published in Brethren magazines and annual reports. Their letters provide rare accounts of the rhetorical strategies the Chinese evangelists employed as they sought to convince non-Christian Chinese that Christianity was not a European religion, and that Christians and Chinese worshipped the same supreme god.

Although some historians have emphasized the stereotyped rhetoric of missionary letters and the formulaic use of Biblical tropes, the most successful Brethren missionaries used the written word to invite the reader to enter worlds that were otherwise unknown to them. The Brethren workers told stories about people and events, but they also laid open their lives for readers, relying on the trope of the questing pilgrim carrying his burden of sin and facing human antagonists. Some letters were routine, but others invited readers to empathetically respond to their aspirations, disappointments, and sufferings. Most Open Brethren were laypersons with little training or interest in academic theology, and Bunyan's questing pilgrim rather than Darby's premillennial dispensational theology inspired their storytelling.

The model of the independent local church proved to be an important tool for indigenization. After the 1835 schism that I discuss in Chapter 2, Groves helped launch the first network of independent indigenous-led churches in Tamil Nadu. And as I discuss in Parts II and III of this monograph, Open Brethren formed a network of local churches in Southeast Asia whose members included Europeans and Eurasians; English- and Tamil-speaking immigrants

[13] The John Rylands Christian Brethren archive in Manchester holds magic lantern slides of *Pilgrim's Progress*, which were shown at Brethren Sunday schools and Bible classes. The missionaries in the Straits Settlements and Malaya also held public showings of magic lantern slides depicting episodes from the book.

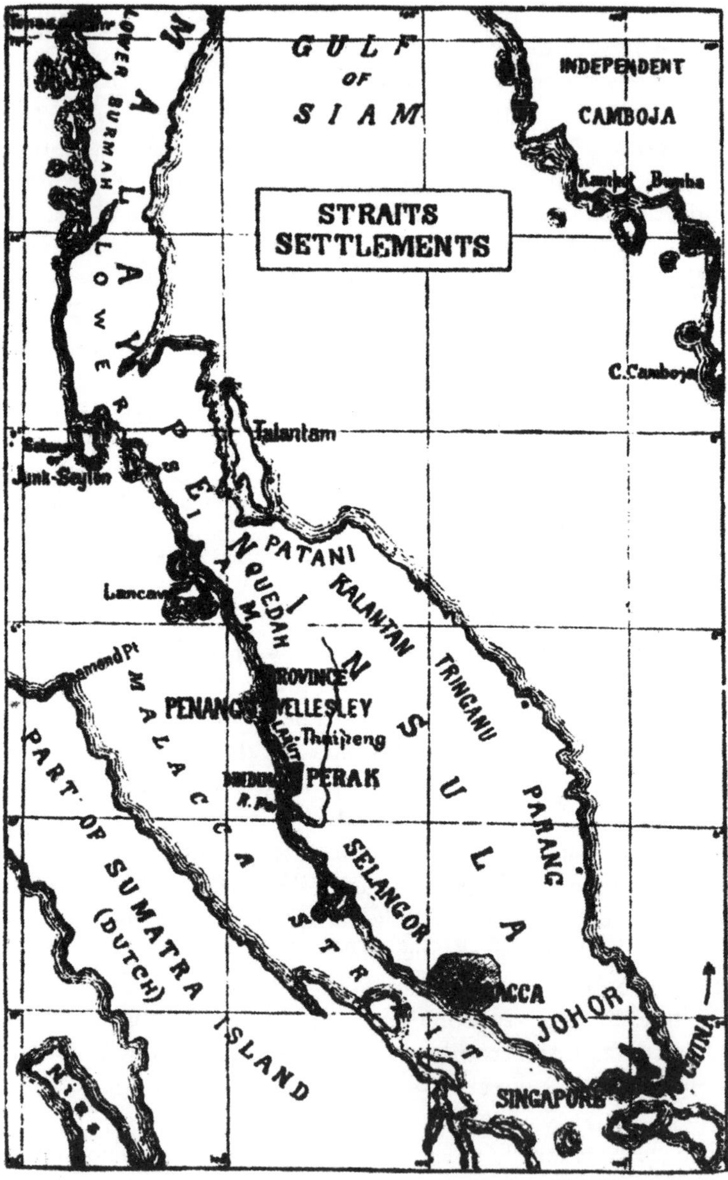

Figure 1 Map of Straits Settlements. The Straits Settlements included Penang, Malacca, and Singapore, which were controlled by the East India Company until 1867, when they came under direct British control as a Crown Colony. After World War II the colony was dissolved. *Echoes of Service* No. 223 (July 1890): 202.

from India; Straits-born Chinese; and Hokkien-, Hakka-, and Cantonese-speaking immmigrants from the coastal provinces of Southeastern China.

Open Brethren missionaries also introduced the local church movement in China, influencing Watchman Nee to launch what was described in 1951 as "the greatest indigenous movement in China today . . . free of all foreign influences and independent of all foreign financial support".[14] As I discuss in Chapter 13, Watchman Nee's influences included Exclusive Brethren in London but also Open Brethren missionaries, including one in Malaya who sought to convince Nee that the Open Brethren assemblies were primitive local churches and not under the control of a centralized mission agency. David Woodbridge concludes that when Nee adopted Brethren-style missionary primitivism, he was able to free Christianity from its association with Western power, and to assert local authority over churches. After the Communist Revolution the Brethren withdrew their missionaries from China, but the Little Flock movement survived and played an important role in the underground church movement (Woodbridge 2019: 155; see also Lian 2010: 215–6).

Christianity, Capitalism, and Social Inequality

Viewpoints on Christian missionaries and cross-cultural evangelism could not be more polarized. Christians publish memoirs that exalt individual missionaries as adventurous explorers of unknown lands and bold social reformers, while many secular scholars denounce them for their imperialist mentality and cross-cultural insensitivity. Even though nonconformist Christians opposed war and attacked social inequality in their own and other societies, Marxists still suspect that Christian ideology is a smokescreen for bourgeois capitalist interests, reinforcing racial, gender, and class inequities. In their pathbreaking research, for example, John and Jean Comaroff proposed that Protestant missionaries in South Africa sanctioned social inequality and reinforced "gendered images of self and society that lay at the core of bourgeois ideology" (Comaroff and Comaroff 1991: 68).[15]

---

[14] "An Indigenous Movement in China", *Echoes Quarterly Review* 3, 2 (April–June 1951): 63. Reprinted from *China's Millions*.

[15] John and Jean Comaroff have explored the encounter between Christian missionaries and the Southern Tswana in South Africa as the "meshing of two social worlds themselves in motion, two worlds of power and meaning whose interplay was only partly predictable" (Comaroff and Comaroff 1991: 39). They propose that nonconformist Christians lent support to capitalist society and the colonial enterprise, cultivating in Africans the "forms of selfhood and subjectivity on which [capitalism] rested" (Comaroff and Comaroff 1991: 66).

But as Robert Frykenberg has observed with respect to India, "there can be no easy summary of the relations between missions and colonialism" (Frykenberg 2005: 107, 112; see also Robert 2000, 2008). Those who label the Brethren as fundamentalists and describe them as socially conservative might be surprised to learn that in a 1972 history of their movement, Brethren historians described their missionary work as "turning the world upside down", a New Testament allusion to *Acts* 17: 6 that also recalls a long history of British radical movements (Stunt et al. 1972; Hill 1984).[16]

When I began my research on Christianity, I attended a Mandarin course at one of Singapore's major churches. Most of those attending were medically trained Chinese Christians who planned to visit China to offer free medical assistance. They took the class so that they could discuss Christianity with individuals whom they met during their sojourn in China. The textbook that we used was designed to prepare them for proselytism, and its anonymous author or authors offered the opinion that Communism was a non-deistic form of Christianity. As the textbook explained it:

> In many aspects the Communist ideal seems quite close to the Christian one. Some passages in the New Testament sounds very "Communist", and social justice is an important theme in the Word . . . . In the same way people in China have abandoned Marxism but are still deeply Marxist in their thinking, Marx (although an Atheist) also was deeply influenced by "Christian" values. Some people go so far as to say Marxism is an atheist sect of Christianity! It's Christianity without God. The values are justice, freedom, equality, the "Saviour" is the proletarian, the "Enemy" is the exploiting class, the "hope to come" is the future Communist society and the "Bible" is the works of Marx, Engels, Lenin, Mao and the others. . . . (*Xinyang Duben,* 信仰讀本 n.d.: 133).

The author contrasted Marxist and Christian strategies for change, observing that Marxists sought to change the economic and political system from the top, while "God's way of changing society is by changing individuals hearts (from the grassroots)" (*Xinyang Duben* n.d.: 134).

In the 19th century, Protestant missionaries in South Asia and China denounced traditional kinship systems as exploitative of girls and women, and

[16] Christians typically cite the Bible by book, chapter, and verse, and only rarely identify the edition they are using. For this reason, I have not put references to specific books of the Bible into the bibliography. Authors cited in this monograph sometimes identify a Bible passage by naming the chapter and verse, and expect their readers to understand the allusion. To explicate these allusions, I have referred to the King James version of the Bible published by Zondervan Press (*The Holy Bible* 1983).

proposed that Christian education would free them. In an 1853 announcement of the formation of women's group to support female education, for example, the author (probably Maria Howard) asserted that: "In China, as in all other lands, the gospel alone is the true remedy for social inequality; it gives happiness on earth, and prepares for glory in heaven."[17]

Darby and other founders of the Brethren movement also concluded that state-sponsored Protestant Christianity was a system of political control devoid of spirituality. They believed that the rise of national churches had resulted in the marginalization of the simple patterns of the early church, and advocated the separation of church and state. In 1814, Thomas Jefferson, a Christian deist, had proposed that "In every country and in every age, the priest has been hostile to liberty. He is always in alliance with the despot, abetting his abuses in return for protection to his own".[18] The Brethren further criticized "priestcraft", which some described as having arisen in the Roman Empire as a syncretic compromise with so-called pagan religions, and rejected the requirement that Christian leaders be ordained.

Some 19th-century Protestant missionaries extended their critique of religion and the state to Asia, contending that the unknown inventors of Indian and Chinese religions had designed them to support social inequality. When Christians translated God with the Chinese term *Shangdi* (literally, Emperor Above), for example, they proposed that China had once been monotheistic, but its rulers had claimed the privilege of being the sole mediators between the people and this supreme god.[19] Protestant Christians urged the Chinese to reclaim direct, unmediated contact with *Shangdi* by worshipping the Christian God.

Although they were not politically radical, the Brethren promoted an egalitarian ethos in their local churches (Wilson 2003: 81). Moreover, Brethren evangelists addressed their message of moral reform not only to the poor, but also sought influence among elites. For example, Lord Radstock (1833–1913) exhorted Russian aristocrats to give up luxuries and to donate their riches to benevolent causes, and influenced Vasily Alexandrovich Pashkov to launch a mass religious movement that promoted brotherhood among all ethnic groups

---

17 "The State of Females in China", *CGMG* 2, 11 (April 1853): 85.

18 Thomas Jefferson to Horatio G. Spafford, 17 March 1814, https://founders.archives.gov/documents/Jefferson/03-07-02-0167 [accessed 1 February 2020].

19 Bible translators Karl Gützlaff, William Medhurst, W.C. Milne, and John Stronach argued that 'God' should be translated as *Shangdi* and not *shen* precisely because they were aware that ancient Chinese rulers had venerated *Shangdi* as a transcendant Supreme Being and claimed *Shangdi* to be none other than the Christian God.

and social classes. Pashkov led services and prayer meetings at his mansion, where "civil officials, domestic servants, cab drivers, factory workers, peasants, and even priests and beggars worshipped with aristocrats and other members of high society" (Wardin 2013: 178–9). The government suppressed Pashkov's movement, forcing him into exile in 1884.

Although Leo Tolstoy had developed his own form of Christian anarchism, he knew of Radstock's teachings and agreed with some of them. Tolstoy also met Radstock's convert Frederick Baedeker (1823–1906), who in 1877 received a licence to visit prisons throughout Russia, and he based two characters in his 1899 novel *Resurrection* on the Brethren evangelist (Wardin 2013: 237). Tolstoy rejected the dogmas and rites of the state-sponsored Russian Orthodox Church, and like Groves took the Sermon on the Mount as his map for spiritual resurrection and social renewal (Wardin 2013: 175). In the final chapter of *Resurrection*, the main character Nekhludoff realizes that the Sermon on the Mount laid out "simple, clear, practical laws" that if "carried out in practice" could create the Kingdom of Heaven on Earth (Tolstoy 1899 [1999]: 481–3).

Two years after the publication of *Resurrection*, the Russian Orthodox Church excommunicated Tolstoy. In 1908 Lenin praised him as the "mirror of the Russian Revolution", but also condemned him as a "landlord obsessed with Christ" who chose belief in God and moral self-perfection over "sober realism" in his criticism of capitalist exploitation and the "growth of poverty, degradation and misery among the working masses" (Lenin 1965 [1908]).[20] The international press took note when the 100th anniversary of Tolstoy's death in 2010 was met with official silence in Russia.

Like the Pashkovians, the Open Brethren in Britain did not recognize social barriers between members of their assemblies, and wealthy members adopted simple lifestyles (Wilson 2003: 81). The Brethren missionaries in Penang and Singapore also revelled in bringing together all ethnic groups and classes at their gatherings. From the start, the Brethren in Penang and Singapore baptized Europeans, Eurasians, and Asians together, and their English-speaking congregations included Europeans, Eurasians, South Asians from India and Ceylon, and Straits Chinese. They trained and promoted Asian Christian leaders decades before the end of the British empire and the rise of new nation states made this a practical imperative for Christians.

---

[20] https://www.marxists.org/archive/lenin/works/1908/sep/11.htm [accessed 15 August 2016].

At the same time, we find paradoxical tensions within the Brethren movement relating to issues of gender equality, their relation to authorities, and European privilege. Although the supporters of female education proposed that that the gospel would free Asian women, some influential Brethren leaders opposed the public ministry of women both "toward the world and toward the church", arguing that men and women should use their gifts in different spheres (Caldwell 1895: 141; see Dickson 1993). This conservatism has persisted in some Brethren assemblies in Singapore, whose members advised me, "You know, Jean, women can't be elders!"

In the 1860s and 1870s Brethren female missionaries were revivalists and did public evangelism in the Straits Settlements. But by the end of the 19th century, female missionaries took work with women and girls as their exclusive sphere. Ironically for modern readers, one essayist described traditional gender roles as an "ancient habit of life" in Asia and Africa, but God's will for the Brethren (Caldwell 1895: 187). As I discuss in Chapter 14, former Brethren whom I interviewed in Penang identified limitations on women's roles in Brethren assemblies as a key factor in the charismatic schisms of 1963.

And although the Brethren sought to separate themselves from state power and many were pacifists, the expansion of the British empire opened doors to Christians that had been closed for centuries. Daniel Bays sees complicity with capitalist agendas among evangelical Christians working in China, observing that although the opium issue and the first Opium War were debated in the British House of Commons, "no China coast missionary was sufficiently concerned about the morality of the opium issue actually to oppose the war and its settlement". He infers that the missionaries were confident that the war was "the hand of providence opening China to the Gospel" (Bays 2012: 47).

The morality of opium sale and use did concern many Christians, including the Open Brethren missionaries in Singapore and Penang, where the government monopoly on the sale of opium was the foundation of the colonial economy. But the Brethren workers relied on colonial authorities for access to prisons, hospitals, and leprosariums, so did not lead a movement to oppose the opium trade. Instead, the missionaries exhorted people that its use was sinful and offered opium addiction treatments at their dispensaries. When two missionaries and a Chinese evangelist did open-air preaching in Singapore, a young listener retorted, "O yes, it is all very well to tell us Chinamen to believe Jesus, and to leave off sinning, while at the same time you send us the opium." The missionary responded by demanding that his listener buy a New Testament portion worth a penny for $1. When he refused, he observed, "If the English Government do send you the opium surely you have the power to refuse to buy it?" But he also confessed that they "inwardly felt ashamed to think that such a thing could be levelled at us as British people".[21]

The anti-opium movement was the cause that made the China Inland Mission famous (Austin 2007: 14–5), and the Quaker-led Society for the Suppression of the Opium Trade (est. 1874) succeeded in pressuring the British government to end the opium trade between India and China in 1913. But despite an anti-opium movement in Singapore and Malaya led by Straits Chinese leaders, including Dr Lim Boon Keng and Dr Wu Lien-teh, the opium trade continued in the Straits Settlements until after the Japanese Occupation (Toda 2012).

Finally, from the start of their movement, the Open Brethren promoted the indigenization of leadership and the formation of independent local churches. But their support for local churches existed in dialectical tension with their desire to continue as fulltime workers in cities like Penang and Singapore. By the 1950s, evangelical Christianity had been established in both cities for over a century. But not until Malaysia and Singapore became independent nation states in the postcolonial period did the era of the foreign missionary end.

Evangelical Christians and the Brethren Movement in Penang and Singapore: An Overview

In this monograph, I investigate the history of evangelical Christianity as a transregional social movement, focusing on Penang and Singapore, British-controlled port cities on the sea highway between India and China. In order to place the history of global Christianity on an enlarged map, I investigate the everyday practices, travels, and network relationships of European and Asian Christians in those two cities from the early introduction of evangelical Christianity in 1819 to the start of a new millennium in 2000.

By the time the London Missionary Society (LMS) launched the Ultra Ganges Mission in Southeast Asia, European nations had been battling for control of the sea highway and its ports for centuries. Britain had waged maritime wars with France, Spain, and Holland, and also the Seven Years' War (1756–63), a global conflict among major powers in Europe, India, and America, and at sea (Mahan 1918: 329). The Seven Years' War left Britain and France deeply indebted, setting the stage for the American and French Revolutions, but it also made Britain the dominant power in India. The sea made Britain wealthy, and the Royal Navy protected its commercial interests.

---

[21] Alfred R. Thoburn, "Among Chinese in Singapore", Singapore, 3 December 1894, *ES* No. 327 (February 1895 Pt. I): 31.

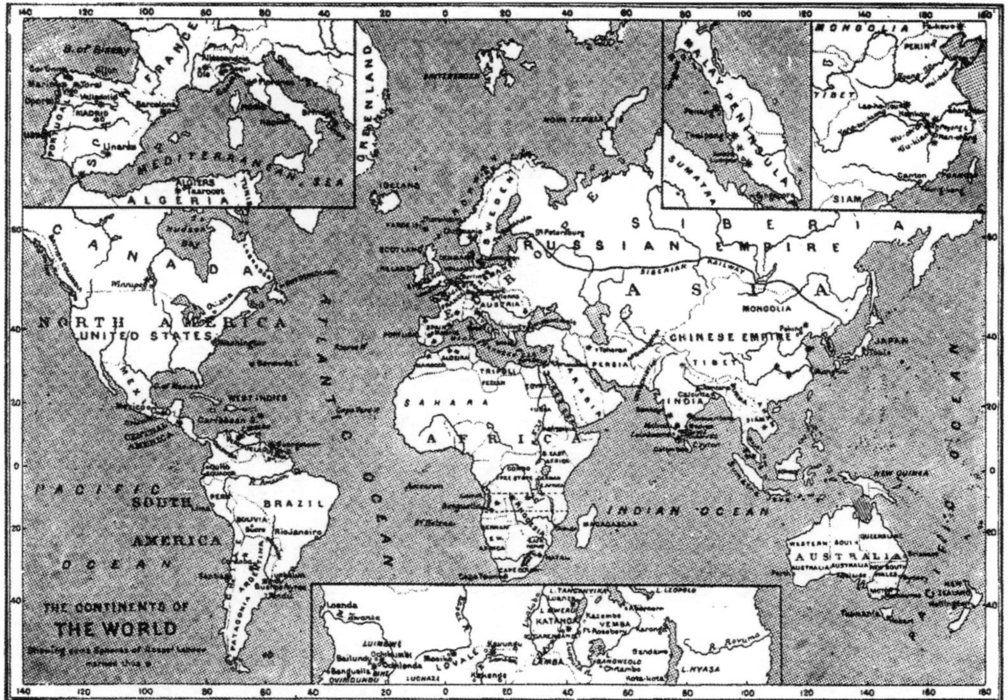

Map of the World, with Enlargements of Spain, Italy, Malay Peninsula, China, and a strip of Central Africa.

Figure 2 Map of the world published in *Echoes of Service* in 1908, showing the sites of Open Brethren missions. Inset maps show the missions in four regions, including the Malay Peninsula and China (top right), in greater detail. *Echoes of Service* No. 636 (Frontispiece January 1908 Pt. I).

In 1786 and 1819, agents of the British East India Company (EIC) negotiated treaties for control of Penang and Singapore islands, both chosen for their location on the sea lanes connecting India with China. In 1786, Captain Francis Light (1740–94) arranged to lease Penang Island from the Kedah Sultanate on behalf of the EIC, renaming it Prince of Wales Island. He founded the city of George Town and served as its superintendant.

Thomas Stamford Raffles (1781–1826) was posted there in 1805, then moved to Malacca. In 1811 he led a successful invasion of Java and was appointed Lieutenant Governor of the Dutch East Indies. Forced to return Java to Dutch control by the terms of the Anglo-Dutch Treaty that concluded the Napoleonic Wars, Raffles was next appointed Lieutenant Governor of the EIC trading centre at Bencoolen (today, Bengkulu) on Sumatra. He negotiated to secure transfer of control of territory on the southern tip of the Malay peninsula to the EIC, and appointed Major William Farquhar as Resident of Singapore in 1819. Malacca had been occupied by the British, but was formally ceded to British control in exchange for Bencoolen by the terms of the Anglo-Dutch Treaty of 1824. In 1826, Singapore, Penang, and Malacca were formed into a single administrative unit known as the Straits Settlements.

Soon after the so-called Pious Clause in the East India Company 1813 Charter Act permitted access to territories that the East India Company controlled, British evangelical Christians started the Anglo-Chinese College in Malacca (1818), and missions in Java and Amboyna (1814), Penang and Singapore (1819). After five treaty ports became open to Europeans in 1843, they moved to China and independent missionaries took over the missions and schools they had abandoned. In Penang, these missionaries continued the educational and evangelical projects at the former LMS mission with support from Brethren in Britain, including the wealthy founders of the Chinese Evangelization Society in London and George Müller, the founder and director of the Scriptural Knowledge Institution in Bristol. The missionaries in Singapore and Penang worked in partnership with Asian evangelists, and corresponded with and visited independent churches that existed in the Malay Peninsula, Java and Borneo, Southern Thailand, and Burma.

In the early years of the Brethren mission, both European missionaries and Hokkien evangelists circulated widely. Take, for example, the career of Alexander Grant (c. 1833–1914), a Scots Presbyterian missionary who worked in the Amoy Mission before moving to Singapore in 1861. Not long after his arrival there, he chose independence, joining the Brethren movement in Penang. In 1867 Grant became resident missionary at Singapore's newly-built Bethesda Free Meeting House, and modern Singaporean Christians regard him as a founder.

Grant's career was transregional, encompassing Scotland, Fujian, Penang, Singapore, Java, London, and North China. Grant worked as an independent missionary at Brethren assemblies in Penang and Singapore between 1861 and 1873, and again between 1878 and 1885. But histories of Christianity in China only record details of his three years in the Amoy Mission in Fujian (1858–61), sometimes mentioning that he was in North China in 1900 during the Boxer Uprising.

Chinese Christians also circulated widely, and travel and communications linked them into regional and transregional networks. Gan Kui (1821–1901), for example, is an important figure in the history of Indonesian Christianity, but he also lived and worked in Singapore, British Malaya, and China. He moved from Amoy to Java in 1856, where he worked with the Society of Internal and External Mission (Genootschap voor In- en Uitwendige Zending or GIUZ) as an evangelist doing outreach to Hokkien immigrants. When the Brethren opened a meeting house in Singapore in 1867, Chinese Christians built a Free Chinese Christian church on adjacent land. The Christians in Batavia sent them a donation, and Gan Kui moved to Singapore. During his long association with the Brethren, the European missionaries sent reports on his work to the editors of *Echoes of Service* from Java, Fujian, Burma, Penang, Singapore, and cities and towns throughout British Malaya.

Historians of China have documented the growth of independent Christianity by examining the work of prominent Chinese Christian leaders and revivalists like Wang Mingdao, John Sung, and Watchman Nee.[22] But they regard the drive towards independence as a 20th-century development in China. Lian Xi concluded that in 1900, "no significant independent Christian communities had endured in China" (Lian 2010: 31), and Daniel Bays observes the "spirit of independence" was undiscernible in the 19th century but became prominent after 1900 (Bays 1996: 308).

In a detailed history of Protestants in Southern Fujian and their social networks, Chris White explores the career of Tan See Boo (whom he identifies by his Mandarin name, Chen Shiwu), a Presbyterian catechist from Fujian who became independent and joined the Brethren Movement in Singapore. He uses this example to demonstrate that interactions and exchanges between Christians in both regions were mutually influential, but concluded that Chen

[22] The Pentecostal Jesus Church is an important early example of an independent church sometimes described as China's first native denomination (see Inouye 2019).

failed when he sought to promote the Brethren movement to Christians in Fujian (White 2017: 100–5).[23]

These historians of Chinese Christianity have paid little attention to local churches formed by independent Christians in Southeast Asia, including the Chinese Free Christian Church in Singapore that Tan led, and the Patekoan Church in Batavia that Gan Kui helped found. Long before 1900 Chinese Christians had formed independent churches in Batavia, the Malay States, and Southern Thailand that Brethren workers visited from time to time, including some that still exist today.

By contrast with denominational missions, the Open Brethren workers fostered independence. Traditional denominations required that their ministers be theologically trained and ordained, producing what the Brethren call the "one man ministry". The Brethren proposed instead that Christians form local churches led by lay people with no priestly mediators. Some of their recognized leaders like Grant were ordained, but on joining the Brethren movement, they gave up the title of "Reverend". The Open Brethren missionaries and Asian evangelists taught the skills of Bible exegesis to male members, a practice known as discipleship. Discipleship created an open structure of teacher-disciple relationships that travel extended through space and time, producing radiating growth.

At the same time as Chinese Christians created local churches in Southeast Asia, they became increasingly connected to global Christian circuits.[24] When Brethren missionaries arrived in the Straits Settlements in 1860, they distributed copies of *Revival* magazine, and in the following years Christians reported waves of revival from Europe, South Africa, North America, and China. With the development of increasingly swift ocean-going steamships and the opening

---

[23] White describes Chen/Tan as having joined "the Brethren Church, or the Plymouth Brethren", whose history he traces to Ireland (White 2017: 103). White also claims that any member of a Brethren church could perform the ritual of baptism, proposing this as a possible reason for his decision to join them. But Bethesda's Assembly Record Book shows that only the missionaries and Chinese fulltime workers like Chen conducted baptisms, likely due to government regulations concerning registration (ARB 1865–1934).

[24] Study of the history and contemporary practice of global Christianity in other world areas would almost certainly reveal striking similarities. To give but one example, Simon Coleman concluded that in the Swedish church that he studied, members regarded their community as global, and valued mass media, conferences, and prayer networks precisely because they sustained a "sense of participation in impermanent, free-flowing structures". Their religion was not tied to a specific denomination, and they regarded it as embracing the whole world (Coleman 2009: 67–8).

of the Suez Canal in 1869, well-known evangelical Christian leaders began to travel internationally to promote their evangelical programmes. Between 1875 and 1892, Brethren philanthropist George Müller and his second wife visited 42 countries in the course of 17 public speaking tours. In 1887 he lectured in Singapore for two weeks.

Beginning in the 1920s, independent Chinese Christian leaders John Sung, Watchman Nee, Leland Wang and his brother Wilson also visited and led revival campaigns in Singapore and Penang.[25] These leaders and revivalists influenced Chinese Christians in Southeast Asia through their campaigns but also through Chinese Christian publications. Although publications had spread the influence of their movement worldwide, the Brethren did not translate their English-language magazines, annual reports, or books into Chinese or other Asian languages. English-educated Christians read them, but other Christian missions, including the North American Christian and Missionary Alliance (C&MA), took the lead in creating a Chinese Christian press.

Chinese Christians in Penang and Singapore were engaged in these publication circuits as readers, authors, and editors. Soon after Watchman Nee published a new book in Shanghai in January 1938, Penang Chinese Brethren wrote to him to say that they had all read it, and sent a donation to support evangelical work in remote regions of China. And although China was the main base for Chinese Christian publishing, because of the disruptions of war, Wilson Wang lived in Penang for almost two decades as the Burmah Road Gospel Hall's international evangelist (1942–60). He co-edited the widely circulated Chinese *Bible Magazine* in Penang, sending it to Hong Kong to be printed, and Teh Phai Lian, who later founded the Charismatic Church of Penang, became a regular contributor.

Historians of Christianity in Singapore and Malaysia observe that the Brethren trained and supported Asian leaders long before the major denominational missions recognized the need to do so (Lee 1992: 132; Sng 2003: 200–2). When the Japanese occupied Singapore and Penang in 1941, the foreign missionaries fled or were interned. During the war years, Brethren churches continued to meet under Asian leadership while the denominational

[25] Allan Anderson (2014: 143) mentions John Sung's campaigns in Southeast Asia as an early Pentecostal influence, and Lian (2010: 151–3) describes his wide itinerations. But in his analyses of the 20th-century growth of independent churches, Bays only describes these revivalists' campaigns on Chinese circuits (Bays 1996: 2012). The terms Singapore, Penang, Malaysia, and Southeast Asia are not found in the indexes of any of these important studies, which demonstrates how marginal Southeast Asia has been to the history of Christianity in Asia.

churches struggled. After the war ended, many of the missionaries returned, and some relocated to Malaysia from Mainland China. But only after the new nation states formed after World War II started setting limits to visas for foreign workers did the era of the foreign missionary end.

After World War II, the Brethren movement and local churches that came out of the Brethren movement met with different fates in China, Penang, and Singapore. In China, the new communist government adopted an atheist ideology, forced foreign missionaries to leave, and enacted programmes of registration and control for China's five legal religions—Buddhism, Daoism, Catholicism, Protestantism, and Islam. Many Chinese Christian leaders fled to Taiwan or Southeast Asia, and from there to North America.

Penang and Singapore, once governed together with Malacca as the British Straits Settlements, were separated in 1965 when Singapore was expelled from the new Federation of Malaysia due to political differences. Penang joined Malaysia as one of 13 states and 3 federal territories, and Singapore became an autonomous nation-state. Since independence, Christians in Malaysia have faced limitations on building new churches, and visa requirements make it difficult to even host short-term speakers. By contrast, Singapore hosts local, regional, and international mission organizations and initiatives, including many that relocated from China after 1949.

In Part IV of this monograph, I write about the modern fate of the local church, including independent local churches that former Brethren elders helped found. These include a Christian Assembly in Singapore (est. 1935) linked to Watchman Nee's local church movement, and an independent church founded in Singapore by Charles Lee, a Chinese evangelist from Shandong who had fled to Taiwan in 1949. The missionaries invited him to hold meetings in Penang and Singapore, but their cooperation ended when he abruptly formed a new local church in 1957. I also explore the events leading to the founding of Charismatic and Pentecostal local churches in Penang and Singapore that 'came out of' the Brethren movement in 1963, and the impact of the Full Gospel movement in the 1980s. In the final chapter, I return to the Brethren movement and its modern fate.

For a generation, the Open Brethren roots of the Church of Singapore and the Charismatic Church of Penang were still visible. The founders of the new charismatic churches disagreed with the Brethren *doxa*, and the Brethren rejected some charismatic teachings and practices as heterodox, but all took the New Testament as their guide to Christian practice and formed local churches. Although many emphasize the newness of Pentecostal practices, I propose that the modern charismatic movement, with its emphasis on revival, networks, and independence from denominational structures, has a deep history in the local church movement that the Open Brethren promoted globally.

But after schism Christians often chose mutually forgetting, emphasizing differences and joining new networks.[26] As Jan Assmann has observed, societies are connective structures that "maintain their identity through the generations by fashioning a culture out of memory" (2011: 4). Religions play a role in fashioning memory culture, joining together past, present, and future by the tie of ideas and practices. But religious unity, like national unity, also requires boundaries and forgetting. This history of the Open Brethren movement is a history of continuity and growth, discontinuity and schism.[27]

The Structure of the Conjuncture

Throughout this monograph, I explore diagnostic events, which Sally Falk Moore describes as events that reveal "ongoing contests and conflicts and competitions and the efforts to prevent, suppress, or repress these" (Moore 1987: 730; see also 1994: 365). In his study of Catholicism in a northern Guangdong Hakka village, Eriberto P. Lozada, Jr. commented that a focus on diagnostic events helped researchers connect local events to the larger world "by making explicit the social, political, and economic ties of a community to the larger system" (2001: 21).

Marshall Sahlins labels the dialectical process of change the "structure of the conjuncture", by which he means "the practical realization of the cultural categories in a specific historical context, as expressed in the interested action of the historical agents, including the microsociology of their interaction . . . this notion of praxis as a situational sociology of meaning can be applied to the general understanding of culture change" (Sahlins 1985: xiv). When faced with

---

[26] Edward K. Pousson, a charismatic Christian who worked as a missionary in China and Malaysia, recognized the similarities between the charismatic approach to missions and those of the "Churches of Christ and the Plymouth Brethren" (Pousson 1992: 19), but does not explore historical reasons for the resemblance.

[27] In a commentary on Joel Robbins' critique of so-called continuity thinking, John Barker observed that the theme of continuity and change is too broad and ambiguous to provide a foundation for the anthropology of Christianity. He recommends that anthropologists focus on the "distinctive content of Christian institutions and expressions, both in recent times and over the long term" (Barker 2007: 18). Although I agree, institutional histories may not document diagnostic events that are turning points in local histories. Historical investigation from multiple perspectives is more likely to uncover aspects of the past that participants chose to forget as they construct new identies (see Connerton 1989).

conflicting intentions and interpretations, people may assign new meanings to cultural categories and enter into novel relationships (Sahlins 1981: 70–2).

As Frykenberg (2005: 129) has observed, much of what happened in the past remains hidden from historians. Mission histories rarely touch on the subject of conflict, and reports about internal conflicts almost never entered the public record (Jenkins 2000: 59). The conflict between German missionary Karl Rhenius and the Anglican authorities that I discuss in Chapter 2 is a striking exception. And at the centre of the controversy was the Brethren movement's first missionary, Anthony Norris Groves. After the Church Missionary Society (CMS) expelled Rhenius from his mission, boarding up his church so that he could not use it (Jenkins 2000: 59), Groves publicized the conflict, raised funds for Rhenius and his co-workers, and convinced them to return to Tinnevelly as independent missionaries. This showdown with the Anglican establishment in India had consequences for the reputation of the Brethren movement and its missionaries.

This study also owes much to Joseph Levenson's magisterial work, *Confucian China and its Modern Fate* (1972 [1958, 1964, 1965]), a study that deeply explored the structure of the conjuncture between Chinese and Western ideologies and practices. As Levenson described it, the encounter with Western nationalism, on the one hand, and Christianity, on the other sparked a 20th-century movement to modernize Confucianism. One Chinese author even compared the movement to the Protestant Reformation, describing the Confucian reformer Kang You-wei as the Chinese Luther (Levenson 1972: 83). Throughout Asia, Hindus, Buddhists, Muslims, and practitioners of popular religions also engaged in programmes of national revivalism and reform (Van Der Veer 2014).[28] As I discuss in Chapter 11, when the leaders of China's nationalist party promoted the New Life Movement in the 1930s, its creators drew on elements of evangelical Christianity to revolutionize Chinese society.

Levenson observed that although Christian missionaries made outstanding contributions to the modernization of China, they lost their religious cause (1972: 124; see also Dunch 2001). But Michael Browne, an Open Brethren missionary who observed the Cultural Revolution (1966–76) from Hong Kong, concluded that the Communists had discredited "ancient ethical codes, ancestral worship and false sects" and replaced all religions with a form of Communism that "closely paralleled Christianity, both in its structure, methods

[28] Frykenberg concludes that in India Christians struck "deep roots among people on the social and territorial margins of India", including the Dalit (or 'Untouchables') and tribal communities, but also "hastened the construction (or invention) of modern, or syndicated, Hinduism and Indian nationalism, as well as Islamic revivalisms" (Frykenberg 2005: 107).

of propagation, and emphasis upon a central charismatic figure". He predicted that after Mao's death, the "Red faith" would have prepared the way for the rapid evangelization of China.[29] He did not foresee the striking comeback of Buddhism, Daoism, and Confucianism, which now receive unprecedented official support.

My approach to the study of global Christianity and the local church is also informed by Pierre Bourdieu's theory of practice. Bourdieu proposed that people are unconsciously constrained by social structures and their *habitus*, a term that he used to describe deeply ingrained dispositions and expertise formed through practice and experienced as common sense (Bourdieu 1990 [1980]: 52–65). But he also observed that as people made decisions and plans, they had agency. He proposed that one motive that directed their choices was the quest for prestige through the accumulation of different forms of social and cultural capital. At the same time, he noted that as they internalized their habitus, people also learned a sense of place and of their limitations, making choices appropriate to their social class.

Bourdieu's work also addressed the social foundations of inequality. He concluded that the dominant classes had an interest in putting the definition of the social world beyond question, a *doxa*, which he calls the "universe of the undiscussed". But he added that the dominated had an interest in "exposing the arbitariness of the taken-for-granted" (Bourdieu 1977: 168–9). When challenged, people may respond by systematizing their doxic assumptions as orthodoxy and labelling their critics' views as heterodoxy or heresy.

The Brethren based doxa on the Bible and were certain that if they took the New Testament as a model for their Christian practice, they could ensure uniformity without centralization or written doctrines. But understanding the Bible is a matter of hermeneutics and exegesis in the time and space of human lives. Although they sought to distinguish themselves from denominational Christians and their institutional practices, critics have repeatedly challenged the Brethren to defend their understandings of Christian practice from the charge of being a human-made set of ideas and practices (an orthodoxy) or a deviation from Christian doxa (heterodoxy or even heresy).

George Simmel compared society to an event in which one individual effects the fate and development of another, and is in turn effected by them (Simmel 1950: 11). In their cross-cultural missions, the Open Brethren sought to be fateful agents of change and urged those whom they addressed to break free of the constraints of traditional social systems. They challenged what they described

---

[29] Michael Browne, "What about the church in China?", *Echoes Quarterly Review* 22, 1 (January–March 1970): 11–2.

as tyrannical family structures and Asian religions whose priests they regarded as oppressive. They employed a strategy sometimes called "controversy", calling on non-Christians to defend their taken-for-granted beliefs and practices. In so doing, they promoted reflexivity and choice over tradition.

In Penang and Singapore, the Brethren evangelists challenged the habitus of Chinese popular religion, which blends elements of the textual and ritual traditions of Confucianism, Buddhism and Daoism with practices like spirit possession and divination. They required those who wished baptism to cease to offer financial support to institutions like temples, and to remove god images, ancestral tablets and genealogies from their family altars, replacing them with scriptures and Christian almanacs. But since ancestor worship was closely tied up with family cohesion, and through Confucianism with Chinese identity, these requirements meant that conversion was potentially deeply divisive within family and community.

British social anthropologists sought to understand how people use kinship systems and voluntary associations to organize themselves separate from the state and its controls. In this study of Christian circulations, I examine the organization of the local church movement and its social impacts in Penang and Singapore. I also employ Clifford Geertz' methodological guidelines for interpretative anthropology. Geertz recommended that anthropologists understand actors' viewpoints by observing and interpreting performances and texts, and translating and explicating key terms (Geertz 1973). Like Geertz and Sahlins both, I also use story to unlock an understanding of change.

In *The Way that Lives in the Heart*, I wrote about Penang Chinese popular religion and spirit mediums using a method that one reviewer described as a "colloquy of differences" (Hopkins 2011). I combined an analysis of the habitus or shared practices and taken-for-granted understandings of popular religious culture with vignettes of four spirit mediums. Each drew on the shared resources of popular religion and textual traditions to fashion new syntheses and interpretations that they offered to their disciples as teachings, personal advice, admonitions, and entertainment. They combined elements from eclectic cultural archives as they constructed authoritative world views for their disciples.

In this monograph, I explore the practice of evangelical Christianity and the Brethren movement in Penang and Singapore as a colloquy of differences. I describe Christianity as a shared structure of meaning and practice, but also provide vignettes of people's everyday lives and ordinary and extraordinary encounters, experiences, decisions, and debates in a world in motion. Taken together, the lives of these individuals provide a perspectival view on the globalization of Christianity and the local church, but also the impact of waves of revival, revolution, and change.

PART I
The Open Brethren Movement

Chapter 1

The Brethren Movement and the Local Church

> Where dwells the religion? Tell me first where dwells electricity, or motion, or thought or gesture. They do not dwell or stay at all. Electricity cannot be made fast, mortared up and ended, like London Monument, or the Tower, so that you shall know where to find it, and keep it fixed, as the English do with their things, forevermore; it is passing, glancing, gesticular; it is a traveller, a newness, a surprise, a secret, which perplexes them, and puts them out.
>
> Ralph Waldo Emerson, 1856[1]

Although most historians of World Christianity have ignored the Brethren, some have appreciated their maverick influence. Robert Krapohl compared the Brethren to a "dwarf star" in the firmament of 19th-century Christianity: "Barely visible, they exerted an undeniable gravitational pull on everything close to them" (Krapohl 1997: 397). Because they sought to connect themselves directly to divine providence, David Bebbington has described them as the most romantic and other-worldly of 19th-century evangelicals, observing that their freedom from institutional structures promoted innovation (Bebbington 2006: 252).

John Nelson Darby is the most famous of the Brethren movement's founders: in *Who's Who in Christianity*, the entry on Darby is found between short biographies of Dante and Darwin (Cohn-Sherbok 1998: 68). Donald Akenson concludes that Darby was the "final catalytical agent in a cascade of concepts, events, and beliefs" that formed the "potent pattern" of Bible interpretation now known as premillennial dispensational theology. Darby laid

[1] Ralph Waldo Emerson (1856: 67).

out a cosmology from eternity to eternity, placing his generation close to the end of time. In the 20th and 21st centuries, the North American wing of the evangelical movement widely adopted his teachings on the pre-tribulational rapture (Akenson 2016: 4–5).

Darby was born into a prominent Anglo-Irish family and studied law before becoming a Church of Ireland priest. He worked as a curate in County Wicklow but abandoned his curacy after growing disillusioned with the Church of Ireland. He began to work independently, but apparently never formally resigned from the Anglican priesthood (Akenson 2016: 300–1). The year after he resigned his curacy, he published an influential pamphlet *Considerations on the Nature and Unity of the Church of Christ* (1828).

In this pamphlet, Darby observed that paradoxically the ritual that Christians called communion symbolized their disunion. He concluded that "So far as men pride themselves on being Established, Presbyterian, Baptist, Independent, or anything else, they are antichristian." He recommended that the Christians unite instead in "the word of the Spirit of God" (Darby 1828: 30).

In a retrospective letter Darby recalled that he had realized that his work was not in agreement with the Bible while working among "poor Irish mountaineers, in a wild and uncultivated district" (Darby 1857–59 [1985]: 182). At that time, he began to question why Christians needed to be ordained before they were allowed to preach or perform rituals:

> I said to myself, "If the Apostle Paul were to come here now, he would not, according to the established system, be even allowed to preach, not being legally ordained; . . . This is not mere abuse, such as may be found everywhere; it is the principle of the system that is at fault. Ministry is of the Spirit, but the system is found on an opposite principle; consequently it seemed impossible to remain in it any longer (Darby 1985 [1857–59]: 184–5).

Darby claimed that many ministers "left nationalism" in order to practice ministry "of the Spirit", and that their meetings had spread throughout England (Darby 1985 [1857–59]: 186).

In 1848, the Brethren divided into wings described as Open and Exclusive. When the Bethesda assembly in Bristol accepted as a member someone associated with Benjamin Wills Newton, an influential Brethren teacher and writer whose teachings Darby had condemned as heretical, Darby objected. Led by George Müller, the members of Bethesda Chapel in Bristol defended their right to chose whom they would invite to their meetings, and Darby excommunicated them. In London, members of the Brook Street Chapel in Tottenham also rejected Darby's demand.[2]

As the unchallenged leader of the Exclusive Brethren, Darby promoted his views widely in Europe. A similar movement had already spread throughout France, and he introduced Brethren principles to Christians in Switzerland (Darby 1985 [1857–59]: 186). He also visited North America five times between 1862 and 1877. He spread his influence through both public lectures and his publications, including translations of the Bible from the original Hebrew and Greek texts into English, German, French, and Italian, and a multi-volume synopsis of the Bible in which he systematized his views (Reid 1876: 17; see also Akenson 2018). Darby advocated a mystical concept of the Church, separation from the world, and a doctrine of "pure grace' that would ensure salvation when "received into the heart by the Spirit" (Darby 1985 [1857–59]: 186).

After the schism, the Open Brethren formed a loose network of autonomous local churches that practised open communion. They were staunch evangelical Christians, but had no officially recognized doctrinal system or leader, although some read Darby's writings and taught his doctrines in their meetings (Reid 1876: 5–6). George Lang argued that the Open Brethren, rather than Darby's revolters, had the stronger claim to be the continuation of the original movement (Lang 1949: 243). But because the Exclusive and Open Brethren still shared many practices, many did not recognize their differences, identifying both as "Plymouth Brethren".[3]

The Open Brethren and the Local Church

Institutions are replicable structures, and denominational religions are among the world's oldest enduring social structures. But the Open Brethren describe themselves as undenominational Christians and formed networks of primitive local churches with no centralized institutions. The New Testament Greek word that is translated into English as church is *ekklesia*, or in English ecclesia. Ecclesia meant "to call out" and referred to a group

---

[2] In 1849, London's Brook Street Chapel posted the Tottenham Memorandum, which is still displayed. This memorandum states the basic principles of the Open Brethren: "We find our centre of union with each other, and with all saints [born again believers] in Christ, as one in Him, and our power of fellowship by the Holy Ghost." https://www.slideshare.net/brookstreetchapel/brook-street-chapel [accessed 22 August 2017].

[3] For a detailed historical account of the first 25 years of the Brethren movement, see Harold R. Rowdon (1967).

of citizens who had been called together. The early Brethren called their meeting places halls or chapels, and did not regard them as sacred space. Anthony Norris Groves' son Edward Kennaway Groves described the assemblies as an expansion of family life, with an "enlarged sphere for love and service" (Groves 1906: 204).[4]

For the Open Brethren, baptism and the weekly breaking of bread service provide them with both cohesion and distinction. The Brethren like Baptists practice baptism by full immersion in water, a symbolic reenactment of the death, burial, and resurrection of Christ that is often described as being "buried with Christ". A person who is raised Brethren must make a personal choice to be baptized, and often does so as a young adult. Once a person is baptized, he or she may then participate in their breaking of bread ceremony.

The ritual of the Lord's Supper is a communion that unites the present moment with past and future events in the Christian salvation narrative.[5] The ritual reenacts Jesus' final meal with his disciples, at which he shared bread and wine with them, saying, "This is my body which is given for you", a foreshadowing of his sacrificial death and resurrection, which Christians believe redeemed them from sin. At the ritual of the Lord's Supper, Brethren also anticipate Jesus' return and the prophesied event that Darby called the rapture.

As one modern Brethren author explains, "the worshipper not only looks back to Golgotha and remembers Him in death, he not only looks upward to the Throne of God and praises Him for an accomplished redemption, but he also looks forward to that moment when the Lord will descend from heaven and take His waiting people home" (MacDonald 1973a: 71). Thus the communion ceremony serves as a regular reminder to look forward to the end of time. As an expression of this expectant attitude, 19th-century Brethren often replaced the standard Christian qualification about future plans "Lord willing" with "If the Lord be not come". Their breaking of bread service initially was small and intimate, and like Quakers, participants sometimes prayed and selected hymns spontaneously (Grass 2006: 98–9). Although spontaneity was an ideal, some

---

[4] Groves described Singapore missionary Alexander Grant as one of George Müller's successors, and praised him as a "discoverer of the Church" for his research on the term *ecclesia* in the New Testament (Groves 1906: 202).

[5] On the significance of ritual commemoration in Christianity and other religions, see Paul Connerton (1989: 41–71).

individuals were recognized to have the gift of teaching and presented carefully prepared teachings based on close study of the Bible.[6]

Although churches are local, Christians describe the Church as a spiritual unity that joins past, present, and future Christians. For that reason, in a 1931 editorial in *Echoes of Service*, editor William Edwy Vine (1873–1949) rejected naming churches for the people of a whole country like "the Church of England" or "the Indian Church". He also rejected the term "indigenous church", noting that it was based on a racial distinction between European and non-European Christians. He argued that a Chinese believer had the same spiritual identity as the "missionary from Europe or elsewhere who brought him the gospel", maintaining that the term "indigenous church" was subversive of the "true and spiritual condition and relationship". He concluded that "Churches of God as such should know no racial distinctions".[7]

Evangelical Christianity and the Brethren Movement

Today the Open Brethren are engaged evangelical Christians and share with other evangelicals four emphases: "*conversionism*, the belief that lives need to be changed; *activism*, the expression of the gospel in effort; *Biblicism*, a particular regard for the Bible; and what may be called *crucicentrism*, a stress on the sacrifice of Christ on the cross" (Bebbington 1989: 3–4). Mark Noll observes that these traits "have never by themselves yielded cohesive, institutionally compact, or

---

[6] In the 1990s, a typical programme at a Brethren assembly in Singapore included an introductory song (sung by an individual), some words from an elder, and an opening hymn followed by a prayer. Next would be a scripture reading, an address by a male elder and a prayer. From time to time, women participated, but traditionally women could not take leadership or speak at the breaking of bread ritual, which was led by the assembly's male elders. Some assemblies in Singapore and Malaysia now employ full-time workers who have had formal training in ministry. But in the traditional Brethren assemblies that I visited, the male elders rotated responsibility to preach at their Sunday communion meeting, and also called on popular speakers from other Brethren assemblies or churches to address them. They often invited travellers passing through Singapore to speak, and the guests (some of them prominent evangelists) opened by conveying greetings from the Christians in the last place they had visited. As the long history of schisms in the Brethren movement shows, if a member's teachings were deemed to be wrong, the elders would meet with that person to correct the error and would also prevent him from speaking publically. If the member continued to defend teachings that the male elders deemed to be heterodox or even heretical, they would expel him.

[7] W.E. Vine, "The Church and Churches", *ES* No. 1042 (September 1931): 195–6.

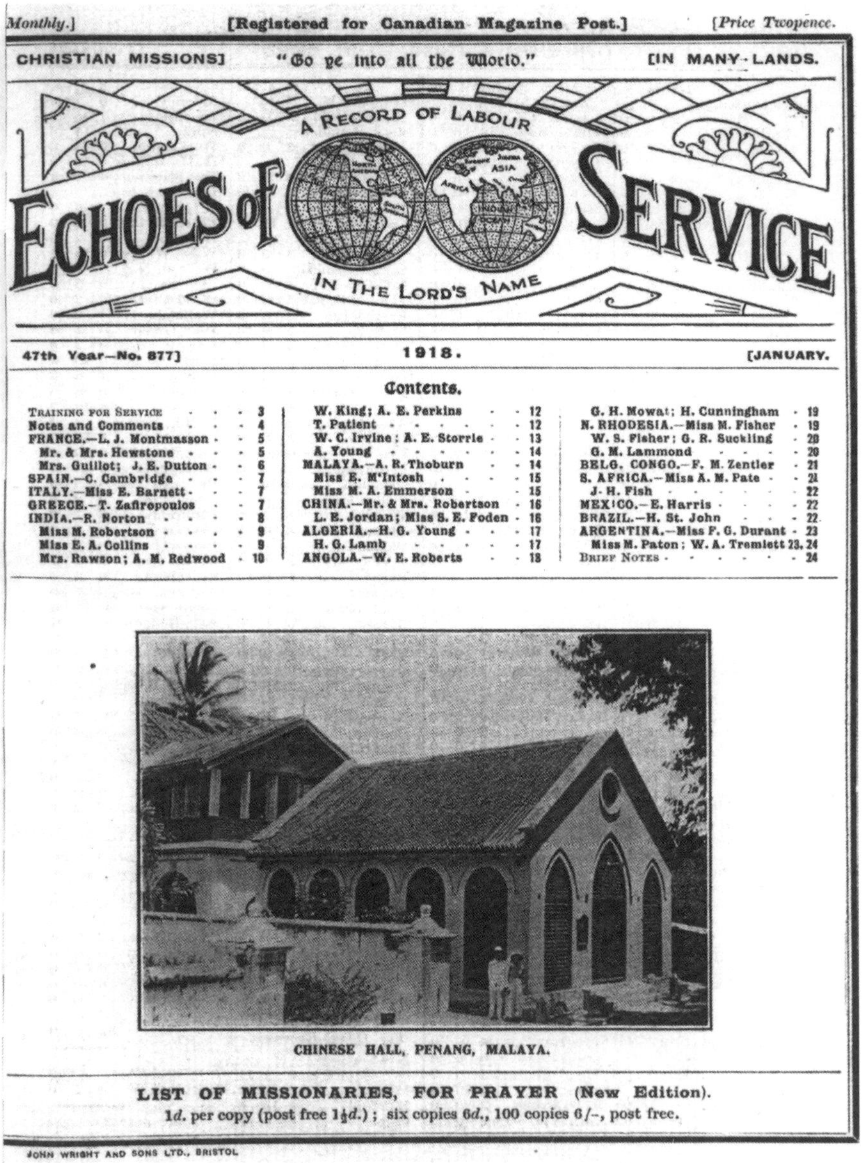

Monthly.] [Registered for Canadian Magazine Post.] [Price Twopence.

CHRISTIAN MISSIONS] "Go ye into all the World." [IN MANY-LANDS.

A RECORD OF LABOUR

ECHOES of SERVICE

IN THE LORD'S NAME

47th Year—No. 877] 1918. [JANUARY.

Contents.

CHINESE HALL, PENANG, MALAYA.

LIST OF MISSIONARIES, FOR PRAYER (New Edition).
1*d.* per copy (post free 1½*d.*); six copies 6*d.*, 100 copies 6/–, post free.

JOHN WRIGHT AND SONS LTD., BRISTOL

Figure 3 Cover page of *Echoes of Service* magazine with a photograph of the Chinese Hall in Penang, Malaysia. *Echoes of Service* No. 877 (January 1918): 1.

clearly demarcated groups of Christians", but they do identify "a large family of churches and religious enterprises" (Noll 2001: 13).[8]

According to a 2011 study by the Pew Forum, 584 million of the world's more than two billion Christians are identified as Pentecostal or charismatic. This study shows that 285 million of the world's Christians describe themselves as evangelical, which some regard as another label for Christian fundamentalism (Pew Forum 2011; see also Noll 2001: 278). Modern Protestant evangelicalism had its origin in waves of revival that swept across Europe and North America starting in the 18th century (Fitzgerald 2017: 13). By the 19th century, these movements had become global, extending to Asia and Australasia.

Many who write about the history of Christianity adopt the modes of national and national-confessional history writing. But evangelical Christians participated in international networks of communication and cooperated across linguistic and national boundaries. As Paul Jenkins notes, this international movement was "bewilderingly diffuse", involving a network of Protestant activists through Europe who cooperated interculturally (Jenkins 2000: 50–1; see also Gierl 2015). Historians have been challenged to write a history of modern Christianity that investigates the growth of multiple regional Christian movements and centres, and their transnational linkages (Stanley 2018: 5–6).

The Open Brethren trace their roots to Dublin and Bristol, Plymouth and Bath, but they also belonged to the diffuse international network that Jenkins describes, and made an early contribution to the global diffusion of undenominational Christianity. The Brethren helped extend Pietist networks well beyond Europe, connecting independent local churches and their leaders in Asia to its formal and informal circuits. They also invited denominational missionaries who had been labelled mavericks and malcontents to become independent, and helped raise funds for their support.

The Pietists urged Christians to pray directly to God in their own words and to expect a response, but they also called attention to their philanthropic programmes through their publications and networked communication (Gierl 2015: 369). As Martin Gierl explains, an individual became a Pietist not by enrolling in an organization but by participating in Pietist discourse, following

[8] In his definition of evangelicalism, David H. Lumsdaine notes that many in the United States use the term evangelical as a "polite substitute" for fundamentalism, and consider it to be an "unreasonable, militant, backward and uneducated" form of Protestantism (Lumsdaine 2009: 7).The term fundamentalism is associated with an American movement that started decades after the Brethren movement, but which has historical connections with it (see also Akenson 2018).

its rules, and publically identifying oneself as a Pietist. Communications, including networked correspondence, extended the scope of that discourse worldwide, creating what Gierl has described as an emerging trans-local public sphere (Gierl 2015: 369).

By the mid-19th century, the invention of the rotary press had increased the speed and efficiency of producing books and magazines, lowering the cost of printing. The development of an international postal system enabled the wide circulation of magazines, and the development of railway networks and faster steamship travel increased the efficiency of postal delivery services.[9]

Improved communications also promoted the electricity of revival. As Ralph Waldo Emerson proposed, religion is not brick and mortar buildings but electricity and motion, a traveller and a newness (Emerson 1856: 67). The 1859–60 event that some call the Second Evangelical Awakening began in Canada in 1857, but by 1859 had spread to Britain, where the revival attracted many British Christians to the Brethren movement. David L. Edwards concluded that the event merited its grand title since "many of its gatherings on both sides of the Atlantic were as full of excitement as the congregations of Whitefield and the Wesleys, and its leaders could travel around and address evening meetings far more easily than the pioneers could, thanks to the steamship, the railway and gas lights" (Edwards 1984: 170). Participants compared the spread of revival to electricity, water flowing, fire, and wind. But trains, roads, and steamships that promoted the rapid movement of people also promoted revival's rapid spread (Gitre 2004: 813).

Print Media and the Open Brethren Movement

Like other Pietists, the Open Brethren promoted their views and philanthropic practices in tracts, annual reports, and magazines, using technological advancements in print, travel, and communications to create a global parish that was held together by "the triad of discourse, media, and communications" (Gierl 2015: 369). In their annual reports and magazines, Brethren missionaries

[9] In Britain in 1837, Rowland Hill had promoted post office reforms based on the use of a uniform rate of postage and prepayment by postage stamp. In 1874 an international postal union was created that was soon named the Universal Postal Union. Member states accepted the stamps of other states throughout the entire route, increasing the efficiency of international mail. By 1914 member states included almost all countries; today the UPU is a branch of the United Nations, http://www.britannica.com/topic/postal-system.

published detailed accounts of their local activities that their editors and publishers circulated worldwide, creating far-flung transregional linkages.[10]

In *Imagined Communities* (1983), Benedict Anderson proposed that print capitalism helped create imagined communities whose members never met face-to-face but who had similar interests and share a common discourse. He focuses on national identity, but the Open Brethren used the printed word to unify a subcultural religious movement. Like other Pietists, the Brethren were committed evangelical Christians, but they had no formal statement of doctrines comparable to the Anglican 39 Articles of Religion, nor did they have any scripted liturgy comparable to the *Book of Common Prayer*. Instead, the editors of their annual reports and missionary magazines used their editorials and commentaries to promote correct ideas and patterns of practice. For the Brethren, writers and editors replaced archbishops and deacons (see also Dickson 2002: 146–8; Grass 2006: 149–51).

Independent missionaries wrote lengthy letters that were edited and published in annual reports and magazines, including *The Missionary Echo* and its successor, *Echoes of Service*. In an early form of crowdfunding, the editors of these publications collected, acknowledged, and transmitted donations on their behalf.[11] The letters offered ongoing diaries of the activities and experiences of Christians, and sometimes resembled serialized fiction, with new episodes in people's lives unfolding issue after issue. Starting in 1898, the publishers illustrated *Echoes of Service* with photographs of gospel halls and workers, as well as reproductions of postcard images of the countries where they worked (see Fig. 3).

The most celebrated 19th-century Brethren missionary was Frederick Stanley Arnot (1858–1914), whose letters were so popular with the readers of *Echoes of Service* that the editors began bimonthly publication of the magazine in 1891. Arnot was born in Glasgow and raised in Hamilton, where

---

[10] As Klaus Koschorke (2014: 185–8) observes, by the early 20th century local Christian publications promoted "cognitive interaction" by reporting events in indigenous Christian churches in Asia and Africa, Argentina, and Canada. Open Brethren publications did precisely this for English readers starting in the mid-19th century; Chinese publications had a similar impact in greater China.

[11] In 1876, a fund known as the Home and Foreign Mission Funds was established to support Brethren missionaries commended by assemblies in Scotland (Stunt et al. 1972: 562). According to the authors of *Turning the World Upside Down* (Stunt et al. 1972: 565), records for the early days of this mission fund are not available, so it is not possible to confirm that missionaries in Singapore and/or Penang received funding from this source.

the family of African missionary Dr David Livingstone lived. Livingstone's daughter was his classmate, and as a child he often visited their house. He and his brother were allowed to explore the attic, where the family had stored many of the doctor's curios, books, and letters (Stunt et al. 1972: 363; see also Burness 2016). He resolved to go to Africa and arrived there in 1881 at the age of 23.

Arnot travelled for seven years in Africa, and his frequent letters to the editors of *Echoes* were detailed with historical background, proto-ethnographic description, and maps. His diary entries and letters were gathered into small pamphlets and published (Arnot 1884, 1887), and on his return to England in 1888, he "found himself famous".[12] The Royal Geographic Society made him a fellow, and Brethren evangelist Lord Radstock invited Princess Mary (later Queen Mary) to attend a reception in his honour. In 1889, Arnot published his first book, *Garenganze, or Seven Years Pioneer Mission Work in Central Africa,* based on letters to *Echoes of Service* and his previously published pamphlets (Stunt et al. 1972: 378–9).

Arnot returned to Africa in 1889 accompanied by 13 new missionaries. Assemblies in England, Ireland, and Scotland commended the new recruits, who included Arnot's fiancée, a former miner, a doctor, a gardener, a merchant, and an evangelist (Stunt et al. 1972: 379). Arnot returned to England in 1892 and published a second book in 1893, *Bihe and Garenganze, or Four Years Further Work and Travel in Central Africa*. In 1896, Arnot worked for *Echoes of Service* and edited a "Missionary Paper for Young People", entitled *Across the Seas: a Selection of Missionary Incidents for Young People*, that included missionary letters similar to those published in *Echoes of Service* but written for youth.

In 1911 the editors of *Echoes of Service* launched a new youth-oriented publication, *Links of Help in Other Lands* (1911–34). They did so in conjunction with a growing Missionary Study Class Movement designed to teach youth about the Brethren contribution to overseas missions and the importance of evangelical practice at home and abroad. In the first issue the new editor T. Mortimore Sparks observed that although "countless volumes of

---

[12] A few months after the editors of *Echoes* reported the publication of one of Arnot's pamphlets, Mr Macdonald wrote from Penang that the account of Arnot's labours stirred his heart and would keep them "up to the mark" when they were "in danger of being cast down". Macdonald, Penang, 8 April 1885, *ES* No. 162 (June 1885): 93. But the success of Arnot's work set a standard that few of his contemporaries in the Brethren movement could match.

Figure 4 Missionary Helps postcard eulogizing Dr David Livingstone and showing a photograph of the tree in Africa under which his heart was buried. The seven African missions that "sprang from his grave" include Brethren missions in Central Africa founded by Fred S. Arnot. Liverpool. N.d. [c. 1912; advertised as having been recently published in *Links of Help in Other Lands* (Vol. II) 1912–13: 67]. Private collection of author.

Figure 5 Missionary Helps postcard commemorating the missionary career of Fred S. Arnot, described as the "Missionary Explorer upon whom Livingston's Mantle Fell", and noting that he was F.R.G.S., a Fellow of the Royal Geographic Society. The postcard shows photographs of Liwanki [Lewanika], King of the Barotse and of King Khama, who had been baptized Lutheran and who founded a Christian state in what is now Botswana, identifying him as Arnot's friend. Liverpool. Undated; after 1914. Private collection of author.

missionary literature" had been published, little of it focused on Open Brethren missionaries.[13]

The new magazine included a series of invited essays entitled "Look on the Fields", which included multi-part essays on Malaya and China, and also reviewed "spheres of labour", including translation, work with lepers, and medical missions. Topics discussed in the magazine included Confucianism, Buddhism, and Shintoism, and it contained remarkable analyses of China's revolutionary climate that I draw on in Chapter 11.

Between 1907 and 1924, both *Echoes of Service* and *Links of Help* advertised striking art postcards and posters that, like the magazine, were designed to support the missionary study movement (see, for example, Figures 4, 5, and 6 in this chapter). A small organization called Missionary Helps designed and sold these postcards between c. 1907–24.[14] In the first decades of the 20th century, *Links of Help* and the Missionary Helps postcards promoted the Open Brethren undenominational missionary movement by commemorating its past and by proposing that past as a model for the present and future. They did so fully aware of rising challenges from religious nationalists in Asia, from Western secularist literature that was being "caught up and read in China, Indian, and Egypt", and from modernist theologians in England and America who rejected "fundamental doctrines".[15]

The British and Foreign Bible and Religious Tract Societies

By the time that Groves went to India and Müller opened his first orphanage, British evangelical Christians had formed a huge variety of charitable societies to promote social improvement and reform. Among the most influential of these were the Church Missionary Society (1799), the Religious Tract Society

---

[13] T.M. Sparks, "To Our Readers", *Links of Help with Other Lands* Vol. 1 (1911–12): 2.

[14] Typically 12 or 20 cards were advertised as available for purchase, and some were sold as posters. Missionary Helps gave their address first as Liverpool, then as West Kirby (near Liverpool), and finally Wimbledon, where they cooperated with Pickering & Inglis, a Brethren publisher based in Glasgow that had extended its business to London in 1919. The head of Missionary Helps was Mr J. Smithard, a member of the Crete Road Gospel Hall in Liverpool, who was also involved in the Missionary Study Class movement. He published a pamphlet entitled "Missionary Studies—By the Use of Eye Gate" (c. 1908), and his organization's postcards used text and striking graphics to teach young people about missionary history and practice.

[15] "Duty and Need", Dr A. Rendle Short, *Links of Help* Vol. I (1911–12): 3–6. Dr Short was a scientist/surgeon who was known for his defence of creation as not contradicting evolution.

(1799), the British and Foreign Bible Society (1804) and the London Society for Promoting Christianity amongst the Jews (1808).[16] New organizations followed, including the Female Education Society (1834), the London City Mission (1835), and specialized programmes like medical missions, outreach to lepers, and work in prisons or at sailors' rests.

Among the most important of these were the British and Foreign Bible Society and the Religious Tract Society, which were among the earliest societies supporting missions in Penang and Singapore. The British and Foreign Bible Society was launched in 1804 as a non-denominational evangelical group whose main purpose was the translation and publication of the Bible so that it could be made available to readers throughout the world. Their earliest outreach was within the British Isles, and one of their first projects was making the Welsh Bible available. Soon after the BFBS was founded, auxiliaries spread rapidly throughout Britain and Europe, including the Russian Bible Society (est. 1813), the Dutch Bible Society (est. 1814) and the American Bible Society (est. 1816).

In 1779, two Methodist laymen founded a Bible Society that took as its goal the distribution of Bibles among British soldiers and sailors in the Navy. When the British and Foreign Bible Society was formed in 1804, this group renamed itself the Naval and Military Bible Society. Both groups distributed Bibles to members of the military, and the BFBS took as an early outreach programme distributing French and Spanish Bibles to foreign prisoners of war from the Franco-Spanish fleet, survivors of the 1805 Battle of Trafalgar who had been imprisoned on boats (Kverndal 2004: 328–9).

In 1813 British sailors began forming floating marine Bible associations that provided a vital link between the British and Foreign Bible Society and the world's port cities. The British and Foreign Bible Society soon could depend on their seafaring co-workers (sometimes the masters of merchant vessels or naval commanders) to transport Bibles in different languages to every corner of the globe (Kverndal 2004: 332–3). As they travelled, they spread evangelical Christianity as a global social movement.

The Bible Society movement also spread to Asia, where local Christians formed branches of the Bible Society, often in advance of the founding of mission stations. In 1814, London Missionary Society missionary William Milne (1785–1822) spent five months in Java, and while there met with Sir Thomas Stamford Raffles (1781–1826), then Lieutenant-Governor of Java. Raffles agreed to form

[16] The eight major evangelical organizations also included the Prayer Book and Homily Society (1812), the British Newfoundland and North America Society for Educating the Poor (1823), the General Society for Promoting District Visiting (1828), and the Church Pastoral Aid Society (1836) (Brown 1961: 342).

an auxiliary Bible Society and served as its president. The society took as its first project printing a translation of the Scriptures in Low Malay dialect, and also distributed Dutch and English Bibles and Testaments supplied by the BFBS to soldiers on service there ("T.S. Raffles and the Bible Society" n.d.). When Batavia was returned to Dutch control in 1817, the Java Bible Society was transferred to the Netherlands Bible Society (Browne 1859: 198).

In East and Southeast Asia, the BFBS funds supported several enterprises. First, the society supported translation work and often paid the salaries of missionaries who had specialized linguistic competence, who were seconded for long periods to the BFBS to engage in the work of Bible translation. Second, the society supported printing enterprises.They sometimes sent (or assisted missionary agencies in sending) modern printing equipment to mission stations so that Christian literature could be printed and distributed locally. Sometimes their funds were also used to pay for the composition and printing of tracts and Testaments.

Finally, the BFBS supplied the Brethren and other Protestant missionaries with Christian literature at subsidized cost and also provided funds for the distribution of scriptures, including paying the salaries of Asian colporteurs who could travel more freely than the European missionaries. In Penang and Singapore, the male Brethren missionaries regularly collaborated with the BFBS agents in their itineration and scripture distribution;[17] female missionaries often visited the homes of local women in the company of BFBS Bible women.

The Brethren also distributed tracts and books produced by the Religious Tract Society (RTS), which published Christian evangelical literature aimed at women, children and the poor. By 1848 the RTS was working throughout Europe, North America, and the near and middle East, and also in many parts of Asia, including Singapore, Borneo, Thailand, Burma, and China. The RTS kept in print popular publications like *Pilgrim's Progress*, which they translated into European and other languages (see Hofmeyr 2004). As Kyle B. Roberts has noted, tracts that blended the oral and the written, the orthodox and the folk were staples of 19th-century evangelicalism, playing a vital role in informing "the personal religious practices and belief systems of generations of evangelicals" (Roberts 2006: 234).[18]

---

[17] Thomas R. Angus, "Reaching Towns and Villages with the Gospel by means of a Bible-van", 30 December 1903. *Echoes of Service* (February 1904): 69.

[18] One tract that Roberts analyses, *The Dairyman's Daughter*, was published in over 40 languages, including Russian, Arabic, and Turkish. Roberts observes that the project of writing, translating, and distributing evangelical tracts fostered "a sense of membership in a religious community that in the eighteenth century crossed the Northern Atlantic, and by the end of the nineteenth century, spanned the globe" (Roberts 2006: 234).

Figure 6 Missionary Helps postcard promoting the network of Bible Societies and listing auxiliary branches in Europe and North America. N.d. [c. 1912; an unedited version was reprinted in *Links of Help with Other Lands* Vol. II (1912–13): 191]. *Echoes of Service* archive.

Conclusion

In the 19th century, print media, travel, and revival connected the Open Brethren to other Pietist Christians, who shared many of their philanthropic and evangelical practices. For that reason, the history of the Open Brethren movement in Asia must be written in the history of their evangelical projects. In Asia, these included education, medical missions, street corner evangelism and the distribution of tracts and testaments, the creation of opium refuges, rescue work with women and girls, and visitation in prisons, hospitals, and leper asylums. The Open Brethren differed from other evangelical Christians, however, in urging Christians to work independently of denominational structures, and to rely on networked communications to raise funds for their projects, a practice called living by faith. At the same time that they promoted independence to British Christians, they encouraged the formation of local churches with indigenous leaders in Asia. To the development of their practices and their philanthropic programmes in Bristol, Bath, and India, I now turn.

Chapter 2

George Müller, Anthony Norris Groves, and the Local Church in India

Open thy mouth wide, and I will fill it.

Book of Psalms[1]

The Open Brethren identify as founders George Müller (1805–98) and Anthony Norris Groves (1795–1853). Both helped develop the practice known as living by faith, Müller as the head of philanthropic organizations in Bristol, and Groves as a missionary in Baghdad and India. As I discuss in Chapter 1, the printed word linked the Brethren into global networks, and was the instrument through which they raised funds for their projects. Revivalists, missionaries, and indigenous evangelists wrote letters reporting on their work, and the editors of their publications in Bristol, London, and Bath collected and channelled donations to them.

British Baptist William Carey (1761–1834), the founder of the Baptist Missionary Society, is sometimes described as the father of modern missions. Although Carey's work marked the "entry of the English-speaking world on a large scale into the missionary enterprise" (Neill 1986: 222), the roots of the European missionary movement are found in 18th-century Pietism. The Danish-Halle mission sent its first missionaries to Tranquebar in what is now Tamil Nadu in 1706 (Fenger 1906: 18), and starting in 1732, Moravian Brethren worked with slave populations in the Danish-governed West Indies, with the Inuit of Greenland, and with North American Indians. A century later, the Open Brethren directly modeled their evangelical practices on those that Pietist Christians had developed in the long 18th century.

[1] Psalm 81: 10.

Figure 7 A 1921 Missionary Helps postcard showing "10 Ambassadors for Christ", including Anthony Norris Groves and George Müller and missionaries Leonard Strong and Frederick Stanley Arnot. A note added that the postcard was available through *Links of Help*, the "monthly magazine of the M[issionary] S[tudy] C[lass] movement". The map was also available as a large poster. *Echoes of Service* archive.

Pietism and the Brethren Movement

Pietism had roots in debates about what religious practice should be. Lutheran theologian Johan Arndt's 1605 book *True Christianity* shaped the Pietist answer to that question (Arndt 1979; Ward 2004: 21; see also Pinson 1934). In *True Christianity*, which by the end of the 18th century had been reprinted over 125 times, Arndt proposed that the Christian should focus on personal renewal, growth, and religious experience rather than doctrinal statements of faith (Erb 1979: 2–3).

In 1675 Philip Jakob Spener—Count Zinzendorf's godfather—published *Pia Desideria oder Wahren evangelischen Kirche* [*Pious Wishes*], as a preface to a collection of Arndt's sermons, popularizing Arndt as a "second Luther" (Oberman 1979: xiii). In *Pia Desideria* Spener put forward six proposals for reform of the Lutheran Church, including spiritual renewal, reform in the education of ministers to train them not only in theology but also in piety and devotion, and reform in their pastoral practice so that they preached sermons that expressed enthusiasm and emotion.

These theologians promoted the importance of a Christian's inner renewal, piety, and ethical concern, over orthodoxy and ritual formalism. But Pietists also assumed an ethical and social responsibility to address the problems of their generation. August Hermann Francke (1663–1727) is credited with transforming Pietist convictions into philanthropic institutions, including orphanages, schools for the poor, a hospital, and a pharmaceutical business.

In 1692 Francke joined the University of Halle as chair of Greek and Oriental Languages and Professor of Theology, also taking on a pastorate in order to support himself. Francke developed an innovative private school system at Halle, starting with a school for the poor at which tuition and board were free, then adding a fee-paying higher elementary school or *Bürgerschule*.[2] He used education to bridge class stratification, allowing orphans to prepare for a university education rather than channelling them towards a trade apprenticeship (Stoeffler 1973: 26). The Halle Pädagogium and Latin School became the model for secondary schools for all of Protestant Germany, and influenced the modernization of the German secondary school curriculum (Adamson 1971: 251–6).

---

[2] In 1695 he founded the Pädagogium, a school for the children of the elite, and in the same year established an orphanage to look after and educate neglected children and orphans. In 1697 he established a Latin School, and in 1698 a Girls School (Adamson 1971: 243–6).

In addition to the schools and orphanage, Francke developed a large pharmaceutical mail-order business, a hospital, and a dispensary. At his orphanages in Halle, Francke developed non-profit dispensaries for the care of the poor, and in the early 18th century employed a physician who, together with his brothers, developed a set of proprietary medications whose recipes were kept secret. The Francke Foundation sold these highly regarded medicines widely, and in the mid-18th century realized net profits of over £6,000 per year (Wilson 1998: 94–7; 2000).

The foundation also had a publishing business, and printed and sold Bibles, tracts, and Christian books on a large scale. Their publications included translations of the Bible into Eastern European languages and later into Tamil. Francke used the profits from its pharmaceutical and publishing enterprises to maintain the schools and medical facilities, and also to provide support for theology and medical students in Halle (Wilson 1998: 85–7, 93).

The University of Halle also trained missionaries, and the earliest missionaries to India were Lutheran Pietists. In 1706 the Danish king invited two of Francke's students, Bartholomäus Ziegenbalg and Heinrich Plütschau, to work in Tranquebar [Tharangambadi], which was a Danish colony from 1620–1845. They established a mission in what is now Tamil Nadu, and translated the Bible into Tamil and Hindustani. The missionaries' letters home were published in German and English translation, and Francke collected donations for this mission from all over Europe in a cooperative effort that involved Halle, Copenhagen, and London (Stoeffler 1973: 35).[3]

Halle-trained missionaries also worked in Europe. At the suggestion of Francke, in 1728 Johann Heinrich Callenberg established at University of Halle an Institutum Judaicum that taught advanced Hebrew, Yiddish and rabbinics to prepare students for work with European Jews. The Institutum also operated a printing office where Callenberg published Yiddish translations of sections of the New Testament. The programme's first two missionaries, Widmann and Manitius, travelled widely in Europe from 1730–35, seeking to strike up conversations with Jews whom they met in the streets or other public places, using Yiddish to explain their interpretation of salvation to them, and distributing Christian publications, promoting a focus on the Bible over Kabbalah.

The Halle-trained Pietist missionaries emphasized language learning for effective oral communication, translated texts into vernacular languages,

[3] In the 18th century the East India Company did not allow evangelical work, but the EIC appreciated the Lutheran missionaries' mastery of Indian languages and their printing skills, and sometimes recruited them to British-controlled areas.

distributed Bibles and tracts, and did street corner evangelism. Their work established a pattern for later generations of evangelical missionaries, including the Open Brethren, who, like them, visited local communities to learn about ordinary people's lives and hardships, entered religious public spaces during services seeking an audience with non-Christians, and engaged non-Christians in debate about sacred meanings and practices (Ariel 2013: 25–6).

Franke also provided a model for the Pietist practice of networked communication. In order to attract donations from evangelical Christians throughout Europe, he wrote *The Footsteps of Divine Providence: or, The Bountiful Hand of Heaven Defraying the Expenses of Faith* in 1701, and updated it with additions for a decade. An English translation of an abbreviated version of the second edition was published in London in 1707 (Herzog 2003: 80). In developing evangelical networks that crossed territorial and denominational boundaries, including cooperation with the Anglican Society for Promoting Christian Knowledge (SPCK) and the Society for Propagating the Gospel in Foreign Parts, Francke contributed to the development of an evangelical movement that "purposively transcended dynastic boundaries" (Wilson 1998: 89).

The title page of an English translation of Francke's book, *The Footsteps of Divine Providence* (1787), has two epigraphs from the Bible: "Except the Lord build the house, they labour in vain that build it" (Psalm cxxvii. 1) and "Length of days is in [wisdom's] right hand; and in her left hand riches and honour" (Prov. iii. 16). The first suggest an agentive and attentive God involved in human affairs, the second human agency in exercizing wisdom and understanding. Francke provided Pietism with the prototype of what came to be called "faith" missions, and a model for the expectation of "concrete answers to prayer" (Stoeffler 1973: 31).

George Müller and the Scriptural Knowledge Institution

The Open Brethren regard George Müller (1805–98), together with Anthony Norris Groves (1795–1853), as the two main founders of the Open Brethren movement. Their biographies are closely linked: Müller married Groves' sister and raised funds for over 60 years to support the mission that Groves founded in India in 1836 (SKI 1897: 47). For decades Müller published letters from and channelled donations to independent missionaries and Chinese evangelists in Penang and Singapore, and supported James Hudson Taylor and missionaries associated with the China Inland Mission.

Müller was born in Prussia and attended the University of Halle to prepare to become a Lutheran clergyman. In 1826 he became interested in becoming a

Figure 8 Postcard, George Müller. *Echoes of Service* archive.

missionary. Uncertain what to do, he bought a ticket in the Royal Lottery and decided that if he won, he would "take it to be His will that he should become a missionary; if not, that he should remain at home." He won a small sum and applied to the Berlin Missionary Society. When they refused him since his father would not give his consent, he decided that his method in relying on the lottery had been both worldly and unscriptural (Warne 1934: 20–3).

In 1829 Müller applied to the London Society for Promoting Christianity amongst the Jews (LSPCJ) and was accepted as a missionary student. The LSPCJ was a combined Bible, Missionary, Tract, and School Society that supported ordained missionaries, unordained missionary agents, colporteurs, and teachers, including a number of Jewish converts to Christianity, at mission stations in Europe, Asia, Africa, and North America. The LSPCJ's foundation marked the starting point of the Christian Zionist movement, and its founder Lewis Way promoted the divine right of the Jewish people to possess Palestine in the LJS journal, *The Jewish Expositor*, in articles published in 1820–22 (see Lewis 2009).

On arrival in London in March 1829, his health was poor and a friend invited him to Devon to recuperate. Soon after his return to London to continue his training, Müller decided to leave the LSPCJ and return to Devon (Müller 1984: 23–9; Stunt 2000: 286). While still in London he had heard about Groves, and in Devon he met many of his associates, including Henry Craik, who had tutored Grove's children, Bessie and Charlotte Paget, and William Hake. In October 1830, Müller married Groves' sister, Mary. Soon after his marriage he renounced his salary and decided to live by faith, meaning that he relied on gifts alone to support his work, a practice that the Open Brethren identify as one of their distinctives (Stunt 2000: 286; Larsen 1998: 69).

As he explained it, he enjoyed living on the brink:

> I had a secret satisfaction in the greatness of the difficulties which were in the way. So far from being cast down on account of them, they delighted my soul; for I only desired to do the will of the Lord in this matter . . . the greater the obstacles, the more abundantly plain the proof, that I had come to a right judgment, if they were removed by prayer (Sims n.d.: 35).

As he made decisions, he prayed and read the Bible seeking to discern God's will, a practice termed bibliomancy.[4]

[4] Bibliomancy is the practice of reading the Bible as a way of seeking guidance from divine providence. To that end, the person opens their Bible at random with a troubling question in mind and reads the page thus found in relation to their question.

Together with Henry Craik, Müller established the Scriptural Knowledge Institution (SKI) in Bristol in 1834 to raise funds for philanthropic work, including Bible printing and distribution and missionary work. Müller also built orphanages in Bristol to look after children who had lost their parents in the cholera pandemic that reached Britain in 1831. Müller noted in his diary that he had read Francke's biography and also seen many times the enormous orphan houses that Francke had founded.[5] In 1835 he wrote: "I have frequently, for a long time, thought of laboring in a similar way, on a much smaller scale; not to imitate Franke (sic), but in reliance upon the Lord. May God make it plain!" (Müller 1861: 111).

Müller recalled that on reading the phrase "Open thy mouth wide, and I will fill it" (Psalm 81: 10) in his Bible, he had prayed "for premises, one thousand pounds, and suitable individuals to take care of the children". Two days later he received the first shilling for the project (Müller 1861: 116). Ashley Down orphanage could eventually accommodate over 2,000 residents (Pierson 1899: 212). Müller's biographer concluded that "George Müller's whole life work at Bristol found both its suggestion and pattern in Francke's orphanage at Halle" (Pierson 1899: 46). Pierson further concluded that every form of "faith work", including Hudson Taylor's China Inland Mission, could be traced "to the example of A. H. Francke, in Halle, or George Mueller in Bristol" (Pierson 1899: 206).

Müller's publication *Narrative of the Lord's Dealings with George Müller* included this entry, which is probably one of the most cited passages from his writings:

> "Nov. 8, 1840.--There was also 1s. put into the box at Bethesda, with the words "Jehovah Jireh." These words have often been refreshing to my soul for many years past, and I wrote them with a valuable diamond ring, set with ten brilliants, which was given for the orphans about twenty months since, upon a pane of glass in my room, which circumstance, in remembrance of the remarkable way in which that valuable ring came, has often cheered my heart, *when in deep poverty my eyes have been cast upon* "JEHOVAH JIREH' (i.e., the Lord will provide) whilst sitting in my room (Müller 1841: 364).

Müller relied on prayer, but he also advertised his work and that of revivalists, missionaries, and indigenous evangelists in his network through an

[5] This is likely to have been H.E.F. Guericke's *A.H. Francke*, which was originally published in German in 1827 and was translated into English as *The Life of A.H. Francke* (1847).

internationally distributed annual report that he both sent and sold to donors. Müller entitled the annual report *A Brief Narrative of Facts relative to The New Orphan Homes of Ashley Down Bristol and the Other Objects of the Scriptural Knowledge Institution for Home and Abroad.* Between 1837 and 1856, Müller also published four installments of *A Narrative of some of the Lord's Dealings with George Müller*, which wove together entries from his diary and the SKI annual reports, a series that he continued in 1861 and 1886.[6]

Like the British and Foreign Bible Society, the Scriptural Knowledge Institution took Bible distribution as one of its major goals. But most of the Bibles that the SKI kept in stock were intended for readers of English and European languages. For example, Müller reported in 1877 that their Bible and Tract Warehouse had in stock 200 different sorts of English Bibles, ranging in price from 6d. (sixpence) to £4 18s, and also 30 different kinds of New Testament. The SKI warehouse maintained a stock of Bibles and Testaments in Welsh, Danish, Dutch, French, German, Italian, Portuguese, and Spanish; of Testaments in Russian, Swedish, Ancient Greek, and Greek and English, and also sold the Old Testament and Psalms in Hebrew (Müller 1877: 32). Their agents often gave away scriptures or sold them at subsidized rates, including expensive large type editions for those who had difficulty reading small print.

The SKI supported an extensive network of missionaries in Britain and Europe, including England, Ireland, Scotland, Wales, Spain, Italy, France, Belgium, Switzerland, Germany, and Norway. In Europe, missionaries and colporteurs used Bible Carriages to travel and circulate the scriptures widely in conjunction with open-air preaching. In his 1877 annual report, for example, Müller reported that the SKI colporteurs had given out many thousands of scriptures at considerable expense to workers in the factories and mills of Lancashire, Yorkshire, Derbyshire, and Nottinghamshire (Muller 1877: 33).

The SKI supplied the missionaries in Penang and Singapore with financial support, but the BFBS sponsored Bible translation into Asian languages, and arranged to have copies of the scriptures printed locally. The BFBS also maintained local staff who engaged in Bible distribution, paid the salaries of Chinese colporteurs (some of whom worked with Brethren missionaries), and later provided their workers with Bible vans that Brethren missionaries borrowed from time to time.

---

[6] As Neil Summerton has observed, although individual gifts were not solicited from specific individuals, and the needs of the work were the subject of prayer, the reports and other publications served to make the SKI's needs widely known (Summerton 2003; see also Summerton 2016: 83).

The SKI started publishing annual reports in 1837, and transmitted donations to independent missionaries working in Europe, England, Scotland, Ireland, and Canada. The recipients of funds sent Müller letters reporting on their activities, and starting in 1858 he published excerpts from these letters in the SKI's annual report. By 1860 Müller forwarded donations to 80 missionaries working in British Guiana, China, Penang, the East Indies, Nova Scotia, Canada, Italy, Sardinia, Switzerland, France, Belgium, Ireland, Scotland, and 21 missionaries working in England and Cornwall (Müller 1860).

One of the earliest missionaries the Scriptural Knowledge Institution supported was Leonard Strong (1797–1874), a former Anglican missionary in the Crown colony of Demerara-Essequibo (today, Guyana), who had seceded from the Anglican missionary agency. The Baptist missionary who had preceded Strong had been convicted of complicity in a slave uprising and sentenced to death. Although John Smith's sentence was remitted, he died in prison awaiting dismissal from the West Indies (London Missionary Society 1824).

British Parliament had abolished the slave trade when it enacted the Slave Trade Act of 1807. But the emancipation of the slaves was not accomplished until the Slavery Abolition Act of 1833. Quakers and Evangelical Christians had led the movement to abolish slavery, and white settlers in the West Indies feared that when evangelical missionaries introduced Christian ideals, they would also influence slaves to demand political liberty (Carson 2012: 115).

The British authorities chose Strong to replace Smith, believing that as an Anglican minister he would be under the government's direct control. But when the establishment learned that Strong also favoured "the Emancipation of the labouring class", they arranged for his transfer (Stunt 2015: 184). He remained in Demerara, but was disatisfied, observing that the officers of a newly formed branch of the Bible Society were fond of horse racing and balls (Stunt 2015: 189). He resigned from the CMS in 1838, joined a Brethren assembly, and remained in British Guiana as an independent missionary with support from the SKI (Stunt 2015: 191).

In the SKI's 19th annual report, Müller listed details of more than 3,000 donations from all over Britain, but also from Australia, Rome, Belgium, and British Guiana. In the entries for May 1858, he included one donor's initials and identified another as a clergyman, but usually only supplied information about the donor's location:

> May 1 From British Guiana, 6s, the proceeds of the sale of a couple of fowls.--£3.10s. "the fruit of one month's praying for the Orphans."--From C. M. S. L.: a gold rose chain, a silver gilt smelling bottle, a gold pencil case, a gold watch hook, a pair of pearl earings, a regard brooch

> set with 2 rubies, an emerald, a garnet, an amethyst, and a brilliant, a ring set with 9 small diamonds, and 13 other gold rings. Another precious answer to my daily prayers for such articles... --May 20. From Cumberland: a nugget of gold from Australia, and a gold brooch set with a carbuncle. --May 22. From Greenock £1 and 3 sets of gold shirt studs (SKI 1858: 42–3).

When Müller reported a gift of six shillings from the sale of two chickens alongside gifts of silver, gold, rubies, pearls, and diamonds, the narrative suggested the inclusiveness of the Open Brethren movement.

Starting in 1860, SKI's list of supported missionaries included independent missionaries in Penang, some of whom moved to Malacca and Singapore. After 1868 Müller frequently published extracts from letters from missionaries and Chinese evangelists in all three cities. In 1869, Tan See Boo wrote to Müller from Singapore to thank him for a five pound donation, and also gave thanks for Müller's love and to God, "our Heavenly Father who condescends to care for us, hearing my prayer, graciously giving this from places where I have not been and persons whom I do not know, from afar" (Müller 1870: 65). The SKI also gave extensive support to James Hudson Taylor and the China Inland Mission (est. 1865), and by the early 1870s Müller reported sending donations to as many as 25 missionaries in China, twice as many as he supported in other countries (Summerton 2016: 94–5).

In the last SKI annual report that he wrote, Müller summarized his fundraising for the 63 years since the SKI's founding. Between March 1834 and May 1897, the SKI had raised £259,776 for the support of several hundred independent undenominational missionaries in China, India, the Straits of Malacca, Palestine, Egypt, Africa, Demerara, Essequibo Berbice, South America, the United States, Canada, Spain, Italy, Scotland, Wales, and throughout England. Sixty-three of these missionaries were from his church in Bristol. He concluded that the many thousands of pounds spent on the missions in Penang and Singapore in the previous 40 years had been well spent (SKI 1897: 51; Warne 1934: 109–11).

Anthony Norris Groves

Contemporary Brethren describe Anthony Norris Groves as one of the main founders of their missionary movement. Like Darby, Groves, concluded that ordination was not required to preach the gospel, and he went to Baghdad in 1829 as an independent lay missionary, taking the Sermon on the Mount as his guide to Christian practice (H. Groves 1869: 39, 43). In a published journal reporting on a year in Baghdad, he proposed that Christians should judge whether or not someone was "fit for their work" not by "their being ordained or unordained by this or that denomination of men, but according to the rule of the apostles, by their doctrine and walking as they had", taking them for "ensamples" (Groves 1832: 262).

In proposing that Christians take the apostles as "ensamples", Groves used an archaic term found in the King James Bible that refers to "a precedent which may be followed or imitated; a pattern or model of conduct". Ensample is also used as a verb meaning "to authorize or instruct by example" (OED Online 2018). Simply put, Groves proposed that Christians take the New Testament as a model not only for doctrine but also for practice. Although uncommonly used, the term 'ensample' precisely describes the Brethren approach to their practice of Christianity.

The Open Brethren took as their main ensample the New Testament, which includes 21 epistles, personal letters that leaders wrote to members of the early churches. The apostles travelled widely in the first ten years after Jesus' death, spreading their religion from Jerusalem to Antioch, Ephesus, and Rome, but also to North Africa and Asia Minor. Nineteen centuries later, the Brethren took the epistles as a model for evangelical outreach in the multilingual, multiethnic British empire and, like the Apostles, wrote letters reporting on the local churches they visited.

The Open Brethren also promoted the lives of Christians as ensamples for practice, and Groves himself took German Pietist missionary Karl Rhenius as a model for his work. He praised Rhenius' methods of proselytism, but also persuaded Rhenius to become an independent missionary and help raised donations for his support. Groves also mentored one of Rhenius' students, Tamil evangelist John Christian Arulappan (a.k.a. Aroolappen) (1810–67), and promoted him to British Christians. The Open Brethren later held up Arulappan as an ensample of the self-sufficient native Christian leader, evidence of the success of their approach.

Groves' legacy was ensured by his second wife, Harriet Baynes Groves, who composed and published his memoir in 1856, and their son, Henry Groves, who was the co-editor of a new missionary magazine, *The Missionary Echo*, that commenced publication in 1872. In 1939, George Lang wrote a new biography of Groves, whom he praised as a "modern pioneer" for faith missions conducted on apostolic principles (Lang 1939 [1949]: 19).

In 1813—the year that the so-called Pious Clause of the Charter Act granted evangelical Protestant missionaries access to territories that the British East India Company controlled—18-year-old Groves had set up a dental practice in Plymouth. Two years later he married his wealthy cousin and moved to

Exeter. There Groves' friends included schoolmaster William Hake, who was co-secretary of the pacifist Society for the Promotion of Permanent and Universal Peace, and Bessie and Charlotte Paget. The Paget sisters introduced Groves into a wider circle of Christians, some of whom were members of the Society of Friends, and Groves became co-secretary with George Dymond of the Devon and Exeter Society for the Abolition of Slavery throughout the British Dominions (Stunt 2000: 121). Groves' second wife credited Bessie Paget, whom he called his "mother, in the things of God" with introducing Groves to the "doctrines of grace" and also to Bible prophecy (H. Groves 1869: 558).

In 1825 Groves published an influential tract, *Christian Devotedness, or The Consideration of Our Saviour's Precept, "Lay not up for yourselves treasures upon earth"*. Groves urged Christians to not hoard wealth but rather to give it up for charitable purposes, basing his arguments on the Sermon on the Mount, in which Jesus exhorted his listeners to "lay up for yourselves treasures in heaven, where neither moth nor rust doth corrupt, and where thieves do not break through nor steal: for where your treasure is, there will your heart be also". He proposed that Christians should base their lives on the teachings laid out in the Sermon on the Mount and give "themselves, their property, time and talents" to the task of making others "happy in time, and in eternity". Groves concluded that care of the soul was far more important than the accumulation of wealth, and that material wealth should be given away to ensure an individual's future in heaven.

The next year, Groves entered Trinity College Dublin as an external student to study theology in preparation to become a missionary with the Anglican Church Missionary Society. John Nelson Darby later claimed credit for creating the Brethren form of religious practice, but Groves' widow and others attributed its invention to Groves. While visiting Dublin, Groves had began to attend an undenominational meeting with a small group of Christians. The initiative to form the group was taken by Edward Cronin, a dental student and convert from Catholicism who as a sojourner in Dublin had sought a church. Cronin discovered, however, that he needed special membership before he could join in the breaking of bread ceremony. In 1825 he began to hold private meetings with a few friends for prayer. In 1827, one of the group's members, John Gifford Bellett, invited Groves to join them, and Darby also joined (Coad 1968: 20; see also H. Groves 1869: 39). Like Darby, Groves observed that although the ritual of the Lord's Supper was supposed to symbolize Christian unity, it instead divided Christians.

In Exeter Groves had a conversation with William Hake, who asked him if he considered war to be unlawful. He agreed that it was, and Hake then asked him how he could affirm the Anglican article of faith that stated, "It is lawful for Christian men to take up arms at the command of a civil magistrate." Groves realized that he could not affirm this article, and consequently could not be ordained as a Church of England minister (Brock 1984: 31). When a thief stole the money intended for his transportation, leaving the rent money behind, Groves regarded this as a providential event that showed that he was not meant to finish his theology degree (H. Groves 1869: 41–2).

Groves still went to London to see if he could arrange to work for the CMS as a lay missionary. But after the CMS informed him that as an unordained missionary he could not perform the breaking of bread ritual, Groves closely read the Scriptures and concluded that "it appeared to him from Scripture, that believers, meeting together as disciples of Christ, were free to bread bread together, as their Lord had admonished them; and that, in as far as the practice of the apostles could be a guide, every Lord's day should be set apart for thus remembering the Lord's death, and obeying his parting command".

Groves closed his dental practice and he and his family lived with Bessie and Charlotte Paget for a year before going to Baghdad as lay missionaries (H. Groves 1869: 35–6). While living with them, he preached to a small gathering of Christians who met in a house owned by Bessie Paget. While living in Exeter, Groves was baptized by immersion, but because he decided that Christians should not be divided by their denominations, he did not wish to be identified as Baptist (H. Groves 1869: 57).

Baghdad and India

Like Groves, many of the early Brethren were educated, well-to-do young men. In 1829, John Vesey Parnell (later Lord Congleton) convinced a friend to take himself, Mr and Mrs Groves, their two sons, and their sons' tutor John Kitto, on a yacht to Russia, from whence the party travelled overland to Baghdad (Dann 2004: 109–40). There, Groves opened a school and the British and Foreign Bible Society's depot in Bombay provided him with Bibles, Testaments and Psalters in Armenian, Arabic, Syriac, and Persian. During his stay, an epidemic of plague devastated the city, followed by a massive flood that led houses to collapse throughout the city. Mrs Groves fell ill with plague and died, followed soon by their youngest child. As these natural disasters unfolded, the city fell under siege, resulting in massive inflation and famine (Groves 1832: 12, 154, 204, 236–7). Through it all, Groves remained confident that God exercized special providence over cities and nations, life and death, and expected miracles in modern times (Whittaker 2016: 38–9).

Groves continued to work in Baghdad until 1833. *Christian Devotedness* had been published in India, and after reading it, British irrigation engineer Arthur Cotton visited Groves in Baghdad and encouraged him to visit India (H. Groves 1869: 273–4). Leaving his two sons with friends, Groves travelled by ship along the Indian coastline, making inland excursions to Tinnevelly, Trichinopoly, Patna and Benares, and meeting with missionaries of all denominations. In Calcutta he met with the Anglican Bishop and chaplains, as well as wealthy and influential European residents. He considered working with Europeans, and thought that Calcutta might prove to be "a sphere of most abundant usefulness" for him (H. Groves 1869: 294).

Groves discovered that *Christian Devotedness* had been widely circulated in India and while in Bombay wrote a new tract. In "On the Nature of Christian Influence", he explained that although people thought that being "great, charismatic, rich, or wise in the things of the world" would give them influence in Christian work, their influence depended instead on the extent to which an individual's life "was controlled by Christian principles", including the universal principal of "unconditional love". The Christian expressed this love by "imparting his riches to the church and to the poor, as his Lord desires, makes a striking exhibition of his love in obeying the Lord, and he encourages the saints to deeds of similar devotedness" (Groves 1833: 41–4).

In his meetings with missionaries, Groves promoted a method of evangelical work based on personal self-denial. He promoted not only a simple lifestyle but also living in "close and real contact" with the natives so as to "leave a lively impression". He characterized this as a "crucifixion of the self" without which nothing could be accomplished (H. Groves 1869: 279). But he also reported that he had privately suggested to some missionaries that they give up "certain expensive and apparently self-indulgent habits" and that they had resisted his recommendations (H. Groves 1869: 230). Groves commented that he was asking people to act in a manner "so contrary to natural principles" that it would call the world's attention to Christians. These included the desire to hoard riches, seek status and charisma, and obtain learned degrees—a list that recalls Pierre Bourdieu's analysis of agents and their strategies as quests not only for wealth but for social, cultural and symbolic capital (Groves 1833: 44; Bourdieu 1984).

In India, Groves met British Baptist William Carey (1761–1834), the founder of the Baptist Missionary Society, who had joined the Danish mission in Serampore in 1793. He also visited German missionaries including Prussian Lutheran missionary Karl Rhenius (1790–1838), who had come to India in 1814 with support from the Anglican Church Missionary Society. Rhenius had worked in Madras for five years, where he proved to be a brilliant linguist who spoke Tamil fluently (Neill 1985: 218–9). But because he was unwilling to conform to Anglican practices, the CMS sent him to work in a remote area, Tinnevelly (today known as Tirunelveli), at a "mission *founded* and *continued by Germans of the same principles with himself*" (Groves 1835: 3 [emphasis in the original]).

The German Pietist Mission

In Tinnevelly Rhenius joined the earliest Protestant mission in India, which had been launched by Lutheran Pietists trained in Halle, Germany. He worked in Palamcottah (Palaiyamkottai), a town in the Tinnevelly district whose chapel school had been built in 1783 with donations from a Brahmin widow. A Halle-trained Pietist missionary had baptized her, and the church is still popularly known as "Clorinda's Church" (Daughrity 2008: 75; Neill 1985: 54).

As Robert Eric Frykenberg described him, Rhenius was a brilliant Prussian military veteran with "Moravian convictions". He trained indigenous workers who spread the Christian movement widely in Tinnevelly:

> Rhenius encouraged, instructed, trained, translated, and held dramatic public debates. His disciples, known as pilgrims, fanned out; thousands, again whole villages, turned Christian. The community doubled and trebled in size each decade thereafter. As congregations proliferated, so did chapel schools and self-help societies, with missions for the homeless, widows, and orphans. Rhenius's wife, a Ceylon-born Tamil speaker of Dutch extraction, ran schools for girls and women, teaching basic literacy and home health—setting a pattern that would soon be followed elsewhere (Frykenberg 2005: 114).

As Rhenius described his methods, he studied Hindu religious books but also engaged in extensive itineration, tracting, and public exhortations, sometimes at Hindu temple festivals. He debated frequently with Indian elites and religious experts, including Hindu Brahmans, Jain priests, astrologers, and others, who both explained their own religion and asked questions about Christianity.

In 1841, Rhenius' son composed and published a memoir based on extracts of his father's journals, papers, and correspondence. Rhenius vividly reported his observations and conversations with them. For example, on one occasion Yogi Narayana Swamiar from Mysore travelled through the region on an elephant with drummers and attendants, visiting wealthy devotees and accepting gifts from them. When he visited Rhenius, they discussed the Hindu concept *maya*, which Rhenius translated as "delusion". Rhenius observed that *maya* existed, not in material objects but in the human mind, which was "captivated and

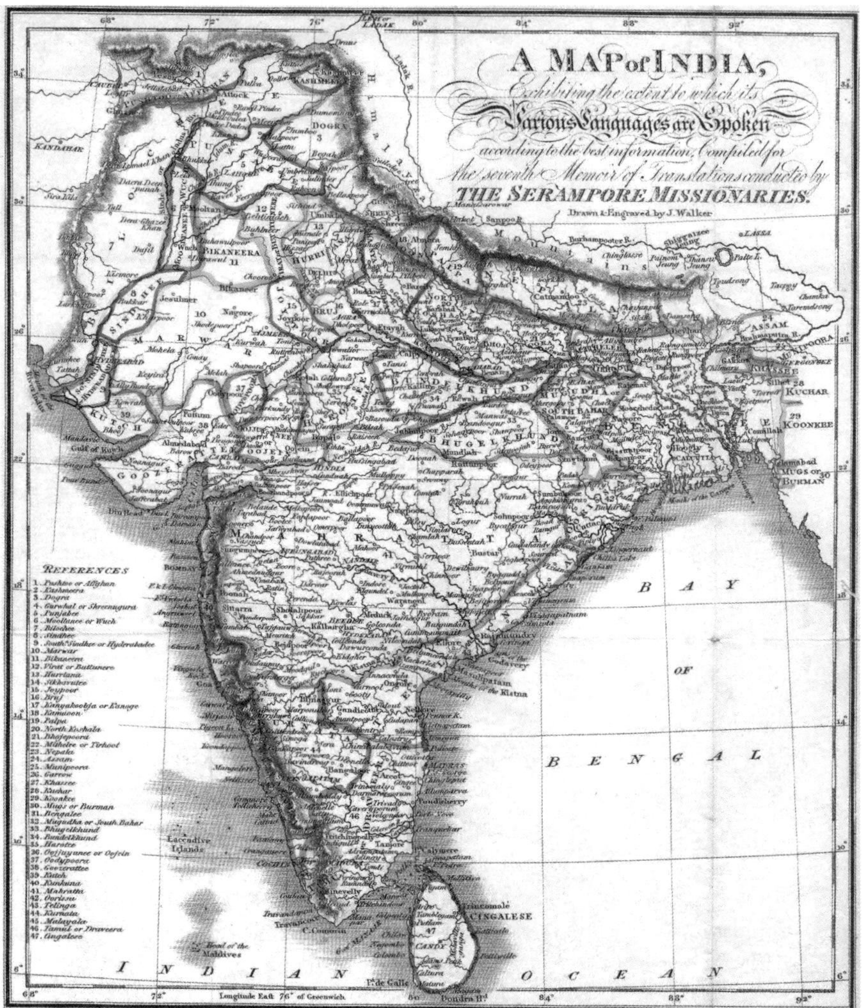

Figure 9 In 1822, the Serampore Mission published a map of India's spoken languages, including Tamul or "Draveera" (today Tamil), which was spoken in southern India including Madras (today Chennai), and at their missions in Tranquebar (Tharangambadi) and Tinnevelly (Tirunelveli). "Map of India and Languages Spoken, 1822" is reprinted with permission of Center for Study of the Life and Work of William Carey, D.D. (1761–1834), William Carey University, 710 William Carey Parkway, Hattiesburg, Mississippi, 39401 U.S.A.

Figure 10 Postcard showing some details of British Baptism missionary William Carey's life, including his early career as a cobbler, and examples of Bible translation into Indian languages. *Echoes of Service* archive.

bewildered by them". The Yogi admitted that he loved riches, and Rhenius offered to teach him an "approved remedy for the evil" of desire. Rhenius gave him Christian books in Tamil and Telugu, and the Yogi promised to return to learn more. Rhenius expressed the pious hope that someday the Guru would find "true riches". But he also added that the Guru had explained how the late Anglican bishop had helped him to obtain his governance, which was the means to his pomp (Rhenius 1841: 447–8).[7]

Rhenius' journals also documented Tamil Nadu's minority religions. He was intrigued by the Jain religion, speculating that it was a "corruption" of Christianity, but he also guessed that Jains regarded Christianity as a corruption of their own beliefs (Rhenius 1841: 189). In North Travancore he visited a Syrian College and attended a Syrian Christian service. Although he deplored their ritual as "childish play with things sacred", he observed that the ritual blessing was gracefully performed, and that the priest looked "very grand" in a "splendid red silk gown" that contrasted with his long black beard (Rhenius 1841: 386).

In his writings, he described people's everyday practices including the on-the-ground workings of the caste system and Hindu rituals. To give but one example, in his journal for 1822, he reported meeting a man on the road who had pierced his cheeks with wire and had heavy chains hanging from his mouth and on his shoulders. The young man explained that he had incurable dysentery, and that on the advice of a priest at a famous temple, he had taken a vow to seek donations for chain links that he could use to draw the "idol car". Rhenius invited him to his house where he "made known to him the plan of salvation", but reported that he did not succeed in convincing him to give up on self-mortification (Rhenius 1841: 233–4).

Rhenius argued that India's underlying religion was monotheistic, and that polytheism had been introduced as an instrument of exploitation. He criticized the caste system, noting that the symbolism of purity and impurity supported

[7] Homi Bhabha comments that in a reported dialogue with an Indian pilgrim, Rhenius placed a "narcissistic, demand" on the pilgrim that the pilgrim resisted (1994: 140). He juxtaposes this dialogue with an excerpt from the sermon of an Anglican Archdeacon, viewing them as similar, but the two texts are different in tone and detail. Rhenius could speak Tamil and he provided detailed exegesis of the metaphorical explanation that the pilgrim offered in response to the question of whether he knew God; the archdeacon mentioned that Indians sometimes explained their rejection of Christianity using "a popular and careless proverb" but gives no examples and offers no exegesis (Bhabha 1994 [2004]: 140–1).

social inequality.[8] Rhenius concluded that the unknown author of the caste system had sought to:

> establish the unlimited power and despotic superiority of the priesthood over every other class. This will be evident from a consideration of the doctrines and ceremonies of the Hindus, particularly from the doctrine of transmigration, from the implicit obedience which the Brahmans demand, and from the manner in which they treat the people (Rhenius 1841: 173–4).

Compare Rhenius' analysis of the caste system with that of Marx, who proposed in an 1861–63 manuscript that in Asia, religion including the Hindu caste system veiled exploitation, an inequality that he viewed as intrinsic to the Asiatic Mode of Production. As a consequence, he concluded, relations of production appeared to both sides as "a relation of masters to servants, of free men to slaves, or demigods to ordinary mortals" (Anderson 2010: 164). Marx was familiar with the writings of Christian missionaries in India and China and, like them, proposed the overthrow of traditional systems of authority.

The German missionaries' method involved forming a network of indigenous Christian churches that they visited from time to time, a practice that the Brethren missionaries in Singapore and Penang also adopted. Rhenius described the Indian indigenous churches as "primitive churches", comparing them to the churches of the first century described in the New Testament. Far from idealizing them, he compared them to a church that an apostle had described as having made a "shipwreck of their faith" (Rhenius 1841: 288). He concluded that new Christians would not immediately be perfect since Hindu notions of deity and sin were so different from those set out in the Bible (Rhenius 1841: 291).

Schism in the Tinnevelly Mission

Groves had learned of the Tinnevelly mission from a sermon that he had heard as a boy and had long imagined visiting India. But when he visited the German mission in 1833, he also knew of a conflict unfolding between the missionaries and their superiors. For more than a century the Pietist missionaries had freely followed practices developed in the early Danish mission. But when Rhenius

[8] Groves also adopted the radical social agenda of breaking down caste. Timothy Stunt concludes that Groves' opposition to caste contradicted his support for indigenization (Stunt 2015: 113–4). But Groves' emphasis on equality and brotherhood logically lead to a critique of the caste system.

requested that the German missionaries be allowed to ordain their Tamil catechists, the Anglican Church Missionary Society authorities insisted that their bishop ordain the Tamil catechists. They further required them to affirm the Anglican Church's 39 Articles and to use "the form of worship prescribed in the Common Prayer only, and no other", even though it had not yet been translated into Tamil. As Pietists, the Tamil catechists rejected the Anglican form of baptism and also practised spontaeous prayer. They refused to affirm the 39 Articles and declined ordination from the Anglican bishop. A crisis ensued (Rhenius 1841: 381–2).

In an 1834 entry in his journal that was reprinted in his *Memoir*, Groves praised the evangelical method that the German missionaries had used, and criticized the Anglican authorities:

> Never was there a more important moment than the present for India; up to this time the Church has been as free as our hearts could wish. Persons have been converted, either by reading God's word, or through one another, and have drank the living waters wherever they could find them full and clear; but now the Church of England is seeking to extend its power, and the Independents and Methodists are seeking to enclose their little flocks. My object in India is two-fold, to try to check the operation of these exclusive systems, by showing in the Christian Church they are not necessary for all that is *holy* and *moral* . . . my earnest desire is to re-model the whole plan of Missionary operations, so as to bring them to the simple standard of God's word (H. Groves 1869: 285–6).

As the conflict between Rhenius and the Anglican establishment unfolded, Groves urged Rhenius to publish a document he had written in defense of his position that Anglican ritual forms should not be imposed on Indian Christians. "A Review of a Work Entitled the Church; Her Daughters and Handmaidens, Her Pastors and People, &c-" appeared as a pamphlet in 1834. Groves returned to Europe in 1834 and arranged to have Rhenius' self-defense published in London in 1835, making the dispute with his Anglican superiors a matter of wide public debate.

In the pamphlet Rhenius rejected the CMS committee's insistence on one set form of prayer as laid out in the *Book of Common Prayer*. "It cannot but bind their spirit, and thus injure their ministrations; which is not that of the letter, but of the spirit. If a clergyman cannot pray in the Spirit, he cannot preach in the Spirit, and such persons should not be put into the ministry" (Rhenius 1834: 24). Rhenius observed that although the Anglican church claimed to be a restoration of the primitive church, the frequent repetition of prayers "ordered to be said at all times and under all circumstances" resembled the practice in the Roman, Armenian, and Greek Churches (Rhenius 1834: 25). He noted that the formulaic nature of Anglican worship deprived the minister of the "liberty" to avail themselves of "passing events and particular conditions of the people". Moreover, he claimed, this form of worship stifled the spirit of prayer, making people into "formalists in religion and vain worshippers" (Rhenius 1834: 26).

As Allan Anderson explains African Pentecostalism, its theology is to be found "in the preaching, rituals and practices of churches that have contextualized Christianity in such a way as to make it really meaningful to ordinary people". He calls this "enacted theology" or "theology in practice", observing that it is to be found in Pentecostalism all over the world (Anderson 2003: 86). The liberty of worship that both Rhenius and Groves promoted precisely allowed people to contextualize Christianity in their lives, a powerful form of emplacement that led directly to the formation of independent, indigenous churches in India.

Rhenius' pamphlet deeply distressed the CMS and in 1835 they dismissed Rhenius, claiming Tinnevelly as their territory and ordering him to leave. Rhenius went to Madras and planned to return to Europe, but Groves urged him to return to Tinnevelly and resume work as an independent missionary. He did so, and in a pamphlet entitled "A Brief Account of the Present Circumstances of the Tinnevelly Mission", Groves claimed that he had "been in God's hand the instrument" of preventing Rhenius from returning to Europe. In that pamphlet Groves noted that the Tinnevelly catechists and students were deeply grateful to him, but he also laid out the expenses of the mission, with the intent of getting as many to subscribe as possible "toward the support of these catechists" and the schools (Groves 1835: 13). Rhenius began to receive donations from all over India and from Europe. At the same time, Rhenius' coworkers Revs. Schaffter, Müller, and Lechler also resigned. Together with Rhenius, they returned to Tinnevelly to continue an independent German Evangelical Mission (Rhenius 1841: 474, 511). As I discuss in Chapter 3, Lechler later left this mission and worked with the London Missionary Society, first in Penang, then in Tamil Nadu.

Throughout the Anglican mission, division soon followed, an event for which Stephen Neill—an Anglican historian who himself was the Bishop of Tinnevelly for a time—blamed Groves (Neil 1985: 408–9). One hundred and seventy-six congregations remained with the Anglicans, 76 followed Rhenius, 15 remained neutral, and 35 divided (Neill 1985: 221). Although some of the churches that followed Rhenius eventually returned to the Anglican church, others remained independent, and some later joined the Open Brethren network.

At the centre of this division was the question of what form prayer should take. As Marcel Mauss observed, prayer—the Pietists' chief technology of the sacred—is both ritualistic and creative:

> Prayer is precisely one of these phenomena where ritual is united in belief. It is full of meaning like a myth: it is often as rich in ideas and images as a religious narrative. It is full of power and efficacy like a ritual and it is often as powerfully creative as a ceremony based on sympathetic magic (Mauss 1909 [2003]: 22).

He further observed that in Protestantism prayer had become "practically the whole of religious life" and had engulfed other religious expressions: "prayer has been the remarkable tree which, having grown up in the shade of other trees, has ended by smothering them under its vast branches" (Mauss 1909 [2003]: 23).

Mauss added that prayer had begun as an obligatory group practice, but as society changed, prayer became increasingly individualistic, following the variations and nuances of individual consciousness, and that as a result, individual became the creators of their own faith (Mauss 1909 [2003]: 24). Rhenius precisely proposed that prayer identified with "thought and an outpouring of the spirit" was superior to scripted group prayer. The practice of spontaneous prayer allowed not only missionaries but also non-European Christians to emplace the religion in their lives by relating their prayers to "passing events and particular conditions" (Rhenius 1835 [1834]: 26).

John Christian Arulappan and the Christian Pettah Revival

Groves visited England in 1834, where he married again. He returned to India with missionaries whom he had recruited in Britain, Germany, and Switzerland, including George Beer, a shoemaker, and William Bowden, a stonemason, and their wives. Beer and Bowden were not highly educated but they had experience as open-air evangelists, and had prepared by reading "avidly such missionary literature as was available" (Stunt et al. 1972: 24–5). That year, Müller and Craik also launched the Scriptural Knowledge Institution, and in 1835, Müller sent £50 to Rhenius in India (Stunt et al. 1972: 30). For over 60 years Müller channelled donations to independent missionaries in India, first to Beer and Bowden, and later to their sons (Müller 1896: 51).

Because the Madras European community did not welcome Groves and his fellow workers, the Brethren missionaries relocated to Chittoor in the Godavari Delta region, where Tamil evangelist John Christian Arulappan joined them. Groves did outreach with Europeans and also mentored English-educated

Indian Christians, but he and his family focused their effort on developing commercial agricultural projects that they hoped would make their Christian work self-sustaining.

When Groves returned to England in 1852, he visited Open Brethren Assemblies in London, and urged them to support the Godavari Delta missionaries. As he described his visit to Mr and Mrs John Eliot Howard, Mary Stacey, and the Tottenham assembly:

> I endeavoured to interest them about missions; spoke of Bowden, Beer, and Aroolappen; and in the evening, brought the subject before the church, and they hope, in union with believers in Hackney, Orchard Street and other places, to form an effectual committee to care for these things (H. Groves 1869: 481).

In 1853—the year of Groves' death—London soliciter James Van Sommer (1822–1901), who met with assemblies in Hackney and Tottenham and who was also involved with the London City Mission, launched *The Missionary Reporter*, proposing that every church could be a missionary society (Stunt 1967; Forrest 1971).[9]

Van Sommer encouraged churches to send donations directly to missionaries and requested that the churches send him their replies to print. In this way, *The Missionary Reporter* both promoted and publicized the work of independent missionaries in British Guiana, India, China, Guatemala, Honduras, and Mauritius.[10]

The first issue included extracts of John Christian Arulappan's journals, and the editor also sent copies of the magazine to him.[11] Arulappan was

---

[9] Partridge, Oakley & Co. produced both *The Chinese Missionary Gleaner* and *The Missionary Reporter* (Forrest n.d.: 30). In the first issue of *The Missionary Reporter*, which appeared in July 1853, the editor noted that because the Chinese Evangelization Society was focusing on China, this left room for *The Missionary Reporter*. *The Missionary Reporter* frequently included news from the China Evangelization Society, and both magazines published letters from James Hudson Taylor and William Lobschied in China. One issue also included information that the Census of Great Britain included 132 congregations called "Brethren", seven called "Non-sectarian", two called "Believers", and others that described themselves as Primitive Christians, New Testament Christians, Free Gospel Christians, etc. (Forrest n.d.: 36).

[10] Although records indicate that the magazine was published until 1861, researchers have not located copies of the issues published between 1858 and 1861 (Forrest n.d.; Personal communication, Graham Johnson, archivist, John Rylands Library, University of Manchester).

[11] *The Missionary Reporter* 1853: 2.

an independent Tamil Christian leader whom Rhenius had trained at the Church Missionary Society mission, and Groves had mentored. He became independent, and in 1840 helped found Christian Pettah, an agricultural settlement where Christians supported themselves through agriculture and a printing press. The Christian Pettah Christians did itinerant evangelism, and by 1859, Arulappan had established 33 congregations (Lang 1939). For the Open Brethren, Arulappan's independent and autonomous work in Tinnevelly became a model for effective indigenization.

As I note in the Introduction, Müller corresponded with Arulappan, who knew English, and published extracts from his letters in the SKI annual reports. And after Arulappan's death in 1867, Harriet Groves added an 81-page Supplement to her 1856 biography of her husband. "Aroolappen and the Christian-Pettah Mission" included reprints of letters and extracts from his journals that had been published in *The Missionary Reporter*. She celebrated Arulappan as a native missionary who for nearly 30 years had worked at a mission that existed unaided by any society, praising him and his many helpers as "instruments used of God to revive others" (H. Groves 1869: 572). In her eulogy to Arulappan, Harriet Groves recalled his early connection with the Church Missionary Society, which had equipped him with an English education, but gave credit to divine providence and Groves for the event that came to be known as the Christian Pettah revival (H. Groves 1869: 620).

After the 1859–60 revival, a new magazine *The Indian Watchman* was launched in Madras and from 1860–64 was the main publication for the undenominational Godavari Delta mission (Stunt et al. 1972: 30). Groves' eldest son Henry Groves (1818–91) returned to Britain from India, and in 1872 he and John Lindsay Maclean, an army captain who had sold his commission on adopting pacifist views, launched *The Missionary Echo* in Bath as a channel through which independent missionaries could publish news of their work (Stunt et al. 1972: 35–43). Like the SKI's annual reports, *The Missionary Echo* and its successor, *Echoes of Service*, promoted the work of missionaries and independent indigenous evangelists who lived by faith, and channelled donations to them.[12]

The Open Brethren's memory of Arulappan was refreshed in 1939 when George Lang published *The History and Diaries of an Indian Christian (J.C. Aroolappen)*. In the book's preface, he explained that he had learned about

[12] Neil Summerton observes that the two publications competed, and concludes that a factor in the emergence of *The Missionary Echo* was on the one hand perceptions of limitations in Müller's method of administering the SKI, and on the other "competitive entrepreneurialism" (Summerton 2016:104).

Arulappan when he read Groves' *Memoir* closely while travelling, then soon after his return to England "happened" on the third edition with its appendix. The next year he "happened" on Rhenius' memoir in a small shop in a country town, and a friend gave him copies of *The Indian Watchman* and *The Missionary Reporter* that included many lengthy letters and reports from Arulappan [quotation marks in the original]. He decided that his providential acquaintance with Arulappan through these books and magazines was meant to encourage and instruct, warn and rebuke himself and his contemporaries.[13]

In *To the Ends of the Earth: Pentecostalism and the Transformation of World Christianity* (2013), Allan Anderson described Arulappan as a radical evangelical Christian who practised an "individualist and anti-establishment form of Christianity that denied the traditions of the time", challenging the need for ordination and emphasizing the "empowerment of the Spirit" for all Christians regardless of their race or caste. He noted that Arulappan's indigenous church was led by a "priesthood of all believers", and that he followed the practice of living by faith (Anderson 2013: 20).

Anderson relied on Lang's 1939 book as a main source for information on Arulappan and the 1860s revival in India. He found it "interesting" that Lang was Brethren, since he believed the Brethren movement to be opposed to Pentecostal manifestations (Anderson 2013: 19). But Arulappan had worked with Groves for four years, and Groves promoted precisely the kind of "individualist and anti-establishment form of Christianity" that Anderson identifies as a precedent for Pentecostalism, and that Lang called on the Brethren to remember.

[13] Because his sources of information were inaccessible, Lang did not provide references for most of the quoted materials in this book (Lang 1939: 8). Neil Dickson notes that Lang's published version of these events, which bring together many accounts of the Christian Pettah revival, including some published in issues of *The Missionary Recorder* that are now lost, is different from Müller's, and infers that Müller edited Arulappan's prose extensively (personal communication; see Lang 1939, reprinted in 1988).

PART II
Penang and China

Chapter 3

The London Missionary Society in Penang, 1819–43

In 1795 Nonconformist Christians cooperated with evangelical Anglicans to form the missionary society that became known as the London Missionary Society (LMS). Their founders sought advice from the Moravians, whose first mission had been established in the Caribbean in 1732 (Hassé 1911: 131). In 1804, the inter-denominational LMS sponsored Scots Presbyterian Robert Morrison (1782–1834), who studied Chinese and went to Canton in 1807. In 1813, Congregationalist William Milne (1785–1822) joined Morrison in Guangzhou.

European missionaries had limited access to China, but Morrison and Milne recognized that many immigrant Chinese lived and worked in British-controlled areas of Southeast Asia and concluded that they could pursue their projects of translation, publication, and education more easily there. On behalf of the London Missionary Society, Morrison and Milne established what came to be known as the Ultra-Ganges Mission, which included missions in Java and Amboyna (1814), Penang and Singapore (1819), and also the Anglo-Chinese College in Malacca (1818). Milne appointed himself the Anglo-Ganges College's first principal. Not long after, the young founders of the Penang and Singapore missions left to escape his autocratic control.

Soon after the First Opium War forced China to open five treaty ports to European residence, the LMS missionaries moved to China. As I discuss in Chapters 4 and 6, independent missionaries took over running the Protestant schools and Mission Chapel in Penang with support from wealthy Open Brethren in London and George Müller in Bristol. Although historians describe the LMS mission in Penang as having ended in 1844, continuities of place, persons, and projects link this early history to the Penang Brethren mission.

The London Missionary Society in Penang

Walter Medhurst (1796–1857) first visited Penang in 1819 to assess the possibility of working there and met David Brown (1778–1825), who invited him to return to work in James Town (today, Bayan Lepas). Brown employed over 1,000 Chinese workers on his plantations, where he cultivated cloves, nutmeg, and tamarind.[1] With Brown's support and the expectation of government funding, Medhurst returned and established two new boys' schools, one for Hokkien speakers, and one for Cantonese, and introduced a New System of Education.[2] When he moved there from Malacca, six Malays and two Chinese accompanied him, which he described as a Moravian method. [3]

They held classes in a God of Prosperity (*Tua Pek Kong*) temple, and on entering the shrine some students bowed to the carved image of the deity and prayed for assistance in learning to read.[4] Their Chinese teachers used a Christian catechism as a textbook, but also taught students the Chinese classics using a set of standard books. The missionaries claimed that no one would attend their schools unless these were included in the curriculum.[5]

Like Walter Medhurst and his wife Eliza, Thomas Beighton (1790–1844), John Ince (1795–1825), and their wives did not seek permission from the LMS directors before leaving Malacca for Penang. They received a grant of land in George Town from the government,[6] and Mrs Ince and Mrs Beighton soon opened a girls' school.[7] Although they had set up schools in different towns on Penang Island, Beighton opposed Medhurst remaining in Penang, and at the end of 1821, Mr and Mrs Medhurst moved to Batavia.[8]

Penang's first Malay-medium boys' school was a mosque, and by 1821 the LMS mission had five Malay schools. When the missionaries circulated an advertisement for one of these schools, the parents wanted to know if the children "were to be allowed to read the Koran, and it appeared that if the Koran was to be treated with so much disrespect as to be denied a place in

---

1 Beighton to Hankey, 7 November 1820 (LMS/IC).
2 Medhurst to LMS directors, 15 February 1819 (LMS/IC).
3 Medhurst to LMS directors, 22 November 1820 (LMS/IC).
4 Beighton to W.A. Hankey, 20 April 1819 (LMS/IC).
5 Report to LMS directors, 1821–22 (LMS/IC).
6 Beighton to Rev. Burden, 27 November 1820; 14 December 1821 (LMS/IC).
7 Ince to RO and Burden, 20 October 1821 (LMS/IC).
8 John Slater had established a Chinese mission in Batavia in 1819, and Medhurst worked there until he relocated to China in 1842 or 1843 (Harrison 1979: 38, 58–9, 62–4, 188–91).

the school, no children would be allowed to attend".[9] As was the case for the Chinese schools, they compromised, teaching the Koran through the medium of Arabic, and Christian scriptures in the Malay vernacular.

In 1823 the missionaries announced their plans to build a Mission Chapel with a full page advertisement in the *Prince of Wales Island Gazette Extraordinaire*. As they explained it, their goal was to exhibit to Asians "the nature and simplicity of that Worship which Jehovah requires", hoping that this would "convince them that the Christian Religion is far superior to their own". The next year, they announced the opening of the Penang Mission Chapel, whose interior displayed Christian scriptures written in English, Malay, and Chinese. Beighton gave the first sermon at a "grand and solemn" evening service, taking as his text the last verse of the 60th chapter of Isaiah: "A little one shall become a thousand and a small one a strong nation: I the Lord will hasten it in his times."[10]

Nonconformist Protestant Christians in Penang founded the Prince of Wales [Penang] Auxiliary Bible Society in 1817, and ordered Bibles and Testaments from the British and Foreign Bible Society in English, Portuguese, Dutch, Malay, Bengalee, Telegu, Persian, and Tamil but not Chinese, since Milne had left them well supplied.[11] And in July 1826—around the same time that the founders of the Brethren movement began to meet with friends in Dublin for prayer—a small group of European Christians created a primitive Church in the Mission Chapel. They wrote:[12]

> That on a serious perusal of the New Testament it appears to us, that the primitive churches were voluntary Societies of men and women, who having believed the Gospel of Christ, did according to his revealed will form themselves into religious communities, that they seriously engaged to unite in maintaining the truth, and worship of God; to walk in all ordinances and commandments of the Lord blameless, and to endeavour to promote each other's growth in faith and holiness.

They proposed to administer the Lord's Supper to their members and to cooperate in "relieving the poor saints". A Dutch Eurasian member of their

---

[9] Report to LMS directors, 1821–22 (LMS/IC).

[10] *Prince of Wales Island Gazette Extraordinaire*, Vol. 10, No. 50, 23 June 1824, enclosed in J. Rodyk to Hankey, 30 June 1824 (LMS/IC).

[11] BFBS Minutes 1815: 30–1; see also Browne 1859: 195–6. Although formally established in 1966 and 1985, the Bible Societies of Singapore and Malaysia claim a longer history that links them to these early auxiliaries of the BFBS.

[12] "Rules and Regulations Mutually agreed upon at the Formation of the Independent Church, Mission Chapel Prince of Wales Island on Tuesday evening July 11 1826" (LMS/IC).

church reported to the LMS directors that worship in the "government Church here on a Sabbath day is but thinly attended", but that a "highly respectable and numerous" congregation assembled in the new Mission Chapel, adding that the missionaries' work with Chinese and Malays had not been too successful.[13]

Figure 11 Etching of the Penang Mission Chapel, c. 1824 (published in "The Society's Mission at Pulo Pinang or Prince of Wales Island", London Missionary Society, *Missionary Sketches* No. XXXVII). Private collection of author.

Student boarders whom the missionaries required to attend services did so, but most of their early converts were Asian orphans or slaves whom missionaries had adopted and educated. John and Abigail Beighton adopted two Tamil children whose father had killed their mother, a Malay infant who had been found alone in a house after her parents had died (who became first a student, then a teacher in the Orphan School), and a Batak slave whom the missionaries had bought from his owner.[14] One Tamil orphan whom they raised, James Gawthorne, later became Penang's acting postmaster and a leader in the Penang Mission Church (see Gawthorne 2014). The missionaries recruited to their Orphan Schools the

[13] J. Rodyk to Hankey, 30 June 1824 (LMS/IC).

[14] The missionaries also reported that they were looking after a girl who was stolen from a "tribe of cannibals" and brought to Penang for sale. Beighton to Ellis, 23 May 1834 (LMS/IC).

children of European men who had formed relationships with local women, but had left them when they returned to Europe (Beighton 1888: 113).

Although some were socially disadvantaged, Eurasians became the core of Penang's early political and economic elite.[15] When Dr Francis King worked in Penang between 1857 and 1865, he noted that David Wardlow Brown (1812–64), who owned two thirds of Penang's cultivated land, was Eurasian, and that his wife was an educated English woman. Brown was the second son of David Brown, the plantation owner who had recruited Medhurst to open Chinese schools in James Town, and was the most important planter on the island. He was one of four racially mixed brothers, none of whom shared the same mother (Walker 2014: 84). As Dr King described it in a letter, "All the respectable islanders are mixed", including Penang's Governor, the Resident Councillor and the principal merchants (Ross 1980: 88–9).

Anglicans and Nonconformist Christians in Penang

Many of Penang's European and Eurasian Christians were members of so-called nonconformist or dissenting Christian denominations. Baptists, Congregationalists, Presbyterians, Quakers, and Methodists advocated religious liberty, claiming the right of free choice in their commitments (Binfield 1977: 7). Although they may have had popular appeal, nonconformist Churches only gradually achieved equal rights with the established churches, including the Church of England.

As they built their economic empire, the British had encountered kingdoms, empires, and sultanates whose rulers were both annointed by and patrons of religions. The East India Company (EIC) demonstrated the moral charter for their rule by making Anglicanism their official church while enacting a policy of indirect rule and religious tolerance that gave formal support to Hindus, Muslims, and Catholics. Many Europeans were members of Freemasonry, the so-called religion of the Enlightenment, which was de-Christianized in the early 19th century, which allowed Jewish, Hindu, Parsee, and Muslim elites to become members (DeBernardi 2004: 57–8).

The so-called Pious Clause in the 1813 Charter of the EIC permitted nonconformist Christians to work in territories under EIC control, but it also strengthened the position of the Anglican Establishment. In 1814, the Crown

[15] Many historians assume uniformity across colonial cities, but as this study shows, Penang's society did not demonstrate the "ossified racial hierachies" sometimes assumed to exist (see Lewis 2016: 5). Lewis' study provides an insightful exploration of cosmopolitan port cities in Southeast Asia, including Penang.

appointed a bishop to Calcutta whose jurisdiction eventually extended to all of Asia, Australia and New Zealand, and even South Africa (Buchanan 2015: 319, 541). Rev. Robert Sparke Hutchings, a graduate of Oxford University, was appointed as Penang's chaplain, and in 1819, the Bishop of Calcutta consecrated Saint George's Church, which is the oldest Anglican Church in Southeast Asia (Buchanan 2015: 438; 539–40). The Anglican chaplains claimed special ritual authority in Penang, taking ministry to the English as their primary concern (Northcott 1992: 35).

In 1823, as they were planning to build the Mission Chapel, the LMS missionaries realized that although they could baptize Asians who wished to become Christian, they were not certain that they had the authority to perform a legally valid marriage ceremony. Ince and Beighton visited Sir Ralph Rice, Penang's Recorder (as the chief legal officer was known). Not only could they not convince him that they had the right to perform weddings, they discovered that he also doubted their right to baptize anyone. They further learned that "he did not consider us anything at all on the Island, and was not aware we had legal right to be here".[16]

Far from promoting Christianity, the East India Company was "officially committed, both in policy and in law, to protecting all religious institutions of India", protections that extended to the diverse populations of Singapore and Penang (Frykenberg 2005:107). In the Straits Settlements, the First Charter of Justice granted to "all the native subjects the free exercise of their religion, indulges them in all their prejudices, pays the most scrupulous attention to their ancient usages and habits" (Purcell 1948: 49; see also Braddell 1921). The Charter allowed residents to follow their religious customs with respect to marriage, divorce, and inheritance issues. Consequently, the Court of Judicature acknowledged that Roman Catholic priests, Muslim imams, and Chinese monks could perform lawful marriages.

Among the first settlers in Penang were Portuguese Eurasian Catholics and their French Catholic priests. The Portuguese were the earliest European traders to establish territorial bases in the Indian Ocean, and in Malacca, Portuguese sailors and local women had intermarried. The Catholic Church had supported missionaries in Asia as early as the 16th century, including Saint Francis Xavier, and the Eurasians practised the Catholic religion and spoke the Creole language Kristang (Barter 2016: 19; Roxborogh 1992).[17] When the Dutch took control

[16] Beighton and Ince to Hankey, 24 September 1823 (LMS/IC).

[17] Catholic missions in Asia went into decline the latter half of the 18th century as Spanish, Portuguese, and French colonial enterprises weakened, and also as a consequence of the dissolution of the Jesuit order (Neill 1986: 173–6).

of Malacca from the Portuguese in 1641, the Portuguese Eurasians fled to the Malay States and Phuket Island in Southern Thailand. Some intermarried with Malays and adopted Malay language and culture; led by French priests, others remained Catholic and maintained a distinct identity (Fernandis 2003: 287).

For about ten years, Light had made Phuket his base and he married Portuguese Eurasian Martina Rozells (Augustin 1970: 11). Soon after moving to Penang Island, Light invited Eurasians living in Kedah to move there. The East India Company made land grants for religious purposes, and in 1786 Eurasian Catholics built the Church of the Assumption on Church Street.

In 1800, Chinese merchants from Fujian and Guangdong cooperated to build the Kong Hok Palace, a Buddhist-syncretic temple on Pitt Street, and in 1801 Indian Muslims established the Kapitan Kling Mosque. Burmese founded the Theravada Dhammikarama Burmese Temple in 1805, and immigrants from Sumatra built the Aceh Street Mosque in 1808. Not until 1819 did the Anglicans build Saint George's Church, and the Protestant missionaries opened a mission chapel in 1823.

The LMS missionaries discovered that although Catholic priests were allowed to perform marriage rites, the Penang court required an ordained minister to perform marriage rites according to Ecclesiastical law for all Protestant Christians, including converts. In practice this meant an Anglican chaplain, since Penang's Court Recorder also judged that Church of Scotland ministers were not qualified to perform this office. Thus the missionaries were forced to have their converts' marriages solemnized at the Anglican Church, or risk having their marriages regarded as not legally binding in Penang's court.

In 1824 Ince wrote to the Court Recorder Sir Ralph Rice to argue the missionaries' case. First, he proposed that since Catholic priests, Muslim imams, and Buddhist monks were allowed to perform marriages, marriages performed by Protestant missionaries should also be deemed lawful. Second, he argued that since the current Marriage Act did not extend to India, English law prior to the Marriage Act applied. Finally, Ince observed that since the LMS missionaries were allowed to perform marriages in other Dutch and English settlements (including Singapore and Malacca), they should be allowed to do so in Penang.

Rice defended the practice of allowing Catholic priests to perform marriages on grounds that they were already performing this function when he came to Penang; however, since there had been no Protestant missionaries in Penang at that time, he concluded that broad respect for the laws and customs of Penang residents did not extend to them. Rice further concluded that there was no legislative recognition of "a power in the Seniors of your Society to ordain, and make Priests, by imposition of hands", and that the earlier law had found marriage according to "Sabbatarian or Anabaptist forms" to be "imperfect".[18] In 1833, Beighton reported again that the missionaries were not being allowed to perform marriages or to baptize the children of Europeans. The official registrar refused to record them, requiring that the Anglican Chaplain perform the rituals.[19]

Baptism and marriage were not the only issues. Whenever there was a burial in Penang's Protestant Cemetery, even for an LMS missionary, by "custom" the Anglican chaplain read the Church of England burial service at the grave. In 1842, a missionary poignantly described a nonconformist Christian father meeting the coffin of his infant son at the gate of the Protestant cemetery, where he delivered a "solemn address and an extempore prayer".[20] This only changed when the old Protestant cemetery was closed in 1892 and a new one opened on Western Road.[21]

---

[18] Although he did not change his decision, Rice donated $100 to the new Mission Chapel before he left his post as Recorder. He also wrote to the missionaries that he hoped that the "civilizing influence of Christianity may be felt amongst our multifarious population. In addition to my duty as an Individual, I feel a professional interest on the subject, knowing how much morality and religion diminish the painful punishments of law." Sir Ralph Rice to the LMS missionaries in Penang. No date; enclosure in letter from John Anderson to Hankey, 11 August 1824 (LMS/IC).

[19] Beighton to Ellis, 21 September 1833 (LMS/IC).

[20] A. Stronach to Tidman and Freeman, 3 July 1842 (LMS/IC).

[21] On the Protestant Cemetery, see Langdon 2017. The issue also concerned Christians in Britain. Under Lord Hardwicke's Marriage Act of 1753, a marriage in England and Wales (but not Scotland) was only valid if performed in an Anglican church after the public announcement of bans or by licence, unless those marrying were Quaker or Jewish. As Sir Thomas Erskine May described it, the Church of England "alone performed the religious services incident to all baptisms, marriages, and deaths" and had sole "custody of the registers". Responding to the dissenters' wish to perform religious services involved interfering with the privileges of the Church and was not quickly remedied (May 1912 Vol. 2: 249–50). In Britain, this situation was resolved with the enactment of the Registration and Marriage Acts of 1836, which created a new system of civil registration of births, marriages, and deaths. In 1852 the Indian government retroactively recognized marriages that had not conformed to the registration requirements and new regulations legitimated marriages performed by ordained Church of Scotland ministers (Williams 1856: 137–46). In the Straits Settlements, provision was made for the government to appoint marriage registrars, but in practice these were ordained Anglican, Catholic, or Church of Scotland clergymen. The Brethren missionaries only started acting as marriage registrars in 1890, a role that they performed until the Federation of Malaya gained independence in 1957.

Samuel and Marie Dyer

After the death of John Ince in 1825, Beighton pleaded with the LMS directors for a replacement to work with Chinese who spoke Fujian dialects, explaining that although the characters were the same, "the difference between the Mandarin and Fuh-kien dialects is as great as it is possible to be".[22] John Halliburton, the Sheriff of Prince of Wales Island, also wrote to the LMS directors, requesting that they send a replacement for Ince who had "the appearance and manners of a Gentleman".[23] In 1827 the LMS directors sent Samuel Dyer (1804–43) and his wife, Maria Tarn Dyer (1803–46) to Penang, where they worked from 1827 until 1835. With support from the Penang government and local residents, they ran boys' and girls' schools at the LMS Mission on Farquhar Street (Murray 1921: 236).

Samuel Dyer (1804–43) had been 'born again' and taught Sunday School at Paddington Chapel, a nonconformist church whose construction in West London in 1813 was led by Thomas Wilson, one of the founders of the LMS. In 1822 Dyer entered Trinity College at Cambridge University to study law. Only after entering Cambridge did Dyer learn that he could not graduate without declaring himself a member of the Established Church, and he anticipated that he could not conscientiously subscribe to the 39 Articles.[24]

The 39 Articles are the foundational statements of Anglican doctrine, issued by the Church of England in 1571 and printed in the Book of Common Prayer. The Articles distinguish Anglican from Catholic doctrine, and Article 19 states that "the Church of Rome hath erred, not only in their living and manner of Ceremonies, but also in matters of Faith". The 39 Articles also drew doctrinal boundaries between Anglicans and nonconformist Christians. Baptists practised adult baptism by full immersion, for example, and did not accept the Anglican position on infant baptism as stated in Article 27: "The Baptism of young Children is in any wise to be retained in the Church, as most agreeable with the institution of Christ." As pacifists, Quakers objected to Article 37, which stated that it was lawful for Christians to serve in wars.

---

[22] Beighton to Hankey, 4 May 1825 (LMS/IC).

[23] F. Halliburton to Hankey, 4 June 1825 (LMS/IC).

[24] Undergraduates at Oxford were required to subscribe to the 39 Articles on matriculation, and at Cambridge at graduation (Binfield 1977: 4). Although allowed to enter and study in those universities, after 1616 nonconformist or dissenting Christians "were debarred from its honours and endowments,—its scholarships, degrees, and fellowships,—and from any share in the government of the university" (May 1912 Vol. 2: 254).

While still a student at Cambridge, Dyer had read an 1818 pamphlet written by Rev. Thomas Lewis of the Union Chapel in Islington. The pamphlet included a funeral oration that Rev. Lewis had delivered for Mrs Mead, a young woman who had hoped to be a missionary but who had died in Penang on the way to Travancore, India. According to Mrs Dyer, after reading the pamphlet, which proposed the "existence, influence, and triumphs of a Divine principle" that compelled individuals to devote themselves to "the service of Christ and his cause", Dyer could no longer study. Dyer became convinced that he should become a missionary, and withdrew from Cambridge after five terms without graduating (Davies 1846: 24).

Dyer next studied at the LMS seminary at Gosport, where Rev. David Bogue had established an institute where the LMS sent men for training to become missionaries. Bogue taught a simple approach to proselytism that emphasized "common sense", believing that people would give up their indigenous beliefs if presented with Christian Truth (Daily 2013: 74–5). Dyer soon discovered that this approach to proselytism was naive, but he also studied printing, punch-cutting and type-founding in Islington (Davies 1846: 42).

Dyer became engaged to Maria Tarn, who was the daughter of Joseph Tarn (1766–1837), a prominent evangelical Christian who had helped found the Evangelical Tract Society. Maria's father belonged to a network of dissenting Christians who had been deeply influenced by 18th-century Methodist revivals. Soon after Maria's birth, he was invited to become a committee member at Spa Fields Chapel in Islington, London, whose congregation was "wealthy and influential". He became a director of the LMS and was also assistant secretary and accountant of the British and Foreign Bible Society (Obituary 1837).

While Samuel and Maria prepared for their missionary work in Penang, both studied Chinese language with Morrison, whose work in translating the Bible into Chinese had already made him famous.[25] On his return to England in 1824, he had presented King George IV with his translation of the Chinese Bible and was made a fellow of the Royal Society. The next year he opened a Language Institute in Holborn, London, where he gave a three-month course of lectures. He taught 13 students: three days a week he met his male students (including Samuel Dyer) at the Language Institution; three days a week he taught a class of women who were preparing to engage in the "education of pagan females" (including Maria Tarn and Mary Ann Aldersey, who later

---

[25] For further detail on Morrison's life and missionary work in China until 1840, see Murray Rubinstein 1996a.

opened girls' schools in Java and Ningpo) at his house in Hackney (Morrison 1839: 302).

Dyer was ordained in Paddington Chapel in 1827 and soon after he and Maria married. They sailed for the Straits of Malacca on 10 March 1827 and worked in Penang for eight years before moving to Malacca. Maria's father reported to the directors of the Holborn Language Institution that within six or seven weeks of arriving in Penang, Samuel and Maria were able to converse in Chinese, and that "Mr. Dyer preached in that language so as to be well understood" (Morrison 1839: 300–2).[26] In fact, Dyer reported that he initially could only communicate by writing, and that after nine months he was still learning Hokkien.[27]

Although his training at the LMS seminary offered limited preparation, Dyer innovated a way to use moveable metal types to print Chinese characters. The style of Chinese type that he created worked as a flexible replacement for woodblock printing that allowed English letters or romanized text and Chinese characters to be combined, which was useful for the printing of dictionaries. Once the steel punches had been cut, they could be reused, which make printing both faster and cheaper (Davies 1846:131–41; see also Zhang 2007: 105–6).

Samuel Dyer also worked in the LMS boys' schools, where the teachers continued to teach the Chinese classics. Dyer described the Confucian classics as "pernicious" and was bothered by the sentence "nature originally good", which the Chinese commentary explained was true "of every man's nature when born into this world". In singling out the sentence "nature originally good" for critique, Dyer precisely identified a crucial difference between Christianity and Confucianism. Christians teach that all humans are born with original sin that Jesus Christ removed for Christians by his death on the cross, and Congregationalists like Dyer believed that only someone with faith in Jesus Christ could be saved. Someone who assumed that human nature was good would not recognize themselves as flawed and in need of repenting their sins and seeking Christian salvation. Dyer claimed that he would rather be without schools than teach "We cannot rightly serve men, how then can we serve God", alluding to Chapter 11 of the Confucian Analects.[28] Despite his objections, students at the mission school continued to memorize Confucian texts in the morning and recite Christian texts in the afternoon.

---

[26] Dyer also studied the collection of Chinese works that Dr Morrison had deposited at the Church Missionary Society's Mission House in Islington (Davies 1846: 37, 42).

[27] Dyer to Hankey, 19 August 1827; Dyer to Hankey, 9 May 1828 (LMS/IC).

[28] Dyer to Hankey, 9 May 1828 (LMS/IC).

The Penang Girls' Schools

Soon after her arrival in Penang Maria Dyer organized a new girls' school that followed the Lancasterian model, a popular method of peer tutoring in which more advanced students taught less advanced students. In 1829, a network of British women helped raise funds to build a Chinese Female School in the Penang mission compound.[29] Three years later they formed an "Association in aid of Chinese Female Schools of Singapore and Penang"[30] whose members made and shipped goods to Penang for Maria Dyer to sell. The committee's treasurer was Mrs Flora Tarn, the wife of Maria's brother William Tarn.[31]

In the 1830s, many of the students in the LMS girls' schools belonged to the mixed linguaculture known as *nyonya/baba* Chinese. Evan Davies (1805–64), a Welsh Protestant missionary who worked at the LMS mission in Penang between 1835–39, observed that Chinese women in Penang were the descendants of "Chinese men by Malay women, some one or two generations back".[32] Because Chinese law prohibited the emigration of women, Chinese immigrants to Penang had married Malays, Thai, and Batak slaves from Sumatra. The creolized subculture that resulted took its name from the Malay word for 'woman', *nyonya*, and the term *baba,* which refers to a Straits-born Chinese.

Since boys spent more time with their fathers and men, and girls with their mothers and females, the boys spoke Chinese, and girls Malay. Fathers wanted a Chinese education for their sons, but the Protestant girls' schools taught female students in Malay. But the Straits Chinese (as they came to be known) also saw value in an English education for their children, and Davies commented that "Commerce, science and British rule are predisposing the public mind in favour of every thing British." Davies noted that three Chinese girls who spoke

---

[29] Beighton and Dyer to Hankey, 21 November 1827 (LMS/IC).

[30] Minutes of a meeting of the Committee of the Association in aid of Chinese Female Schools of Singapore and Penang (27 November 1846) included in the FES Minutes, meeting chaired by Mrs Tarn, 10 December 1846.

[31] This association was one of many that British women formed to support female missionaries and their educational projects (see Midgley 2007: 94–8). William Tarn was also involved in evangelical work, following his father in becoming the assistant secretary of the Religious Tract Society, a position that he held for 20 years (Jones 1850: 54–5).

[32] Davies to Ellis, 15 February 1837 (LMS/IC). Davies observed that the women in this creolized subculture spoke Chinese with their husbands and "formed a distinct class from Malay women".

only Malay were brought to them by their Chinese father, who wanted them to learn English and "English habits".[33]

The wives of London Missionary Society missionaries, including Maria Dyer, founded and ran girls' schools in Penang, but initially their work was known only through their husbands' reports. That changed after David Abeel visited England in 1834 and circulated an "Appeal to Christian Ladies on behalf of Female Education in China". Rev. Baptist Wriothesley Noel (1798–1873), an evangelical Anglican minister from an aristocratic family, invited elite women from different denominations to meet with him at St John's Chapel, where he read Abeel's appeal to them and urged them to form a new society (Bebbington 1972; FES 1847: 7).[34] In response, they formed the Society for the Propagation of Female Education in the East to recruit, train, and support single female missionaries.

The Board of Directors invited Maria Dyer's sister-in-law Flora Tarn, who had been raising funds for more than a decade to support the "Chinese Female Schools of Singapore and Penang", to join them, and the new society supported girls' schools in Penang, Malacca, and Singapore with donations and workers.[35] The Female Education Society (FES), as it came to be known, drew attention to the work of female missionaries by publishing their letters, first in an 1847 volume commemorating their first 12 years, then in a new magazine the *Female Missionary Intelligencer* (1853–99).

The Prince of Wales Island Christian Association and Tamil Christians

In 1836, Penang's Christian residents organized the Prince of Wales Island Christian Association to support schools and to provide Christian books and tracts. They recruited three Tamil Christians from Ceylon—two men and one woman—to distribute tracts and Bibles in Tamil, and to teach in new boys'

[33] Davies to Ellis, 15 February 1837 (LMS/IC).

[34] Minutes of the Female Education Society. Record of a meeting held at the Vestry room of St John's Chapel, Bedford Row, Friday, 25 July 1834.

[35] After Mr and Mrs Dyer left Penang in 1835, Mrs Beighton took over the running of the girls' school, and in 1838 received a donation of £25 from the FES, which the LMS matched. Davies to Ellis, 8 January 1838; Mrs Beighton, 9 December 1838 (LMS/IC). Mrs Beighton wrote to the directors to thank them for their gift, and to request scissors, needles, thread, chintz, spelling books, and scripture pictures for use in the girls' school.

and girls' schools.[36] But the Anglican chaplain soon tried to claim the most promising of the new recruits. The Bishop of Calcutta and an archdeacon interviewed Samuel several times, confirmed him and encouraged him to go Bishop's College in India to be trained and ordained.[37] In an 1839 resolution, the Christian Committee rebuked the Bishop for his plan to remove Samuel from Penang, "leaving 7000 souls bereft".[38]

In connection with the new initiative to work with Tamil speakers, Beighton invited John Michael Lechler (1804–61) to move to Penang from Madras. Lechler was an ordained German minister who had come to India from England around 1834.[39] He joined Karl Rhenius at Tinnevelly, but as I discuss in Chapter 2, the Church Missionary Society dismissed Rhenius in 1835. At the urging of Anthony Norris Groves, Rhenius returned to Tinnevelly as an independent missionary, and Lechler resigned from the CMS mission and joined Rhenius and the new German Evangelical Mission. Tamil Christians also withdrew from the CMS mission and formed new churches.

After Rhenius' death in 1838, Lechler left the Tinnevelly mission, moving first to Madras, then to Penang (Rhenius 1841: 474, 511, 602; Frykenberg 2008: 255). The Anglican establishment in India had not been forgiving towards Rhenius and his coworkers or Groves, and not long after Lechler's arrival, Penang's chaplain "powerfully counselled" Christians to keep to their own Church.[40] Sir William Norris and his wife continued to attend services at the Mission Chapel, as did soldiers and their wives, but most of Penang's respectable Christian elite complied with the chaplain's decree. Lechler soon returned to India,[41] and the Christian Association gave up on their aspiration

---

[36] Printed Prospectus for the formation of the Prince of Wales Island Christian Association, 3 November 1836. See Beighton and Davies, *Report of the Penang Station for 1835–36* (LMS/IC).

[37] Davies to Ellis, 30 March 1838 (LMS/IC).

[38] Resolution from Christian Association, 18 June 1839.

[39] Davies to Ellis, 8 January 1838; Davies to Ellis, 30 March 1838 (LMS/IC),

[40] Beighton commented that if Penang's Protestants did go to the Mission Chapel, it might appear that they had become Methodists, "which would not do at all". Beighton to Ellis, November 1838 (LMS/IC).

[41] Lechler worked for the next 21 years at the LMS mission in Salem near Coimbatoor in Tamil Nadu (Whitehouse 1896: 120).Widowed in 1840, he married an agent of the Female Education Society soon after her arrival and after only two days' acquaintance (Seton 2013: 15). In 1854 he visited England and Germany and returned with artisans who could teach trades, developing a successful School of Industry in Salem (Lovett 1899, Vol. 2: 71). Mr and Mrs Lechler had a close relationship with members of the Groves family, a topic beyond the scope of this study.

to launch a Tamil mission, transferring the funds they had raised to the Chinese boarding schools and dissolving their organization.[42]

Confronting the Queen of Heaven

After 1839, the LMS missionaries in Southeast Asia began to report doing public proselytism at Chinese temples, timing their visits to coincide with festivals and other religious observances. The missionaries regarded the Chinese veneration of a pantheon of gods as an empty tradition, with the exception of their worship of the Lord of Heaven (天公, *Tiangong*), whom they equated with the Christian god *Shangdi*.

In Southeast Asia and Southeastern China, they took as a special target the goddess Mazu (媽祖), whom the Chinese state regarded as a special protector and who had received the title of Queen or Empress of Heaven (天后, *Tianhou*). Mazu is believed to offer special protection to sailors and fishermen, and the Chinese built temples dedicated to her in coastal cities in China, Taiwan, and Southeast Asia, including Penang and Singapore. When LMS missionary James Legge visited Walter Medhurst in Batavia in 1839, Medhurst took him to a temple dedicated to the Queen of Heaven. A festival was in progress, and Medhurst immediately engaged a crowd of worshippers in a loud debate, denouncing the "folly" of the service (Girardot 2002: 38).

The Protestants probably first read about Mazu worship in the writings of German missionary Karl Gützlaff (1803–51), whose 1834 book described three journeys along the China coast. Gützlaff observed that the Fujianese rivalled Rome in the "adoration of images" and that they were especially devout after a "profitable journey or an escape from storm" (1834: 183). On his first journey on a Chinese junk, he observed how the boat's crew venerated Mazu:

> When a vessel is about to proceed on a voyage, she is taken in procession to a temple, where many offerings are displayed before her. The priest recites some prayers, the mate makes several prostrations, and the captain usually honours her by appearing in a full dress before her image. . . . Afterwards, the good mother . . . is carried in front of a stage, to behold the minstrels, and to admire the dexterity of the actors; thence she is brought back, with music, to the junk, where the merry peals of the gong receive the venerable old inmate, and the jolly sailors anxiously strive to seize whatever may happen to remain of her banquet (1834: 58–9).

[42] Beighton to Tidman and Freeman, 5 November 1841 (LMS/IC).

On their journey, he repeatedly spoke out against Mazu worship. When asked to make food offerings to her image, he threatened to throw the statue overboard.

On his departure for England in 1839, Evan Davies passed the Penang mission library, including Gützlaff's book, to newly-arrived LMS missionary Alexander Stronach (1800–79).[43] In journal entries for 1840 and 1841, Stronach noted that he had made public exhortations at Chinese temples and festival events:[44]

> For 3 Oct: As this evening the Chinese had a great feast for their idols and their deceased ancestors, I went to speak to those I found in their temple, and to the multitudes congregating outside. With great companies of them I spoke of the vanity of their idolatrous worship, and on the excellence of the true religion revealed from heaven. I distributed seventy books among them.

Near a stage, he joined people sheltering from the rain in a covered walkway. They took a candle from a lantern so that he could read:[45]

> I read to them one of Dr. Milne's Chinese Sermons, and expatiated at considerable length on the truth there briefly enforced. "Neither is there salvation in any other etc." I had a congregation of about fifty Chinamen, many of whom had heard me before, seemed to attend with understanding and feeling to the truths I advanced. Oh, may the Holy Spirit impress these glorious truths in every heart.

Stronach returned to the temple few months later, boldly put books on a table, then went to the centre of the temple, where he sat down and read out loud to the crowd.[46]

Initially Chinese devotees welcomed the missionaries to their temple events, perhaps because they found the spectacle of Europeans speaking Hokkien, however badly, to be entertaining. But just as Gützlaff and Medhurst had done, the missionaries disparaged the veneration of deities in their orations. Once

---

43 22 August 1839, list of Davies' property (LMS/IC).

44 He does not identify the temple, but he likely visited the Kong Hok Palace (*Guangfu Gong*) on Pitt Street, which faced the sea and had been dedicated to Mazu but which became known as the Guanyin Temple. For a list of major festival events in 1857, see the Appendix "Chinese Festivals Celebrated in Penang, Malaysia" in DeBernardi 2004.

45 From Alexander Stronach to LMS directors, journal entry for 3 October 1840 (LMS/IC).

46 From Alexander Stronach to LMS directors, journal entry for 8 March 1841(LMS/IC).

they understood the purpose of these exhortations, temple managers sought to evict the missionaries and Chinese evangelists from the temple grounds.

Controversy and the Malay Mission in Penang

Murray Rubinstein has noted that congruencies between Chinese religion and evangelical Christianity promoted conversion in Taiwan (Rubinstein 1996b). But in the case of Islam, congruencies did not promote Christian conversion. The Christians offered a sacred book of great antiquity, but Muslims already had the Koran. The Christians placed Jesus at the centre of their practice, but Jesus was already known to Muslims as a holy man and a prophet, one inferior to their own founder. The Christians offered converts access to a global Christian network, but Muslims had an Islamic network whose diversity they came to know firsthand when they made the pilgrimage to Mecca. The Christians opposed idolatry, but Muslims strictly prohibited any sort of visual representation of the human form. Muslim leaders were well organized in their opposition to Christian evangelism and had the support of the Malay sultans. Finally, the British treaty with the Sultan of Kedah did not allow any interference with Islam.

Although most of the LMS missionaries studied Chinese languages, Beighton studied the Malay language and sought converts among Muslims with his translations and "controversies" (Carey 1850: 436; Obituary 1845: 172). Beighton often walked through town to converse with Asians in groups, especially at festivals. He also visited wealthy Asian merchants in their homes (Carey 1850: 436–7), and exchanged printed materials and long letters with a number of Muslims, including the "opulent Mahometan Seyd", who wrote a letter to Beighton explaining that he came to Penang from Arabia not to change his religion but to obtain wealth.[47] He also corresponded with local imams.

Muslim leaders objected to several of Beighton's Malay tracts including his translation of a section of London Anglican Bishop Bielby Porteus' *Lectures on the Evidences of Christianity*. Bishop Porteus had bluntly declared Christianity to be true and Islam to be a fraud, dismissing Muhammed as an "enthusiast and an imposter" (Porteus 1801: 40–1). The tract so upset members of Penang's Muslim community that they went as a group and presented a petition to the Governor requesting that Beighton's evangelical work be stopped. The Governor called the missionaries to a meeting, and they were gratified to learn

[47] Beighton to Ellis and Tidman, 24 March 1841 (LMS/IC).

that because the press was free in India, the government planned to take no action to stop them from circulating the offending tract (Carey 1850: 436).[48]

One of the LMS teachers in Penang used an English edition of *Pilgrim's Progress* as a text, and Beighton sought support from the Religious Tract Society (RTS) and the LMS directors to translate and print *Pilgrim's Progress* in Malay. The missionaries used the 17th-century allegory to convey the Christian teaching that the individual needed to go on a spiritual journey in order to reach heaven. Beighton tried to convince the LMS directors that reading it would also induce some Malay Muslims "to leave the city Destruction in search of a better country . . . the Heavenly Jerusalem, the Celestial City."[49]

The challenges of translation were many. Beighton finished translating Part One of *Pilgrim's Progress* in 1841, but reported that some of the passages made no sense. He decided to add explanations in the text, using the Malay equivalent of 'viz'. Because he did not think that readers would refer to a Bible to read the Bible references (which many English editions supply in notes), he also added the most important of these to the text itself, thereby ensuring "at least a portion of the Word of God being read with the Pilgrim". He gave numerous examples of his technique: "a great burden on his back—*viz.* his sins"; "a book in his hand *viz.* the Gospel"; "the comforter *viz.* the Holy Spirit"; "be always at a place somewhat ascending *viz.* Mount Calvary where Christ was crucified".

He also altered the allegorical street names in Vanity Fair to reflect Penang's ethnic mix, so instead of "the British Row, the French Row, the Italian row, the Spanish row, the German row" (Bunyan 1984: 73), he offered: the English Protestant Road, the French Road, the Arabian Road, the China Road, the Hindoo Road, the Siam Road, and also the Barbarian Road, all streets where every kind of merchandise was available. As Beighton described it, the English Protestant Road was narrow and few people walked in it "but the other streets are exceedingly large and broad and vast multitudes walk there under the Government of . . . the King of Vanity Fair".[50]

Beighton also took liberties in rewriting the text of *Pilgrim's Progress* seeking to convince Muslim readers of the alleged folly of their religion. His free translation was more likely to have given offense than to have achieved his goal. In Beighton's revision of the story, for example, the Pilgrim preached against Islam—the religion of the 'Arabian prophet Mahomet'—which, following

[48] Carey provides no date for this event. In 1826, the LMS directors approved Malay printing in Penang on a small scale, and the Penang mission soon published tracts in Malay. Beighton to Ellis, 14 December 1836 (LMS/IC).

[49] Beighton to LMS directors, 20 August 1840 (LMS/IC).

[50] Beighton to Ellis and Tidman, 24 March 1841 (LMS/IC).

Bishop Porteus' example, he condemned as an invented, vain and worthless religion. And when he translated a conversation between Christian and the character named Ignorance, he represented Ignorance as a Muslim:[51]

> Ignorance: "I know my Lord's will. I am very correct and pure in my conduct. I pay all my debts. I pray five times a day—making 17 prostrations in all. Moreover I fast a whole month every year. I give alms and pay tithes of all I possess, ...[I] go on pilgrimage to Mecca so that I may have the praise of men. I heartily oppose all infidels and would kill them if I had the power. I am not wicked like other people, thus our religion is exceedingly good."
>
> Christian: "But you did not come in at the wicket gate, etc."

Beighton noted that he deliberately put Mohammed's name into his translation, hoping that this would prevent Muslims from destroying it.

Although Beighton aspired to a handsomely produced book printed in England or Harlem and illustrated with engravings, he and his assistants printed his Malay translation in Penang using the LMS press. He claimed that after he corresponded with one imam and sent him tracts, the imam's faith had been shattered, adding, "The Press is too powerful an engine for him to cope with—I have sent him the Pilgrim as promised."[52] But despite his optimism, most agreed that the LMS missionaries in Penang had failed in their efforts to convert Muslims.[53]

After Siam conquered the Sultanate of Kedah in 1821, the exiled Sultan and his family lived in a house next to the LMS mission. In 1825, Beighton reported to the LMS directors that the Sultan had "half-promised to come some Sabbath Day", and that he had invited him to return with him to Kedah if he was reinstated on his throne.[54] The Sultan did not visit a Christian service, but Beighton's son John became a favourite companion and a frequent guest at royal feasts and dramatic dances staged for the king. When they parted, the Sultan gave him a massive gold and diamond ring as a memento of their friendship (Beighton 1888: 17–8).

---

[51] Beighton to Ellis and Tidman, 24 March 1841 (LMS/IC).

[52] Beighton to LMS directors, 2 September 1842 (LMS/IC). He died before his translation of Volume II was published, and his wife supervised the teachers in printing it.

[53] Although the Malay-medium LMS schools were well funded by the East India Company and popular with students, after his death a co-worker commented that "it was not Mr. Beighton's happy lot to see much fruit in the *conversion* of Many Mahomedans to God" (Anon 1848: 173).

[54] Beighton to LMS directors, 30 June 1825 (LMS/IC).

Penang had been ceded to Sir Francis Light in 1786 on the understanding that the British would offer protection to Kedah. But Light had not received the approval of the East India Company when he promised protection, and the Sultan struggled to maintain control of Kedah in the face of Siamese claims. Finally the East India Company formally recognized Siam's right to the territory, and by 1837 the Sultan was a state prisoner on a ship in Penang's harbour.

The government allowed Beighton to visit him on his boat, and asked him to persuade the Sultan and his entourage to leave for Malacca. Beighton refused, telling everyone that he had nothing to do with politics. When they met, the Sultan hinted that he would regard Christianity with some favour if he were restored to his throne, and others told Beighton that if the Sultan was restored, "all the people would believe the Gospel".[55] Centuries earlier, the people of Kedah had followed their ruler in becoming Muslim, so the missionaries believed this could happen. But the Sultan left Penang without regaining control of the Sultanate of Kedah, and the promise of mass conversion was not realized.

From Penang to China

The Treaty of Nanking ceded Hong Kong Island to Britain and opened five port cities—Canton, Amoy, Foochow, Ningpo, and Shanghai—to foreign trade. In December 1842, James Legge, Samuel Dyer, and John Stronach sold the Anglo-Chinese College Building in Malacca, the dwelling house, and other property, handing over control of the Mission Chapels at Malacca and Batavia to the care of trustees. In 1843 they relocated the Anglo-Chinese College to Hong Kong, and most of the LMS missionaries shifted their activities from Penang, Malacca, Singapore, and Batavia (where Medhurst had worked for decades) to China. Many moved to the newly-opened treaty port in Amoy (Xiamen) in Fujian Province, where the population spoke Amoy Hokkien, the language that most of the LMS missionaries had sought to learn in Southeast Asia. Although they supported a Malay mission in Singapore for a few years, the LMS dedicated their financial resources to the evangelization of China and left others to take up the work in the Straits Settlements and Java that they had begun decades earlier.

When the LMS mission's Chinese work ended, John Stronach and his assistant William Young departed from Singapore for Amoy. His brother Alexander Stronach joined him soon thereafter, abruptly abandoning Penang's Chinese boys' school, even though the students were under long-term contracts. Although the missionaries who had studied the Chinese language moved to

[55] Beighton to Ellis, April 1837 (LMS/IC).

China, Beighton had worked with Malay speakers, albeit with limited success. As he was preparing to leave, Alexander Stronach wrote to the LMS directors to recommend that the Penang Malay mission also be closed and the printing press moved to Singapore. The directors eventually approved keeping the Penang Mission open, but by the time they had made this decision Beighton had died. The directors decided to continue the Malay mission in Singapore and moved the printing press there, leaving the Singapore station under the control of Benjamin Peach Keasberry (1811–75).

Because they have relied on histories of denominational missions, most historians are unaware that independent missionaries continued to work in Penang and elsewhere in Southeast Asia after the LMS moved to China. David Scott, for example, reports that for 40 years after 1842, only a few Protestant missionaries worked in Singapore, and all work ended in Penang (see Scott 2016:3).

From the London Missionary Society's perspective, the mission in Penang ceased to exist when Beighton died in 1844 (Lovett 1899, Vol. 2: 627, 439). And from the Open Brethren perspective, the history of the Penang Mission did not start until John Chapman and his wife went to Penang in 1859 from Bristol with support from George Müller and Bethesda and Salem Chapels (Stunt et al. 1972: 250). But after the London Missionary Society stopped supporting the Penang Mission, local Christians continued to meet in the mission chapel, and independent missionaries directly continued the LMS educational and evangelical projects at their former mission.

Chapter 4

The Brethren Movement and the Penang Mission

> Mr. Beighton died [in 1844] and the Penang Mission came to an end. … During the first twenty-five years of its corporate life the Society began a number of missionary enterprises which never took vigorous root, and some of which were barely more than experiments.
>
> Richard Lovett's *History of the London Missionary Society*[1]

> We have a church and school, and the London Missionary Society has long since abandoned it, and would, no doubt, be glad to grant the premises to any persons desirous of labouring here.
>
> 1855 letter from Penang lawyer J.D. Vaughan to George Pearse[2]

The Brethren movement first reached Penang by way of a funding opportunity. In 1851, George Pearse, a wealthy London stockbroker, wrote letters to missionaries to introduce the Chinese Evangelization Society and their programmes. John George Bausum replied with enthusiasm to their proposal to "promote the Gospel through a Native agency", and described his and his second wife's work in running boarding schools in Penang.

---

[1] Lovett 1899 Vol. 2: 439, 627.

[2] J.D. Vaughan to George Pearse, Foreign Secretary of the Chinese Evangelization Society (Penang, 19 August 1855), *The Chinese Missionary Gleaner* (*CMG*) Vol. 2, No. 30 NS (November 1855): 241. The Chinese Evangelization Society publications cited in this chapter are held in the archives of the Council for World Mission at the School of Oriental and African Studies, University of London (SOAS CWML 0190). They are also available through Nineteenth Century Collections Online.

Bausum was born in Germany on 8 June 1812 and was baptized Lutheran.[3] He started working with Chinese and Malays on the Malay Peninsula in 1837, and by 1842 had moved to Province Wellesley, where he ran a "flourishing school".[4] When the London Missionary Society relocated its missionaries to China, Bausum took over their schools in Penang.

Maria Tarn Dyer had been widowed in Macao in 1843, and her British supporters urged her to return to Penang and to run her girls' schools as an independent missionary. There she met and married Bausum. In 1845, the treasurer of the Association in aid of Chinese Female Schools of Singapore and Penang reported that ladies' working parties in England and Scotland, groups of friends, and students in a Sunday school in Paddington had donated "useful and fancy articles" to her for the support of the Penang girls' school.[5]

After her husband's death, Mrs Beighton had been unable to sell the mission property, and George Felix Gottlieb, who was then Magistrate and Harbour Master, wrote to the LMS directors to advise them that if what had been bought by local subscription was subtracted, then only the Mission House would be left for sale.[6] One of the two schools had been built by Mr Dyer at his private expense, and the other by the Penang Christian Association, and both, he added, would be very useful for a Protestant missionary or missionary society. He recommended Mr and Mrs Bausum to them, and in 1846 the LMS directors allowed them to continue using the mission premises in Penang.

At the time that the Bausums assumed control of the Penang Mission and schools, the LMS properties included the Mission House, which combined a library, printing and bookbinding equipment, outhouses, and a garden; the Chapel, including an organ and a silver communion service; grounds that were planted with coconuts and plantain trees; and a half-dozen school houses. In

---

[3] The CMG editors gave his birthplace as Wirtemberg (see *CMG* No. 8 NS (1 August 1856): 97). Other sources state that he was born in Rodheim vor der Höhe, near Frankfurt am Main.

[4] Maria Dyer to LMS directors, 31 January 1845 (LMS/IC). Possibly he cooperated with the American Board of Commissioners for Foreign Missions, which started work in Singapore in 1834 and by 1837 had 19 missionaries working in Penang and Province Wellesley, Malacca, and Singapore (Sng 2003: 37). But like the LMS, the ABCFM moved its missionaries to China after the first treaty ports were opened.

[5] The *Evangelical Magazine and Missionary Chronicle* 1845: 704.

[6] In the 1830s, Gottlieb was the first Harbour Master of Penang and became Penang's Postmaster in 1858. Both of his sons were lawyers (Khoo 2006: 24). He attended the LMS mission church and was a monthly subscriber to the boys' school. After Bausum's death he took responsibility for looking after the LMS property.

addition, the mission owned a brick building in Beach Street, attap houses in Pulau Tikus, and a large piece of land in Province Wellesley.[7]

But not long after, Maria fell ill and died. The Female Education Society directors resolved to send a new teacher to Penang, but found no one for the post.[8] Two years later Jemima Poppy (1818–69), a female missionary who had come to Southeast Asia to work in Borneo with support from the FES but who had left after her coworker died, visited Singapore, met Bausum and married him. As a married woman, she could no longer work as an agent of the FES, but she took over the running of the Penang girls' schools with the support of Maria Dyer Bausum's network of fundraisers.

Although the boys' schools received government assistance, Bausum found that his independence had acted "detrimentally on funds".[9] Bausum applied to the Anglican Church Missionary Society for support, and when they refused to help him, he approached Penang's Anglican chaplain. But in an interaction that recalls Rhenius' conflict with the Anglican establishment in India, Bausum reported that the Anglicans would only give him financial assistance if the native church conformed to their form of worship. He studied the Book of Common Prayer, and because as a Pietist he did not accept the ritual of infant baptism, found that he could not affirm the 39 Articles. He withdrew his application for ordination.[10]

Penang's Anglican chaplain next proposed to purchase the mission premises. Bausum opposed the sale, noting that Scots residents and other dissenters in Penang had built the chapel, "and all who contributed, did aid to erect a dissenters, and not an Episcopalian place of worship". He appealed to the Free Church of Scotland hoping that they would "extend their efforts to Penang and ordain me as one of their missionaries for this place".[11] But instead they sent their own minister to Penang.

Bausum agreed to shared use of the Mission Chapel, noting that Presbyterian families had contributed to its building, but asked the Presbyterians to pay a

---

[7] Letter from John T. Beighton to Read, 19 December 1845 (LMS/IC).

[8] FES minutes, 14 January 1847; 11 February 1847 (AM2 Minutes 1583–3939; 1846–63). The records of the Society for Promoting Female Education in the East, including General and Finance Committee minutes, annual reports and copies of their magazine the *Female Missionary Intelligencer*, are held at the University of Birmingham, Cadbury Research Library, Special Collections (GB 150 FES). The society is often called the Female Education Society, abbreviated FES.

[9] Bausum to Tidman, 23 March 1855 (LMS/IC).

[10] Bausum to LMS directors, 31 May 1849 (LMS/IC).

[11] Bausum to LMS directors, 31 May 1849 (LMS/IC).

monthly rent. When they argued that the chapel was intended for the use of any Protestant congregation with their own minister, he countered that it was built for the agents of the LMS "who were appointed to labour here among the Chinese or Malays".[12] The Anglican minister offered help but only on the condition that Presbyterians discontinue having services in the Mission Chapel.

On receiving the letter from Pearse, Bausum immediately applied to the Chinese Evangelization Society for funds to train three Chinese students and a Malay Muslim convert whose sister had also been baptized. The Malay had been Thomas Beighton's student in the LMS boys' school, and Bausum proposed that he could use Malay to do outreach to the Chinese in Penang. On his baptism, the young man took the name Nathaniel April (aka Asrel).[13]

In their 1854 annual report the directors of the CES described their aspirations in supporting Bausum's recruits:[14]

> The Board continues the support of the four native youths under the charge of Mr Bausum. The accounts received of their progress are satisfactory; they go out into the neighborhood of Penang, speaking to the people of the glad tidings of salvation. It is hoped that one day some, if not all, these youths will enter China as heralds of peace. From the difficulties of the language and the peculiarities of the Chinese people, the Board looks to a native agency as the most efficient instrument for the Evangelization of China. The present aspect of the country, its politics and religious excitement, induce a strong hope that the day is approaching when many will throw off idolatry and become preachers of the gospel to their countrymen. The Lord appears to be preparing wonderful things for China that such vast numbers should, at the bidding of one man, cast away their idols and worship one Supreme Being, is indeed marvelous in our eyes.

The religious excitement to which the CES directors referred was the Taiping Rebellion, whose leaders sought the overthrow of the Qing dynasty. The rebels claimed to worship the same God as the Christians, and British Christians imagined what it might mean for them if the Taiping Heavenly King ruled China. Of this more below in Chapter 5.

---

[12] Bausum to the Presbyterian committee (n.d.), enclosure in Bausum to the LMS directors, 4 February 1852 (LMS/IC).

[13] Bausum to Pearse, in *The Chinese and General Missionary Gleaner* (*CGMG*) Vol. 2, No. 10 (March 1853): 76–7.

[14] "Fourth Annual Report of the Chinese Evangelization Society" in *CMG* Vol. 1, No. 12 NS (May 1854): 90.

Karl Gützlaff and the Chinese Evangelization Society

Karl Friedrich August Gützlaff (1803–51) is rarely mentioned in histories of the Brethren Movement, and both the Chinese Union that he founded and the Chinese Evangelization Society were shortlived. Nonetheless his influence on the Open Brethren movement was great. Like Karl Rhenius, Gützlaff promoted the rapid indigenization of Christianity, proposing that European Christians support local evangelists and independent primitive churches. This strategy influenced the Open Brethren missionaries in Penang and Singapore long after the CES dissolved.

Gützlaff attended the Jänicke Missionary Institute (1800–27), a small seminary in Berlin that was one of the earliest schools to offer missionary training (Herppich 2016: 3). Rhenius had written to the King of Prussia Frederick William III, urging him to support missionary training. In response, the king gave support to the Missionary Institute and sponsored Gützlaff, who entered their missionary training programme in 1821. Before leaving Europe, Gützlaff wrote to Rhenius to thank him for being "the instrument in his hand of fulfilling my wishes" (Rhenius 1841: 258–9).

In 1826, Gützlaff sailed to Batavia with sponsorship from the Netherlands Missionary Society, but by 1828 he had become independent. He married Maria Newell, a female missionary in Malacca, and they worked together in Thailand. After losing her and their child in 1831, he made three voyages along the China coast, including Fujian, Canton, and Macao, and published accounts of his journeys that circulated widely (Gützlaff 1834). He held an official post as Chinese secretary to the government of Hong Kong from 1843 until 1851, and continued to publish in English, Chinese, and German (Lutz 1985: 63–7). In addition to founding the Chinese Union, Gützlaff did Bible translation, including an 1840 Chinese translation of the Old Testament, which the leader of the Taiping Heavenly Kingdom later used as the basis for the Taiping Bible, promoted medical missions, and was instrumental in forming the interdenominational and international Basel Hakka Mission in 1846 (Lutz and Lutz 1998: 4–6).

Gützlaff founded the Chinese Union in 1844 in Hong Kong in order to sinify Christian evangelism. To that end, he proposed "to have Chinese present the essence of Christianity in local dialects, compose tracts that were Chinese in tone and style, and supervise the proselytizing" so that in the end "Chinese would win China for Christ" (Lutz 1985: 67). As Gützlaff described it, the movement started in Canton, but in just a few years had spread to all 18 provinces and even to adjacent countries. The society raised funds to train Chinese colporteurs to carry tracts and New Testaments to the interior of

China, and the Chinese workers had reported spectacular successes. Gützlaff reported that the cost of supporting one of these workers for a year was only £15 per annum, far less than the cost of supporting a European missionary who required years of study to learn to speak and read Chinese.[15] Although Gützlaff never met Rhenius face-to-face, they continued to exchange letters after he went to Asia. In his proposal to rely on indigenous evangelists rather than foreign missionaries to spread Christianity, his movement resembles Rhenius's methods of expansion in India.

Gützlaff also proposed that European missionaries should be medically trained and should offer medical assistance as a way to demonstrate "a lively interest in the welfare of individuals" in order "open the heart for the reception of truth":

> By imitating our Saviour and his apostles in well-doing, we shall prove our claim to be called his disciples. . . . But it should never be forgotten, that it is the most sacred duty of all to alleviate sufferings, and thus to show that the gospel is indeed a message of mercy. . . . It is by the irresistible power of this noble quality that we hope to gain ground (Gützlaff 1835: 568, cited in Grundmann 2005: 55).

Although he was not formally credentialed, Gützlaff had practised medicine in Thailand (1828–31), Macao (1833–39), and as a ship's surgeon (Grundmann 2005: 51–6).

Concurrently, the first medical mission was launched in Canton by Dr Peter Parker (1804–88), who as a student at Yale had pursued both a divinity degree and medical training. Ordained as a Presbyterian minister, in 1834 he went to China with support from the American Board of Commissioners for Foreign Missions (ABCFM). He opened a popular free clinic with the support of the local business community in 1835, and in 1838 he and his supporters formally launched the Medical Missionary Society in Guangzhou (Canton) (Grundmann 2005: 59–71). With its foundation, the role of the medical missionary who conjoined the provision of free medical care with the preaching of the gospel found formal recognition and support.

In 1850 Gützlaff travelled in Europe giving public lectures and promoting his method. Gützlaff's writings had long been popular in Europe: they influenced David Livingstone to become a medical missionary in Africa, and provided early reports of the Taiping Rebellion that intrigued Karl Marx. In England Gützlaff found interest among wealthy members of the Brook Street

---

[15] *The Gleaner in the Missionary Field* (*GMF*) Vol. 1, No. 3 (May 1850): 18.

Figure 12 Karl Friedrich August ('Charles') Gützlaff wearing Fujian dress. Lithograph by Richard James Lane, after George Chinnery, published 1835. ©National Portrait Gallery, London.

Chapel (est. 1839), including businessman and chemist John Eliot Howard (1807–83).

The Howard family were former Quakers who had withdrawn from Quaker meeting after the Beaconites of Manchester seceded in 1836. Quaker founder George Fox taught that people were fundamentally good since all had the "inward light" of Christ in them. But the inward light doctrine gave no theological justification for Christian proselytism or spiritual revival, and some British Quakers, drawn to evangelical Christianity, questioned it. Some of the seceders joined the Brethren movement (Cantor 2005: 359; West 2016: 19), although Howard refused to call himself Brethren, noting "I cannot pledge myself to any brethren but the sect which were called Christians first at Antioch" (Howard 1885: 118). In 1839, the Howard family helped found the Brook Street Meeting House (later known as the Brook Street Chapel) in Tottenham, North London.

In response to Gützlaff's appeal, a small group met in the Howard home and founded "The Chinese Association". The founders of the small organization included members of two Open Brethren Assemblies. One of these was the Hackney Assembly, which later moved to Paragon Road, and its prominent members included George Pearse, the wealthy London stockbroker who wrote to Bausum, and naturalist and geologist Philip Henry Gosse (Forrest 1971: 34, 42).[16] The other was Brook Street Chapel in Tottenham. CES founding members also included Richard Ball, a former Quaker who had been baptized in Exeter by Benjamin W. Newton, the Brethren leader whose conflict with Darby had precipitated the 1848 schism in the Brethren movement (Stunt 2015: 49).

The CES also promoted female education in China and affiliated with the "London Central Ladies' Association in Aid of the Work of the Native Evangelists", a group that Mrs J. Eliot Howard had cofounded in 1851 to receive contributions for female missionaries.[17] The London Central Ladies' Association cooperated with the Female Education Society to support female missionaries working in Ningpo, China and in the Penang and Singapore girls' schools.

In March 1850 the Chinese Association published the first issue of *The Gleaner in the Missionary Field* (1850–51). In 1851 they took as their name "The Chinese Society for Furthering the Promulgation of the Gospel in China,

---

[16] Philip Gosse's son Edmond Gosse wrote a well-known memoir based on his recollections of growing up in a strict Brethren household (Gosse 1907).

[17] *GMF* Vol. 2, No. 2 (February 1851): 12–3.

and Adjacent Countries, by Means of Native Evangelists" and renamed their publication *The Chinese and General Missionary Gleaner* (1851–53).[18] As I discuss in Chapter 2, after Anthony Norris Groves visited Brethren assemblies in London in 1852 to raise interest in independent work in India, James Van Sommer, another member of the Tottenham assembly, launched *The Missionary Reporter*. After he commenced the new magazine, members of the Chinese Association narrowed the scope of their work to China, calling themselves the Chinese Evangelization Society (CES), and their magazine *The Chinese Missionary Gleaner* (see Forrest 1971).

The editors of their magazine described the CES as founded on a "broad and unsectarian basis", and its leaders as evangelical Christians connected with various religious denominations. They noted that previous evangelical organizations like LMS, the Bible Society, and the Religious Tract Society had failed in their attempts to cooperate, and praised the London City Mission as proving that "all denominations can work peaceably as brethren".[19]

Historians observe that the British Brethren had no historical relationship with the Moravian Brethren. But British Christians had read their memoirs, magazines, and annual reports, and in an 1851 editorial, the CES founders promoted them as a model. The editors further described the Moravian Brethren as having launched the modern missionary movement, and praised them for their asceticism, philanthropic spirit, and globality (see Gibbs 2020). The Moravian motto was "Joy in poverty and shame!" and they observed that their founder Count Zinzendorf (1700–60) and his wife kept only a "small portion of their large income" for their expenses, donating the rest. The London Brethren further observed that this work had been launched by a single congregation—a small colony of religious refugees at Herrnhut—that had made its influence felt in North America and the British West Indies, South Africa and Australia, and that this community had perpetuated itself from generation to generation. The CES noted that their own generation had "means and appliances" that had not been available to the 18th-century missionaries, but proposed that

[18] Another ex-Quaker, Richard Ball, and George Pearse were together elected to the role of secretary of the association; John Eliot Howard and his brother Robert were on the Board of Management. The members of the Board of Management are listed in the annual reports of the *CGMG* (see May 1851: 94; May 1852: 93).

[19] *CGMG* Vol. 2, No. 10 (March 1853): 74. The London City Mission's founders included Rev. Baptist W. Noel, who had also promoted the British and Foreign Bible Society and the Female Education Society. Noel had been a prominent evangelical Anglican, but his promotion of undenominational cooperation had put him at odds with the Anglican establishment, and in 1848 he had become Baptist (Bebbington 1972).

many churches would be "saved from extinction" if their members imitated the Moravians' "arduous and self-denying exertions".[20]

Following Gützlaff, the founders proposed that the preferred strategy for evangelism was to support a small number of European missionaries to instruct and supervise a large network of Chinese Christian evangelists and indigenous churches. The CES founders further proposed that their missionaries be medically trained. They described medical missionaries as imitating Jesus, who had healed the sick, adding that even those who oppposed the work of missionaries found their medical work praiseworthy. They also concluded that medical missions were a highly effective strategy for evangelism, noting that "in the time of sickness the mind is more disposed to receive the consolations of the gospel".[21] To that end, the CES also cooperated with the Association at Hackney in aid of Medical Missions to China.[22]

The CES was well placed to promote medical missions due to the support of the Howard family, whose successful pharmaceutical manufacturing business, Howard & Sons, had made them wealthy. John Eliot was elected a Fellow of the Royal Society in 1874 for his research on quinine, which was Howard & Sons' most successful product. The Howard brothers supplied missionaries with medicines, including palliatives to help opium users overcome their addiction, at reduced costs or for free (West 2016: 6; Austin 2007: 242).

Among the first missionaries to apply to the CES for funding was Bausum; the CES also supported James Hudson Taylor in China. The CES aspired to extend the range of missionary work in China from the treaty ports to the "vast cities of the inland parts of the country".[23] The CES dissolved in 1859, but in 1865 Taylor founded the China Inland Mission with precisely that goal, and recruited missionaries to work in China's interior cities and towns. Taylor promoted medical work including the treatment of opium addicts, and historian Jesse Lutz concludes that CIM directly continued the work of the CES (Lutz 2008: 311).

---

[20] "The Missionary Labours of the Moravian Brethren", *CGMG* Vol. 1, No. 3 (August 1851):17–8. They cited an 1833 "United Brethren's Missions: Centenary Retrospect of the Missionary Labours of the Brethren", which was translated and reprinted in *The Missionary Register for 1833* (May 1833): 229–32.

[21] *CGMG* Vol. 2, No. 1 (June 1852): 1.

[22] "Third Annual Report of the Chinese Evangelization Society", *CGMG* Vol. 2, No. 12 (May 1853): 92, 96.

[23] *CGMG* Vol. 2, No. 3, 2nd ed. (August 1852): 17.

Transition

When Mr Bausum died suddenly in 1855, Mrs Bausum (Jemima Poppy) took responsibility for running the Penang mission, including supervision of the boys' and girls' schools, and advising the Chinese catechists and "members of our native church". She reported to the CES Board that Penang had a church with 37 members, 2 of whom were "native missionaries" who still required superintendence. Two of these received support from the CES. Nathaniel April, she noted, preached "exceedingly well every Sabbath", but when she proposed to members of the mission church that they choose a pastor from among themselves, to her surprise they elected a newly baptized convert named Je Moy (or Yee Moy).

The missionaries and Nathaniel April spoke Malay, but the native Christians were Chinese and chose Je Moy since he could read the Scripture to them in their language, a dialect of Hokkien. She advised them that they needed to raise funds from among themselves to pay him, and they each pledged a small amount.[24] Lawyer Jonas Daniel Vaughan proposed to the directors of the London Missionary Society that these three be confirmed as ministers, and that the LMS consider dispatching an ordained missionary to Penang.[25] They declined both requests.

Both Nathaniel and Je Moy wrote letters that were published in *The Chinese Missionary Gleaner*, and the editors listed their names as supported workers and collected donations on their behalf. As Nathaniel described it, after Mr Bausum died, he took his place leading the Malay-speaking congregation. Their schools had 47 boarders, who met in the Mission Chapel both morning and evening to hear him read and comment on a chapter in the bible, ending in prayer. Je Moy reported that Mr Bausum had converted him, and that he was living at the Chinese school as a teacher and Catechist. He held meetings twice a week in Chinese to a congregation of about 30 persons besides the school children, and also did itinerant evangelism, seeking to "do good to our lost countrymen".[26]

When she wrote to Mr Pearse at the CES, Mrs Bausum proposed that supporting a new missionary in Penang would cost little beyond the person's salary:[27]

---

24 Mrs Bausum, Penang, to Mr Pearse, 11 September 1855. *CMG* NS No. 2 (1856): 23.

25 J.D. Vaughan to Tidman, 19 August 1855 (LMS/IC).

26 Nathaniel and Jemoy, Penang, 16 and 18 July 1856, letters to George Pearse, *CMG* NS No. 10 (1 October 1856): 127–8.

27 Mrs Bausum, Penang, to Mr Pearse, 11 September 1855, *CMG* NS No. 2 (1856): 23.

> ... everything is on foot, and some subscriptions and government allowance can be obtained for the boys' school, and undoubtedly the ladies would continue to grant their support to the girls' department as hitherto. Here are depositories of Bibles and tracts, and everything for a missionary's use. Here is a dwelling house, two schoolhouses, and a chapel; which I doubt not, the London Missionary Society would freely lend to any truly evangelical society. . . . I commit these hints to your committee's consideration, and trust the Lord will direct and enable you to act as shall be most for his own glory.

She also described her students and teachers to the FES:[28]

> My girls' school is interesting. We have at present four girls who have from conviction embraced Christianity, two of whom are shortly to be married to catechists. Two baptised in infancy, being the children of native Christians, also seem well-inclined, besides several who seem desirous of coming out and being separate.

A Singaporean Christian had pledged to send $3/month to pay the Chinese teacher until another missionary was sent, but the outlook for the mission was poor.[29] Vaughan reported to the LMS directors that although Mrs Bausum wanted to continue her work at the girls' school, Mr Bausum had mortgaged a failed nutmeg plantation for $1000 and she was destitute.[30]

Unable to raise funds for her school, and with a throat infection that left her unable to speak for months, in July 1856 she left Penang for Ningpo (today, Ningbo).[31] There she and her three children joined Mr Bausum's stepdaughters (the children of Samuel Dyer and Maria Tarn Dyer), Maria and Burella Dyer, who were teaching in a school run by Mary Ann Aldersey.

The LMS directors did not send a missionary to Penang, but the CES directors recruited independent missionaries for Penang. Richard Ball took up a special collections to pay for the travel expenses for Dr Pruen and Mrs Pruen, who had volunteered to work with no salary, and to fund Miss Chandler, the

---

[28] "Recent Intelligence: Extracts of a Letter from Mrs Bausum", Penang, 15 October 1855. *Female Missionary Intelligencer* (*FMI*) Vol. 2, No. 30 (February 1856): 23.

[29] Extracts of a letter from Mrs Bausum, Penang, 15 October 1855. *FMI* Vol. 3, No. 30 (February 1856): 23.

[30] J.D. Vaughan to Tidman, 19 August 1855 (LMS/IC).

[31] Mrs Bausum to Tidman, 21 December 1855; Mrs Bausum to Tidman, 18 July 1856 (LMS/IC). Mrs Bausum to George Pearse, 23 October 1856, *CMG* Vol. 2, No. 13 NS (1 February 1857): 35. Some sources suggest that she returned to England first, but this correspondence confirms that she went directly to Ningpo.

daughter of a surgeon in Bristol, who planned to work as joint superintendent for the girls school with Mrs Pruen.[32]

Later Open Brethren publications did not list donors by name, but the CES listed the donors for the special collection for the Penang Mission. Miss Chandler's main donor was the Female Education Society, but donors also included a number of prominent Open Brethren, including John Eliot Howard, the Earl of Cavan, Captain T. Hull and "Christian Friends at Barnstable", who would have been associated with Open Brethren Robert Cleaver Chapman (see Pickering 1918 for biographical details on all of these individuals). Her donors also included Conrad Finzel, junior, Esq., the son of a wealthy businessman who supported George Müller and the orphanages in Bristol. Conrad Finzel (1793–1859) had founded a sugar refinery in Bristol that in 1866 was described as the "busiest sugar refinery in the world", and donated the modern equivalent of over a million dollars per year (£10,000 annually) to the Ashley Down orphanage (Bourne 1866: 20).

Dr and Mrs Pruen and Miss Chandler departed for Penang on 4 September 1856 and arrived in Penang on 20 October. Mrs Bausum had already gone to Ningpo, but members of the native church and Gottlieb were there to meet them. Mr Pruen reported that a Chinese Christian ran the Penang boys' school, which with 92 students, including 32 boarders, was full.[33] The girls' school had 38 girls, including 22 boarders who attended the regular services in the Mission Chapel. Mrs Pruen described her students as a "medley of nations", and they included 18 Chinese, 10 Burmese, 4 Malays, 3 Armenians, 1 Siamese, 1 Tamil, and 1 European, all of whom learned to read both Malay and English. In addition to learning Scriptures and hymns, they studied history, geography, arithmetic, and writing (in both Arabic and Roman script), and spent the afternoon studying needlework of all kinds.[34]

The CES also continued to support the Chinese and Malay-speaking "assistants" whom Bausum had trained, Je Moy and Nathaniel April. As Je Moy described his activities in 1858, he taught every morning in the school for two hours, preached in the chapel on Sunday to a congregation of about 50 persons, and did street corner proselytism and distributed tracts.

[32] "Seventh Annual Report", *CMG* Vol. 2, No. 17 NS (1 May 1857): 72. The Peninsular and Oriental Steam Navigation Company also reduced the cost of passage.

[33] *CMG* Vol. 2, No. 17 (1 May 1857): 66.

[34] "Native Girls' School at Penang", Mrs Pruen, *FMI* NS Vol. 1, No. 3 (1 March 1858): 33–5.

May 1, 1857.] THE CHINESE MISSIONARY GLEANER. 73

lege. Men of faith, filled with love to souls, will be required for the work. May the Lord of the harvest raise up such labourers to go and gather in the harvest.

MISSIONARIES AND OTHERS, AND THEIR STATIONS.

~~Rev. W.~~ Lobscheid	Hong-kong (temporary.)
Dr. Parker	Ningpo.
~~Mr. J. H.~~ Taylor	Shanghai.
~~Mr. J.~~ Jones	Ningpo.
Dr. and Mrs. Pruen	Penang.
~~Miss~~ Chandler	Penang.
Rev. C. J. Hall	Ningpo.
Miss Magrath	Hong-kong.

NATIVE ASSISTANTS, &c.

UNDER REV. W LOBSCHEID.

Fu-Sitom and Ayut	Preachers.
Pun-yu-chun and Hau-fuk	Colporteurs.
Aloi	Medical Assistant.

Also three Teachers in boys and girls' schools, containing about 57 pupils.

UNDER DR. PARKER.

Dzing	Evangelist.
Dziang-Sung	Medical Assistant.

Also a school containing 15 boys.

IN PENANG.

Nathaniel, April and Jemoy	Native Assistants.

Boys and girls' schools, under Dr. Pruen, Mrs. Pruen, and Miss Chandler; containing altogether about 60 pupils.

Figure 13 CES List of missionaries and "native assistants" (annotations in the original). The individuals whose names were crossed off had resigned from the CES by 1857. *CMG* Vol. 2, No. 17 (1 May 1857): 73.

As part of his public outreach, Je Moy debated with non-Christian Chinese, and he described visiting a Chinese schoolmaster and trying to convince him that idol worship was futile. When the schoolmaster asked him if he worshipped and followed Confucius, he replied that Confucius was "but a man", whereupon the schoolmaster abused him. He also did open-air evangelism at the Chinese temple, but when a crowd gathered to listen, the priest dispersed them and called him a vagabond. He added that although people in the town insulted him and sometimes attempted to assault him, "rude and barbarous" people living in the valleys and hills listened and begged him to stay and teach them.[35]

Dr Pruen baptized 11 converts, but also reported that of 30 adults baptized by Mr Bausum, 15 had returned to China, possibly due to the global economic crisis of 1857.[36] But their effort was shortlived. Miss Chandler soon married a government worker and retired from teaching.[37] Their Malay evangelist Nathaniel April took new work at a distance, and after Dr Pruen died in 1859, Mrs Pruen left Penang.

In 1857, the CES Board had reported that their association had fallen into debt and that they could not meet their missionaries' expenses.[38] Two years later, in their 10th and final annual report, the Board announced that their association had been dissolved. They recalled that they had raised £13,000 and had been able to send out "seven missionaries, and eight ladies, support many natives, circulate the entire Scriptures, and publish a monthly journal for about ten years".[39] The missionaries and Asian evangelists whom they had sponsored found other means of support. Although they could no longer support them, in the final pages of the final issue of *The Chinese Missionary Gleaner*, the CES directors reported that new missionaries were on the way to Penang.

I began my account of the Penang mission with the London Missionary Society and the independent missionaries who took over their schools and projects. But the early Brethren missions in Penang and Singapore also had links with persons and events in China, and to China I now turn.

---

[35] Yee Moy, Catechist under Dr W. Pruen, to George Pearse, 29 June 1858, *CMG* Vol. 3, No. 34 NS (1 October 1858): 130–1.

[36] *CMG* Vol. 3, No. 27 NS (1 March 1858): 32.

[37] *CMG* Vol. 3, No. 29 NS (1 May 1858): 60.

[38] "Seventh Annual Report", *CMG* Vol. 2, No. 17 (1 May 1857): 71–2.

[39] *CMG* Vol. 4, No. 44 NS (1 October 1859): 92.

Chapter 5

Revival and Rebellion in China

> In many respects, Scotland may be called God's second Israel. No other land has its Sabbath as Scotland has; no other land has the Bible as Scotland has; no other land has the gospel preached, free as the air we breathe, fresh as the stream from the everlasting hills.
>
> Robert Murray M'Cheyne[1]

Many date the "explosive starburst" growth of Pentecostal Christianity to the early 20th century, and pinpoint its origin to the Los Angeles Azusa Street Revival.[2] But sociologist David Martin observes that Pentecostalism is "an extension of Methodism and of the Evangelical Revivals (or Awakenings) accompanying Anglo-American modernization" (Martin 2002: 7). Allan Anderson concludes that "Pentecostalism that is made in the USA is only one part of the total picture of many forms of Pentecostalism" and urges scholars to study local histories in order to reconstruct the movement's grassroots expansion (Anderson 2014: 11; see also Chong and Goh 2014).

As I discuss in Chapter 6, Brethren missionaries went to the Straits Settlements in 1859, and soon after their arrival gave copies of *The Revival* to friends and donors in Singapore and Penang. But revivalism also came to Southeast Asia indirectly via the influence of Scots Presbyterian missionary

---

[1] Robert Murray M'Cheyne, in Bonar 1845: 449.

[2] Martin describes the 1906 Asuza Street Revival as an "explosive starbust" that sent people in all directions with a fusion of the faiths of culturally despised poor blacks and poor whites (Martin 2002: 5). He does note that the 19th- and early 20th-century history of revivals in India "would even support the claim that the movement was as much generated there as among North American poor whites and poor blacks", but does not pursue this insight further (Martin 2002: 154). Allen Anderson recognizes that non-denominational faith missions, including the China Inland Mission, from 1865 promoted a form of revivalism but still dates the introduction of Pentecostalism to China to 1906 (Anderson 2009: 119–21).

William Chalmers Burns (1815–68). Burns travelled widely in Fujian with his Chinese partners, where they made converts and sparked a revival known as the Pechuia Awakening in 1854. Historians of Pentecostalism have overlooked this event, but S. Wells Williams later described it as the first "outpouring of the Holy Spirit in China" (Burns 1870: 489, 510). Those whom Burns and his coworkers converted amazed the missionaries in Amoy by going to a nearby town and seeking to convert the residents.[3]

I first learned of Burns when I visited the Wilkie Terrace Christian Assembly in Singapore, a local church whose early leaders included former Brethren elder Wong Kai Seng and Faithful Luke, an associate of Watchman Nee. I noticed books by a Singaporean Christian Timothy Tow (1920–2009) in their library, and followed up by visiting the Far Eastern Bible College (FEBC). In 1955, Tow had led a secession from the Chinese Presbyterian Synod and formed the Bible Presbyterian Church. Singapore's Bible Presbyterians founded FEBC in 1960, and Tow was FEBC's principal for almost 30 years.

Tow's publications included a biography of famous Chinese evangelist John Sung (Tow 1985) and a short biography of Burns, whom Tow described as the "grandfather" of Singapore's Bible Presbyterians (Tow 1994). In the book's Introduction, Tow commented that Burns was the first missionary of the English Presbyterian Mission to China, but that under the "deadly haze of liberalism and ecumenism", Presbyterians had forgotten him. The Bible Presbyterians, Tow claimed, derived their faith directly from Burns and had transmitted Burns' form of Christian practice, including revivalism and evangelism, in Southeast Asia, India, Africa, and Australia (Tow 1994: 10). I discovered that Burns had worked in Fujian with Brethren missionary Alexander Grant and his coworker Tan See Boo, as well as other Chinese Christians who migrated from Fujian to Southeast Asia. I concluded that Burns should also be described as the grandfather of the Brethren movement in Penang and Singapore.

Burns was the first missionary to work in China with the Presbyterian Mission. He followed strategies of indigenization that he learned both from reading missionary memoirs and from Chinese evangelists who had worked with Karl Gützlaff and the Chinese Union. Burns left the pastoral work of building churches to others, and historians like former Anglican bishop Stephen Neill do not regard Burns as a significant figure in the history of Christian missions

[3] Calvinists like Burns described their revivals as "outpourings of the Holy Spirit" because they attributed the emotional response that accompanied being "born again" as evidence of the role of the Holy Spirit in an individual's regeneration. But unlike Pentecostal revivals, these manifestations were not accompanied by speaking in tongues or healing.

in China (Neill 1986: 242).[4] But Presbyterian mission historian Edward Band concluded that Burns influenced thousands through his itinerant work and revivals (Band 1948: 71). Burns may not have established brick-and-mortar churches, but his charisma combined with effective indigenization contributed to his success in China.

Burns had influence through his partners and his Chinese converts. One of these partners was James Hudson Taylor, a young independent missionary who had been baptized in a Brethren assembly in Hull before going to London and associating with Brethren there. Taylor went to China in 1853 with support from the Chinese Evangelization Society, the organization that started funding John George Bausum and the Penang Mission in 1852. The CES founders included members of the wealthy Howard family, former Quakers who had joined the Brethren network in 1836. Taylor later founded the China Inland Mission with support from George Müller and the Open Brethren.

Burns also worked in Fujian with Presbyterian missionary Alexander Grant (c. 1833–1914). Grant was sent from Amoy to Singapore in 1861, but joined the Brethren movement in Penang before becoming the Singapore Brethren assembly's first missionary. One of Burns' best-known converts in Pechuia, Tan See Boo, was also sent to Singapore to work with Chinese immigrants. In 1867, he and the Chinese congregation that he led joined the Brethren movement, building a Chinese gospel hall next to the new Bethesda Hall. British Brethren in the Straits Settlements who wanted to learn to speak Hokkien often went to Fujian and lived in Tan's home town, the site of the Pechuia Awakening. Pechuia is as much a part of this history of the Brethren Movement in Penang and Singapore as are Bristol and Bath.

Revivalism: Britain and Canada

When he was only 24, Burns became famous for sparking the Kilsyth Revival of 1839 at his father's church. As he preached, he recalled a 1630 revival that inspired him to plead with the "unconverted before me" to "flee to Christ". He continued to do so until "the power of the Lord's Spirit become so mighty" that it carried all before it "like the rushing mighty wind of Pentecost!" As he

[4] In a letter Burns' coworker Carstairs Douglas cast doubt on Burns' reputation for doing pioneering work (Carstairs, cited in Burns 1870: 586–7). His contribution may be disputed, but Burns cooperated with the interdenominational American Board of Commissioners for Foreign Missions, the American Methodist Episcopal mission, and the English and Irish evangelical Church Missionary Society. In Fuzhou he influenced the Xu brothers, the first Chinese Methodists to be ordained as ministers in Fujian (Burns 1870: 493–9; Dunch 2001: 19).

described it, "During the whole of the time that I was speaking, the people listened with the most riveted and solemn attention, and with many silent tears and inward groanings of the spirit; but at last their feelings became too strong for all ordinary restraints, and broke forth simultaneously in weeping and wailing, tears and groans, intermingled with shouts of joy and praise from some of the people of God" (Burns 1870: 95).

Although he had intended to go to India as a missionary, after he found himself in the "midst of a great spiritual awakening", he decided to stay in Scotland. He accepted a short-term engagement at a church in Dundee, where he replaced Robert Murray M'Cheyne while M'Cheyne travelled to Palestine (Burns 1870: 56). In 1840 the *Aberdeen Herald* published a verbatim report of one of Burns' meetings together with a critical attack. The newpaper account so alarmed the Presbytery of Aberdeen that they appointed a committee to interview him and requested testimonials from others, including Robert Murray M'Cheyne.

The journalist reported that Burns had proclaimed, "This is the outpouring of the Spirit", and was asked by the committee members to explain what he had meant. He described observing physical manifestations of grief, including weeping, audible prayers for mercy and crying out loud "as if pierced to the heart". He also noted that sometimes "strong men in the prime of life" fell down or fell into convulsions (Burns 1870: 178–80), behaviours that modern Pentecostal and charismatic Christians call being "slain in the spirit". Following their investigation, the committee members concluded that the revival movement was a genuine "outpouring of the Spirit of God", but that perhaps Burns should not have protracted his meetings to such a late hour (Burns 1870: 185–6; 569–73; see also Band 1948: 6; Bonar 1845: 496–504).[5]

In 1843 conflict over the issue of state control of the appointment of ministers led to the schism known as the Disruption, and the evangelical wing of the Presbyterian Church in Scotland became independent. When the dissenters seceded from the Established Church to form the new Free Church of Scotland, 454 ministers—37.9% of the 1,195 ministers of the Church of Scotland—gave up claims to support by ancient endowments and lost the buildings in which their congregations had worshipped (Latourette 1953: 1193; Brown 1987: 39):

> All over Scotland, ministers left their manses and elders and congregations left their parish churches to meet the following Sunday in farmyards, graveyards, public halls, barns, gravel pits, on hillsides and on board anchored ships. The event was to become symbolic of a great

[5] According to Neil Dickson, if the committee had judged otherwise, his licence to preach would likely have been withdrawn. Personal communication.

> sacrifice of money and security, and as the ultimate statement of social and religious self-determination (Brown 1987: 38).

Burns' father, William Hamilton Burns, lost his manse in Kilsyth in the Disruption, but a large proportion of his congregation followed him, and they built their own building in 1843 (Hutchison 1986: 72).[6] Although they quickly replenished their financial resources, the evangelical Presbyterians lost control of the foreign missions of the Church of Scotland.

After the Disruption, Burns' uncle, Dr Robert Burns (1789–1869), went to Canada where he became the new minister at Toronto's Knox Presbyterian Church, then took a position at Knox Free Church Theological College. Montreal had a large population of Scottish immigrants, and when Dr Burns visited, people asked him, "Have you brought your nephew with you?" (Burns 1870: 257). The Canadian Free Presbyterians arranged William Burns' free passage to Montreal, where he preached to troops stationed in Montreal and spoke on street corners (Burns 1870: 265). He then toured throughout the Canadian dominion for two years, speaking Gaelic in Inverness, English to a congregation of former slaves in Amherstburgh, and by interpreter to an assembly of First Nations peoples at a Methodist mission (Burns 1870: 269–88).

Burns returned to Scotland in 1846, uncertain whether he should continue to be an itinerant evangelist or go to a "heathen field". He found no openings in India, but the convener of the Foreign Missions Committee in Scotland received a letter from the English Presbyterian Church Missionary Committee asking him to recommend someone to work for them as their first missionary in China. The convener saw this as a "providential coincidence" and recommended Burns to them (Burns 1870: 293–4). Doubtful at first, Burns finally agreed.

Evangelical missionaries had only gained access to China's so-called treaty ports in 1843; but as we have seen, the China mission effort had begun a generation earlier. Burns' cousin William Chalmers, who had preached at his ordination, was born in Malacca. And in 1841 Burns had worked for a few months at High Bridge Church, which London Missionary Society missionary and Chinese Bible translator Robert Morrison had once attended (Burns 1870: 296–7).

In preparation, Burns studied Morrison's translation of the Chinese Bible and practised Chinese by translating the New Testament and comparing his results with Morrison's translation. After many months of anticipation and preparation, Burns saw a Chinese person for the first time when they reached the Java Sea (Burns 1870: 318). As the ship approached the coast of China,

[6] I thank Neil Dickson for providing information about the impact of the Disruption on Burns' father.

he studied Morrison's *Memoirs* (1839), praying for the grace to follow in his footsteps, and Robert Philip's *Life and Opinions of Rev. William Milne, D. D.* (1840), whose Chinese tracts he praised highly (Burns 1870: 322).

During his sea voyage, Burns also read the *Memoirs and Remains of Robert Murray M'Cheyne* (Bonar 1845), the evangelical Scottish minister whom Burns had replaced in Dundee in 1839. The *Memoirs* included letters that M'Cheyne had written to Burns while he travelled throughout Europe and Palestine visiting Jewish communities, and also the "Evidence on Revivals" that M'Cheyne wrote for the Presbytery of Aberdeen when they investigated Burns in 1840 (Bonar 1845: 496–504).[7]

In one sermon, M'Cheyne explained that although the Jews were God's chosen people, because they had rejected Jesus, they would be first to be judged and punished. Meanwhile, he told his audience, God's special regard had passed to Scotland:

> In many respects, Scotland may be called God's second Israel. No other land has its Sabbath as Scotland has; no other land has the Bible as Scotland has; no other land has the gospel preached, free as the air we breathe, fresh as the stream from the everlasting hills. Oh, then, think for a moment, you who sit under the shade of faithful ministers, and yet remain unconcerned and unconverted, and are not brought to sit under the shade of Christ, think how like your wrath will be to that of the unbelieving Jew! And think, again, of the marvellous grace of Christ, that the gospel is first to you. The more that your sins are like scarlet and like crimson, the more is the blood free to you that washes white as snow; for this is still His word to all His ministers, Begin at Jerusalem (Bonar 1845: 449).

Burns found, however, that unlike Scotland, China had neither the Sabbath, nor the Bible, nor the gospel preached.

In Hong Kong, Burns studied Cantonese, then moved to Amoy in 1851, where he learned Hokkien. There he engaged in open-air evangelism and held meetings in a chapel in Tai-hang, translated part one of *The Pilgrim's Progress*—a favourite childhood book of his—and revised the Amoy hymnal (Burns 1870: 388). In Amoy, he lived near the American Reformed (Dutch) mission and often cooperated with them, as well as with the LMS missionaries.

On Indigenization and Rhetoric

Soon after Burns arrived in China in 1847, he began travelling with Chinese evangelists who had worked with Karl Friedrich August Gützlaff (1803–51)

[7] In his devotions, he followed Mr M'Cheyne's calendar for daily reading of the Scriptures.

and the Chinese Union, which Gűtzlaff and seven Chinese had formed in 1844. As we have seen, John Eliot Howard and other wealthy London Brethren formed the Chinese Evangelization Society after Gützlaff visited Britain in 1850 on a speaking tour. But while Gützlaff was in Europe, the missionary acting as the Chinese Union's director became certain that members had never travelled to the places where they claimed to have distributed copies of the New Testament, and launched an investigation (Lutz and Lutz 1998: 239). In their defence, Burns testified that he had employed one Chinese Union member as a teacher and two others as assistants on his itinerations, and that they were knowledgeable about Christianity and honest (Lutz 2008: 250, 306). But after Gützlaff died in Hong Kong in 1851, the Chinese Union dissolved.

As Jessie Lutz observes, "several of the more aggressive, bold, and innovative missionaries were either instructed by Gützlaff or inspired by his example; they include Issachar Roberts of Taiping fame, the individualistic Scotch Presbyterian William Burns, and J. Hudson Taylor of the China Inland Mission" (Lutz 2008: 118). Burns followed evangelistic patterns that Gützlaff had promoted, travelling widely with local evangelists and supporting the creation of self-sufficient, self-supporting indigenous churches, practices that the Open Brethren later followed in Penang and Singapore.[8]

Burns was a strong orator and charismatic revivalist, but he found the task of addressing a Chinese audience daunting. In an 1849 letter to his mother, Burns wrote that perhaps one Chinese listener in Amoy was open to his message. He contrasted this with his work as a revivalist in Scotland, where audiences fell to the floor, crying:

> But ah! when I speak thus you must not judge of such as case as if it were similar to those which we remember at Kilsyth, Dundee, and Perth, in days that are past! There is among this people no Sabbath, no Bible, no distinct knowledge even of the existence of one only living and true God; and in my present circumstances it is not a little encouragement to find tokens even of a distinct and cordial apprehension of the simplest principles of divine truth (Burns 1870: 359).

Although he remained convinced that God had sent him there, he admitted that the situation was overwhelming.

In a short biography published on the centenary of his birth, the author described Burns' oratorical skills:

> His voice was of such range and power that he had been known to hold 10,000 people spellbound. But he had few graces of rhetoric or oratory,

[8] The Amoy church supported two native evangelists, "entirely supported by the native church in Amoy, under the care of American missionaries" (Burns 1870: 490).

> and certainly he sought none. His appeals in early days were carried home rather by a kind of terrific energy, so that "the words 'no cross, no crown,' pealed from his lips not so much like a sentence of ordinary speech as a shout in the thick of battle. . . . his greatest efforts were made through the medium of clear and simple speech, steeped in spiritual emotion and directed by an irresistible force that could be none other than the Spirit of God (Connell 1915: 123).

As his brother described it, Burns appealed to his hearers with story and metaphor, speaking with a "vividness and energy" that reminded him of George Whitefield, whose revivals had helped launch the first transatlantic awakening, and also the day of Pentecost as described in the second chapter of *Acts* (Burns 1870: 98). From all accounts, Burns was able to communicate in Chinese languages with equal vividness and energy.[9]

A foundation of classical rhetoric is the concept of *kairos*, or the opportune moment. How does a given context for communication both call for and constrain speech? First, there is the question of time of speaking. For example observing the Sabbath was and is crucial to the identity of evangelical Christians. In Scotland, 19th-century evangelical Christian leaders passed laws to close pubs and museums, and even restricted travel on Sunday, causing M'Cheyne to boast that the Scots were God's new chosen people (Bonar 1845: 449). But the temporality of the seven-day week with a day of prayer and/or rest was not shared by the Chinese, who followed a lunisolar calendar.

Second, there is the place of speaking, and the evangelists performed their Christian message in Chinese spaces. When they travelled, the missionaries and local colporteurs (as distributers of Christian literature are called) distributed tracts and testaments and also spoke wherever they could gather an audience. Just as the German missionaries had done in India and before that in Jewish communities in Europe, in China, the Christians did open-air evangelism at events that attracted large crowds.

Burns accommodated to Chinese social rhythms by going to markets that followed a regular rotation throughout the region; when the market day fell on Sunday, he took advantage of this to go to the marketplace to preach for three hours (Burns 1870: 357). In his street-corner orations, he reported focusing on a few points:

> Today I have been out, and have had more encouragement in the aspect of the people, and also in my ability to communicate to them the great

[9] The author of an obituary described him as having quick linguistic apprehension and mother wit, but lacking the elements that "constitute the enthusiastic and exciting preacher" (Obituary 1868: 184).

truths, (1) That there is but one true God, His character, &c.; (2) That all men are sinners—idolators, &c.; and (3) That there is a Saviour and only one, Jesus the Son of the living God (Burns 1870: 362).

The message was simple and easily translated, but in order to convince his listeners that they needed redemption, he needed to put his audience in touch with powerful emotions. With satisfaction, Burns reported tears among his Chinese listeners.

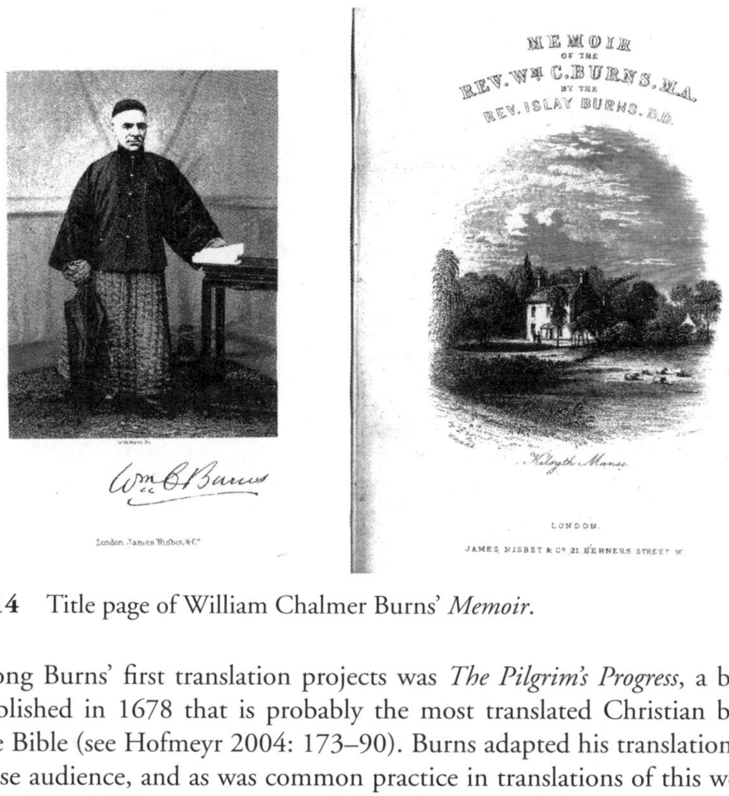

Figure 14 Title page of William Chalmer Burns' *Memoir.*

Among Burns' first translation projects was *The Pilgrim's Progress*, a book first published in 1678 that is probably the most translated Christian book after the Bible (see Hofmeyr 2004: 173–90). Burns adapted his translation for a Chinese audience, and as was common practice in translations of this work, the Scottish artist who did the illustrations represented the characters and the settings as Chinese (Burns 1870: 398–9; see Hofmeyr 2004).[10] Burns' brother and biographer reported that for Burns, "it was a subject of continual interest to watch the effect of the mystic allegory on another mind, and especially on a

[10] Patrick Hanan notes that at times Burns departed quite far from the original, in particular in his translation of Part II, a topic that would repay further study (Hanan 2004: 73).

Chinese mind." Burns observed that "the imagery of the dream fell singularly in with some of the familiar incidents of Chinese life" (Burns 1870: 398). Traditional Chinese sometimes interpret dreams as spiritual communications, and the missionaries reported that individuals sometimes came to see them after dreaming about Jesus. Hong Xiuquan, the leader of the Taiping Rebellion himself had come to Christianity as the consequence of a dream that he interpreted to mean that he was Jesus' younger brother.

In January 1854, Burns set out on a tour with Chinese Christians, including Chieng-choan and Tiek-choan, who were members of Amoy's American Reformed Church. They encountered so much interest at the first town that they visited, a market town for the region, that they remained for two months, teaching day and night (Burns 1870: 403). Market days occurred 12 times a month, attracting large crowds on those days.[11] In a letter from Pechuia, Burns wrote, "What I see here, makes me call to mind former days of the Lord's power in my native land" (31 March 1854, cited in Johnston 1860: 17).

After a "good number were born in the spirit" at Pechuia, Burns asked Reformed Church missionaries John Van Nest Talmage and Elihu Doty (who had worked with Hokkien immigrants in Batavia and Pontianak for eight years before moving to Amoy) to examine the candidates for baptism and to baptize them, forming a church.[12] Burns' and the Chinese evangelists' two-month campaign later came to be known as the Pechuia Awakening.

More than a few Chinese Christians in Singapore credited their conversions to an encounter with Burns. Among them was Tan See Boo, whom the Brethren in Singapore claim as their first Chinese evangelist. The account of

[11] The CES reported on this event. "The Missionary Summary", *CMG* Vol. 1, No. 19 NS (December 1854): 153.

[12] After Burns' departure, the English Presbyterians wanted to claim Pechuia for their own mission. But since Burns' replacement could not speak Hokkien, the American Reformed Church missionaries continued to visit until Carstairs Douglas was able to assume control of the new church. They retained control of an offshoot church at Chioh-be (Shi-ma) that Burns' Chinese converts had founded on their own initiative. Despite this minor territorial skirmish, in 1860 the American Reformed and English Presbyterian missionaries recognized their common cause by forming a united Church in China. In 1862 they further organized a "Great Elders Meeting" (*Tai-Hoey*), or presbytery, whose members included missionaries and elders from both churches, and which was empowered to administer their organized congregations (Cheung 2004; Fagg 1894: 194). This decision led to considerable opposition from the American Reformed Church, some of whose leaders wanted to maintain a clear hierarchy of control and who consequently objected to this hybrid form of organization. For a detailed study of the development of the "first native Protestant church" in South Fujian that focuses on the period from 1842–63, see Cheung (2004).

his conversion was often reprinted (Johnston 1860: 44–6; Burns 1870: 411–4; Fagg 1894: 160–3).[13] Burns had met Tan on his first visit to Pechuia in 1854 and found him to be "amongst the foremost and most interesting of his listeners". At that time, See Boo was 18 or 20 years old and worked at carving wooden idols in a variety of styles for home altars. He showed interest in Burns' teachings and after his conversion "cast himself on the providence of God", carving beads and ornaments instead of god images.

When Tan joined the missionaries for evangelistic journeys on their gospel boat, he brought his tools and olive stones along, working until they reached their destination and asking for no compensation. Tan was diligent in his Bible studies: "Morning, noon, and night, you might hear his clear and cheerful voice, reading aloud some portion of Scripture or Christian classic; or in the same loud tone, for almost all Chinamen read aloud, and that often at the full pitch of their voice, committing to memory some favourite passage of the Word of God" (Burns 1870: 413).

While Burns was visiting Scotland in 1854, the new Christians in Pechuia sent letters to both Burns and Talmage begging the mission boards of their two churches to send someone to help them. Tan See Boo was one of the nine who, after praying over every sentence, signed and mailed the letter to the two missionaries (Burns 1870: 422–3). Doty also wrote to Burns while he was visiting Scotland to report that his Chinese converts were carrying out new evangelistic work:

> But what shall I tell you of the Lord's visitation of mercy at Chioh-be? Again, truly, are we as those that dream. The general features of the work are very similar to what you witnessed at Pechuia. The instrumentality has been native brethren almost entirely. Attention was first awakened in one or two by I-ju and Tick-jam, who went to Chioh-be together.
>
> This was two or three months ago. This was followed up by repeated visits of other brethren from Pechuia and Amoy. Shortly the desire to hear the Word was so intense, that there would be scarcely any stop day or night; the brethren in turns going, and breaking down from much speaking in the course of three or four days, and coming back to us almost voiceless (letter from Doty to Burns [1854], cited in Fagg 1894: 163–4).

But when Burns returned to China in 1855, he did not rejoin the missionaries in Fujian but continued on to Shanghai, where he sought to travel to Nanjing to meet up with the leaders of the Taiping Rebellion.

---

[13] Burns' brother based his account of Tan on letters not from Burns but from other missionaries.

The Taiping Rebels and the Nanking Monument of the Beatitudes

The Taiping Rebellion raised Christian hopes that a new government whose leaders claimed to be brothers with the Christians might overthrow the Qing dynasty. On 19 March 1853, the Taiping rebels had taken Nanjing (Nanking), and on 29 March their leader Hong Xiuquan was carried into the city on a golden palanquin, wearing a yellow robe and yellow shoes—signs of his claims to imperial sovereignty (Spence 1996: 171). Among the Taiping leaders' first acts was to print copies of the Book of Genesis and Exodus, and by the end of 1853 they had also printed Leviticus and Numbers, all based on Gützlaff's 1840 translation (Spence 1996: 177–9). The government retook Nanjing in 1864, and the remaining rebels retreated to remote mountainous areas. Others left China, including 12 refugees who were buried in Penang's Protestant Cemetery.

Between 1853 and 1854, representatives of the British, French, and American communities in China met with the Taiping leaders and reviewed their decrees and messages, which many found unreasonable and bizarre (Spence 1996: 192–209). But the directors of the Chinese Evangelization Society saw evidence of the influence of Gützlaff's Chinese Christian Union (*Han-Hwuy*) in the Taiping movement. They knew that some of the insurgents had studied in Hong Kong, and that one of the rebel leaders had worked with Swedish missionary Theodore Hamberg while he was a provisional director of the Union in Hong Kong. They guessed that some of the Taiping rebels had been "Gützlaff's disciples" and that they had borrowed their ideas from Chinese Union tracts. But they also distanced themselves from the Taiping rebels' political aims, accepting Walter Medhurst's assessment that there were both Christian and political influences at work, and that the Taiping leaders were using Christianity as a stepping stone.[14]

A French boat had visited the rebels in Nanjing in November 1843, and Medhurst reported that Sir George Bonham had brought back four volumes of scriptures, including Gützlaff's translation of the Old Testament and a translation of the New Testament that he and Gützlaff had prepared in 1835. The date of publication was given as the third year of the Taiping dynasty, and a large red stamp on the first page stated that the book was "given out by imperial

[14] "Origin of the Religious Views of the Rebel Army", *CMG* Vol. 1, No. 5 NS (October 1853): 33–5.

authority". Hong had employed 400 printers to print the Bible, supervising the work himself.[15]

The CES directors responded to this news by plans to print and circulate Gützlaff's translation of the Bible, but they first consulted with missionaries and Chinese scholars, who praised the translation for its elegant style. Knowing that the Taiping king had adopted his translation, they further concluded that "the Chinese therefore have pronounced in favour of Gutzlaff's version". If his rebellion succeeded, they predicted that the Gützlaff's translation would be imperially endorsed and that the Chinese Bibles that they were printing would be widely circulated.

They also reported an "Extraordinary Scene in a Chapel". Medhurst claimed that when he had preached "on the folly of idolatry and urging the necessity of worshipping the true God", a man had stood up and proclaimed:[16]

> "that is true, that is true, the idols must perish, and shall perish. I am a Kwangsi man, a follower of Tai-ping-wang; we all of us worship one God (*Shangte*) and believe in Jesus, while we do our utmost to put down idolatry, everywhere demolishing the temples and destroying the idols, and exhorting the people to forsake these superstitions. When we commenced two years ago we were only 3,000 in number, and we have marched from one end of the empire to the other, putting to flight whole armies of the mandarin troops that were sent against us. If it had not been that God was on our side, we could not have thus prevailed against such overwhelming numbers. . . . What is the use, then" he asked, "of you Chinese going on to burn incense and candles, and gilt paper; which if your idols required it, would only show their covetous disposition; just like the mandarins who seize the men by the throat, and if they will not give them money, squeeze them severely, but if they will give, they only squeeze them gently?"

The Taiping speaker adopted *Shangdi* as the name for God and described the veneration of Chinese deities as mirroring their subjection to Mandarins, an analysis that many Western analysts of Chinese popular religion would endorse (see, for example, Feuchtwang 2001). He also announced to the assembled

---

[15] "The Trip of the French Ship 'Cassini' to Nanking". Reprinted from the *North China Herald*, 24 December 1853 in *CMG* Vol. I, No. 11 NS (April 1854): 82–4; "The Printing of the Scriptures by the Rebels", Extract of a letter of Dr Medhurst—"Patriot", *CMG* Vol. I, No. 2 NS (April 1854): 84.

[16] "Extraordinary Scene in a Chapel", *North China Herald*, 17 December 1853, reprinted in *CMG* Vol. I, No. 11 NS (April 1854): 84–5.

churchgoers that the Taiping king had forbidden opium, tobacco, snuff, wine, and that all offences against God would be punished.

As conflict with the Qing government escalated, Hong Xiuquan's cousin Hong Rengan had taken refuge in Hong Kong, where he worked with the Basel Mission and also as an assistant to LMS missionary James Legge. Hong provided Hamberg with written and oral accounts of the Taiping movement's founding on which Hamberg based *The Visions of Hung-siu-tshuen, and [the] Origin of the Kwang-si Insurrection* (Hamberg 1854; Spence 1996: 269–70). In April 1855, the Brethren magazine *The Missionary Reporter* published extracts from Hamberg's book under the title *The Chinese Rebel Chief, Hong-siu-tsuen; and the Origin of the Insurrection in China.*

These excerpts included a detailed account of Hong Xiuquan's dream of a visit to heaven where he encountered God and received from him a demon-expelling sword. The editor James Van Sommer denied implying that Hong was a hypocrite or insane, but noted that the Taiping rebels regarded their opponents as demons to be exterminated, much as Christians rulers like Constantine had done. He proposed that Christians practise intercessory prayer, the conversion of adults, and the establishment of schools for children rather than seeking the patronage of worldly rulers.[17]

The Taiping Heavenly King invited Hong Rengan to Nanjing and in 1859 named him to the post of "Shield King". On joining the Taiping rebels in Nanjing, he proclaimed that missionaries were free to travel in the Kingdom of Heavenly Peace, and some visited Nanjing and preached in the streets (Jenner 1911: 35). The Shield King promoted Christianity, but he also proclaimed his intention to introduce newspapers, railroads, steamboats, and insurance companies "for the good of China" (Jenner 1911: 35).[18]

Hong Rengan had a large stone stele made and placed at the entrance of his palace in Nanjing. When they suppressed the rebellion in 1864, imperial troops

---

[17] Editorial, *The Missionary Reporter*, Vol. II, No. 4 April 1855: 29–31; Extracts from "The Chinese Rebel Chief, Hong-siu-tsuen; and the Origin of the Insurrection in China", pp. 31–5.

[18] A Taiping commander identified Issachar Roberts, an American Baptist missionary with whom both Hong Xiuquan and Hong Rengan had studied in Hong Kong, as "the spiritual instructor of his prince, Tai-ping-wang". In 1854, the Taiping king wrote to Roberts and invited him to visit and bring "many brethren to help to promulgate the gospel, and administer the ordinance of baptism" so that they would obtain "the true doctrine". Roberts tried unsuccessfully to reach the Taiping camp twice, supported in part by a £25 donation from the board of the CES. He was finally able to go to Nanjing in 1860, and accepted a post in the Taiping government as minister of foreign policy (Spence 1996: 286).

THE NANKING MONUMENT OF THE BEATITUDES.

FROM THE RUBBING IN THE BIBLE HOUSE, QUEEN VICTORIA STREET.

(By kind permission of the Directors of the British and Foreign Bible Society.)

[Frontispiece.

Figure 15 The Nanking Monument of the Beatitudes, from a rubbing made by Alexander Wylie (Jenner 1911: x). Private collection of author.

destroyed the stele. But for many years the British House in London displayed a rubbing of the stone engraving donated by Alexander Wylie to the Bible Society (Canton 1904: 405; Jenner 1911: x).[19]

The stele that Christians called the Nanking Monument of the Beatitudes displayed a huge engraved character *fu* 福. Those who practise Chinese popular religion often pray for *fu*, which means prosperity and blessings, and many display the elegantly written character in their home as a wish for good fortune (see DeBernardi 2006: 57–61). Christian translators made the felicitous decision to use *fu* to translate the word 'gospel' (*fuyin* 福音, or 'good news') and also to translate "blessings" (Jenner 1911: Frontispiece, 37–9).

Above the large *fu* character was an engraving of the text known as the Beatitudes or the Sermon on the Mount (Matthew ch 5: 3–12). This text was also the foundation of Anthony Norris Groves' understanding of Christian practice: "Blessed are the poor in spirit; for theirs is the kingdom of heaven." The word for blessings (*fu*) was marked in red every time it appeared in the text. The engraver further elevated the characters for God (*Shangdi* 上帝) and Heavenly Kingdom (*Tianguo* 天国) above the text, a visual icon of God and Heaven's transcendent importance. The stone stele expressed in material form a powerful synthesis of Chinese values and Christianity.

The Million Testament Fund

In 1850, an interdenominational committee had completed the translation of the New Testament known as the *Delegates Version New Testament*.[20] Encouraged by the prospect that a Christian dynasty could one day rule China, in 1853 Rev. J.A. James and Thomas Thompson proposed to launch a fund for printing and circulating a million copies of the new translation in China (see DeBernardi 2011). Rev. James further proposed that the British and Foreign Bible Society would be the best-suited organization to carry out the project.[21]

---

[19] I have been unable to confirm whether or not the Bible Society's Archives at Cambridge University Library has this rubbing in its collection.

[20] At the Bible Society Library at Cambridge, I was shown a copy of the Delegate's New Version New Testament but was not given permission to photograph it. The text was printed on thin paper, and the book was small and flexible.

[21] J.A. James, "Something Must be Done, and Done Immediately, for China.—What? An Appeal to the Protestants of the United Kingdoms of Great Britain and Ireland", in *The British Banner* 14 September 1853; reprinted in *The Patriot*, 26 September 1853 (Bible Society Library, Million Testament file, 1853).

Supporters of the project had learned that Burns had printed a new translation of *The Pilgrim's Progress* at a low cost in Amoy. The total cost of preparing the manuscript had been £40, and he anticipated the cost of printing a single copy to be fourpence to sixpence.[22] Promoters of the Million Testament Fund concluded that a new translation of the New Testament could be printed at a cost of fourpence a copy, and were confident that their goal of printing a million copies would be easily accomplished.[23]

The BFBS had started to plan its Jubilee Year, and in 1853 adopted a resolution to take "upon themselves all the measures necessary for printing, with the least practicable delay One Million Copies of the Chinese New Testament". A number of British newspapers rallied support for the interdenominational project and a torrent of donations followed. Most of the donors were British, but donations also came from South Africa, Canada, the United States, Barbados, Antigua, and even Syria and the Holy Land, where students in a mission school donated funds—"a gift of the Bible from the Bible's birth-place to Eastern Asia".[24] In only six months they had collected over £30,000. The BFBS committee noted that contributions had come from "Rich and Poor, Churchmen and Dissenters, Ministers of Religion and Minister of State, Sunday School Teachers and Scholars" (Bible Society 1854: 74).

In 1855, Burns returned to China from England. Only ten days after arriving in Shanghai, Burns and a Chinese assistant set off by boat for the headquarters of the Taiping rebels in Nanjing. Burns later revealed that at the time he made "most meager allusion" to this trip in his letters, fearing the mandarin officials might suspect him of having a relationship with the rebels (Burns 1870: 427).

Burns travelled towards Nanjing, distributing books as he went, but on reaching Dantu, his boat crew refused to go further and advised him to complete his journey on foot (Burns 1870: 430). He accepted their recommendation that they return to Shanghai by way of the Grand Canal. He distributed books (presumably the *Delegates Version New Testament*) as they travelled, sometimes to men who swam up to the book, then tied it to the tops of their heads with their long queues (Burns 1870: 435). Burns never reached the Taiping rebels, but a few years later the Taiping Shield King Hong Rengan reported that the

[22] Editorial, *The Patriot*, September 1853 (Bible Society Library, Million Testament file, 1853).

[23] Editorial, *The Watchman*, 21 September 1853 (Bible Society Library, Million Testament file, 1853).

[24] BFBS *Monthly Extracts* No. 38 (30 June 1854): 431.

Heavenly King had a new favourite book, *The Pilgrim's Progress*, and that he liked Burns' 1853 translation best.[25]

Although Christian missionaries in China had celebrated when the Taiping rebels printed the scriptures, the rebels' endorsement of Christianity put their agents in danger. LMS missionary William Muirhead wrote to the BFBS after two of their colporteurs were arrested and imprisoned that the mandarins had concluded that books with the name Jesus in the title identified them with the rebels, who were widely known to have adopted the "religion of the Heavenly Father and Jesus". The colporteurs were imprisoned for a month and only freed after the British consul intervened.[26] Meanwhile, the outbreak of the second Opium War (1856–60) further hampered their efforts, and in 1857 Dr Legge announced that colportage would have to be suspended (Bible Society 1857: 189).

James Hudson Taylor, the Brethren Movement, and the China Inland Mission

After his effort to reach the Taiping rebels in Nanjing failed, for a time Burns distributed scriptures by riverboat in connection with the Million Testament Fund. He first travelled on China's network of inland waterways with a Chinese Christian colporteur, then with James Hudson Taylor (1870: 445–6), who came to China with support from the Chinese Evangelization Society (CES).[27]

Before going to China, Taylor had learned about Gützlaff's evangelical work in China from reading *The Gleaner in the Missionary Field*, and wrote a letter of inquiry to George Pearse. Pearse was a stockbroker at the Bank of England who later became a missionary first in France, then in North Africa. He was also a member of the Hackney Brethren, whose members, together with Brethren at

[25] Jonathan Spence speculates that Hong Rengan might have brought a copy of Burn's illustrated 1853 translation to Nanjing in 1859, but also notes that several editions existed by the mid-1850s and Hong Xiuquan could have obtained a copy earlier (Spence 1996: 281–2). Spence cites several sources that Hong Rengan had stated that Burns' translation was Hong Xiuquan's favourite (Spence 1996: 365, fn. 46).

[26] Bible Society. *Monthly Extracts* (30 December 1857): 84–5.

[27] In 1854, George Müller observed that the Scriptural Knowledge Institution sought to "make use of the remarkable opening which the Lord has been pleased to give for the circulation of the Holy Scriptures in China" and gave funds to a missionary in China to circulate about 3,000 copies of the New Testament in Chinese (SKI 1854: 39). He does not identify the missionary but almost certainly the "remarkable opening" was the Million Testament Fund.

Figure 16 Young James Hudson Taylor. Echoes of Service archive.

the Brook Street Chapel in Tottenham, supported the Chinese Evangelization Society (West 2016: 16–7). Pearse was one of the society's secretaries, and on their behalf had written to John George Bausum in Penang in 1851, inviting him to apply to the CES for funding.

In 1851, Taylor had been baptized in a Brethren assembly in Hull, and after he moved to London to pursue medical studies, became a regular visitor to Brook Street Chapel. Through Pearse Taylor met John Eliot Howard and Luke Howard, the wealthy pharmaceutical manufacturers who had started the Brethren meeting in Tottenham in 1838 after separating from the Quakers (West 2016: 234). On Sundays he sometimes visited John Eliot Howard, whom he described as the "Great Manufacturing Chemist", then spent the rest of the day with another former Quaker Miss Mary Stacey, who was one of the early members of the Brook Street Chapel.[28]

The Brethren resemble Quakers insofar as they thought that by depending on their God rather than human rules to guide them, they were opening themselves up to providence and inspiration. Taylor praised Brethren fellowship in a letter to his mother:[29]

> You don't know how sweet it is to be dependent on the Lord for every thing, whether it be the singing of a hymn, reading of the word, or prayer, or exhortation, or silent waiting on Himself, all, all is best as He sees fit to provide for whatever we need, whether spiritually or temporary he will and does provide as long as we trust in Him, and do not, by our casual arrangements, spoil, and set aside the Lord's own blessed order by usurping the position of the Head, present by the Spirit, in all assemblies of Saints, who do not meet from form, but in His name.

Although he did not attend the mid-week meeting, Taylor probably knew that Anthony Norris Groves had spoken at the Brook Street Tottenham Assembly in 1852 and had urged them to form a committee to support independent faith missionaries (H. Groves 1869: 481; West 2016: 17). As we have seen, soon after Groves made this appeal, Van Sommer started publishing *The Missionary Reporter* (Forrest 1971). In the first issue, he explained that the purpose of this magazine was to lend help and sympathy to missionaries in foreign lands who

[28] Letter, J.H. Taylor to sister Louisa, 22 May 1853 (SOAS GB 102 CIM/03/02/08). James Hudson Taylor and Maria Dyer's correspondence is held at the School of Oriental and African Studies Archives (SOAS), University of London, China Inland Mission Archive.

[29] Letter, J.H. Taylor to mother, 11 October 1852 (SOAS GB 102 CIM/03/02/08).

were unconnected with any missionary society. He also promoted the idea that every church could be a missionary society.[30]

Taylor studied medicine to prepare for work in China, but before completing his training, he applied to the CES for support to go to China as an independent missionary.[31] Because the CES was nonsectarian, its leaders included not only prominent Brethren but also ordained ministers and Taylor worried that they might reject him. In a letter to his mother, Taylor noted that in his interview with the CES, he had told them that he "did not believe in the division of the Church into Clergy and Laity . . . being persuaded that "**priestcraft has in all ages been the greatest curse to the Church and the world** [emphasis mine]". He also affirmed, as the Brethren did, "the right of all Christians to preach, baptize, and administer the Lord's Supper—the equality of Saints etc." The CES accepted him.[32]

When Taylor landed in Shanghai in 1854, the city was in turmoil. But soon he joined up with Burns, and the two missionaries spent seven months doing itinerant evangelism. As Taylor described it, they followed "the course of the canals and rivers which here spread like a network over the whole face of the rich, fertile, country" (Taylor 1986: 76).[33] When travel in the Shanghai region became too difficult, a Christian sea captain offered them free passage to Swatow (Shantou), and they travelled there together in March 1856. In June, Taylor wrote to *The Chinese Missionary Gleaner* that he and Burns had been travelling both together and separately in the Swatow region to preach and distribute books, including the New Testament. He observed that people were suspicious, and was resigned to focus on medical work as a strategy to "opening the door for Evangelistic efforts".[34]

Taylor next moved to Shanghai, but first lost his medical supplies in a fire, then was robbed. Like the other missionaries whom CES had sent to China, he also discovered that his expenses in China were greater than expected. By

30 "Introductory Observations", *The Missionary Reporter*, No. 1, July 1853.

31 In a letter to his mother, he expressed his concern that if a missionary society paid for his medical training, he would be subject to their rules and removed from the "direct and immediate leadings of God". Letter, Taylor to mother, 1 May 1852 (SOAS GB 102 CIM/03/02/05).

32 Letters, Taylor to mother, 19 June 1853; 9 July 1853 (SOAS GB 102 CIM/03/02/08).

33 Taylor's letters published in *The Chinese Missionary Gleaner* include a detailed diary reporting on their travels together in 1855. See "Extracts from Mr J.H. Taylor's Journal" *CMG* No. 6 (1 June 1856): 69–73.

34 J.H. Taylor, Swatow, 14 June 1956, letter to George Pearse, *CMG*, No. 10 NS (1 October 1856): 123–5.

1857, the CES could no longer meet its commitments to Taylor and other missionaries. Taylor separated from them and worked with Chinese Christians to establish an independent Ningpo Mission.[35] In December 1857, George Müller sent him £40 ("which I have obtained from the Lord simply in answer to prayer") together with a letter of encouragement:

> I was glad to find that you had resolved to trust in the Lord alone and to look to Him alone for the supply of all your necessities. I have myself proven him thus faithful for more than 27 years, during which time I have to him alone made known my wants.[36]

Müller added Taylor to the Scriptural Knowledge Institution's list of supported missionaries, and began to publish accounts of his work in Ningpo.

Taylor's missionary career in China, which included founding the China Inland Mission, which historians regard as continuing many of the CES's programmes and values, is beyond the scope of this study. But in Ningpo he met and married Samuel and Maria Dyer's daughter Maria, who was teaching in a girls' school. Some opposed the match on the grounds that Taylor was an unordained lay worker with Brethren connections, but Maria reasoned that her mother had married an independent missionary and resolved to do so herself with the support of her stepmother, Jemima Bausum Lord.

Although they offered little information about Taylor's Brethren commitments, Taylor's early biographers—his son and daughter-in-law—recognized Burns' influence. As they described it, Burns was a "practical and methodical" worker who cooperated with Taylor while maintaining his independence. They added that "William Burns was better to him than a college course with all its advantages, because he lived out before him right there in China the reality of all that he most needed to be and know" (Taylor and Taylor 1911: 349). But Taylor's biographers also described Burns as "cultured, genial, and overflowing with mother-wit", a "delightful companion" who entertained with a fund of anecdotes from his work in Britain, Canada, and China. They also noted that he had a gift for friendship: "Such a friendship is one of the crowning blessings of life. Money cannot buy it; influence cannot command it" (Taylor and Taylor 1911: 347–8).

---

[35] In his *History of Christian Missions*, Stephen Neill mentions the Chinese Evangelization Society, which raised funds to support both the Penang Mission and Taylor's first trip to China, but describes it as a "curiously incompetent body which almost wholly failed to meet its obligations, and after an inglorious career went into dissolution" (Neill 1986: 282).

[36] Letter, Müller to Taylor, 9 December 1857 (SOAS GB 102 CIM/04/08).

In 1860 Taylor and his family returned to England, where Taylor completed his medical training at the Royal London Hospital in 1862. In 1865 he founded the China Inland Mission together with William Thomas Berger, the mission's home director, and published the first edition of the magazine that became *China's Millions*. He and his family returned to China with a party of 21 missionaries in 1866.[37] By 1870, Müller's list of supported workers included 25 missionaries in China (SKI 1870: 48).

Swatow, Amoy, and Alexander Grant

While Taylor returned to Shanghai in 1856, then moved to Ningpo, Burns remained in Swatow with two Chinese Christian workers. In August all three were arrested. In his summary report, Commissioner Yeh Mingchen deemed it to be "exceedingly improper that William Burns (admitting himself to be an Englishman) should change his own dress, shave his head, and assuming the costume of the Chinese, penetrate into the interior in so irregular a manner", and questioned whether Burns was truly who he claimed to be (Burns 1870: 460–1).[38] The magistrate had Burns escorted to Canton to the care of the British Consul, and had his two Christian workers returned to their home towns, where they were imprisoned (Burns 1870: 456). As soon as he was free to travel, Burns returned to Swatow, where he interceded on behalf of his two assistants (Burns 1870: 464).

Burns remained in Swatow where he worked with Dr De la Porte, a missionary connected to the Free Church of Scotland, to open a medical clinic. Burns interpreted for the doctor while two native evangelists provided "spiritual healing" for those waiting (Burns 1870: 465). When the doctor returned to England in 1858, Burns returned to Amoy where Rev. Alexander Grant, M.A. (1832–1914) became his new coworker (Burns 1870: 479).[39] Grant had studied at Aberdeen, where he trained to be a Presbyterian minister, and was ordained on 19 October 1857. He left eight days later for China, and joined Carstairs

[37] For further information on Taylor, see Alvyn Austin' study of the China Inland Mission (Austin 2007), which includes an extensive bibliography of sources.

[38] Burns' *Memoir* includes a complete translation of the Chinese Commissioner's 1856 declaration to the British Consul at Canton (Burns 1870: 458–61).

[39] Grant's father had been a schoolmaster and missionary to Scottish immigrants in rural Aberdeenshire, but in 1843 joined the Free Church of Scotland and was ordained. The next year he took an appointment at Lumphanan Free Church (Scott 1925: 458). I thank Neil Dickson and also Grant's descendants Ann Anderson and Hazel Andrews for information about Alexander Grant and his family.

Douglas and George Smith in Amoy in April 1858.[40] Like Burns, he joined the English Presbyterian Mission in Amoy.

Burns and Grant worked together closely for almost a year in 1859. While Burns was still in Swatow, Douglas had written to him of problems that had arisen in Pechuia, rebuking him for failing in his "pastoral duty" towards the "immature Christians". Burns and Grant visited the Chinese Christians in August and found that they had organized a period of prayer and fasting. One preacher who had been converted in 1854 even sobbed aloud, which Burns took to be evidence that "the Lord was in the midst of us" (Burns 1870: 488), while Grant observed that "the shaking of the tree had only fastened the roots the more" (cited in Burns 1870: 489).[41] Grant also noted that Burns had arranged renovations to a chapel in Maping, a town ten miles from Pechuia, which made it possible for foreign missionaries to live there, and that he had met with no opposition to his staying there (Johnston 1860: 31).

They also travelled up an estuary by Gospel boat to a major prefectural city, Zhangzhou. Since they could not rent a place to stay, they lived on the boat and went into the streets every day to preach (Band 1948: 52). But extension of their work to the Zhangzhou region proved impossible, and in October 1859 Burns moved on to Fuzhou, where he divided his time between preaching on shipboard at the Pagoda Anchorage and studying the Fuzhou dialect (Burns 1870: 494).

In 1861, the Amoy Mission decided to send a missionary to Singapore to work with Chinese-speaking Christians.[42] They considered sending Burns, but sent Grant instead.[43] Grant almost immediately went to Penang and joined the Brethren movement, ending his relationship with the Presbyterian mission. On giving up his relationship with the Presbyterian mission, he began corresponding with Müller; on his return to England, he and his family joined the London Brethren network in Tottenham.

Burns also left—not for Fujian but Beijing, where he attempted to negotiate a settlement on behalf of native Christians whose property had been attacked, seeking for Protestant converts an exemption from the obligation to support

---

[40] Letter from Matheson to Barbour, 23 October 1857 (SOAS, South Fujian/Amoy [Xiamen], PCE/FMC Box 17); Johnston 1860: 31–4; Cheung 2004: 285.

[41] In 1860, the Presbyterians established a formal system of church governance by a committee of elders and also a superordinate Presbytery to oversee the diverse stations and missions in Amoy (Band 1948: 48–9, 68).

[42] They likely sought to replace Rev. Thomas Mackenzie Fraser, who had left Singapore for Australia in late 1860.

[43] Letter, Burns to Matheson, 4 June 1861 (SOAS PCE/FMC South Fujian, Box 119).

temple and ancestral worship, a privilege that Catholics had been granted in 1862 (Band 1948: 6). He remained in Beijing and retranslated parts I and II of *The Pilgrim's Progress* into a more elegant Mandarin style. In 1867 he moved to Nieu-chwang (today Yingkou), a treaty port in what was then Manchuria, where he died the next year (Burns 1870: 499–540; Band 1948: 69).

Although they did not work together long, Grant and Burns exchanged letters until Burns' death. Four decades later, Grant visited Burns' grave in Nieu-chwang as he fled from Jehol during the Boxer Uprising.

Chapter 6

Crisis in the Penang Mission

> What can I say to you, dear reader? What you have to do is to come at once to Jesus, just as you are, in all your sins, polluted and filthy to the very core of your heart, whatever or whoever or in whatever position you may be moving, you are yet in your natural condition, loving the world and its vain empty amusements and compliments; remember you cannot trust in God for anything, your conscience would fly in your face and condemn you. You know you cannot trust in God as a loving, gracious, tender-hearted Father. . . . An unregenerate man cannot serve or worship God; his worship is solemn mockery, and helps him doubly to deceive himself.
>
> John Chapman, 1865 report on the Penang Mission Schools[1]

In 1859, John Chapman and his wife embarked for Penang from Bristol with support from Bethesda and Salem Chapels and George Müller's Scriptural Knowledge Institution (SKI), accompanied by Miss O'Callaghan and Bee, a Chinese Christian girl.[2] The Chinese Evangelization Society and the Female Education Society provided travel funds for John George Bausum's widow Jemima Poppy Bausum, who had returned to England to seek support for a new school for orphans in Ningpo, and who stopped in Penang to help the new missionaries on her way back to China.[3] Müller had sent them off with tracts and Bibles for their ship's crew, and the missionaries had nightly meetings on shipboard. On their arrival in Singapore in January 1860, Miss O'Callaghan wrote Müller to report the conversions of the chief officer and the ship's carpenter, the one Welsh, the other Scots (SKI 1860: 63).[4]

---

[1] Chapman 1865: 4.

[2] *CMG* Vol. 4, No. 44 N.S. (1 October 1859): 103.

[3] FES Minutes, 16 July 1859.

[4] Arthur Rendle Short reports that John Chapman published a letter in 1861 in the final issue of *The Missionary Reporter* (Short n.d: 88), but the 1860 and 1861 issues were not preserved.

The new workers went to Penang at the height of a revival that Christian historian James Edwin Orr called the Second Evangelical Awakening (Orr 1955, 1964). The revival broke out after an 1857 economic crisis that had led to business failures and massive unemployment in the United States and Britain. Britain had experienced earlier economic fluctuations, but with the development of steam navigation and the telegraph in Europe and Britain, the 1857 catastrophe spread with unprecedented speed. Within weeks, a crisis that had started in New York had paralyzed the world's major industrial and commercial centres (Hughes 1956: 194). Almost certainly the first worldwide commercial crisis was a factor in the insolvency of the CES, whose directors were unable to meet their commitments in 1857 and were forced to dissolve the organization.

Karl Marx was certain that the economic crisis would ignite a revolutionary wave, and focused that year on writing the critical analysis of capitalism now known as the *Grundrisse* (Kratke 2008: 169). But Christians in the United States and Canada responded to the crisis not with revolution, but with a revival that soon spread to Ireland, Scotland, and Wales. Although their meetings may not have been as ecstatic as 20th-century Pentecostal revivals, 19th-century revivalism "preceded the Fundamentalist age, and represents an ebullient populist Christianity" (Lineham 2006: 155).

In the 1860 report of the Scriptural Knowledge Institution, Müller provided many first-hand accounts of the revival, including this one from a "Scotch brother":

> We have had two successive waves of Divine power. The first rushed along with a noise and force that were startling in the extreme. Cases of bodily affection, something like entire relaxation of power, epilepsy, catalepsy, and trance occured to awaken public attention and excite concern. . . . The town seemed to be shaken as at the storming of Jericho. . . . The second wave of power was not so noisy as the former, but deeper, wider, and fully as enduring (SKI 1860: 55).

Müller followed up with the revivalist's converts, ensuring that they received additional instruction. Many subsequently joined the Brethren movement, drawn by the vision of a renovated society that was both ethical and utopian (Dickson 2002: 73).

In 1859, Richard Cope Morgan, a publisher associated for a time with the Brethren movement, began publishing news digests that became popular with the Open Brethren. *The Revival* (1859–70) reported on and promoted the work of itinerant revivalist preachers, creating the impression that revival had broken out throughout Britain (Bebbington 1989: 116–7; Grass 2006:

152).[5] The newspaper started with a run of 8,000 copies, but reached 80,000 within a few months (Piggin 1994). Soon after their arrival in Penang, Mr and Mrs Chapman and Miss O'Callaghan gave copies of *The Revival* to their friends and donors, and the editors asked its readers to pray for "blessing on copies of the *Revival* circulated in the Straits of Malacca".[6] Renamed *The Christian* (1870–1969) in 1870, circulation rose to 15,000 subscribers a week (Scott 1972: 9).

These newspapers were nonsectarian, but the publishers used their influence to support "schemes as made for national righteousness" (Morgan 1909: 56). In 1862, the editors of *The Revival* collected funds for famine relief for the Lancashire cotton mill workforce, which had been put out of work by an interruption in the importation of raw cotton from the United States due to the Civil War. The downturn was further complicated by a falling rate of profit due both to increasing prices for raw cotton and an oversupply of finished cloth.

By 1859 Britain had abolished slavery throughout its empire, but British cotton producers continued to rely on American cotton that had been grown by slaves. In one of many letters to the Editor, the author observed that "slavery only existed in South Carolina because cotton was required at Manchester, and that, if we would but close our ports to slave-grown cotton, we should rid the States of slavery". He concluded that God had "dissolved the connexion for us which we would not dissolve for ourselves; and we have at this time to feed 200,000 for an indefinite period".[7]

Mrs Chapman responded to the 1862 call for donations for famine relief in Lancashire with a letter and three pounds from herself and Alexander Grant. She also forwarded a dollar donated by a Chinese Christian, who had wrapped the money in a piece of paper on which he had written in Chinese characters: "For the poor in England who are out of work." In her letter, she added, "We greatly enjoy *The Revival* papers, which we circulate here and at Singapore." She

[5] Baptist minister J. Edwin Orr identified this event as the Second Evangelical Awakening (Orr 1955, 1964), but David W. Bebbington critically notes that the movement's spread in England was limited to fishing communities in Cornwall and North Devon. Bebbington concludes that Morgan used the publication as a "novel technique" to further spread the revival (Bebbington 1989: 116–7).

[6] Anon. "Requests for Prayer &c", *The Revival* No. 177 (11 December 1862): 280.

[7] "The Present Crisis and Our Duty", Samuel Garrett, *The Revival* No. 176 (30 October 1862: 198).

also asked them to pray for Penang, "which needs the power of God to arouse the Europeans, and those who have heard the gospel".[8]

Evangelistic Outreach in Penang

In 1861, the Amoy Presbyterian mission sent Alexander Grant (c. 1833–1914) to Singapore to work with Chinese immigrants in a cooperative effort with a new Anglican Mission, but he almost immediately moved to Penang and became Mr Chapman's coworker. Grant may not have met James Hudson Taylor in China, but through his association with William Chalmers Burns, he almost certainly knew something of Taylor's connection to the Open Brethren movement, including his relationships with Müller and the London Brethren who had founded the Chinese Evangelization Society. However he might have learned of the Penang mission, he chose independence and living by faith over remaining in the Presbyterian mission.

In Penang Grant contracted typhoid fever, and after making a full recovery "walked down into the water and by baptism publicly confessed his burial and resurrection with Christ".[9] He remained with the Chapmans, and by 1862 George Müller was collecting donations on his behalf. Between 1863 and 1867 the Scriptural Knowledge Institutions' Annual Reports included lengthy extracts of letters from Mr and Mrs Chapman, Miss O'Callaghan, and Mr Grant.[10]

---

[8] "India-Penang", M[ary].C[hapman], 19 January 1863, *The Revival*, No. 191 (19 March 1863): 137. She reported that there was much encouraging news in Singapore and that the Young Men's Christian Association was well attended. The YMCA was first organized in London in 1844 and became popular in the 1850s (Lewis 1986: 113–4).

[9] "Our Departed Brother Alexander Grant", Lucy A. Grant, *ES* No. 786 (March 1914 Pt. 2): 104–6. According to Mrs Grant, as the result of his aunts' influence, Grant was quite "exercised on the subject" of adult immersion baptism, but had never baptized an infant himself. His younger brother William J. Grant (1849–1930) was a Baptist pastor in Ayrshire, Scotland, but he too joined the Brethren movement in 1880, apparently seeking to escape sectarian limitations (Dickson 1990: 374; 2002: 116). Although Grant was in China during the 1859–60 revival, he would have learned about it from his associates in Penang and also through letters from home. In Scotland, the revival had attracted many new members into the Brethren movement, including Baptists who were attracted by the Brethren's "lay ethos, furtherance of aggressive evangelism, and appeal to the primitivism of the early Church" (Dickson 2002: 141).

[10] Müller identified the missionaries whose letters he summarized by initials not names, but the number of individuals is small enough that they are easily identified.

The missionaries ran the girls' and boys' schools with local teachers and also held meetings for Bible study three times a week. In their letters to Müller they reported conversions, especially from among the students in the Penang Mission Schools, and group baptisms, often of Europeans and Asians together. Miss O'Callaghan and Mrs Chapman reported leading lively meetings of soldiers' wives and children at the Fort, attended by 55 men, 20 women, and 60 children. The two women took turns meeting with women, and Mr Chapman and Mr Grant were "among the men" (SKI 1864: 76–7).

Chapman and Grant received permission to distribute tracts to the captains and crews of English vessels in Penang's harbour and held services on shipboard. They were also allowed access to the inmates in Penang's debtor's prison, where they distributed English and Malay tracts and scriptures in Tamil, Chinese, and Hindu (SKI 1862: 59–61). On one occasion, a wealthy Chinese who spoke English, Chinese, and Malay invited them to his home and requested tracts, asking them about their views on the transmigration of the soul (SKI 1864: 76).

They often travelled widely with Chinese and Tamil partners, visiting villages on Penang Island and on the mainland, and their letters describe the hospitality of local people who offered them exotic foods and invited them to sleep on the floor. Grant had learned to speak Hokkien in Fujian, and Chapman could speak Malay. As they travelled, they exhorted groups of Chinese and Malays, distributing tracts in Malay, Chinese, Tamil, Hindi, and English. Although he reported some debates, more often Chapman observed that people listened to them politely without responding.

Grant observed that Malays and Chinese responded differently to their exhortations based on their existing religious practices:

> The Malays are more prepared for the Gospel, in as far as they believe in one God, and are conscious of sin, and know not how to obtain forgiveness; at the same time they are more fortified against it. The Chinese, again, have no conscience of sins, and no craving for atonement; their sacrifices being rather thank-offerings, than sacrifices for sin. Yet, among both alike, God is able to gather to His Son Jesus a people for His Name. 'The Salvation of God is now sent to the Gentiles, and they will hear it' (SKI 1866: 51).

He later reported that Penang's Muslims openly rejected "the preaching of Christ", but that the Chinese would listen, then return to hear more. But most of the conversions they reported were of European soldiers and their wives (SKI 1868: 46).

Living by Faith in Penang

The Protestant boys' and girls' schools received support for decades from government grants and donations from Penang's respectable residents. During John George Bausum's tenure, the schools' supporters had included the East India Company, Colonel Butterworth, the Governor of the Straits Settlements, and Penang's major landowners. Other elite supporters included the Bishop of Calcutta, who donated the proceeds of a sermon preached on behalf of the Protestant Mission School, E.A. Blundell, Penang's Resident Councillor, and George Felix Gottlieb, Penang's Harbour Master.[11]

Chapman sought to live by faith and modelled his fundraising methods on Müller's. In his 1862 report, Chapman noted that he objected to the previous practice of supporting the schools through subscription, preferring "a more excellent way", namely, "to look to Him alone, for the means to carry it on". He also announced that he had taken oversight of the schools "without any Committee or Treasurer" (Chapman 1862: 2). Despite these declarations, the 1862 report included the information that an annual grant from the government had supplied a third of the funding for the school, and the Anglican Chaplain and a respectable community member had signed off on the accounting to attest to its accuracy.

Müller reported on his work by supplying diaries of his accounts, and Chapman adopted this method of reporting. As he described it, he had started the year in a financially precarious state, with only 77.42 Straits dollars in hand. He reported that he prayed and received a stream of donations, always in time to meet his expenses. In the middle of this record of donation after donation, he exclaimed, "Thus the Lord answers our prayers again and again, asking in the name of Jesus" (Chapman 1862: 3–6).

He concluded his 1862 report on the Penang Protestant mission schools with a passionate statement that has the cadence of the revivalist's spoken exhortation:

> The object in giving this report is to shew that God the living God is to be trusted in as in days of old; and you who do not know Him as a loving gracious kind Father, seek by earnest prayer to get acquainted with Him, ask Him through Jesus to lead you in the right way, and if

[11] In 1851, the financial committee for the Protestant mission school had included the Presbyterian minister Rev. C. Moir, G.F. Gottlieb, Esq., A. Rodyk, Esq., and L. Nairne, Esq. as treasurer (Bausum 1851: 2). Part of Bausum's "Report of the Protestant Mission School in Penang for 1851" was reprinted in *CGMG* Vol. 2, No. 3, 2nd ed. (August 1852): 24.

> you have not come to Jesus, come now, just as you are, He is willing and reading to receive you, and sure I am you will never regret the choice; and to Him be all the praise and glory (Chapman 1862: 5–6).

By contrast, about a decade earlier Bausum had concluded his 1851/2 report on the Penang Protestant Mission Schools by noting a decrease in donations, politely advising his readers that the smallest gift would be appreciated (Bausum 1852: 4).

In 1865 Chapman published a report for the previous three year's work at the schools. He observed that he had not been publishing reports since they were "not to be trusted in, for the purpose of getting money" (Chapman 1865: 12). The 1865 report included a diary describing his and his Grant's evangelical itinerations and donations, together with a simple accounting for those three years. To avoid serving the status needs of donors, Müller did not identify them by name in his annual reports, and Chapman followed this practice.[12]

Chapman noted that he had been able to sustain the mission and schools without depending on the rich or worldly, and it seems highly likely he no longer had the patronage of the government or the Anglican establishment:

> And again, that this may be a testimony for the Lord Jesus, the blessed Jesus, to those who lean upon an arm of flesh, whether it be in the way of looking to a rich man, because he has plenty of money; or to a benevolent man, because he is accustomed to give when asked, but who are, nevertheless, worldly-minded men, who shew by their conduct that they love not the Lord Jesus, but are full of pride, and self-importance, and hatred to the truth (Chapman 1865: 3).

Chapman further exhorted his readers to be reborn, accusing them of hypocrisy and self-deception:

> What can I say to you, dear reader? What you have to do is to come at once to Jesus, just as you are, in all your sins, polluted and filthy to the very core of your heart, whatever or whoever or in whatever position you may be moving, you are yet in your natural condition, loving the world and its vain emply amusements and compliments; remember you cannot trust in God for anything, your conscience would fly in your face and condemn you. You know you cannot trust in God as a loving, gracious, tender-hearted Father. . . . An unregenerate man cannot serve or worship God; his worship is solemn mockery, and helps him doubly to deceive himself (Chapman 1865: 4).

---

[12] In the 1865 report, he did not mention government funding and the accounting lacked the Anglican chaplain's signature. In dispensing with independent accounting and not providing regular reports, Chapman may have risked raising suspicions of financial impropriety.

Chapman emphasized that the majority of the schools' donations came from "those who believe in Christ, and love Him, and love those who are engaged in his work".

He explained to his readers that this method of fundraising was based on the New Testament:

> We believe the way the Apostles were supported and our blessed Lord Jesus himself, was, by godly persons giving of their means voluntarily; and we don't think that the development of modern Christianity has made any improvement on the way in which the Apostles were supported in their day (Chapman 1865: 18).

In his blunt refusal to depend on the wealthy or the benevolent for the success of his efforts, Chapman almost certainly offended the Penang establishment, whose good opinion he relied upon for the mission's continued support.[13]

The Opium Treatment Centre

Like other evangelical Christians, the Open Brethren opposed the utilitarian economic system that gave rise to war and exploitation, including the slave trade, the opium trade, child labour, and prostitution. In Penang, the morality of opium sale and use was a matter of particular concern for them. In the colonial Straits Settlements, the British raised revenue by farming out monopolies on the sale of spirits and opium, and the government realized a substantial profit from the opium monopoly (Trocki 1990: 2).

The Brethren missionaries often publically exhorted people to stop using opium, and Chapman offered treatment for opium addicts at the mission. He reported to Müller: "We have in the Mission eight opium smokers, and have had applications from others to enter to receive medicine, but could not take them in until some of those that are in be cured" (SKI 1862: 60).[14] By 1862

[13] Historian Tim Grass observes that the new generation of Brethren leaders who emerged after the revival tended to insist on rigid conformity to New Testament church practice (Grass 2006: 118). Perhaps strict patternism explains Chapman's exultant insistence that in relying on providence and prayer alone, he was adhering to the method of the New Testament.

[14] In the 1840s the American Reformed Missionaries in Borneo working with Chinese in Pontianak had used a compound of opium, tartar emetic, and ipecac in pill form to induce vomiting, which caused the addict to develop an aversion to the smell and sight of the drug (De Jong 1987: 55). Chapman does not mention the medicine used, but the Howard family offered quinine and other medicines to medical missionaries for free or at a low cost.

the number seeking treatment at the Penang Mission had increased to a dozen (SKI 1863: 62).

The recovering addicts lived in the Mission compound, where they received medicine daily and were also exhorted in Malay, Hokkien, or Hakka. Chapman described one as "impressed by the truth" and two more as "under conviction" (SKI 1863: 62). In 1863, Chapman mentioned that they were thinking of building a hospital for them, adding, "We tell them plainly, that medicine of itself will not enable them permanently to give up opium; the power of the Lord Jesus alone can effectually cure them" (SKI 1864: 77).

At their medical clinics, the Christians exhorted patients while they waited to see the doctor, advising them that if they were healed, they should be thankful not to the doctor but to God. This argument was congruent with popular religious practice. Chinese traditionalists pray to their gods for help in urgent life matters—passing an examination, recovering from illness, winning a lawsuit, etc. If they believe that the gods have assisted them in overcoming these difficulties, then they will feel obliged to return to the temple to repay a debt of gratitude (*baoen* 報恩). Chinese patients sometimes joined Christian circles to show their gratitude on being healed.

In his 1865 report on the Protestant schools, Chapman announced that he sought to raise $600 to build the opium hospital, where addicts would live while taking medicine, reading scriptures, and hearing the preaching of the gospel. He affirmed his belief in prayer: "I know not from what quarter the Lord will send in the means, but I know the promise of Jesus, 'all things whatsoever ye ask in prayer, believing, ye shall receive'" (Chapman 1865: 12). By February 1865 he had $461.86 in hand for building the new hospital (Chapman 1865: 20). Despite his success at fundraising, the opium addiction treatment centre that Chapman envisioned was never built.

Crisis and Change

When a Christian sea captain visited Penang in 1865, he reported to Müller that the Mission Chapel and schools were thriving:

> With the exception of the missionaries, the church consists of native Christians, Chinese (principally), Malays and Klings [Tamils], numbering 67 adults with 30 communicants in the schools. There are 45 boys, boarders, 20 girls, boarders, 20 day scholars, and 5 native teachers; 55 men and 12 women have been baptized. . . . One Chinaman in particular appears very serious; he walks a distance of 10 miles to meeting every Sunday morning. The others are very attentive during worship, and the singing is very good: the words in their own tongue are set to psalm tunes (SKI 1865: 59).

The London Missionary Society's mission chapel had served as a primitive church for Penang's nonconformist Christians, but this visitor mentioned no European service.

Mrs Chapman returned to England in January 1865, and Mr Chapman followed soon after he published his 1865 report on the schools and mission. Chapman stayed there for 18 months, leaving Grant in charge (SKI 1867: 44).[15] When Mr Chapman returned in November 1866, he brought three new recruits: Mr and Mrs William Macdonald and Miss Lucy A. Judd.

After his return from England, Chapman was deeply discouraged:

> The people have no desire for salvation. I turn from one to another, Chinese, Malays, Klings, Hindoos, Europeans, but, 'who hath believed our report?' My comfort is, the certainty of being led by Him, and therefore of my being in the right way, and in the right place. If I were not sure of this, I should be miserable (SKI 1867: 47).

The schools may have been thriving when he left for Britain, but he reported to Müller, "The Girls' School has been most disappointing, the boys' also, and the native church *most mournful*; so many walk no more with us" (SKI 1867: 48). But he added that he had free access to the jail, where he believed that Malays listened with interest, and he addressed an audience of ten English-speaking sailors in the House of Corrections (SKI 1867: 47–8).

In 1867, Penang's Lieutenant Governor, Colonel Archibald E.H. Anson wrote to the LMS directors and offered the unflattering assessment: "The people who now have the use of the Chapel and other buildings do not, as far as I can learn, succeed well with their mission. Indeed, I don't think it is a very desirable one, so far as I can judge of it."[16] In that letter, he also sent the LMS director a map of the mission property, complaining that a piece of the property was "empty and untidy", and asking if they would allow them to build a library there. This was precisely the land that Chapman had hoped to use for the opium treatment centre.

The Penang Mission was located in a seaside area where the wealthy built bungalows in large treed compounds. One of their affluent neighbors had donated the tract of land next to the mission around 40 years earlier, on condition that it remain empty so that his house would enjoy sea breezes and an unobstructed view of Penang Hill. Anson noted that a Chinese merchant

---

[15] Müller explained Chapman's 1865 return to England in terms of health issues (SKI 1867: 44); Mrs Chapman had already returned (Chapman 1865: 18).

[16] Col. Anson to Ellis, 10 November 1867 (LMS/PD).

now owned the house opposite the open space, and argued that the original agreement was no longer valid.

Thomas Beighton's son John, who lived in London, helped the LMS gather information about the property. He wrote to George Felix Gottlieb, who reported that the Chapel, Mission House, Girls' School, and Boys' School, stood together on a piece of ground, but that a portion of that land still belonged to Mrs Lord (formerly Jemima Poppy Bausum). Gottlieb thought that it would be a pity to sell the mission properties, but suggested that they consider selling the empty piece of ground that Mr John Anderson had donated to the mission, and sent Beighton a copy of the title deed. Gottlieb added that Chapman had told him five or six years earlier that he "wanted to build a hospital there to treat Chinese opium smokers", which suggests that his plan had been long known to Penang residents, including the wealthy residents of seaside mansions on Farquhar Street.[17]

The LMS directors claimed to know nothing of the 1846 agreement with Mr and Mr Bausum that they be allowed to use the mission properties in exchange for their upkeep or any subsequent arrangements.[18] In October 1868 the LMS Board decided to sell the property—not just the empty lot but the entire mission—with the help of Col. Anson. Gottleib had given Chapman the Penang mission property deeds, which he sent to London; his wife surrendered them to the LMS lawyers.[19]

In 1867, Miss Judd and Grant married and moved to Singapore, where Grant became the missionary for the newly built Bethesda Free Meeting House. The next year, Miss O'Callaghan moved to Malacca, where she opened a girls' school. Chapman also left Penang in 1868, and by 1869 was working in South Africa among "Malays, Africans, and Europeans". Some Malays, he claimed, were interested in the Gospel, while others opposed, but he was certain he could convert Muslims in his new situation (Müller 1870: 67).[20]

William Macdonald (1839–1911) and his wife were the last to leave Penang. Macdonald was from Shoreditch, London, and had worked as a lawyer's clerk.

---

[17] Gottlieb to Beighton, 2 November 1868 (LMS/PD).

[18] Ellis to Mullens, 3 January 1868; Bausum to LMS Board of Directors, 1 August 1846 (LMS/PD).

[19] Mullens to Woolacott, 16 June 1870 (LMS/PD).

[20] Müller listed a European "labouring at the Cape of Good Hope" in his annual reports for four years, from 1869–73. In focusing on Malay immigrants in South Africa, it would appear that Chapman had adopted the same strategy as the LMS, when they decided to work with immigrant Chinese who were living in British-controlled areas of Southeast Asia, far from the Chinese state.

He had been converted at a New Year's Eve watch-night service in 1861, and in 1865 married Bessie Sinel (1833–78), whose brother was a Brethren evangelist in France. They attended the Paragon Road Assembly in Hackney after their marriage, and went to Penang with support from Müller.[21] When Macdonald thanked Müller for a donation in 1869, he mentioned a long period of trial in the "work of the Lord", which is the only published mention of the crisis at the Penang mission (SKI 1869: 78). He and his wife finally moved to Singapore, but he continued to make short visits Penang until returning to England in 1872 (SKI 1872: 54–5).

By 1868 the schools had closed and the Mission House was rented out. But the Asian and Eurasian members of the Penang Mission Church continued to meet with the help of Ang Kang Kin, a Chinese evangelist who moved to Penang from Singapore. On seeing a printed notice that the property was for sale, they sent a petition to the LMS requesting that at least the Mission Chapel not be sold, arguing that the sale of their central meeting place would create a hardship for them. The petitioners included Mr and Mrs Macdonald, Ang Kang Kin, Chinese members of the church, and James Gawthorne, the acting Postmaster of Penang, the multilingual Tamil who had been adopted and educated by Mr and Mrs Beighton. After the British missionaries left Penang, he took responsibility for managing the property.[22]

The petitioners reported, "That for some time previously and up to about the month of April 1868, the same premises were by the kind permission of the Society occupied by Mr Chapman, a missionary then labouring in the gospel in Penang along with a girl's schoolhouse adjoining the Society's land and premises." The LMS directors wrote notes in the margin indicating that they knew nothing of how they had come to use the mission property: "from when? Who gave permission?"

As the petitioners described it, their church consisted primarily of "Chinese and East Indian people who assembled in the Chapel for the purpose of religious worship." Even when no missionary was present, they claimed, they assembled for worship in the chapel three times a week and on special occasions. The petitioners noted that if the chapel were sold, they would not have the means to acquire another building suitable for their assembly, adding that if they were deprived of a central meeting place, the native Christians would scatter, and the "blessings which has so far acted upon the work which was introduced

---

[21] Carol Richardson, "Bessie Sinel", http://www.theislandwiki.org/index.php/Bessie_Sinel [accessed 4 February 2017].

[22] The Gawthorne family history traces the education and careers of his children, who were members of Penang's elite (Gawthorne 2014).

into Penang by the Society's means would be greatly lessened".[23] After almost 50 years, they noted, the Penang Mission was well known in the region "as a place of reference to strangers in the various parts of the Island of Penang, and Province Wellesley". The petitioners reminded the LMS directors that the chapel was built "with money subscribed in Penang, and for the benefit of gospel work in that place, and will no doubt consider that the Native Church has at the least a moral claim on the Society to be allowed to continue to use the chapel as heretofore."

Gawthorne also wrote directly to LMS foreign secretary Rev. Joseph Mullens. He explained that the Penang Christians did not ask them to return, but "to treat with kindness the Mission Church here". He described the church as both a "child of the Society" and "a fellow labourer with the society in the grand and glorious work of the Gospel", observing that a "sacred duty" had been entrusted to the society to "raise and support churches in heathen lands". He concluded that "The proposed sale if carried out would be a first step on the part of the society towards the destruction of the Mission Church."[24]

Ignoring the petition, on 15 December 1869 the LMS lawyers authorized Penang lawyer James Richardson Logan to sell the property if he could obtain $3,000 for it.[25] The LMS directors insisted that the Brethren missionaries had simply been allowed to occupy the premises from year to year, and that they had acknowledged their rights when they surrendered the title deeds. Their lawyers later recognized Gawthorne's claim to retain possession since he had done maintenance on the property as per the initial agreement with Bausum, but still advised the LMS directors to proceed with the sale of the property, observing that "under present circumstances it is not desirable to open the question".[26]

Although they had advertised the property for sale, the LMS did not have clear title to one piece of land. In 1847, Mr Bausum had bought additional property on the East side of the mission and used it to extend the Girls' School. In 1850 he built a two-storey girls' school that was attached to the Mission House by a bridge, which he described as a brick building that "cost £600 but will last a generation".[27] Although he wrote to the LMS directors to advise them that he intended this property as a "small addition to the Mission Premises", he did nothing to formally convey it to the LMS.[28] On his death in 1855, his

23 Petition to the London Missionary Society, 8 May 1869 (LMS/PD).

24 Gawthorne to Rev. Mullens, 6 December 1969 (LMS/PD).

25 Mullens to Woollacott and Leonard, 15 December 1869 (LMS/PD).

26 Woolacott and Leonard to LMS, 23 June 1870 (LMS/PD).

27 Bausum to Tidman, 6 December 1850 (LMS/IC).

28 Bausum to LMS Board of Directors, 1 August 1846 (LMS/PD).

second wife Jemima Poppy Bausum had inherited "1/2 of the Girls' School House and premises".[29]

At that time, Vaughan noted that the school was "built in part on mission property, in part of a piece of land bought by Mr Bausum", adding that Mrs Bausum would be "most distressed if the Society sells this".[30] But because she only owned half of the girls' school, she herself could not easily sell the property. The title remained in her name, passing to her heirs on her death in Ningpo in 1869. Although they were aware of the problem, in 1870 the LMS directors sold the mission property to Mr David Aitkin, leaving it to him to seek a means to establish legal title.[31]

After the property was sold, William Macdonald returned to Penang and occupied the disputed property.[32] The Penang lawyer who arranged the sale reported that Mr Aitkin had offered Macdonald money for mission purposes if he agreed to leave, but that he still persisted "in retaining possession of the Girls' School partly built on this piece of ground and partly on the Society's property. He will neither pay rent for it nor permit it to be taken down".[33] But finally Macdonald withdrew to Singapore.

In 1872 Anthony Norris Groves's son Henry,[34] together with John Lindsay Maclean, an army captain who had sold his commission on adopting a pacifist views, launched *The Missionary Echo* to promote undenominational missionaries (Stunt et al. 1972: 35–43). Macdonald was one of the first to write them. In a letter published in their March issue, he reported that he and Mr Grant wanted to lay the facts of the mission in the Straits Settlements "more extensively and systematically before Christians at home, so as to bring other labourers into it, if such should be the Lord's will".[35] He and his family returned to England, soon followed by Mr and Mrs Grant.

---

[29] Gottlieb to Beighton, 2 November 1868; A. Logan to Woolacott and Leonard, 10 September 1870 (LMS/PD).

[30] J.D. Vaughan to Tidman, 19 August 1855 (LMS/IC).

[31] A. Logan to Woolacott and Leonard, 3 February 1871 (LMS/PD).

[32] In 1870, Mr Macdonald took an American guest to visit Mahomet Noordin, a wealthy Tamil Muslim who offered them wine and cheroots on a silver platter. He described Macdonald as the only missionary in Penang (Prime 1874: 199–200).

[33] Logan to Woolacott and Leonard, 3 February 1871 (LMS/PD).

[34] Groves' two sons jointly superintended a sugar refining factory in South India; after that business closed, Henry Groves worked for an Assembly in Bristol, and in 1872 became coeditor of *The Missionary Echo* (Stunt et al. 1972: 35–7). He also coedited an early Open Brethren magazine *The Golden Lamp* (1870–90).

[35] Macdonald, Penang and Singapore, 28 December 1871–26 January 1872, *ME* No. 5 (May 1872): 60.

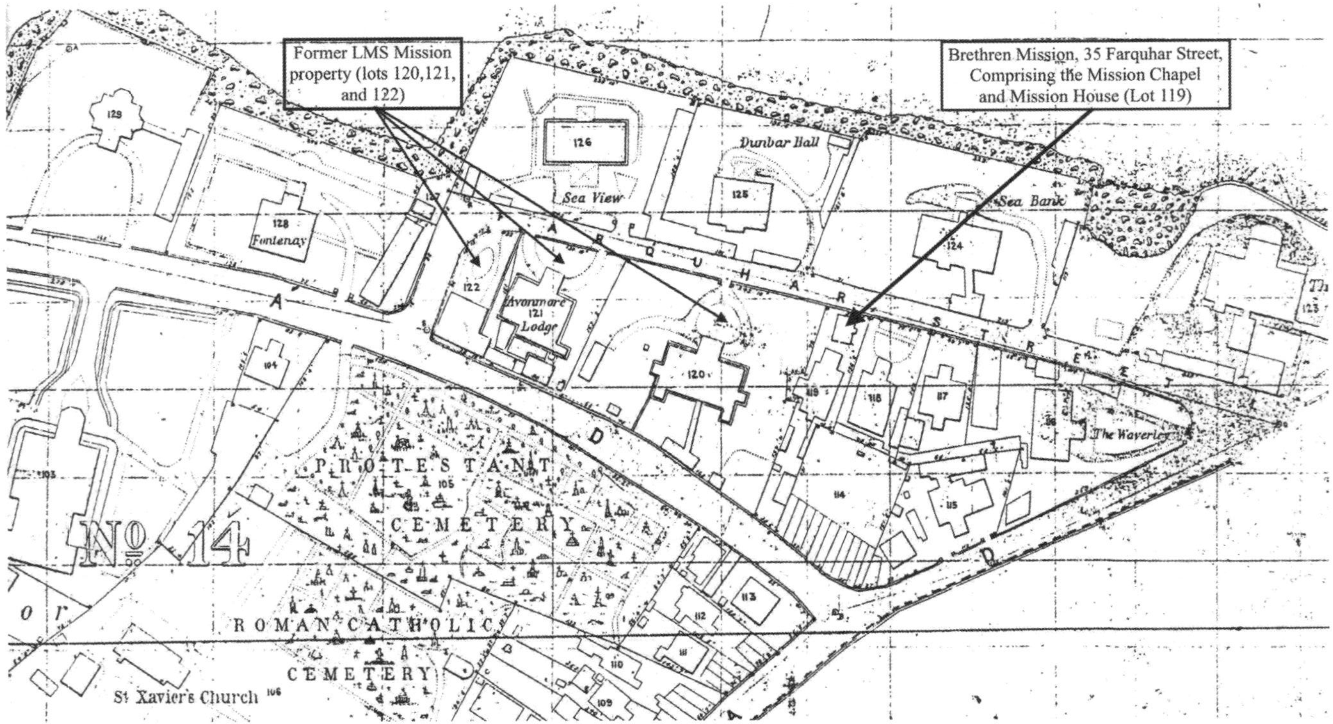

Figure 17 1893 Map of Farquhar Street. After the sale of the LMS mission, Macdonald rebuilt the mission on a strip of land on the east edge of the property (lot 119). The LMS mission property had included lot 120, where a mansion with a circular drive was built, and lots 121 and 122, the land donated on condition that it remain undeveloped. Courtesy of Khoo Salma Nasution; annotations by author.

Rebuilding the Penang Mission

Although the LMS sold their property in Penang, Macdonald managed to obtain a small lot on the East edge of the mission property, which was likely the property inherited by Jemima Bausum Lord's heirs. He and his family returned to Penang in 1874, and he resumed work with support from George Müller and the editors of *The Missionary Echo*.

He soon built a new Mission Chapel with donations from Christians in Penang and Singapore,[36] and also from Padang in West Sumatra. In celebration of the opening of the new chapel in 1876, Macdonald published an announcement describing their work "in connection with The Gospel of Christ At Penang Evangelical—Undenominational", and sent a copy to the LMS directors together with a handwritten note.

The announcement reported that they were performing regular services at their new Mission Chapel on Farquhar Street, and also distributing tracts in "various Western and Eastern languages". In his note to the LMS directors, Macdonald pointed out that their donation of £150 had been entered into the anonymous list of contributors, which were identified not by donor's name but only by location.[37]

[36] *Assembly Record Book*, 26 March 1876: 171.

[37] "The Gospel of Christ Penang Statement by W. Macdonald Missionary", August 1876. Sent by Macdonald to Dr Millers. A handwritten note adds "Please note your Society's donation [of £150] entered in the list of contributors No. 21" (LMS/IC).

Chapter 7

Hokkien Evangelists

> The Lord has sent me, a preacher, from Singapore to Penang now five months, and has opened a way to preach in Penang. At the gospel-station daily preaching; at times going out in neighbouring suburbs, in the town, in the province, on the mainland, or in the distant places. There are those who hear gladly, those who oppose, and those who treat it as a pastime to hear.
>
> Chiam Kim Kak, 1875 letter to the Brethren in Bath[1]

As he prepared to return to England in 1872, Mr Macdonald reported to the editors of *The Missionary Echo* that he had asked two Chinese Christians to take charge of the Penang mission. He described Ang Kang Kin as a preacher and Chiam Kim Kak as a "teaching and preaching brother", who like Tan See Boo was able to do Bible exposition. He added that a third unnamed Chinese Christian also had an aptitude as a "helper in word and doctrine".[2] Although these three could only correspond with him in Chinese, James Gawthorne wrote to him in English and kept him informed of the state of the Penang mission.

In this chapter, I focus on letters from Chinese evangelists that were translated and published in *The Missionary Echo* and George Müller's Scriptural Knowledge Institution's annual reports between 1868 and 1877.[3] Tan See Boo was the first to write, followed by Penang's catechist Ang Kang Kin, then Chiam Kim Kak, who wrote letters from Penang from 1875 to 1877. Some of the translated letters were published in the period of disruption in which

[1] Chiam Kim Kak, letter to the editors of *The Missionary Echo*, 11 January 1875, *ME* No. 40 (April 1875): 52–3.

[2] Macdonald, Penang and Singapore, 26 January 1872, *ME* No. 5 (May 1872): 61.

[3] These included three letters from Ang Kang Kin, five from Chiam Kim Kak, and three from Tan See Boo published in *The Missionary Echo*. Müller published two letters from Ang Kang Kin and a third letter from Singapore whose Chinese author was unnamed in the Scriptural Knowledge Institution's annual report.

the Brethren lost use of the London Missionary Society property, then rebuilt the mission.

The Chinese Christian evangelists in Penang visited people in their homes, but also publically debated non-Christians at temples, clan halls, and worksites. In their public exhortations, Chinese evangelists sought to convince non-Christians of the futility of idol worship and that both Chinese and Christians worshipped the same God—*Shangdi*.

On Translation and Rhetoric

By the time the Open Brethren started work in Penang, the project of translating Christian texts into Chinese was well advanced. The missionaries and their Chinese coworkers could rely on organizations like the British and Foreign Bible Society and the Religious Tract Society for Bibles and tracts in many languages including Chinese. The translators and authors of these publications had already chosen Chinese equivalents for terms like God, Jesus, the Holy Spirit, and the devil. Earlier missionaries in Southeast Asia and China had also developed rhetorical strategies for open-air proselytism that they described in memoirs and published letters that new missionaries studied and adopted. They had also created a Chinese hymnody (see Charter and DeBernardi 1998).

Chinese migrated to Southeast Asia from China's coastal provinces, and the immigrants included speakers of three Chinese regional languages—Southern Min, Yue (Cantonese), and Hakka. But the majority of the immigrants in Singapore and Penang came from Fujian province or Hainan Island, and spoke one of several dialects of Southern Min, a regional language spoken in Fujian, Taiwan, and among diaspora Chinese in Southeast Asia.[4] In Penang and Singapore, the Amoy [Xiamen] dialect of Southern Min is imprecisely termed *Hokkien oe* (*Fujian hua*), meaning 'the language of Fujian'.

Speakers of Southern Min were among the first Chinese population that British Protestant missionaries sought to convert. London Missionary Society missionary Walter Medhurst lived and worked at the mission in Batavia (today Jakarta) until he moved to China in 1842; in Batavia he studied Southern Min and in 1832 completed *A Dictionary of the Hok-këèn Dialect of the Chinese Language: According to the Reading and Colloquial Idioms: Containing about*

[4] Southern Min is spoken by an estimated 40 million people in Fujian, Taiwan, and by diaspora Chinese in Southeast Asia (DeBernardi 1991).

12,000 Characters.[5] The first complete translation of the Amoy dialect Southern Min Bible was completed by the mid-19th century, and the Protestant missionaries in Fujian had also created a Hokkien hymnal that William Chalmers Burns revised in 1851.

Although the missionaries initially translated the Bible into Chinese characters using an elite literary style, they aspired to translate into more accessible vernacular styles of Chinese. Before the standardization of Mandarin as a national language, speakers of China's diverse topolects could read Chinese characters using the literary register of their language. But the missionaries also created romanized versions of Chinese topolects, including Hokkien, which they taught to Chinese who could not read and write Chinese characters. They taught romanized Hokkien in the schools and used it to compose hymns. When the missionaries introduced metal types to print Chinese characters, this allowed Christian texts to be published in characters and romanization.[6]

But before they could translate texts into any variety of Chinese, they needed to decide on equivalents for Christian terms for spiritual entities like God, the Holy Spirit, angels and the devil; moral vocabulary like terms for sin and repentance; and terms that distinguished the Christian heaven and hell from those of other religions that also posited an afterlife.

Birgit Meyer has proposed that there are four alternatives for the Christian translator. The first is the use of pre-Christian religious vocabulary, the second the direct borrowing of a loanword from the source language, the third the borrowing of secular words from the target language or a closely related dialect, and the fourth finding an equivalent entity (Meyer 1994: 51). Chinese translators of the Bible and tracts used all four strategies.

In Chinese translations of Christian terminology, loanwords were used for names, including Jesus Christ, which is phonetically rendered as *Yesu*, and Satan, which is transcribed as *Satan*. Translators also borrowed Chinese religious vocabulary to translate Christian concepts. Protestants translated the term gospel, for example, as *fuyin* (福音) meaning 'good news', and the

[5] Medhurst collaborated on the Delegates translation of the New Testament that I discuss in Chapter 5 (see also DeBernardi 2011). He is, however, better known for having completed a translation of the Bible into Classical Chinese in Shanghai in 1847 that the Taiping rebels adopted.

[6] In Singapore and Penang, Hokkien speakers still use the romanization systems devised by missionaries for everyday purposes like writing personal names, the names of local foods, and business names. Although many still prize the romanized Hokkien Bible and hymnals, contemporary Hokkien-speaking Christians are most likely to use Mandarin in their churches.

Brethren called their Chinese meeting place a *Fuyin Tang* (福音堂) or Good News/Gospel Hall. In Chinese popular religion, the term *fu* means prosperity or blessings, and the character is often displayed as a wish for good luck (see DeBernardi 2006: 57–61). With this translation, Protestants "connected the Chinese pursuit for happiness with their brand of Christianity", making the "foreign import seem local and familiar" (Zheng 2017: 14).

Buddhism also supplied Christian translators with equivalents for their moral vocabulary. When historian Daniel Bays analyzed more than 20 of the must crucial terms in *The Two Friends*, a popular 19th-century Christian tract, he discovered that all but two or three had "definite usages and meanings somewhere in the corpus of Chinese Mahayana Buddhist terms". These included terms for heaven (*tiantang* 天堂), hell (*diyu* 地獄), sin (*zui* 罪), repentance (*hui* or *huigai* 悔改), redemption (*shu* 贖), savior (*jiushizhu* 救世主), and spirit or soul (*linghun* 靈魂) (Bays 1985a: 131; see also 1985b).[7]

Because Protestant Christians had produced different translations of the Bible in Chinese, in 1847 several mission societies decided to collaborate on a new union translation of the New Testament. But the project failed when translation committee members could not agree whether to translate God as *Shangdi* 上帝 (the Emperor Above) or *Shen* 神 (spirit or deity).[8] They produced about 600 handwritten pages debating the alternatives, many of which were published in the *Chinese Repository* and *Chinese Recorder*. After their collaboration failed, the London Missionary Society translators completed their translation projects separately with support from the British and Foreign Bible Society (DeBernardi 2011: 389–90; Zetzsche 1999: 82–3).

The missionaries who preferred to translate God as *Shangdi* argued for their choice in light of claims about China's ancient history, including the claim that the supreme deity of ancient China was none other than the Christian God. In James Legge's *The Religions of China* (1880), for example, he offered two epigraphs to introduce his discussion of Confucianism. The first was a phrase from Chapter 19 of the Confucian *Doctrine of the Mean*: "In the ceremonies of

---

[7] Translators were aware that the use of the Buddhist term for hell was potentially a source of confusion. Like Catholics, Buddhists imagined a tortured journey through purgatory, but they also regarded the material body as insignificant and believed in reincarnation.

[8] Catholics had translated God with *Tianzhu* 天主, which means 'Heaven's Ruler', and the term *Tianzhujiao* 天主教 'The Religion of Heaven's Ruler' is the Chinese name for the Catholic Church. Protestants sought to distinguish themselves from Catholics, and translating 'God' as either *Shangdi* or *Shen* would have accomplished that goal.

the altars of Heaven and Earth, they served God (*Shangdi).*" The second was a line from the New Testament: "They knew God" (Paul, Romans i 21).

Legge concluded that China's ancient religion was monotheistic, and that this original monotheism was still practised in state worship. The Chinese people only turned to polytheism, he claimed, after the introduction of Buddhism and the development of the Daoist religion (Legge 1880: 51, 182; see also Chen 2016). The Brethren missionaries and the Chinese catechists in Penang and Singapore adopted the LMS translation and called God *Shangdi*. They could then justify the rejection of "idol worship" as a rejection of newer traditions, including Buddhism, which they identified as foreign, in favour of the restoration of China's most ancient spiritual traditions.

Christian translators sought character equivalents for Christian terms, but they also had to adapt their translations to China's diverse topolects. In Hokkien, the term for deity is *sin* (*shen* 神) or *angkong*, a Southern Min term that has no agreed upon equivalent in Mandarin. *Siongde* (*Shangdi*), the term that some Protestant missionaries selected to translate God, refers to an ancient Chinese deity, but for Hokkien speakers, it is also the name for the Emperor of the Dark Heavens (*Xuantian Shangdi* 玄天上帝), whom they call *Siongde Gong* (上帝公). The supreme Daoist deity is called the Jade Emperor (*Yu Huang Shangdi* 玉皇上帝), but Hokkien speakers simply refer to him as *Tikong*, or the Lord of Heaven (*Tiangong* 天公) (see DeBernardi 2004: 143–8).

The missionaries and Chinese evangelists often exhorted Chinese traditionalists to give up idol worship, just as the Jews had done when they rejected the polytheism of Babylon and Egypt (see Assmann 1998). Hokkien speakers refer to deity statues respectfully as "Golden bodies" (*gim sin* 金身, Mandarin *jin shen*), and Daoist priests perform rituals to "open the eyes" of these images to enliven them. But when Christians translated 'idol', they selected a term meaning 'image' (Hokkien *ngo siong*, Mandarin *ouxiang* 偶像). The term foregrounds the materiality of deity statues, and when they exhorted Chinese, they denigrated them as powerless blocks of wood.[9]

As we have seen, the British Christians who founded the undenominational Chinese Evangelization Society accepted Karl Gützlaff's proposal that Christians should train Chinese evangelists to do the work of proselytism, and provided funding for the training of Chinese evangelists. Chinese Christians not only had superior language skills, they also had a social advantage in not

[9] On the contrasting use of these terms, I rely on notes on Hokkien language lessons with Ch'ng Oon Hooi (28 June 1980). For an in-depth study of Chinese god statues in Taiwan, see Lin 2008.

being Europeans, and were vital to the work of introducing Christianity both in China and among Chinese-speaking populations in Southeast Asia (Tiedemann 2008: 206).[10]

Like the European missionaries, the Chinese evangelists in Penang distributed tracts and testaments and did open-air evangelism in public settings, including temples, clan halls, and worksites. In their open-air evangelism, they used the method of "controversy" or "friendly disputation", engaging with non-Christians by debating with them (Carey 1850: 436–7). In response to their exhortations, traditionalists often accused the Chinese evangelists of adopting a foreign religion, abandoning their Confucian heritage, and neglecting their ancestors.

Ang Kang Kin (洪 or 汪康慶)

As the Penang mission's Chinese catechist, Kang Kin was the first name on the 1869 petition that James Gawthorne had sent to the directors of the London Missionary Society, requesting that they reconsider their decision to sell the mission. Macdonald wrote to Müller that Kang Kin "had entered the Lord's work without any agreement for wages and appears to be faithful". He added that before the arrival of a check from Müller, they were "very poor", but that when someone gave Kang Kin three dollars, he had given two dollars to them (SKI 1869: 78). No details are given of his life, but his family lived in Fujian and he worked at the Penang mission for 16 years.

Between 1870 and 1872, Macdonald translated letters from Ang that were published in the Scriptural Knowledge Institution's annual reports for 1870, 1871, and 1872. In January 1870 Ang wrote to Müller to thank him for a donation that enabled him to make a trip to Malacca and Singapore, where he spent time with his nephew and convinced him to be baptized (SKI 1870: 66). On 17 May 1871, he wrote to Müller again, reporting on open-air work in Singapore with Alexander Grant:

> I beg your prayers respecting the work at Penang, so that the Gospel may flow like water, Amen. Two months back I went to Malacca and Singapore and visited our brethren. Along with Mr. G[rant], I was every

[10] Philip Yuen-Sang Leung has observed, "in the Christian historiographic tradition—as far as the China field is concerned—missionary heroes, martyrs, the mainline denominations, and the home missions based in Europe and America dominate the shaping forces of history". As a consequence, he concludes, Christian historians have not paid sufficient attention to the role of the Chinese converts and to sociocultural forces (Leung 2002: 61).

> afternoon preaching the Gospel by the wayside in Singapore. There were many people who liked to hear. I met a countryman there, who was formerly an enemy to the Gospel and to me, but now he is very friendly and has asked me many times to visit him at his shop (SKI 1872: 55).

He also reported that in Penang he had done open-air evangelism, but with little result: "I am continually going into town preaching, but as yet have no new people believing."[11]

In 1872 the new Brethren missionary magazine, *The Missionary Echo*, published English translations of four letters that Ang sent to Macdonald while he was absent from Penang, first in Singapore, then in Britain. Almost certainly Ang's letters were part of Macdonald's campaign to restore the Penang Mission.

In the first of his letters in *The Missionary Echo*, Ang reported that he had travelled around Penang Island, hoping to convert a young man who lived in a village 11 miles from George Town. Ku [Khoo] had learned something about Christianity in China, and also from a Christian neighbour, and had paid Ang a visit to the gospel hall. But Ku's parents "pressed him to worship the idol"[12] and Ku threatened to leave home should they seek to force him to do so. Ang described a visit with Ku at his neighbour San's house:[13]

> [Ku] now receives me with honour and pleasure, notwithstanding that he suffers reviling from his acquaintances and relatives, who reproach him, saying of me, 'This is his teacher and his elder brother, who comes to give him advice!' To this he answered, 'Not only is he my teacher or elder brother, but he is my father; for he has taught me the way of salvation of the soul'—and this with so much boldness that the people were silenced.

He stayed the night at San's house, where he and Ku spent hours reading and discussing Christian teachings.

Ang continued his journey, exhorting a "heathen man" who sought to borrow money to pay the cost of praying to a deity:[14]

> I went to the back of the Island, and stayed a night in the house of a Roman Catholic, where there was at the same time a priest and his catechist. I read and exhorted from Acts xvii., verse 16 to the end. I chose this portion because a heathen man, whose wife was sick, came to borrow a little money from the master of the house for making worship

11 Ang to Macdonald, *ME* No. 5 (May 1872): 63.

12 Ibid.

13 Ang to Macdonald, Penang, 30 July 1872, *ME* No. 12 (December 1872): 154.

14 Ibid.

> to his idol, that he might obtain [the idol's] assistance for his sick wife. When the Romish priest heard it, he said to his catechist, 'Listen to this gospel, which is true.'

In the New Testament book that he cited (*Acts* Chapter 17, verses 16–end) Paul reported on debates with the Jews at the synagogue and market. He argued that since God was Lord of heaven and earth, he did not live in manmade temples, and that because he gave life, he did not need any offerings from humans, all of whom are "made of one blood" as his offspring. Paul also noted that God commanded all men everywhere to repent in preparation for the return of Christ and the resurrection of the dead. Similarly, Ang sought to convince his audience that temple worship and ritual offerings were not pleasing to God, and that people should instead repent of their sins and seek salvation from Jesus Christ.

Ang also passed on the news to Mr Macdonald that a revival was taking place in Amoy [now known as Xiamen]. He did not provide details, but in spring 1871 some district magistrates had spread the rumour that foreigners were poisoning wells and refusing to give an antidote unless the afflicted individuals paid large sums of money or converted to Christianity. In Amoy, mobs attacked one English missionary and a number of Chinese preachers, and for a time the missionaries did not dare travel (Pitcher 1893: 151–7; citing Talmage 1871).

Following the crisis, the Chinese "showed themselves remarkably ready to receive the Christian message", and the Amoy Mission established four new chapels to look after their new members (Band 1948 [1972]: 225). These included new meeting places in Zhangzhou and Tong'an, where the first converts had been baptized in 1870 (Pitcher 1893: 121–2). Members of the Pechuia Church that Burns founded also started evangelistic work in a market town, Phu-kiong, at this time (Band 1948 [1972]: 226).

In his 1872 letter, Ang reported:[15]

> I have received a letter from Khee in China, in which he states thus: 'This letter to brother Kang Kin, who is beloved. The Lord has opened a door of faith in China. This year I have baptized twelve persons, and there are four more desiring baptism. Many people like hearing the gospel. . . . I, Khee, send salutations to the missionary at Penang Island,

---

[15] Ang to Macdonald, Penang, 30 July 1872, *ME* No. 12 (December 1872): 155. The person whom Ang called "Khee" and "Lym" was probably Lim Khee Saw, who later emigrated to Singapore then moved to Penang. But since Lim is a common surname in Fujian, this is impossible to know for certain.

> with his wife, and salutations for the brethren at Penang also.' I have answered this letter, and sent a little money for him.

The revival continued, and Ang sent more news to the British missionary:[16]

> I have received letters from brother Lym at Amoy, in which he records that the Holy Ghost has moved the hearts of many people to desire to obtain the salvation of the soul. Brother Lym, with Kwee [Gan Kui], evangelist from Batavia, have hired a place to teach the gospel, because many people are there.

The Chinese Christians in Penang, excited by these reports, urged Ang to return to China, and he departed on Christmas day 1872.

News of the Amoy revival spread through the exchange of letters among Chinese Christians in Singapore, Penang, Java, and Amoy. On receiving this news, Gan Kui and Ang both returned to China, where they may have obtained salaried positions as leaders for new Christian gatherings. Although Ang returned to Penang, his letters ceased.

Chiam Kim Kak

In 1875, 1876, and 1877, *The Missionary Echo* published five translated letters from Chiam Kim Kak. Chiam had worked in Penang in 1870 and 1871, but after Macdonald returned to England, Chiam moved to Singapore, where he did open-air preaching to Chinese sailors and coolies at Tanjong Pagar.[17] A few months after Macdonald returned to Penang, Chiam Kim Kak joined him there "for a season of preaching the gospel".[18] In Penang, he lived and worked in a rented gospel hall, and travelled widely to proselytize (SKI 1875: 48).

In his letters, Chiam reported details of his debates with non-Christians and the experiences of Chinese Christians who were the targets of organized harassment from the sworn brotherhoods. These letters offer rare insight into the rhetorical strategies that Chinese evangelists used in their street corner addresses to Chinese audiences, but also the non-Christian response to their offer of salvation.

The missionaries saw advantage in the fact that the Chinese evangelists spoke Chinese languages fluently and could claim Chinese identity. But religion defined ethnicity, and Chinese regarded Christianity as the European's religion. On a visit to a sawmill, for example, a worker said to Chiam, "You preach

---

[16] Ang, Penang, n.d., *ME* No. 16 (April 1873): 58.
[17] Ibid.
[18] Macdonald, Penang, 27 July 1874; *ME* No. 36 (December 1874): 175.

the red-haired men's doctrine."[19] In response, Chiam's coworker, a Cantonese-speaking evangelist, replied "that it was not so, but that it was God's doctrine; that God sustained Chinese and English people alike, giving to all food, clothes, houses, and comfort; that God is the Lord and ruler of heaven and earth, and that He is the Father of mankind".[20]

Chiam travelled widely in Penang, and often received hospitality from non-Christians. When he visited Blackwater village (Malay: Ayer Itam), a stranger who had heard his street evangelism in George Town gave him a meal and lodging.[21] He travelled to a village where many residents were Roman Catholics, and then went to the coast. At Kompa Bay, "Brother Kim Hee and the friends there assembled for evening worship, and I was lodged there for the night."

But when Chiam preached in front of the "clubhouse of my tribe", referring to a *gongsi* or clan hall, he met with insults:[22]

> One man violently opposed and reviled, telling me that I was not a man. I said, "I am one with you, and the Lord commands his gospel to be preached; the believing and baptized obtain salvation, but unbelieving men are under wrath." He said no more, but left, and the others remained and listened to the gospel.

In Penang, Christian converts often faced what the missionaries described as "persecution" from non-Christians, including members of the sworn brotherhoods that the British colonial authorities called secret societies. In an 1875 letter, Chiam described a visit to a Chinese Christian who begged him not to sing hymns in his house for fear of persecution from "the society men" who might overhear them:[23]

> Later went to Kompa to preach and visit. Were in Bro Kin Hee's house, he asked them not to sing, "or after you leave the opposers will come back to abuse and injure me. They have already said they will not allow my house to be made a place of worship; and the society men have agreed that none of the Christians shall be allowed a passage in any of the passage boats going to or returning from town, and that the barber

[19] Macdonald, Penang, 5 May 1876. Translation of letter from Chiam, *ME* No. 56 (August 1876): 113. "Red haired men" (or "red haired ghosts" 红毛鬼) is Southern Min slang for Europeans, and "doctrine" probably is a translation of the Chinese word *dao* 道, which means 'way' but also refers to a philosophical tradition.

[20] Macdonald, Penang, 5 May 1876. Translation of letter from Chiam, *ME* No. 56 (August 1876): 113.

[21] Chiam, Penang, 11 January 1875, *ME* No. 40 (April 1875): 53.

[22] Ibid.: 53–4.

[23] Chiam, Penang, 7 July 1875, *ME* No. 48 (December 1875): 168–9.

shall not be allowed to shave the heads of the Christians, and that no dealings in trade shall be had with them." I said that we came as visitors, and that his wishes must be respected, and suggested that we should worship together within the house, and that we might in this way sing, and that we should fear God rather than man. Kin Hee said we could read and pray together, but not sing. Pray God to forgive our sins and assist the brethren with endurance.

Seeking Unity: The Lord of Heaven

In his August 1876 letter, Chiam reported that he had done public outreach at the fort on the morning of the eighth day of the first lunar month. On the ninth day of the first lunar month, Hokkien Chinese offer special worship to the Lord of Heaven. He opened his exhortation at the Penang fort by preaching against idol worship:[24]

> [Chiam] Kim Kak, at Penang, this 1*st Chinese moon*, with God's preserving blessing, has preached at the Gospel Hall, in the town, fort, bazaar, sea-side, and country-places. 8*th day*. At the fort preaching; many were passing to and fro at eight in the morning as I stood by the wayside. I read a hymn about putting away the false and adopting the true way of worship. Spoke of God having created the heaven and earth, and that He was the preserver of all men. The Sampan boat men listened, and I exhorted them not to worship idols, for that they could not assist us; that they were like their boats, made of wood, and could only be moved from place to place by men's exertions; that if men carrying an idol fell, the idol would fall with them. Many heard and were convinced, and did not gainsay.

Although he criticized the veneration of idols, Chiam did not persuade the boatmen that the Lord of Heaven was a useless idol—and indeed no image is made of him, since worshippers face the night sky with their offerings—but rather that they were not using the proper ritual form in worshipping the *true* Lord of Heaven:[25]

> I reminded them that to-morrow was said to be the birthday of the Lord of heaven [*Tiangong*], and that many would bring flesh-meat and other offerings, and worship; but that God, the true Lord of heaven, dislikes this, and was not worshipped as though He needed to eat. If you call men to a feast, and give them grass, the food of the lower animals, they

---

[24] Chiam, Penang, March 1876, *ME* No. 56 (August 1876): 111–2.

[25] Ibid.: 112.

> would not eat; so God, being far above men, being a Spirit, needed not to eat, but commands men to repent, and believe, and worship Him, that they may receive forgiveness and blessing, and giving up all wickedness, may live virtuously; then if the body died the soul would enter heaven. The company dispersed, each man to his boat.

Having identified the deity whom his hearers venerated on the ninth day of the first lunar month with the true God, he then argued that the ritual forms that they were using were incorrect and even offensive to God, arguing that God was a spirit and did not need food, and that the offerings made to him were useless. He urged instead repentance, belief, virtue, and worship so that they would be fit to enter heaven.

Exhortations at the Guanyin Temple

The Brethren believed themselves to be calling people "out of nations" to form a new spiritual community. But as Chiam's letters reveal, traditionalists in Penang accused the Christians of abandoning their Chinese identity. Just as baptism and the Lord's Supper defined Brethren identity, the rituals of ancestor worship, the events of the annual festival cycle, and the obligations of membership in Chinese associations linked Chinese in kinship and community networks. The Christians did not encourage the blending of the traditions but insisted instead that people could not follow "two masters". On conversion, Chinese were asked to destroy their wooden and paper god images and ancestral tablets and to withdraw their financial support for community festivals and the sworn brotherhoods, thereby severing those traditional bonds.

Chiam visited Penang's Guanyin Temple on Pitt Street, where he argued with the priest at a Chinese temple, who accused Chiam of calling his hearers to join a foreign tribe:[26]

> The Lord has sent me, a preacher, from Singapore to Penang now five months, and has opened a way to preach in Penang. At the gospel-station daily preaching; at times going out in neighbouring suburbs, in the town, in the province, on the mainland, or in the distant places. There are those who hear gladly, those who oppose, and those who treat it as a pastime to hear. The first day of the Chinese tenth moon I stood outside the large idol temple in the town. Many worshippers were coming and going; several stopped to listen to the preaching. A priest of the temple, seeing people listening to the gospel, came out. He was very angry, and called to the people to go into the temple and sit

[26] Chiam, Penang, 11 January 1875, *ME* No. 40 (April 1875): 52–3.

> down, and not to remain and listen to the gospel. He told them I was calling them to enter a foreign tribe. I replied by telling the priest that he himself had entered a foreign tribe, so that he had shaved off the touching—that is the Chinese pigtail—and had put on the jacket and trousers of a foreigner, and that he now called on people to worship an idol that had been imported from among Hindoos. The priest was not brave enough to reply, but went into the temple again. No one followed him in, but the people remained outside, and continued to listen to the gospel. One of the listeners, when I had ceased speaking, invited me to his shop, where I drank tea with him, and spoke further to him the word of the gospel.

The comparison of Buddhism with Christianity is apt: Buddhism came to China from India, and Buddhist bodhisattvas and devas had analogues among Hindu gods.

In 1875 Chiam described a second confrontation at the Guanyin temple in Penang, which he identified in Hokkien as *Koan-im-teng* (*Guanyin Ting* 觀音亭). This time, the issue was not only whether Chiam was preaching a foreign doctrine, but also whether he had the right to preach within the temple compound:[27]

> Letter to God's churches, pastors, elders, deacons, with all brethren and sisters to give information. From 5th to 6th month, [Chiam] Kim Kak has preached in the town of Penang, country places, in the Gospel Hall, and Laroot (a Malayan kingdom on the main land), preaching to many persons. Some rejoice to hear, some oppose. The 15th day of 5th moon is a day of much worshipping idols by the Chinese people. On that day I was at the outside of the great idol temple of Penang, called Koan-im-teng (the hall of Koan-im, the idols' name). About 35 men stood listening to the preaching, when a man suddenly rushed out of the temple, and asked, "What doctrine do you preach?" I replied, "My book is printed in Chinese characters, and the name of God and of Jesus Christ are here in it, not the names of foreigners. The preaching is of God, the Lord of heaven and earth, who sustains both Chinese and foreigners."

For Chiam, the fact of translation into Chinese was proof enough that Christianity was not foreign, and he identified God, the Lord of Heaven, as a supreme god shared by all.

[27] Chiam, Penang, 7 July 1875, *ME* Vol. 40 (December 1875): 168.

But the man immediately countered that the temple courtyard belonged to the Goddess of Mercy and to the Chinese, not to the British government or the general public:

> He pointed to the pavement on which we stood—a considerable paved but unenclosed space in front of the temple, used for burning paper sacrifices, assemblies of spectators to witness the theatrical performances connected with the temple, &c.—and said: "This ground is the idol's ground, and not the ground of the governor or of the public."

Chiam refused to leave, insisting that because he was not exhorting people to do anything illegal, no policeman would arrest him.

> I replied that ground had been purchased with money contributed by the Chinese people; that I was a Chinese, and had come to exhort Chinese people to repent of sin, and to believe on the Lord Jesus and obtain forgiveness of sins, and to lead virtuous lives, and not to enter that temple to worship idols, and sin against God; that I had come, not to destroy men with wickedness, or to seduce people to gambling, so that if the police-officer came he would not arrest me. This man then went back into the temple; and a number of people remained, and others also came to hear the preaching until I bade them farewell, to return to my abode at the Gospel Hall. Thanks be unto God for this opportunity!

Although the priest retreated, he had grounds for his claim to sovereignty over the temple courtyard.

The assertive claim that the temple belonged to the Goddess of Mercy and not to the Governor or the public alluded to a history of conflict between the temple and British Christians. Cantonese and Fujian merchants in Penang had cooperated to build the Buddhist-syncretic Guanyin Temple on Pitt Street in 1800. Nineteen years later, the Bishop of Calcutta consecrated Saint George's Anglican Church on a site near the temple.

Chinese immigrants brought images of protective patron deities with them from their home towns, and the temple housed a dense pantheon of gods. Consequently the temple hosted many festival events distributed throughout the lunar year (DeBernardi 2004: 229–36). When these events fell on Sunday, the noise from the opera performance disturbed Christians in Saint George's Anglican Church.

In a spirit of accommodation, the Chinese had rescheduled their festival events so that they would not coincide with Sunday worship, but the Anglicans also worshipped on other days of the week. In 1856, the Indian government had enacted a new law that allowed the colonial police greater control over festival events. The next year, led by a brash new deputy commissioner of police who was the son-in-law of Edmond Blundel, the colonial governor, the Penang police attempted to dismantle the stage on Saturday night in order to prevent the stage performance from continuing on Sunday.

Chinese leaders sought advice from James Richardson Logan, who pointed out that the British had built their church next to the temple, and not the other way around (Logan 1857). With his help, the Chinese leadership addressed their complaints directly to the Governor-General of India, who supported them and admonished Blundell. As a consequence, Penang's Chinese community won recognition and protection for their religious organizations and events, including recognition that the temple ground was not public space, nor was it the property of the governor (DeBernardi 2004: 44–52).

Competing Perspectives on Morality

When curious individuals visited him to ask questions about Christianity, Chiam promoted the Christian way to salvation as superior to Buddhist or Daoist salvific practices. In one instance, for example, he reported that he had explained to a visitor that those who believed in Jesus would have eternal life. The visitor defended Buddhism and "idol priests", saying that they were vegetarian and had good hearts. In response, Chiam argued that only Christianity offered "forgiveness with salvation":[28]

> I invited him to sit down, and told him that God so loved the world, that He gave His only begotten Son, that whosoever believeth in Him should not perish, but have everlasting life. He replied, that to eat ox-flesh was not good; and asked, Did I eat it or not? I replied, that the fulness of the earth was given to us to eat by the Lord of heaven and earth, and that we could eat beef with a thankful heart to God; that Christ said, that what we eat did not defile us; but that the outcome of the heart, and evil words, and the doings of the hand, and the walk of the feet, defile men. He replied, Idol priests abstain from flesh, and live according to a good heart. I replied that idol priests spoke fairly, but led bad lives. They said, that to kill animals was wrong; but they used drums made from ox skins. This was not of an upright heart, but of hypocrisy. I begged him not to hope that being a vegetarian would save his soul; but to believe in the Saviour Lord, and obtain forgiveness with salvation, and so hereafter to enter heaven. He took a gospel tract and said he would come again.

[28] Chiam, Penang, March 1876, *ME* No. 56 (August 1876): 112.

Although the person promised to return, perhaps the purpose of his visit was to seek to convince Chiam that moral virtue could be discovered in Asian religious practices and that priests, far from being "bad" as Chiam claimed, in fact lived "according to a good heart". But Chiam did not allow that there could be more than one path to salvation.

Chiam returned to the fort the next month, where he debated with members of a small crowd. One person raised questions about the relevance of his teachings; another observed that despite his promises of eternal life, both Christians and non-Christians died and were buried in the ground:[29]

> 2nd Moon, *1st day to 30th day*. Thus far God has preserved and given blessing to preach in the Gospel Hall [and many other places]. *7th day*. At the fort eight people heard. One man opposed, saying "To-day we eat food; that is enough; it is needless to hear your preaching." Kim Kak [*sic.*] replied, "Man has a body, but he has a soul also. The body being fed, it is well; but the body is of short duration. The soul certainly should feed, and get eternal life and heavenly blessing." The man asked if I had seen the soul. Kim Kak answered that the soul was not material, to be seen with the body's eye; with the heart we believe in the Lord Jesus Christ, that He died for our sins, was buried, and on the third day rose, and forty days after went to the right hand of God, and is now the Saviour Lord for us men. Thus believing, we obtain eternal life. This man said no more. Another man remarked, "You God-worshipping men die, and your bodies are committed to the ground the same as those of idol-worshippers." I replied, "Now we are not yet manifested; but after death the saved believers in Jesus get the eternal life with heavenly blessing, and those not believing, it is quite certain, descend into torment."

Chiam also compared the forgiveness of sins to "getting good wages for their work", which he claimed would make them happy and help them live virtuous lives. He concluded his letter with a prayer, "begging that God's grace may be poured out, and that men may repent and get eternal blessing. Amen."

Conclusion

In his public exhortations, Chiam sought to convince non-Christians both of the futility of idol worship and that Chinese and Christians both venerated the same supreme God—*Shangdi*. At the same time that they claimed congruency, the Chinese evangelists drew inflexible boundaries between Christians and non-Christians. In particular, the Brethren insistence on "Jesus only" meant

[29] Chiam, Penang, March 1876, *ME* No. 56 (August 1876): 113.

that a Chinese who saw virtue in vegetarianism, for example, or recognized moral value in the teachings of an Asian religion would not be encouraged to blend those elements of moral practice or teaching with Christianity.

John Sydenham Furnivall concluded that by the early 20th century, utilitarianism's economic man had been cast out of Europe only to find refuge in the "tropical dependencies" of Southeast Asia. As he described it, these were plural societies in which a medley of peoples lived under a shared political system, each holding to their own religion, culture, and language, meeting only in the marketplace in pursuit of cheap goods and economic gain. He compared the plural society to the Hindu caste system, but noted that caste had the sanction of religion, while the plural society's only common deity was Mammon. Under laissez-faire rule, he concluded, the outcome was "mass individualism" (Furnivall 1948: 304–12, 318; see also Coppel 1997: 563–4).

Although Furnivall described the plural society's medley of peoples as meeting only in the marketplace and caring only for money, evangelical Christians crossed social boundaries in their quest to convince all of their sinfulness and need for salvation. Ang Kang Kin and Chiam Kim Kak reported that their efforts rarely resulted in conversion, and often aroused anger and opposition. Although they often met with counter-arguments and derision, the Chinese evangelists started a long conversation with non-Christian Chinese about values and systems. By the early 20th century, the rivalry between Christianity and Chinese moral cultures had helped ignite both anti-foreign movements and movements of revival and reform.

PART III
Circulations

Chapter 8

Singapore: Visiting Every City

> Let us go again and visit our brethren in every city where we have preached the word of the Lord, and see how they do.
>
> *Acts of the Apostles* 51: 36

Today the Brethren in Singapore regard businessman Philip Robinson (1831–86) as their founder. Robinson was born in Bristol and baptized at Tewkesbury Baptist Church in 1847. He emigrated to Melbourne, Australia in 1850, but in 1857—the year of the global commercial crisis—he and his wife Eliza moved to Singapore. Eliza joined Sophie Cooke, the head of the Chinese Girls' School, to organize a Ladies Bible and Tract Society that held monthly prayer meetings. Together with a few friends, the Robinsons formed a primitive church in their home, then in 1864 rented 108 Bencoolen Street as a Mission Room so that they could do public outreach. When they built Bethesda Free Meeting House in 1867, Alexander Grant moved there from Penang as Bethesda's missionary. Led by Tan See Boo, Chinese Christians built a Free Chinese Christian church on adjacent land.

Singapore, 1819–42

In 1819 Stamford Raffles (1781–1826) negotiated a treaty to establish a post on Singapore, an island at the tip of the Malay Peninsula (Turnbull 2009: 19–32). Danish missionary Rev. Claudius Thomsen soon moved there from Malacca. Abdullah bin Abdul al Kadir (aka Munshi Abdullah, 1796–1854) accompanied him and for a time commuted between Malacca and Singapore (Van Der Putten 2006: 413).

In Singapore, Thomsen developed extensive printing works of three buildings jointly owned with the Anglican chaplain (O'Sullivan 1984: 79). He took on debt in the name of the London Missionary Society, and although they paid these bills, they demanded that he repay them. In order to settle this debt, he sold land, the printing press, and type fonts to the American Board of Commissioners for Foreign Missions (ABCFM). He also rented the mission house to the Americans, and the LMS chapel to a High Church Anglican chaplain, who would not allow the American missionaries to use it. He had put all properties in his own name, and after he returned to England in 1834, the LMS directors learned that the Singapore mission "owned no land, no mission house, no chapel, no schools, no press, and had no congregation" (Bowman 2016: 72–3; see also O'Sullivan 1984: 79–80).

By 1837 the ABCFM was running a successful printing press and had opened schools and a medical clinic in Singapore. The printing establishment that they purchased from Thomsen gave them all the tools they needed to print in Asian languages, including "a set of matrices in Malay, another in Bugis, another in Javanese, and a fourth in Siamese". They owed the latter as well as large metallic Chinese type to the work of Samuel Dyer.[1] The ABCFM reprinted tracts that had been created by the LMS missionaries, including Milne's popular "Dialogues between Two Friends" (ABCFM 1837: 89–90; see Bays 1985a and 1985b). For a short time they also printed a newspaper that Karl Gütlzlaff had first produced, the *Eastern Western Monthly Magazine* (Gützlaff and Huang 1833–38). Historians consider this to be the first Chinese periodical published in China and a model for modern Chinese journalism (Zhang 2007: 39–41; see also Inouye 2016).

The ABCFM opened mission stations in Malacca, Penang, and Province Wellesley (Sng 2003: 37–8), and possibly John George Bausum worked with them in that town before moving to Penang. They also cooperated with Benjamin Peach Keasberry (1811–75), an LMS missionary who had been born in India and raised in Batavia, where he had studied printing and bookmaking with Medhurst from 1830 to 1834. Although he worked for the LMS, Keasberry was closely connected with American Board missionary David Abeel (1804–46), who described Keasberry as one of his "spiritual children" (Williamson 1848: 205).

Abeel had gone to Asia in 1830 with support from the American Seamen's Friend Society and worked as a chaplain to foreign sailors in Canton. He visited Southeast Asia and spent five months in Java, where he met Keasberry at the LMS mission in Batavia. In 1834, Abeel travelled in Europe and North America to raise support for evangelical work in Asia. As I discuss in

[1] The American missionaries reported employing 11 Chinese block-cutters, a copyist, and 8 or 10 printers. On behalf of Karl Gützlaff, these workers published 12 tracts and also cut blocks for his revised translation of the New Testament (ABCFM 1837: 89–90).

Chapter 3, after he circulated an "Appeal to Christian Ladies on behalf of Female Education in China", elite British women formed the nonsectarian Society for the Propagation of Female Education in the East (also known as the Female Education Society, or FES) to raise funds for girls' education in Asia and to recruit and train single female missionaries.

On this tour, Abeel also returned to the United States, where he recruited four missionaries for work in the Dutch East Indies: Elihu Doty, Elbert Nevius, William Youngblood, and Jacob Ennis, all graduates of the New Brunswick Seminary in New Jersey. Although they intended to work in Borneo, the colonial government required them to stay in Batavia for one year, and they went to Java with their wives and Mrs Nevius' sister (De Jong 1987: 15).

In 1935—not long after their arrival in Java—Keasberry entered the New Brunswick Theological Seminary himself. On completing his programme, he and his new wife accompanied Abeel to Canton. They had intended to start an undenominational mission, but they arrived in 1839 just as the Qing government was taking steps to ban the opium trade (Williamson 1848: 169, 179–203). When the First Opium War broke out, Mr and Mrs Keasberry went to Singapore, where he relaunched the Malay Mission on behalf of the LMS. LMS missionaries John and Alexander Stronach had begun working in Singapore with Hokkien speakers in 1838, and Samuel and Maria Dyer briefly joined them in 1842.

For a time Abeel made Singapore his base, but after the treaty ports were opened in 1842, he and the American Board missionaries moved to China.[2] The LMS had long disputed the legitimacy of their purchase of property that they regarded as rightfully theirs, and on their departure, the American Board missionaries returned the land and buildings to the LMS without any compensation (Haines 1962: 214).

In 1842, Maria Dyer received permission to start a school for homeless girls in Singapore in a small building in the LMS compound. But after her husband Samuel Dyer died in 1843, she moved to Penang as an independent missionary to resume running the girls' schools. The directors of the FES sent Arabella Grant to manage the school (see FES 1847). On her departure in 1853, Sophia Cooke (1814–95) took charge and ran it until her death.[3]

[2] After British troops occupied Kolongsoo (Gulangyu) Island near Amoy, Abeel moved there (Williamson 1848: 234). Not long after, the American Board missionaries working with Chinese immigrants in Southeast Asia relocated to the treaty ports.

[3] When the FES dissolved in 1899, the Church of England Zenana Missionary Society took over management of the Chinese Girls' School, which later became St Margaret's Primary School.

The LMS moved Penang's printing press to Singapore for Keasberry's use, and in 1843 he built a new Malay chapel with local subscriptions for Malay-speaking Straits Chinese. But after the LMS Board decided to cease paying his salary in 1844, he became independent (O'Sullivan 1984: 96). Keasberry and Munshi Abdullah continued to collaborate to publish works in Malay, including a new translation of *Pilgrim's Progress*, many tracts, and Abdullah's well-known memoir, *Hikayat Abdullah* (*Tale of Abdullah*) (Lovett vol. II 1899: 439; Band 1948 [1972]: 529; Van Der Putten 2006: 417).[4]

Presbyterian Christians in Singapore

In 1834—the year that Thomsen sold the LMS mission properties—Singapore's Scots Presbyterians cooperated with Anglicans to build a church.[5] They were major donors to the building fund, and the new church was named for Saint Andrew, Scotland's patron saint. But in 1838 the Anglican chaplain allowed Bishop Wilson of Calcutta to consecrate the building according to Church of England rites, which Scots Presbyterians (who came from Established, Free and United branches) regarded as a "breaking of faith" (Greer 1959: 15; Buckley 1902: 287–8).

The Presbyterians felt further betrayed when on a visit to Singapore in 1842, Bishop Wilson had objected to the church looking like a Town Hall or Assembly Room, and ordered a tall spire added to the building. But the builder neglected to add a lightning rod, and the church was twice struck by lightning. Having no alternative, the Scots Presbyterians used the Anglican Church until it was declared unsafe in 1852, then demolished (Buckley 1902: 292). Keasberry had been using the old LMS Mission Chapel as a shop for commercial and

---

[4] Keasberry published a deluxe edition of Abdullah's memoir *Hikayat Abdullah* (*Tale of Abdullah*) in 1849 on his lithographic missionary press (Van Der Putten 2006: 428), making it the first Malay literary text to be published commercially. Abdullah had developed a close working relationship with Alfred North, who came to Singapore to work for the ABCFM as a printer and who studied Malay with Abdullah (Van Der Putten 2006: 413). With encouragement from North, who recommended that he expand notes he took on a trip as an interpreter into a travelogue, in 1840 Abdullah undertook the task of writing a personal memoir that he completed in 1843 (Van Der Putten 2006: 417).

[5] Sir Stamford Raffles had allocated the land in 1822, but it was not built until the community raised sufficient funds.

government printing (Greer 1959: 20–2),[6] and the Anglicans and Presbyterians renovated it to use again as a church (Greer 1959: 31).

In 1856, Dr Thomas Guthrie, one of the leaders of the Free Church of Scotland and the founder of Edinburgh's Ragged Schools (est. 1847), helped Singapore's Presbyterians to recruit Rev. Thomas McKenzie Fraser (1822–85). Rev. Fraser immediately approached the LMS directors to ask if they would transfer title for the mission property to Singapore's Presbyterians (Grier 1959: 30–2). But in a negotiation similar to that which occured in Penang, the directors sought a higher price than the Singaporean Christians could pay.

Soon after Fraser's arrival, the Anglicans and Presbyterians together launched Saint Andrew's Church Mission in the compound of the Chinese Girls' School. Fraser recruited William Chalmers Burns' convert Tan See Boo (陈时武, 1833–84) as the new mission's Chinese catechist in 1856. But Tan objected to Anglican ritual practices, and after a year refused to work at the mission.[7]

In 1861 Fraser also resigned and moved to Australia to take a new position. But before he left, he requested that the Amoy Mission send a missionary to Singapore to work with Hokkien-speaking immigrants, and they chose Alexander Grant. In 1861 the new Anglican church was finally opened, and in 1862 the Society for the Propagation of the Gospel (SPG) sent Rev. Edward Sherman Venn, a graduate of Wadham College, Oxford, to Singapore as their missionary. The mission's subscribers, including the Governor and the Anglican Bishop, decided to put Saint Andrew's Church Mission under the management of the SPG, with Rev. Venn as its superintendent (Buckley 1902: 299–300). Although no reasons are given for his departure from Singapore, Grant likely objected to this arrangement. By the time Rev. Venn had arrived, he had moved to Penang and joined the Brethren movement as an independent missionary (see Chapter 6).

Bethesda Free Meeting House

Singapore's Bethesda Hall (Ang Mo Kio) has in its private archive a large bound *Assembly Record Book* that contemporary Brethren rely on for an understanding of their origins (see Finlay 1964; Lim 2006; Tong 2014; Wee 1996). The secretary entered the group's first Annual Report on 3 July 1865, recalling that

[6] Keasberry and his family founded and ran Malay-medium schools attended by the children of the Malay ruling class, and many of the schools' graduates occupied positions in government administration (Sng 2003: 52–5).

[7] According to one historian, when he resigned, Gan Kui replaced him (Greer 1959: 50–1).

a year earlier, seven evangelical Christians had met in rented rooms to celebrate the Lord's Table. They had no minister but trusted in the "Spirit of God" to lead them:[8]

> A few believers who had been led to see the duty as well as the privilege of assembling together on the first day of the week after the manner of the earliest churches planted by the apostles, viz., for the breaking of bread and Christian Worship, were meeting together privately for these religious exercises. Seeing however that such a gathering, profitable through it might be to their own souls, could not be a sufficient witness for Jesus in showing forth His deed to others, or give an opportunity of preaching the Gospel to those who have not already embraced it, and which is the bounden duty of every Christian Church—they were led to seek the opening of a place for public worship where these desiderata could be enjoyed. . . .
>
> Believing that the revealed and inspired Word of God is a sufficient rule not only for faith but practice, they have framed no written creed, trusting by the Spirit of God to be led into all truth and desiring to be known among men by no other name than Christians so that while one is of Paul and another of Appollos, they would desire to know the truth as it is in Jesus.

The report also noted that members of almost all evangelical churches had joined them.

When the LMS directors finally sold their Singapore property in 1866, the Presbyterians purchased it. Robinson and the members of his primitive church also obtained a parcel of land in 1876 (perhaps at the public auction of the LMS mission property?) and the next year built Bethesda Free Meeting House at 77 Bras Basah Road near North Bridge Road. They called the new gaslit meeting house Bethesda, a name that alludes to a pool in Jerusalem where Jesus performed a miraculous cure. But Brethren assume that this name connected them to Bethesda Chapel in Bristol, the assembly where George Müller preached. Bethesda's founders believed in the "revealed and inspired word of God" and invited evangelical Christians of all denominations to attend and speak at their meetings.

Contemporary Singaporean Brethren guess that Robinson came under George Müller's and Henry Craik's influence in Bristol before he left Britain (Tong 2014: 15–6). But Robinson was a Particular Baptist, and there is no evidence that Robinson and Müller ever met (see Lim 2004). He may not have met Müller, but Mr and Mrs Chapman sent copies of *The Revival* to Christians

---

[8] First Annual Report, *Assembly Record Book* (*ARB*), 3 July 1865: 21.

ALEXANDER GRANT OF SINGAPORE.
DISCOVERER OF THE CHURCH.

Figure 18 "Alexander Grant of Singapore, Discoverer of the Church". Illustration in Edward Kennaway Groves' *George Müller and His Successors* (1906).

in Singapore, and reported news about Singapore to the magazine's editors and to Müller (SKI 1860: 63).

Tan gave the Presbyterians his resignation just as they purchased the LMS mission property at the auction. Soon after the new Brethren meeting house was built, he brought his entire congregation to join the new Brethren assembly. Three months later, Mr and Mrs Grant moved from Penang to Singapore, where Grant became Bethesda's missionary. Gan Kui and A Tak also joined the Brethren, as did another Presbyterian minister, Robert Jeffrey (Greer 1959: 57). The Chinese Christians had obtained a plot of land adjacent to the new Brethren meeting house, and built a new gospel hall that the Brethren called the Free Chinese Christian Congregation.

The Singaporean Christians invited naval officers to their meetings, and the First Annual Report noted that "commanders of vessels in the Harbor have preached with considerable acceptance and have brought their crews to hear the Word". Two early members were William Burrow Haffenden, commander of the ship *Union*, who had been baptized in Penang in 1864; chief officer of the *Union* Edwin Buckley Tarn, who had been baptized in Exmouth, Devon in 1862; and Henry Morgan and Robert McBay, Second and Third Officers of the *Union*, both of whom were "buried with Him in Baptism" in Singapore. Their secretary wrote that after one captain preached every evening, their group grew to 17. But when the *Union* was dispatched to China, only three members remained at Bethesda.[9]

They also invited soldiers and sailors to tea meetings that offered refreshments and exhortations, and they distributed 2,000 tracts in their first year.[10] Miss O'Callaghan had been a popular revivalist in Penang, and the Bethesda records note that on an 1867 visit to Singapore, she held regular meetings for soldiers at the fort. When she gave a farewell address, she "preached with manifest power and blessing", and "some souls found some peace in believing".[11] A few months later, she and Mr Phillips organized a tea meeting for soldiers and sailors, and Bethesda's secretary reported: "the power of the Spirit accompanied the message of the Gospel. Two sailors were much affected and were spoken to after the meeting broke up."[12]

Miss O'Callaghan and the Curse of Eve

Soon after the LMS directors began to explore the possibility of selling their property in Penang, Miss O'Callaghan had moved to Malacca and opened a new girls' school. Müller listed her as a missionary, collected donations on

9 First Annual Report, *ARB*, 3 July 1865: 22–3.

10 Ibid.: 24.

11 *ARB*, 15 August 1867: 55.

12 In 1868, the *Assembly Record Book* recorded the conversion of two seamen, one officer, and two chief officers of vessels. *ARB*, 2 January 1868: 63.

her behalf, and published her reports on her new school and converts made.[13] Miss O'Callaghan reported her new school a success, and Müller described her Malay and Tamil converts. These included a Tamil man who worked as an interpreter for the Magistrate in Malacca and a Malay Muslim, Samat (SKI 1869: 79–80).

On the loss of the Penang mission property, Mr and Mrs Macdonald also moved to Singapore. As a female missionary, Miss O'Callaghan could not baptize her converts, and she brought both to Singapore, where Mr Macdonald baptized them. But Miss O'Callaghan abruptly left Malacca in 1870 after meeting a visiting Dutch evangelist.

Mr Grenwold gave public lectures in Singapore and distributed a tract from the Church of Jesus in South Africa. According to Bethesda's secretary:[14]

> The tract declared that the Lord Jesus had "come again," that the woman clothed with the sun is the Church of Jesus in South Africa brought forth by the spirit of life from God; through which it pleased the Lord to give anew to men the Gift of the Holy Ghost and he further won on their hearts by picturing a place of unalloyed happiness where "they look not after the manner of the world, they gather no more earthly treasures like the heathen, they trouble themselves no more and say like those who have no living God: what shall we eat, what shall we drink, and wherewith shall we be clothed? They do not any longer work in their fields with sorrow all the days of their lives, for these bring forth no more thorns and thistles, as of old; their wives who have become as fruitful vines by the sides of their houses, have no pains when they are with child, and they are delivered without sorrow; they are also no more servants of their husband's as if the punishment of the transgression of Eve still rested upon them." With these foolish notions, corrupt doctrines, and ready speech beguiled he them away from the way of truth. Giving them to understand that in these days the Bible is of itself insufficient but that God's will to man is manifest by revelation through the Church in South Africa. And Miss O'Callaghan is gone to the place they call the "City of God" as the messenger of the few who have been deceived and misled by this man Grenwold.

Not long after learning of the utopian Church in South Africa, which the tract described as a place of "unalloyed happiness" where the curse of Eve had been lifted, Miss O'Callaghan left Malacca for the "City of God".

---

13 The Tamil man had been involved in a denominational mission, hence was already Christian. *ARB*, 30 September 1868: 73.

14 *ARB*, 17 February 1870: 101.

Müller soon ceased collecting donations for Malacca, and he published no further reports from Miss O'Callaghan. By May of 1870, Bethesda had three preachers but only two believers attending Sunday service. Apparently Robinson was among those who had been convinced by Grenwold's teachings. He was only received back to communion after he acknowledged giving up these false doctrines.[15]

Tan See Boo and the Free Chinese Christian Congregation

Bethesda's Chinese evangelist Tan See Boo came to Singapore at the invitation of Rev. Fraser, who had contacted Carstairs Douglass in Amoy seeking a Chinese catechist who could work with Hokkien-speaking immigrants. Douglass recommended Tan, who had received formal theological training in Xiamen before going to Singapore in 1856. He travelled to Singapore together with a friend, Gan Kui (1821–1901), who so impressed Douglass that he gave him his Chinese Bible (Grier 1959: 50).[16]

Before Tan arrived, Sophie Cooke and the Anglican chaplain had established St Andrew's Church Mission in the Chinese Girls' School compound and had hired an Anglican catechist as Tan's coworker. The Presbyterian and Anglican ministers took turns baptizing the Chinese converts. But in a clash which recalls the situations of the Tamil catechists in India, and John George Bausum in Penang, Tan objected to Anglican ritual practices, and after a year refused to work at the mission. Tan continued to work with the Presbyterian Church and also formed a partnership with Keasberry.[17]

In 1864, Rev. Swanson visited from Amoy and proposed that the Chinese Presbyterians form a congregation with elders and deacons. He ordained Tan See Boo and A Tak, who had been converted in Penang, as elders (Grier 1959: 55).[18] But just as the Presbyterians purchased the LMS mission property through an auction, Tan submitted his resignation and became independent. Grant later recalled that Tan had already decided

---

15 *ARB*, 31 July 1870: 105. I could not locate any information about the Church of Jesus in South Africa.

16 Grant, Samarang, 26 June 1883, *ME* No. 141: 122. In 1883 Grant gave Gan Kui's age as 62.

17 Tan and Keasberry also cooperated to found the church that later became Glory Presbyterian Church (Sng 2003: 53–4).

18 In the early 1860s, Tan had returned to Xiamen, hoping to study medicine and be ordained, but his requests were rejected (White 2017: 102).

to become independent and live by faith in 1862 because he could not rely on the Presbyterians to pay his salary.[19]

Singapore's Chinese Christians chose to build their own church just as the LMS sold its properties in Singapore and was taking steps to sell its Penang properties. In both cities, the LMS had not acknowledged the claims of local Christians that it was their donations and efforts which had built these properties. Aware of the risks in vesting ownership in a denominational missionary agency, they might well have seen an advantage in using their funds to build an autonomous local church.

Tan's Chinese congregation had held union prayer meetings every Friday morning for three years and four months before buying land to build their gospel hall (*Fuyin Tang* 福音堂; Southern Min: *Hok Im Tng*) in 1867.[20] Tan donated a large portion of the funds, drawing on income from the sale of medicine to opium addicts, and raising funds from the sale of his wife's jewellery, a detail that recalls George Müller's appeals to wealthy British Christians to sacrifice their jewels to support philanthropic work.[21] The Brethren took up a collection for the Free Chinese Christian Congregation and gave them use of Bethesda while they were waiting for their gospel hall to be built.[22] They also received a £9 donation from Chinese Christians in Batavia.[23]

19 Grant reported that: "In 1862 he left the denomination he had been connected with, *not* for conscientious reasons, but owing to the fact of the treasurer being unable to pay his usual salary, on which he determined to renounce payment for doing gospel work, and, as he said, 'show all Singapore that there was a God'. From that time various traditional views and practices were by degrees given up, and it became the aim of his life to follow the word of God only." Grant, Singapore, 15 December 1883, *ME* No. 146 (February 1884): 25–6.

20 Editorial preface to letter from Tan See Boo, Singapore, 15 October 1872, *ME* (March 1873): 38–9. The Brethren Free Meeting House and the new Chinese Gospel Hall were both close to the old LMS mission, which suggests that they may have obtained parcels of the LMS mission property. According to one source, the Presbyterian mission leased them a 5,000 square foot compound on land that adjoined Bethesda Chapel for $60; since the Presbyterians had purchased the LMS mission property the previous year and did not build on it themselves, this is plausible (Lee 2010).

21 Editorial preface, Tan See Boo, Singapore, 15 October 1872, *ME* No. 15 (March 1873): 38–9.

22 *ARB*, 20 January 1867: 45. The Chinese gospel hall existed until it was bombed in 1941. Tan's grandson sold the land in 1945 and used the proceeds to build a new Chinese gospel hall in Geylang (Lee 2010).

23 Gan Kui and A Tak also joined the new church (Greer 1959: 57).

Tan was the first Asian to be received into fellowship at Bethesda, and the *Assembly Record Book* described his baptism together with five other Chinese converts:[24]

> Tan See Boo, a Chinese catechist who has been laboring in Singapore for ten years past in connection with the Presbyterian mission, but about eight months since resigned his connection with them, resolving to look alone to God for daily bread, and has since been successfully engaged in building up a church of Chinese Christians, and preaching the Gospel to the heathens, was with five others of his countrymen baptized by our brother Chapman. The meeting was conducted in the English, Chinese, and Malay Languages.
>
> So far as known these were the first converts from heathenism ever scripturally baptized in these Settlements.

Tan See Boo was a convert from Presbyterianism, not "heathenism", and many of the Brethren's new members in the Straits Settlements were already Christians when they joined. Nonetheless, if they had been baptized with a ritual that the Brethren regarded as unscriptural, the Brethren baptized them again, fully immersing them in the sea, or in a stream or river.

Only a week after his own baptism, Tan baptized another "Chinese convert from heathenism" and John Chapman, visiting from Penang, baptized Major Hailes. The Chinese and European Christians sometimes joined together for Sunday worship at Bethesda, "prayer, praise and exhortation being rendered both in English, Chinese and Malay". But some of Bethesda's members complained that the long services were tiring. All agreed that it would be better to meet for the breaking of bread ceremony only on the first Sunday of every month.[25]

In 1869 Tan was the first of a small number of Chinese evangelists in Singapore and Penang to receive support from Brethren in Britain. In a letter published in the Scriptural Knowledge Institution's annual report for 1870, Tan thanked George Müller for a £5 donation, and also gave thanks for Müller's love and to God, "our Heavenly Father who condescends to care for us, hearing my prayer, graciously giving this from places where I have not been and persons whom I do not know, from afar" (SKI 1870: 65).

24 *ARB*, 8 May 1867: 51. Although the *ARB* reports that he had resigned only eight months earlier, Grant gave 1862 as the date on which Tan See Boo adopted Brethren principles, which suggests that he continued to work for the Presbyterian mission even as he changed his practices and viewpoints.

25 *ARB*, 5 July 1868: 67; 8 April 1874: 149.

In 1873, the editors of *The Missionary Echo* also published a letter from Tan, noting in a prefatory comment that they were "glad to make known something of native labourers in the gospel, as upon them, under God, the evangelizing of their countrymen so much depends". The editors described Tan's conversion by Burns in Pechuia, China, stressing that he led an indigenous gospel hall in Singapore that had been built with local donations.[26] Tan's letter described fundraising for repairs to the Chinese gospel hall and closed with the wish: "May the winds of Pentecost blow there and here."[27] The letter is elegantly composed; at the end of his next published letter, his 13-year-old son also sent greetings, revealing himself to be the letter's author.[28] This letter may be the first English-language publication of Tan Teck Soon (1859–1922), who as an adult became an influential reformer and author.[29]

Evangelical Projects in Singapore

When *The Missionary Echo* was launched in January 1872, Macdonald and Grant met and decided to return to England so that they could meet with the editors and explain to them details of the work in the Straits.[30] The Grants went in 1873, and remained in Europe for five years. For at least three years, they lived in Tottenham North, London and attended Brook Street Chapel, the Brethren assembly founded by members of the Howard family.[31]

---

[26] Editor's Introduction, Tan, Singapore, 15 October 1872, *ME* No. 15 (March 1873): 38–9.

[27] Tan, Singapore, 15 October 1872, *ME* No. 15 (March 1873): 39.

[28] Tan, Singapore, May 7 1873, *ME* No. 20 (August 1873): 111–2.

[29] Tan married a pupil in the Chinese Girls' School, and their eldest son Tan Teck Soon (1859–1922) was born in Singapore. Tan Teck Soon attended the elite Raffles Institute, then went to China for his university education, studying at the Anglo-Chinese College in Amoy. He returned to Singapore where he worked in business and publishing ventures, and in 1883 was a founding member of the elite Straits Philosophical Society, only one of two non-Western members (Doran 2006; Hee 2009).

[30] Macdonald, Penang and Singapore, 28 December 1871–26 January 1872, *ME* No. 5 (May 1872): 60.

[31] In 1901, the editors of *Echoes of Service* reported that for many years Mrs Robert Howard gave hospitality to missionaries in Tottenham, and some missionaries visiting England were provided with a temporary furnished home at 7, Bruce Grove, Tottenham. When Mr and Mrs Macdonald visited in 1901, they lived there for free (Miscellaneous, "Temporary Home for Missionaries", *ES* No. 491 (December 1901 Pt. 1): 460. After the Grants returned to London in 1885, he gave as his address 6, Tottenham Terrace. Grant, Tottenham, n.d. *ES* No. 173 (May 1886): 8.

In 1878, the Grants returned to the Straits Settlements, and he worked in Singapore until his retirement in 1885.[32] In a letter written in Tottenham, Grant recalled the everyday activities of the Singapore mission. One day they did outreach to the small Jewish population and tracting on shipboard; another day they attended to the English—"the sick, the sorrowing, the backsliding, those who like to see you come in", and also the hundred of soldiers in the barracks and at the fort. On yet another day they visited Chinese Christians, including some in the countryside, and paid visits to sick people in hospital. Finally, they had meetings in their gospel hall, including English worship, gospel preaching, prayer meetings and Bible readings.

Grant noted that they all spoke Malay, and that on Friday when Malays gathered at the mosque, the missionaries were there to address them. Grant added that they sometimes had a day of rest when they went to the seaside to bathe. Grant observed that the city was "frequented by busy European and Asiatic traders" who were in "hot haste" to make money.[33]

Like London, Singapore was a crowded, multi-ethnic city, and Grant's approach to his work in the years between 1878–85 appears to have been modelled on that of the London City Mission (LCM), an undenominational mission that David Naismith had founded in 1835. Brethren philanthropist John Eliot Howard was their "liberal supporter" and proposed the London City Mission as a model for interdenominational evangelical cooperation. His involvement appears to have been both financial and personal: the author of his obituary commented that a striking feature of his funeral was the presence at the cemetery of both elite mourners, including the Lord Mayor of London and prominent scientists, and poor people who had been "recipients of Mr. Howard's bounty" (Obituary 1884).

The LCM's projects included providing education to youth in so-called "ragged schools", prison and hospital visitation, and outreach to minority populations, including Irish Catholics, Jews, the Welsh, Italians, Gypsies, and Asians. The LCM lay workers also engaged in specialized ministries to occupational groups, including soldiers, sailors, police, dock workers and prostitutes. Finally their workers sometimes focused on specific locations, including public houses, coffee shops, hospitals, and workhouses (Lewis 1986: 205). Even though London's working class proved largely indifferent to the pan-evangelical effort to convert them from "heathenism", historian Donald M.

[32] Grant developed neuralgia and he and his family returned to London together with Hocquard's two daughters. They returned to Tottenham. Misc., Grant, Singapore, 3 June 1885, *ES* No. 164 (August 1885): 128.

[33] Grant, "Work in Singapore", Tottenham, n.d. *ES* No. 173 (May 1886): 76–8.

Figure 19 Missionary Helps postcard describing Jewish history and God's covenant with the "Hebrew race", representing their return to Palestine in 1920 as reclaiming the "land of promise". The postcard offered a historical account of the Jewish diaspora together with Biblical prophecies regarding Jesus' return and its connection to Israel's restoration, but does not reference John Nelson Darby's premillenial dispensational theology or the rapture. Private collection of author.

Lewis concludes that the size of the urban mission, its superb organization, and its duration made it an important religious crusade to the Victorian working class (Lewis 1986: 276).

Perhaps influenced by LCM work with the Jewish enclave in the crowded impoverished East End, in 1878 Grant announced that he was drawn to do work with Singapore's Jewish population.[34] As Grant described it, he met with an "intelligent Jew" who could speak Malay and Hebrew, and read him Isaiah Chapter 53. This is a well-known Old Testament passage that Christians interpret as prophesizing that Jesus will sacrifice himself for the absolution of human sins. He reported that the man listened to the news that he had been saved with "surprise".[35]

Although he described Singapore's Jewish community as "haunting the slums with the natives", the small Jewish communities in Singapore and Penang also included well-to-do traders and property owners whose families had immigrated from Baghdad to India in the 19th century. The Indian Jewish diaspora, who are sometimes called Mizrahi or "Eastern" Jews, included the Sassoon family, the so-called Rothschilds of the East, who grew wealthy in the textile and opium trade and extended their investments throughout Asia (Roland 2017). When the Sassoons established business interests in Singapore in 1840, a small number of Baghdad Jews moved there, building a synagogue large enough for 40 worshippers that they rebuilt in 1878.[36] Grant may have been drawn to the Jewish community, but he reported no conversions from his outreach efforts.

Grant and his Chinese coworkers also visited the jails, both English and native. The Superintendent of the Singapore prison intended that "all who pass through his hands should hear the Gospel", and the wardens, who were British soldiers, also came to Grant's house for a weekly Scripture reading (SKI 1878: 51). Grant described an exhortation of the Chinese prisoners in which he claimed that all peoples anticipated a great saviour who would rescue them:[37]

---

[34] As I discuss in Chapter 10, after his retirement to London in 1885, Grant's daughter Lucy taught Jewish children in a Sabbath school in London and studied Yiddish in Prussian Poland.

[35] Grant, Singapore, 10 April 1878, *ME* No. 78 (June 1878): 98. Grant requested that people pray for the Jews of Singapore as "the remnant according to the election of grace". Grant later described Singapore's Jewish population as "precious sons of Zion, comparable to fine gold". Grant, Tottenham, n.d. *ES* No. 173 (May 1886): 77.

[36] "History", website of the Jewish Welfare Board, http://www.singaporejews.com/history.html; "Jewish Community of Singapore", http://www.bh.org.il/jewish-community-singapore/ [accessed 28 May 2016].

[37] Grant, Singapore, 8 December 1880, *ME* No. 110 (February 1881): 27.

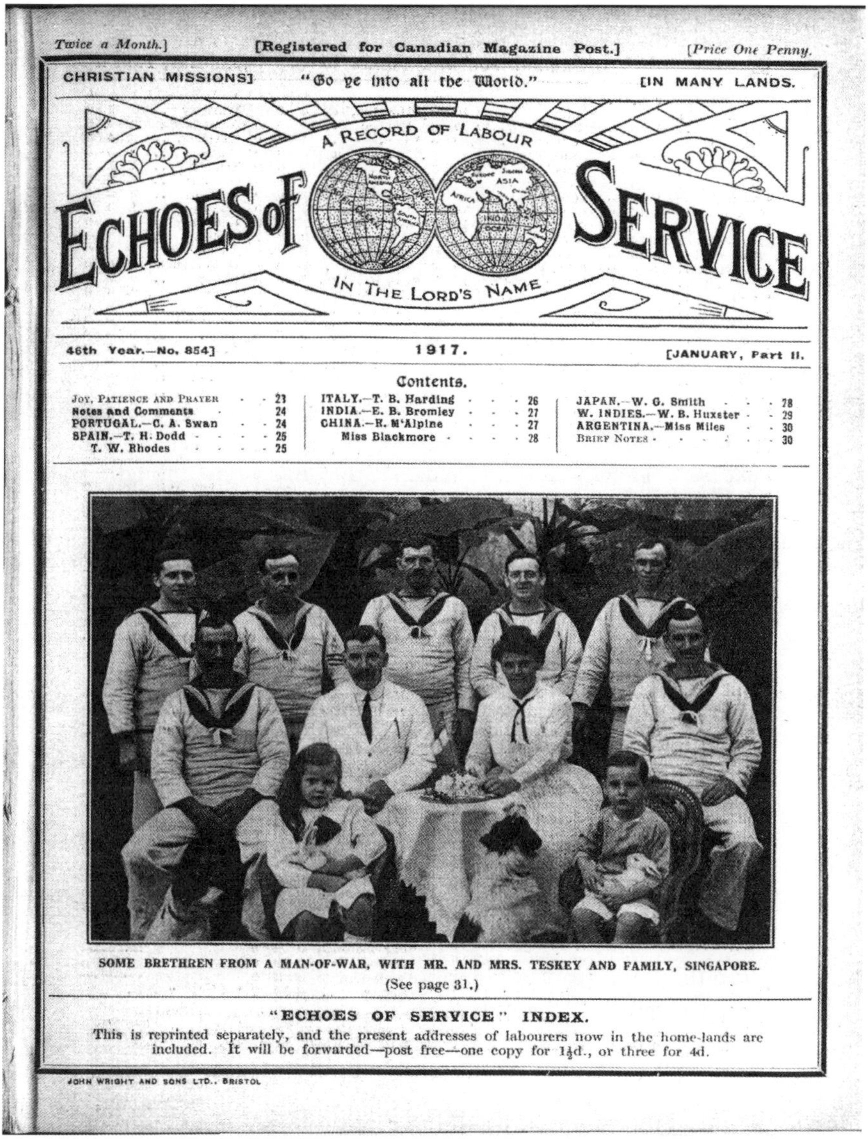

Twice a Month.] [Registered for Canadian Magazine Post.] [*Price One Penny.*

CHRISTIAN MISSIONS] "Go ye into all the World." [IN MANY LANDS.

A RECORD OF LABOUR

ECHOES of SERVICE

IN THE LORD'S NAME

46th Year.—No. 854] 1917. [JANUARY, Part II.

Contents.

SOME BRETHREN FROM A MAN-OF-WAR, WITH MR. AND MRS. TESKEY AND FAMILY, SINGAPORE.

(See page 31.)

"ECHOES OF SERVICE" INDEX.

This is reprinted separately, and the present addresses of labourers now in the home-lands are included. It will be forwarded—post free—one copy for 1½d., or three for 4d.

JOHN WRIGHT AND SONS LTD., BRISTOL

Figure 20 Photograph of British sailors from a Man-of-War with missionaries in Singapore. Teskey, Singapore, n.d., *ES* No. 854 (January Part II 1917): 21.

> On Lord's-day, in the jail, I spoke to about seventy-five prisoners, showing how as soon as man sinned God revealed His purpose or mercy, which gave rise, as among other nations, so among the Chinese, to an expectation of a great Deliverer. Whether a sage, an emperor, a lawgiver, or a warrior, they know not. But the first promise showed He would be a suffering deliverer. . . . Then See Boo, the Chinese preacher, rose and asked them how many of those present believed this, when four or five decidedly said they did.

As I discuss in Chapter 9, the Brethren missionaries frequently reported the conversion of prisoners both before and after they left prison.

Outreach to sailors and soldiers was also part of the everyday practices of the Open Brethren missionaries in Singapore. They often visited the ships in harbour to distribute tracts and Scriptures, and invited sailors to visit them at their Mission Houses. When sailors and their commanders were baptized in Singapore, the Brethren gave them letters of commendation to take with them to their next port. These letters attested that they had been "brought into the liberty of the Gospel, through the preaching of the word" in Singapore and had been baptized.[38]

Singapore's port was busy, and the missionaries visited as many as three ships every morning. Singapore also had a population of sailors in need, and in 1882, Sophie Cooke and Philip Hocquard started a Sailors' Rest in South Bridge road to offer them material assistance and weekly Bible classes (Sng 2003: 67). In the first year, Hocquard reported that 6,654 sailors had visited them (SKI 1884: 46–7).[39]

Many of the ships they visited were in transit from or to battlefields. Hocquard had found Hokkien difficult to master but spoke French fluently, and in 1884 received a grant of 3,500 French scripture portions from the British and Foreign Bible Society to distribute to French soldiers and sailors. He had hoped to go to Tonkin to distribute these tracts on the return journey from Fujian (where he had gone to try to learn Hokkien), but did not have sufficient funding.[40] Instead he distributed them on French transport boats as they passed through Singapore en route to Tonkin, where they were to fight the Franco-Chinese War (1884–85), the outcome of which the French assumed sovereignty over Vietnam. Although the soldiers and sailors were almost certainly Catholic, the French military authorities allowed him to board their ships to distribute scriptures, and by 1885 he had given out 4,550

---

38 *ARB*, 5 January 1868: 64.

39 Grant, Singapore, 17 August 1882, *ME* No. 130 (October 1882): 140.

40 Hocquard, Amoy, 28 April 1884, *ME* No. 151 (July 1884): 114.

portions.[41] Later he visited French soldiers in hospital when they returned from battle injured.

In doing outreach to members of the military, the Brethren did not confront power, and indeed supported Britain's sailors and soldiers. Brethren founder Anthony Norris Groves was a pacifist, and for that reason could not endorse the Anglican 39 Articles and become an ordained Anglican missionary. Although the Open Brethren did not openly promote pacifism (and Macdonald enthusiastically endorsed British military actions in Perak), some prominent military and naval officers resigned from their commissions after joining the Brethren movement (Pickering 1918; Stunt 2014; Wilson 2003: 85).

Hocquard focused on outreach to European soldiers and sailors, but Grant was Bethesda's missionary, and his duties included work with Hokkien speakers. Grant had studied Amoy Hokkien while still working with the Presbyterian Church in Fujian and was a fluent speaker of the language. He worked with Chinese partners and frequently reported on their travels in his letters to the editors of *Echoes*. As Grant's letters show, Hokkien-speaking immigrants to Dutch Indonesia had formed local churches independent of European control. To his Chinese coworkers and their itinerant work I now turn.

Visiting Every City: Batavia and Depok

As travel between Fujian and Southeast Asia became more efficient and affordable, Fujian Chinese emigrated in increasing numbers to Singapore, Penang, the Philippines, and the Dutch East Indies (Pitcher 1893: 37; White 2017). By the latter part of the 19th century, locally-led Chinese churches existed wherever Chinese had migrated, from Burma and Thailand to Borneo and Java. Grant and the Chinese evangelists in Singapore and Penang exchanged letters with Chinese Christians who lived throughout Southeast Asia, and from time to time travelled to visit them.

Grant often travelled in the region with Chinese partners, including Tan See Boo and Gan Kui, who travelled with Tan to Singapore in 1856 before moving to Java. Presbyterian historian Rev. Robert Greer claimed that Gan Kui worked at Saint Andrew's Church Mission in 1857 and left the Presbyterian Church for the Brethren movement in 1867 (Greer 1959: 50–1, 57). But Greer appeared to be unaware that in the intervening decade, Gan Kui had worked in Java.

---

[41] Hocquard, Singapore, 23 February 1885, *ME* No. 161 (May 1885): 75.

Similarly, historians of Christianity in Indonesia describe Gan Kui's work in Java with little awareness of his Singapore connections. As they describe it, in 1856 a Dutch lay Christian Frederik Lodewijk Anthing (1818–83) recruited Gan Kui from Amoy to work with Hokkien Chinese in Batavia (Aritonang and Steenbrink 2008: 908; End 1999: 24). They make no mention of his relationship with Tan or his work with Saint Andrew's Church Mission, noting only that he moved to Singapore in 1873 (Aritonang and Steenbrink 2008: 908).

In 1851, Anthing had established the Society of Internal and External Mission (*Genootschap voor In- en Uitwendige Zending* [GIUZ]), which like the Chinese Union and the Chinese Evangelization Society, proposed that indigenous Christian workers not missionaries should spread Christianity. Anthing trained a number of Javanese to work as evangelists and employed Gan Kui to work with Chinese immigrants. Between 1856 and 1868, Gan Kui travelled extensively in Java doing itinerant evangelism, and in 1868 his first 12 converts were baptized (Aritonang and Steenbrink 2008: 908).

In 1874, wealthy businessman Gouw Kho and his wife, who had studied in the Singapore Chinese Girls' School and had been converted by Grant, joined a small Chinese congregation in Batavia. In 1884 he donated four houses on Patekoan Street in Batavia to the church.[42] Today, Gan Kui and the Gouw family are regarded as founders of this congregation, which some describe as the oldest Chinese Christian church in Jakarta (Aritonang and Steenbrink 2008: 908, 915). Grant and Tan both knew and corresponded with members of this church and with Gan Kui while he worked in Java.[43]

Like Penang and Singapore, Batavia had a long history of Christian evangelization. From 1811 to 1818, Java was under British control, and in 1814 the London Missionary Society sent one Dutch and two German missionaries to open a mission in Batavia, which was the administrative capital for the Dutch East Indies. Governor Stamford Raffles encouraged Morrison and Milne to consider Batavia as the site for the Ultra-Ganges Mission, but they chose Malacca because it had better communications (Lovett 1899 vol. II: 437–8).

Even after the Anglo-Dutch treaty of 1814 required that the East India Company return Java to Dutch control, the LMS mission continued in Batavia. From 1822 until the opening of the treaty ports, missionary and Sinologist Walter Medhurst worked among Chinese and Indonesians

[42] *Patekoan* is Southern Min for Eight Teapots, referring to a practice of offering free hospitality to passers-by.

[43] They also credit Gan Kui with helping found a Chinese church in Probolinggo in Central Java (Aritonang and Steenbrink 2008: 908).

and completed Bible translations, and Keasberry studied printing and bookmaking with him. When the Chinese Christians built a new gospel hall next to Bethesda in 1867, Chinese Christians in Batavia sent them a donation. Could an independent Chinese church with roots in the Batavia LMS mission have persisted?[44]

In 1870, Grant and Robert Jeffrey, a Scots Presbyterian minister who had joined Bethesda, visited the Chinese Gospel Hall in Batavia and went to Semarang, where they preached to Chinese Christians and to Malay-speaking Javanese.[45] Grant and Jeffrey also went to Depok because they had heard that there was a community of Christians there, formed when a well-to-do Dutchman had left his estate to his former servants on condition that they became Christian.[46]

The Christians in Depok were descendants of the former slaves of Cornelis Chastelein (1657–1714). They were originally from Bali and Sulawesi, and had been baptized between 1696 and 1713. Chastelein opposed slavery, and converted them to Christianity in order to free them, deeding land to them in his will (Aritonang and Steenbrink 2008: 650). In 1870, Grant reported that over 100 persons gathered together to study *Pilgrim's Progress* and the sermons of Spurgeon. His widow recalled that when he and Jeffrey taught them, "The field was white to harvest, and they drank in the Scriptures with great avidity and joy."[47]

---

[44] Robert Hefner explains the lack of success of Christian missions in Indonesia in light of the fact that "mission overseers forbade natives from forming their own church councils or synods", which remained in European hands (Hefner 2017: 92). No doubt this was true for denominational missions, but by the 1860s independent Asian-led churches existed in Java.

[45] "Visiting the Churches: Between Java and Singapore", Grant, 1 September 1902, *ES* No. 513 (November 1902 Pt. 1): 411. Mr Jeffrey, like Grant, was an ordained Presbyterian minister. He left the Scots Church and joined Bethesda, and was often listed as one of the preachers in the Singapore Assembly Records Book.

[46] Grant mentioned that when he addressed Malay speakers in Singapore while Keasberry was ill, there had "not yet been any such manifestation of blessing as there was in Java". He reported that a "Chinese brother" who worked as an evangelist in Batavia (probably Gan Kui) and two Chinese Christians had invited him to return, claiming that interest in Christian teachings was increasing. He commented that although a Presbyterian ("Mr. K.") and an evangelical minister lived in Batavia, neither of them could speak Chinese (SKI 1871: 57).

[47] "Our Departed Brother Alexander Grant", Lucy A. Grant, n.d., *ES* No. 786 (March 1914 Pt. II): 106. Mrs. Grant described the 1870 visit to Depok in his obituary.

Tan See Boo as Mediator and Teacher

In 1872, Gan Kui and Ang Kang Kin, who was then in charge of the Penang Mission, both returned to Amoy, drawn by news of a revival. Tan remained in Singapore, where he was supervising renovation work to the Chinese Gospel Hall, and the Chinese Christians in Batavia wrote to him to ask for help in resolving a conflict. Grant was in London, and Tan wrote him a long letter reporting on his trip. At that time, the Christians in Batavia had two meetings places—a home and the gospel house (*Hok-Im-Koan*) in Pinang-town. They had 30 members, but Tan observed that they were weak since Brethren were "deficient in feeding them with the word of the Lord".[48]

As a pastor, Tan mediated a dispute that had arisen when an individual felt slighted when another member did not bring two visitors from Amoy to see him. By the time Tan arrived, Low Bun Chiang—the person at the centre of the controversy—"had fallen back into the world" and was threatening to leave the church. Although he was pessimistic about the outcome of his intervention, on his return to Singapore Tan received a letter from Low reporting that he had been revived.

The Chinese Christians in Java also expected Tan to teach them. After he spent the afternoon with Mr R. and his family and answered questions, he reported that he felt his heart empty. But on his way home,

> the Holy Spirit of the Lord filled me with fresh teaching on the subject of the Christian's holiness. These three things especially: 1st. He cleanses the *sinner* with the blood of the Lord Jesus. (Heb. ix. 14, 15) 2nd. He cleanses His *branches* clear of man's wisdom, the elements of man, with His word of truth. (John xv. 3, 4.) 3rd. He cleanses the Christian from the lusts of the flesh and of the world with His *glory*. (I John iii. 2, 3.) At that time I thanked the Lord much for not leaving me in my emptiness, teaching me on the road with His word...

On his return to the place he was staying, Tan repeated this to his host Lim Cheng Seng, who liked it so much that he wrote it down.

The identification of cleansing with holiness would have resonated with speakers of Southern Min. The word for 'pure' in Hokkien is *chhengkhi* (*qingjie* 清潔), which refers to both cleanliness and purity. Purity is a desirable religious condition that practitioners of Chinese religions achieve by following a vegetarian diet and abstaining from sex, ascetic practices that the Christians

---

[48] Letter from Tan to Grant, Singapore, 16 August, 1873. *ME* No. 24 (December 1873): 171–2.

taught were useless in the absence of salvation through Christ's sacrificial death and resurrection.

Those practising popular religion contrast purity with impurity (Southern Min: *lasam*), and count as impure blood, including menstrual blood and the blood of childbirth, and contact with death. For a Southern Min listener, Tan's teaching almost certainly would have highlighted the apparent paradox of Christ's blood and death being not polluting but cleansing. This letter shows that Tan had studied the Chinese translation of the New Testament and knew it well, and that the Chinese Christians looked to him for instruction.

The Restored Apostolic Mission Church and the Winds of Doctrine

The Grant family returned to Singapore in 1878, and the next year Grant reported that Gan Kui had been with them for some time. When Gan accepted an invitation to visit a small group of Chinese Christians from Swatow [Shantou] living in Pontianak, Borneo, members of the Chinese and English assemblies in Singapore collected $13 and $14.30 to pay for his travel costs. No missionary had lived in Pontianak since Elihu Doty had moved to Amoy in 1844, and Grant observed that "this seems a work entirely through native agency". He thought this church had existed for 30 years or more, which suggests that it had started not long after the American Board mission moved to China.[49]

On the way to Pontianak, Gan Kui baptized someone in Billiton (now Belitung), who then moved to Deli on the East Coast of Sumatra. Grant commented, "We cannot but rejoice with trembling over these half-taught wandering persons, destitute of opportunity of hearing further" (SKI 1880: 45).[50]

The Chinese Christians in Batavia again asked the Brethren in Singapore for help in 1883, perplexed by the introduction of new practices from Europe. Grant waited for Gan Kui to return from China so that they could travel there together. Grant discovered that Anthing, the Dutch judge who had recruited Gan Kui to Java, was now an "apostle" of a denomination that he had joined while visiting Europe. In a preface to Grant's letter, the editor of *Echoes* noted that "It is instructive to observe how far winds of doctrine reach."[51]

---

49 Grant, Singapore, 4 December 1878, *ME* No. 86 (February 1879): 23.

50 The Open Brethren missionaries also made repeated visits to Sumatra, hoping to encourage isolated Christians to form primitive churches, but apparently with no success.

51 Grant, Semarang, 26 June 1883, *ME* No. 141 (September 1883): 122.

Anthing had been born in Batavia of a Dutch Lutheran father and a mother of German ancestry (perhaps Eurasian), and was educated in the Netherlands. As noted above, in the 1850s he became involved in doing evangelical outreach to indigenous populations in the area of Batavia, and he recruited Gan Kui to work with immigrants from Amoy. He retired in 1870, and expended all his resources in support of mission work. He turned to the Hersteld Apostolische Zendingkerk (Restored Apostolic Mission Church) for funding, and in 1879 they ordained him as Apostle for the East Indies. Anthing also married a Dutch woman who was a member of this church (End 1999: 24; Aritonang and Steenbrink 2008: 651).

The Restored Apostolic Mission Church had its origins in the Catholic Apostolic movement that Edward Irving had launched in Britain around 1831. The movement had spread to Germany, but disagreement over the calling of new apostles resulted in German members deciding to separate from the British branch of the movement. Like the Brethren, they adopted premillennial theology, teaching that their members would become Christ's bride when Jesus returned.[52]

Anthing and his new wife, who claimed to have the "gift of prophecy", together sought to spread this movement among the Christians in Java, naming prophets and apostles among Anthing's friends. As Grant described their meetings:[53]

> The way Mr. A[nthing]—has proceeded is this. His wife stands up, and in an excited manner, in language resembling that of the prophets of Israel, delivers a few sentences in Dutch, which are then written down and translated. On such occasions she names someone for a special office. Mr. A— then lays his hands on that person, and he is said to receive the Holy Ghost. In this way a Javanese has been appointed apostle; and a Java-born Chinese, the son of a Christian recently departed, to be a priest.

With the exception of Gouw Kho and his wife, the local Christians apparently accepted these new practices.[54]

Grant visited Anthing, and three times spent two or three hours conversing with him, "reasoning with him out of the Scriptures". Since Grant did not

---

[52] "New Apostolic Church International: About the NAC", http://www.nak.org/en/about-the-nac/ [accessed 8 October 2016].

[53] Grant, Samarang, 26 June 1883, *ME* No. 141 (September 1883): 123–4.

[54] Although *Echoes* gave the name of the Chinese who opposed the new teachings as "Koah", I am confident that this individual was Gouw Kho, whose name they also spelled as Gao Ko.

speak Dutch, Anthing read him some of the prophecies in Malay. Grant asked him how he had shown the signs of apostleship, and Anthing explained that he "was called by Prophecy", and that a Dutch apostle "who had at first refused him, was constrained to lay hands on him". Grant closed his letter noting that Mr Anthing planned to return to Europe to try to unite the English and continental branches of his denomination, adding that the Europeans had broken off with the English since "they did not see why the twelve Apostles should be Englishmen". He was certain that he had not convinced him of the error of claiming to be an apostle with the gift of prophecy.[55]

Several months later, Mr Grant asked for help in supplying the Christians in Batavia, with books and periodicals. On returning home from his gospel work, Grant added, Mr Anthing had fallen as he stepped off a steam tram, and been crushed beneath the wheels, dying the same night. When Grant reported Anthing's "striking and solemn" death, he hinted that God had taken him to end his "mistaken efforts for Java".[56]

Gan Kui continued to circulate between Singapore, Java, and China. In Singapore, Gan Kui worked as a street evangelist. Hocquard had not been successful in his attempt to learn Hokkien in the Straits Settlements, and Gan Kui went with him to China as his host and language teacher in 1884.[57] The next year, Gan Kui returned to Java,[58] but when W.D. Ashdown went to Chioh-be to learn Hokkien a few years later, Gan Kui visited him.[59] He was living about 10 miles from Chioh-be and had meetings in his house, and a former Penang evangelist, Sun Liong, worked as a doctor in a nearby city.[60] William

---

[55] Grant, Semarang, 26 June 1883, *ME* No. 141 (September 1883):123–4.

[56] Grant, Singapore, 29 October 1883, *ME* No. 145 (January 1884): 15. Almost 20 years later, Grant reported that Christians in Java continue to be confused by "apostasy". "Visiting the Churches: Between Java and Singapore", Grant, 1 September 1902, *ES* No. 513 (November 1902 Pt. 1): 411.

[57] Grant, Singapore, 29 October 1883, *ME* No. 145 (January 1884): 15. They first went to the American Reformed Mission Gospel Hall, and from there to Chang-chiu (Zhangzhou), where the English Presbyterians had opened a mission station in 1861. Mary Hocquard, Singapore, 4 December 1883 *ME* No. 146 (February 1884): 27; Hocquard, Amoy, n.d., *ME* No. 146 (February 1884): 27.

[58] Grant, Singapore, 13 April 1885, *ES* No. 162 (June 1885): 92–3. When Grant went out himself to do street evangelism, he encountered Gan Kui "discoursing on the day of Christ from 2 Thes. ii.".

[59] In 1891, Alf Green also stayed in Chioh-be to study Hokkien in temporarily vacant rooms that the American Reformed Mission allowed him to use. Green, S.S. Peninsular, near Singapore, 24 August 1891, *ES* No. 249 (November 1891 Pt. 1): 264.

[60] Green, Thaipeng, 6 September 1893, *ES* No. 297 (November. 1893 Pt. 1): 248.

Chalmers Burns had preached in Chioh-be 30 years earlier, and people still recalled Grant, but no foreign missionary worked there.[61]

Gan Kui returned again to Malaya and spent almost a year working in the Taiping Gospel Hall, where he gave Edgar Hill Hokkien lessons, made almost daily visits to the prison, and taught in the Chinese assembly.[62] While in Taiping he exhorted a prisoner to seek salvation through faith. No letters from Gan Kui were published, and his work was rarely described, but Alf Green reported this encounter:[63]

> One man in the prison here has given us joy by a great feat of memory. One day Gan-Kui asked him to read a little from John's Gospel, chapter xii, as he knows the characters well. We were surprised when he gave his book to another man and *repeated* the portion *by heart*. He told us he had learnt the first *eighteen chapters*, that Gospel having been given him by us some twelve months ago. He said when he gets back to his cell after his day's work he has prayer, and then studies his Book. Gan-Kui said he would give him *three characters* to remember, "Sìn Iâ-so," *i.e.*, "Believe Jesus"; for, said the old man, though you know these chapters so well, yet if faith in Jesus in not added, you will profit nothing. . . . What a power for good a man with such a knowledge of God's Word may be, if possessed mightily with the Holy Spirit!

Like contemporary born-again Christians, the Brethren saw belief in Christ as the only means to salvation, but they also hoped that their converts would be "possessed mightily" by the Holy Spirit and act as agents in the conversion of others. Gan Kui visited the Chinese assemblies in Kuala Kangsar and Tongkah, and in June 1894 returned again to Fujian.

Lim Khee Saw

Another of Burns' converts in China, Lim Khee Saw (1827–1921) emigrated to Singapore in 1878.[64] When he had first arrived in Singapore Lim had refused to take a leadership role in the Chinese Gospel Hall. As Grant described it, he was deeply discouraged:

---

[61] Ashdown, Choih-bé, Amoy, 12 February 1889, *ES* No. 209 (May 1889): 145–6.

[62] Hill, Thaipeng, 16 November 1892, *ES* No. 278 (January 1893 Pt. 2): 22; Green, Thaipeng, 13 December 1892, *ES* No. 279 (February 1893 Pt. 1): 31; Green, Thaipeng, 16 May 1893, *ES* No. 290 (July 1893 No. 2): 166–7.

[63] Green, Thaipeng, 6 September 1893, *ES* No. 297 (November 1893 Pt. I): 248.

[64] Ashdown reported that Lim Khee Saw passed away in June 1921 having been a Christian for over 70 years. W.D. Ashdown, 24 July 1921, *ES* No. 922 (October 1921): 231.

> Then there is Kee Saw, lately come from China, in hopes of escaping from an atmosphere of form and law, but disappointed, so that he now rarely speaks, thinking that as there is so much talk among us already, and so little holiness and love, he would avoid adding to the preponderance of the former. However, if he does speak, it is very valuable, for he has deep experience and knowledge of God.[65]

No details are offered on the difficulties he experienced in China, but the missionaries often reported that Chinese Christians were strict disciplinarians, and that conflicts arose among male elders.[66]

Like Tan, Lim was one of Burns' early converts in Fujian and spoke often of Burns and his contemporaries.[67] In 1896, an article in a Brethren children's magazine recounted his 1851 conversion:

> HEARTS OPENED IN CHINA
>
> A Chinaman, in the province of Fuhkien [Fujian], lay a-dying. His wife and son Ki-saw [Khee Saw] in their distress sent for the priests with their drums, &c., to propitiate the demons that were devouring father. When the dying man heard the drums beating he cried out that they must stop that, he believed in God only, not in demons, and would rather die than be cured in that way. This was long ago, before there were many missionaries in China, but he must have heard something from someone of God, who made heaven and earth. The man died. Some time afterwards, Williams Burns, one of the earliest missionaries to China, went to preach in the town where the widow and her son Ki-saw lived. She heard that a foreign preacher had come; the poor woman, with her tiny feet all bound around with bandages, could not walk to where the missionary was preaching, so she sent Ki-saw to tell the foreign preacher to come and preach opposite her door. "Why do you send for the foreign devil?" her son replied; "What can he tell you that Confucius has not told you before?" Still, she persisted, so Ki-saw went, but determined to oppose and contradict the preacher. Mr. Burns was explaining the first chapter of Romans, which shows how God may be known by the things He has made, and also speaks of the wickedness of man. Ki-saw's mouth was shut; he knew that what was being said was all too true, so he delivered his mothers' message. William Burns went with

[65] Grant, 4 December 1878, *ME* No. 86 (February 1879): 22.

[66] The year before Lim came to Singapore, the Presbyterians had ordained Tan Soan-Leng as their first Chinese pastor in Bai Shui Ying (Pechuia). As the missionaries described him, Tan was a man of "absolute integrity" and had a "fearless straight-forward way of upholding what he considered right" (Band 1948: 227). Possibly Lim had aspired to the position, which offered a £30/year stipend and a "manse".

[67] Ashdown, 24 July 1921, *ES* No. 922 (October 1921): 231.

> him, took up a position opposite to his mother's door, and preached the same Gospel message over again. Both the widow and her son were after a while converted.
>
> Ki-saw is living now in Penang, an island which belongs to England, in the Straits of Malacca (Arnot 1896: 39).

The Brethren missionaries praised Lim for his "splendid gifts", and for a time he was a fulltime worker in Penang.

In May 1879, Lim travelled with Grant and Gan Kui to Burma, passing through Penang on the way. Grant reported that Lim and Gan Kui were "abundantly provided for", partly by what he paid them, and partly through voluntary gifts. They travelled together to Moulmein (today Mawlamyine), a major seaport in southeastern Burma, where the Chinese Christians went out seeking immigrants from Fujian. They were surprised to find that many "had heard of the gospel being from the Amoy region" and learned that some had been favourably impressed with it, while others were not. The Chinese evangelists moved on to Rangoon, and Grant remained in Moulmein, where he gave a series of well-advertised and well-attended Bible readings in the European community.[68]

Soon thereafter, the Chinese Christians contributed to the cost of Lim moving to Penang together with his wife and three children to help the newly arrived Hocquard to learn Hokkien. Hocquard read with Lim and accompanied him when he did street corner evangelism, but he found Hokkien difficult to master and was unable to speak in public.[69] After Hocquard moved to Singapore, Lim decided to enter into trade and to teach his 17-year-old son business. Lim remained in Penang, and his son and daughter were married in the Mission House in 1897 and 1898, but he ceased doing evangelistic work.

Conclusion

In 1891, evangelist Henry Varley passed through Singapore on his return to London from Melbourne. In his letter to the editors of *Echoes of Service*, Varley described Singapore as a "small but important island" and "one of the busiest ports on the great highway between India, China and Japan". He reported that 40 believers met at the Chinese Mission House for an English service at 9

[68] Grant, Straits of Malacca, 15 May 1879, *ME* No. 92 (August 1879): 113–5.

[69] Hocquard, Batu-kawan, 24 June 1879, *ME* No. 93 (September 1879): 126; Macdonald, Penang, 10 July 1879, *ME* No. 94 (October 1879): 140; Hocquard, Penang, 4 September 1879, *ME* No. 95 (November 1879): 158.

am, and 20 Chinese Brethren met at 10 am for a Chinese-language service.[70] Seven or eight Chinese led the service, together with two missionaries, W.G. Honywill and Alfred R. Thoburn, both of whom he claimed spoke Chinese with "freedom and power". Because his departure was delayed, he held Bible readings and revival meetings at the Singapore Town Hall, on the HMS *Hyacinth*, and at Miss Cooke's school for Chinese girls. He reported that many residents reported a "real awakening", and that "civilians, officers, soldiers and sailors, alike speak of blessings received". He hoped that his lines would reach Alexander Grant.[71]

In 1885, Grant had retired to England, and he and his family again lived in Tottenham. But in 1899 he returned to Singapore and met up again with Gan Kui, who had visited Tongkah with Ashdown before joining him. Gan Kui was 78 years old, but Grant reported that he still did open-air preaching and taught in the Chinese assembly:[72]

> He was pointing out to us the other day in his teaching that while Confucius and other leaders in the three great sects of China confine their teaching to cultivating the mind and disposition in various ways, Moses taught Israel to go outside themselves—"Thou shalt love Jehovah thy God with all thy heart and with all thy soul and with all thy might."

Together Grant and Gan Kui visited Kuala Lumpur, where Grant held a week of special Bible addresses in the English Hall and Gan Kui addressed the Chinese meeting. Grant returned to Singapore, and from there went to China, where his daughter and son-in-law were working at the Schofield Memorial Hospital in Taiyuan.[73] He arrived just months before the Boxer Rebellion shattered their world.

---

[70] White ants had destroyed Bethesda, which was rebuilt in 1891.

[71] Varley, 20 August 1891, *ES* No. 248 (October 1891 Pt. 1): 229.

[72] Grant, Singapore, 12 May 1899, *ES* No. 435 (August 1899 Pt. 1): 230.

[73] Green, Kwala Lumpur [sic], 25 September 1899, *ES* No. 442 (November 1899 Pt. 2): 345.

Chapter 9

Penang and Its Networks, 1874–1912

> When God set us apart to this life of trust, He separated us to a life of rare blessedness. *Never sure* as to how much help will come, but *always sure* that enough will be sent. *Never sure* as to when the help will come, but *always sure* that our Father will never fail us. Oh! this blessed state of *uncertain certainty*. Oh! holy conditions of careful carelessness. In a life like this the soul learns to *cling* to God, and to find in His will the highest attainable life.
>
> Letter from Thomas Baird to George Müller's successor (1905)[1]

In the last three decades of the 19th century and the beginning of the 20th, the Open Brethren in Penang and Singapore distributed tracts and testaments, opened (and closed) girls' schools, and exhorted people in prisons, on street corners, on shipboard, and at the entrance to opium dens. When the British authorities opened leprosariums, they added visitation to lepers to their activities. Competing for attention and donations, some aspired to break new ground in the Malay States, Southern Thailand, Borneo, and Sumatra. Their letters described adventurous travel, the moral failings of Europeans, their religious competitors, and social and political obstacles to realizing their ambitions. In this chapter, I offer a kaleidoscopic view of Brethren travels and practices as they sought to expand their work from their base in Penang to the Malay States, Borneo, Southern Thailand, and Sumatra.

In this period, European and Asian Christians travelled widely and sought opportunities for expansion.[2] The Brethren missionaries sought the leadings of

[1] Letter from Thomas Baird to George F. Bergin [George Müller's successor at the Scriptural Knowledge Institution in Bristol] (SKI 1905: 72).

[2] Because this monograph focuses on Penang and Singapore, Kuala Lumpur is beyond the scope of this study. In 1880 Kuala Lumpur became Selangor's capital, and the Bluff Road Gospel Hall was completed in 1897. A girls' school that female Brethren missionaries founded in Kuala Lumpur in 1893, later renamed the Bukit Bintang Girls' School, became one of Malaya's premier schools.

providence rather than the directives of superior authorities to decide where they should be and what they should be doing. They encountered many closed doors, but the patronage of a single individual—a British administrator, Asian ruler, or Chinese businessman—was sometimes enough to launch work in a new location. Although they enjoyed describing arduous journeys by elephant and ox-cart, by the end of the 19th century the editors of *Echoes of Service* advertised modern amenities to potential missionaries.

Expansion to the Malay States

A 1972 history of Echoes of Service, *Turning the World Upside Down*, dated the beginning of the Taiping [Larut] mission to 1889, which is the year in which British Brethren missionaries moved there (Stunt et al. 1972: 251). But long before, a government official and his wife had launched a primitive church in their home, a female missionary had opened schools, and a Chinese evangelist had moved there to open a Chinese Gospel Hall.[3]

When the Macdonalds returned to Penang from England in 1874, Miss Emma S. Kidner (1836–81) returned with them.[4] She looked after their six children, including teaching the older boys, and soon opened a small day school. But after the sale of the LMS property, they only had a two-storey house that they used both as their residence and for their work. In 1875, Macdonald wrote that when the donation sent by the editors of *The Missionary Echo* was delayed, they had the "remarkable experience of being a whole month without money".

By 1875, the Penang Brethren competed with James Hudson Taylor's new China Inland Mission (CIM, est. 1865) for donations and workers. The Scriptural Knowledge Institution gave extensive support to Taylor and the CIM missionaries, and by the early 1870s Müller reported sending donations to as many as 25 missionaries in China, twice as many as he supported in other countries (Summerton 2016: 94–5). The editors of *The Missionary Echo* published many letters from CIM missionaries and maps of Chinese provinces,

---

[3] The author of a modern history of the Taiping Gospel Hall takes 1880 as their founding date. She guessed that Macdonald introduced the Brethren movement to Larut, Kopa, and Taiping in the late 1860s, but apparently did not have access to *The Missionary Echo*. She relies on later letters published in *Echoes of Service* when she takes 1880 as the date of their establishment (Phang 1981: 8). Tatford does mention Kidner's earlier work in opening schools in Penang and Larut (Tatford 1984:167–8).

[4] The 1871 England Census shows an Emma S. Kidner born in Surrey about 1836 and who lived in London in 1871. If this is the same person, she would have been 38 at the time that she moved to Penang.

and in 1875 announced that Taylor had launched a new magazine *China's Millions*.[5]

A changing political situation soon offered the Christians in Penang new opportunities. Hakka and Cantonese Chinese had emigrated to Perak to work in tin mines and formed sworn brotherhoods as self-government for their workers. In alliance with competing Malay political factions, two of these societies fought for control in a series of conflicts that the British called "wars". When the third of these conflicts broke out in 1872, the British intervened "in the interest of the commerce of the Straits Settlements".[6] Both Perak and Selangor became British protectorates, establishing indirect rule in the Malay States. As Malaya began to export tin and agricultural products, modern transportation and communication networks were put in place to link Malaya to world markets. By the 1880s, British Malaya had become the largest tin producer in the world.

After the Sultan of Perak and the Straits Settlements governor signed the Pangkor Treaty in 1874, James W.W. Birch was appointed as a consultant at the court of the Sultan of Perak. In mid-1875, Miss Kidner went to Larut to visit a "lonely Christian", and Mr Macdonald and Chiam Kim Kak followed to look into opening a mission station. But a few months after their visit, the followers of a Malay chief (who were not alone in opposing the extension of British control to Perak) murdered Birch.[7] Although Groves and other Brethren were pacifists, Macdonald supported British "interference" as being for the benefit of "mankind in Perak".[8] After deploying military force to overcome opposition in mid-1876, the British appointed a new resident. Taiping, whose Chinese name "Great Peace" commemorated the Taiping Rebellion (1850–64), became Perak's capital in 1876, and Kuala Lumpur became the capital of Selangor in 1880.

On their first visit to Larut, Mr Macdonald and Chiam Kim Kak had visited scattered tin mines in the Kinta Valley on foot while Miss Kidner remained in town. Her friends took her to visit a Chinese woman who had attended the Penang Girls' school before it closed and who urged her to open a school. She had a meeting with a group of women, and promised them that she would return. She noted that Mr Macdonald was the right person to open a new

[5] "China", n.d., *ME* No. 43 (July 1875): 98.

[6] Macdonald, Penang, 11 July 1875, *ME* No. 47 (November 1875): 155.

[7] "Straits Settlements", Editorial note, *ME* No. 48 (December 1875): 167.

[8] When the British dispatched troopships to transport soldiers to the Malay states, Macdonald visited the ships in the Penang harbour and invited the soldiers to a special meeting. Macdonald, 29 January 1876, *ME* No. 52 (April 1876): 58.

station,[9] but the next year returned to Larut alone.[10] Friends at home sent her letters and donations that she used to buy teaching supplies.[11]

E.M. Marples, the new state treasurer and magistrate, and his wife had organized a local church in their home near the new courthouse, and for a time Miss Kidner lived with them. On Mrs Marples' sudden death in January 1877, Mr Marples rented a Chinese house for her use next door to parents of her pupils.[12] There, she privately taught two Portuguese Eurasian girls and a Chinese student to read and write in English, intending to train them to work in her school.[13] She soon opened a boys' school with 17 students.

The next year, friends of the Penang mission published a "Cry from the Straits Settlements" in *The Missionary Echo*. They explained that Mr Macdonald hoped to recruit more workers to help reopen the schools and to extend their work; Miss Kidner added that many were going to China and passing by the Straits "where there are thousands of Chinese". In her letters, she also observed that the Roman Catholics were already opening stations and getting converts in Larut.

Miss Kidner aspired to be a public evangelist, and when Chiam Kim Kak made a sweeping tour of Perak, they visited the home of a master miner who had 30 miners living with him in Kuminting (now Kamunting). He claimed that when he and "missy" addressed the miners, "all listened gladly".[14]

Miss Kidner also borrowed a magic lantern from a friend in Penang so that she could show views of "The Pilgrim's Progress from the City of Destruction to the Heavenly City" in her schoolroom. On the first night Mr Marples explained the story in Malay, and on the second a court interpreter translated her explanations into Chinese. She observed, "The people seemed deeply impressed, and have not ceased to talk about the man with the load of sin on his back, and how he lost it by looking at the cross. I do think it an excellent way of teaching these interesting people."[15]

---

9 Kidner, Penang, 1 July 1875, *ME* No. 46 (October 1875): 142.

10 She reported that she and the Macdonalds' two eldest sons had done street corner exhortations, to the astonishment of their audience. Kidner, Laroot, 14 July 1876, *ME* No. 61 (January 1877): 13–4.

11 Kidner, Laroot, 14 July 1876 *ME* No. 61 (January 1877): 13–4.

12 Kidner, Laroot, 22 March 1877, *ME* No. 66 (June 1877): 93.

13 Kidner, Laroot, 14 July 1876, *ME* No. 61 (January 1877): 13–4.

14 Chiam Kim Kak, 10th moon, *ME* No. 66 (June 1877): 94.

15 Kidner, Laroot, via Penang, 21 June 1877, *ME* No. 69 (September 1877): 149–50.

But after Mr and Mrs Macdonald lost two of their children to diphtheria, they returned to England, and on the journey Mrs Macdonald fell ill and died. In Mr Macdonald's absence, Miss Kidner returned to Penang to look after the mission. Robert Garling Van Someren (1852–1931), a prominent Dutch Eurasian lawyer, wrote to Macdonald in England:[16]

> All Penang seems to have heard that meetings go on. Some have asserted that it is the right thing; others again seem indignant at the idea that unordained persons, such as we are, some of us unable to speak even, should presume to lead the services.

Not long after, Philip Robinson visited Penang from Singapore and reported that Miss Kidner was "the only resident missionary—a valuable help to the young converts, and deaconess to the little church".[17]

Alexander Grant had stayed in London for five years, but he and his family came back to Singapore, and he went to Penang to help. Miss Kidner took the opportunity to return to England.[18] In 1873, Mrs Gawthorne, who like her husband was Tamil and who knew English and "three Eastern languages", had opened an English-language school for boys in the stone-paved veranda in front of their house. At that time she had 40 students, most of whom were Chinese, and she and her husband also had English scripture readings and prayer in their house twice a week that was attended by soldiers and sailors.[19]

But Mrs Gawthorne planned to close her school by the end of 1878, and in England Miss Kidner sought to recruit someone to open a new English-medium boys' school.[20] When she and Mr Macdonald returned, Mr and Mrs Hocquard accompanied them.[21] Mrs Hocquard opened a school for English-speaking children, and Mr Hocquard visited hospitals, barracks, and ships in the harbour, and studied Hokkien with Lim Khee Saw.[22]

---

16 R. G. v. S., Penang, January 1878, *ME* No. 76 (April 1878): 60–1.

17 Philip Robinson, Penang, 13 February 1878, *ME* No. 77 (May 1878): 77–8.

18 Kidner, North Brixton, 4 May 1878. *ME* No. 78 (June 1878): 92–3.

19 "Miscellaneous, Penang", Macdonald, *ME* No. 18 (June 1873): 88.

20 Kidner, North Brixton, 4 May 1878 *ME* No. 78 (June 1878): 93. She did not identify Mrs Gawthorne by name but stated that Penang's only Protestant English school would close by the end of 1878.

21 Macdonald, Mediterranean; Hocquard, Off Crete, 7 November 1878, *ME* No. 84 (December 1878): 177–8; Macdonald, Penang, 12 December 1878, *ME* No. 85 (January 1879): 23–4.

22 Hocquard, Penang, 8 March 1879, *ME* No. 90 (June 1879): 86; Batu-kawan, 24 June 1879, *ME* No. 93 (September 1879): 126.

Although she would have preferred to return to Larut, on her return Miss Kidner remained in Penang, where she launched a school for Chinese girls in the home of a wealthy Chinese, later renting a house at 21 Penang Road.[23] Soon Ada Lear joined her to help her run the girls' school.[24] But just as her new school seemed likely to succeed, Miss Kidner fell ill. She went to Singapore, but treatment by an apothecary failed, and she died in a rented room.[25] Mr Macdonald had remarried, and his second wife continued to run the English day school, which had received government accreditation, for a decade. Ada Lear kept Miss Kidner's school open for two years, but after she married, she and her husband moved to Taiping.[26] With that, the Penang Protestant girls' school that Miss Kidner had opened in 1878 was closed.[27]

Most of the female missionaries who followed in Penang learned Malay and did visitation to sequestered women and some teaching. But they could not compete with the Catholic girls' schools, which were well established and better funded. Moreover, starting in the 1880s, Methodist missionaries began to develop educational and social ministries, laying the groundwork for a successful Christian school system (Goh 2003, 2005). By 1890, Hocquard described Protestant schools in Penang as a "sorry blank" as compared with Rangoon and Singapore.[28]

Chinese Evangelists in Larut

In 1877, Chinese evangelist Oon Thoan moved to Bukit Mertajam in Province Wellesley, a district on the mainland that investors had developed into large

---

[23] Kidner, Penang, 22 February 1879, *ME* No. 90 (June 1879): 87; 15 December 1879 *ME* No. 98 (February 1880).

[24] Kidner, Penang, 4 January 1881, *ME* No. 111 (March 1881): 40–1.

[25] Grant, Singapore, 27 June 1881, *ME* No. 118 (October 1881): 148–9; "Straits Settlements", *ME* No. 116 (August 1881): 117.

[26] Her husband Joseph L. Greene had worked in a government school in Penang, and started a class for soldiers and organized a reading room for them in his wife's school. Macdonald, Penang, 12 September 1881, *ME* No. 123 (March 1882): 43; Greene, 20 May 1882, *ME* No. 127 (July 1882): 98. In 1883, he was appointed headmaster of a new Central Government School (est. 1883) in Taiping. This school is now known as King Edward VII School and recognizes J.L. Greene as their first headmaster.

[27] Macdonald, Penang, July 1883, *ME* No. 145 (January 1884): 14; Penang, 10–21 April 1884, *ME* No. 152 (August 1884): 129.

[28] "Later Tidings", Hocquard n.d., *ES* No. 220 (April 1890): 120.

commercial plantations, to open a new mission station.[29] When he returned from England in 1878 after his wife's death, Macdonald visited him there:[30]

> The preacher's little thatched house is at the end of a considerable village of chiefly Chinese inhabitants; the rest are mostly Madras men of the coolie caste, who keep bullock or pony carts for hire. The principal room is the preaching-hall, where seats are placed near the table, on which are some testaments and hymn-books; the customary teapot, with half-a-dozen tiny cups in a tray the size of a dinner-plate; and also a small quantity of tobacco for cigarettes. The door is nearly always kept open, and visitors are made welcome when the preacher is not outside engaged in visiting or preaching. There are many Romanists in this part.

He described their competition—the Catholic Church and its mission—and laid out the expenses of the station for the readers of *The Missionary Echo*; he sent a similar letter to Müller (SKI 1879: 53).

In 1880, Marples raised funds in the European community to build a new Chinese gospel hall and meeting room in Larut, and invited Oon Thoan there to lead it. Soon after Macdonald travelled there with Ah Moy, a vegetable farmer who had helped build an independent gospel hall in Ayer Itam, a town at the base of Penang Hill.[31] On Sunday they had a gospel meeting for Europeans in the courthouse, visited the prison, then attended the Chinese meeting, which over 150 individuals (but only one woman) attended. Mr Macdonald later baptized two men and they had a breaking of bread ceremony.[32] He returned again with Koan Ip, a Hakka evangelist whom Oon Thoan had converted, and approved six Chinese and one Portuguese Eurasian for baptism.[33]

---

[29] Kidner, Penang, 29 November 1877, *ME* No.74 (February 1878): 33; R.G. v. S., Penang, January 1878, *ME* No. 76 (April 1878): 60–1. In what may have been a related initative, landowner David Brown—wealthy plantation owner David Brown's second son—and the Anglican Bishop formed a Mission Committee for Province Wellesley in 1878 and planned to develop schools for the children of Tamil plantation workers (Orsler n.d.: 2).The 'old' Tamil headmaster was named Nathaniel, which raises the possibility that he was John George Bausum's protegé Nathaniel April, who spoke Malay, English, and Tamil (Orsler n.d.: 11).

[30] Macdonald, Penang, 13 January 1879, *ME* No. 87 (March 1879): 35.

[31] Macdonald, Penang, 16 August 1882, *ME* No. 131 (November 1882): 155–6.

[32] Macdonald, Penang, n.d., *ME* No. 113 (June 1881): 83–4.

[33] Macdonald, Penang, 12 September–30 December 1881, *ME* No. 123 (March 1882): 43.

When Oon Thoan moved to Singapore in 1884,[34] Voon Kiong (a.k.a Ah Kiong), a Hakka-speaking evangelist who had been working in Province Wellesley, replaced him in Larut.[35] Ten of the Chinese Christians in Larut were charcoal burners who lived near each other but at a distance from town.[36] They could not come to the Chinese Gospel Hall often, and on one of his trips to teach candidates for baptism, Macdonald and Ah Kiong visited them.[37] They travelled through jungle and along tracks where buffalo drew timber, and found three small groups of men cutting wood and burning it in a kiln to make charcoal. At the first and second sites, the men stopped work for Scripture reading and prayer in the jungle clearing. He claimed that as Christians, they preferred this isolated work to mixing with non-Christians in the tin mines.

In 1886, Macdonald's report of work in Penang included details on mission stations in Ayer Itam, Bukit Mertajam, Tongkah, and Larut.[38] He described the Chinese mission station in Larut:

> *Larut.*--In Kota village, about a mile and a half from the chief town of Thaiping, a mission station was commenced in January, 1880. About eighty names have been on the roll from the first, and now there are about fifty; many removals occur, and the believers are scattered about. Voon Kiong preaches, and Jap Koon Hai, a charcoal burner, and Su Hok, a gardener, help in the work. A day-school, attended by five children of Christians, has just been commenced by two sisters, who themselves know very little even of reading Chinese and Malay in Romanised characters. The neighborhood is crowded with mines, and there is an immense field for evangelising. A small piece of garden land was given by the government to trustees for mission work, and the meeting-house of wood and thatch, which has been erected in the centre of it, holds about a hundred persons. Attached to it are a couple of rooms for the preacher, and there are six cottages of Christians on the ground. At the back it is bounded by a stream in which we baptize believers.

---

34 Macdonald, Penang, 10–21 April 1884, *ME* No. 152 (August 1884): 128.

35 It seems likely that the Basel mission in Guangdong, which focused on Hakka speakers, may have trained some of the Chinese evangelists who worked with immigrant Hakka communities in Larut and elsewhere. However, the Brethren missionaries gave no information on this point. On the Basel Mission, see Lutz and Lutz (1998).

36 Macdonald, Penang, 10–21 April 1884, *ME* No. 152 (August 1884): 129.

37 Macdonald, Laroot, 30 June–28 July 1882, *ME* No. 129 (September 1882): 123–4.

38 "Brief general statement of work in Penang and neighborhood", Macdonald, n.d., *ES* No. 177 (September 1886): 139–40.

Chinese Christians continued to meet in their gospel hall and English-speakers in the homes of British Christians. But all of their Chinese converts in Larut belonged to "the migratory class of males" and, Macdonald observed, were likely to move off any time.[39]

Expansion

In 1886, Macdonald sent a summary overview of "work in Penang and neighborhood" to the editors of *The Missionary Echo*, hoping to entice new workers. As he described it, there were about 70 "Chinese believers" in Penang and Province Wellesley, and also scattered in various places, and also about 25 "English speaking believers, of considerable variety as to social status, parentage, etc." Macdonald described their evangelical outreach, which including visiting civil, military, and pauper hospitals, European and Asian boats in harbour, and evangelising among "100,000 of Penang, 150,000 of Province Wellesley, 50,000 of Junk Seylon [Tongkah], and the whole peninsula".[40]

New workers soon came to the Straits Settlements from England, Scotland, and New Zealand. These included: T. Angus (Kuala Lumpur, 1897–1948); W.D. Ashdown (Tongkah, Kuala Lumpur, Singapore, 1888–1934), Thomas Baird (Kuala Lumpur, 1893–1906), D.W. Cooper (Penang and Bukit Mertajam, 1894–1902), Edward Eagger (Larut and Selangor, 1888–97; to China 1897–1920), Alfred Green (Taiping, Singapore, 1890–1912; to Bristol in 1912 as director of the George Müller Foundation), H.C. Hill (Taiping, 1889–98), his brother Edgar Hill (Taiping, 1893–1901, to China 1904–33), W.G. Honywill (Singapore, 1889–96, to Italy 1898–1906), Henry Freeman Marks (Taiping, 1899–1952), James Moore (Penang, Malacca, Borneo, 1889–1904), Alfred R. Thoburn (Singapore, 1889–1920), and George Wilson (Taiping, 1899–1942).[41] Female missionaries included Mary B. Langlands (Kuala Lumpur, 1893–95, married to Mr Moore, Malacca 1895–1900, Borneo, 1900–02); M.E. Davies (Penang, 1899–1903); M.A. Emmerson (Singapore, 1894–1918); Rose Hosegood (Singapore, 1891–99); Elizabeth (Bessie) Maclay (Kuala Lumpur, 1894–1915); and M. Reeve (Penang, 1899–1903).

The Open Brethren missionaries typically learned to speak Malay, and most of the men also studied one Chinese language. Often their Chinese coworkers tutored them, but the missionaries complained that it was difficult to acquire

[39] Macdonald, Penang, 6 May 1881, *ME* No. 115 (July 1881): 95.

[40] "Penang", Macdonald, n.d., *ME* No. 177 (September 1886): 138–40.

[41] For a complete list of missionaries working in Malaysia and Singapore, see Stunt et al. 1972: 623–4.

Figure 21 Postcard showing the locations of Brethren missionaries in the Straits Settlements and Malaya (July 1911). *Echoes of Service* Archive.

these languages since they could not immerse themselves in a community where they constantly heard and were forced to speak that language. Since Hokkien was widely spoken in Penang and Singapore, most of the new male missionaries went to Fujian Province to study the Amoy dialect of Southern Min. They stayed in communities where Protestant missions existed, but also in Chioh-be, a large village near Amoy that early converts from Pechuia had independently evangelized in 1854, and where no foreign missionary was ever permanently resident (Cheung 2004: 225–51). Only a few went to Swatow or Hong Kong to study Hakka, and in 1898 Miss Maclay went to Canton to learn Cantonese.[42]

Of the new male missionaries, only James Moore chose not to study a Chinese language and moved instead to Bukit Mertajam to study Malay intensively. He intended to "seek an entrance into the very heart of Malay influence", perhaps in Perak. Hocquard advised him that the Rajah would not allow it, but Moore was sure that if it was the "Lord's purpose", it would be accomplished, anticipating that God would "take all the arrangements into His hands and to work in me to will and to do of His good pleasure".[43]

He made exploratory tours of Pahang and Trengganu, and when he failed to get permission to live in Trengganu from the Sultan and Prime Minister, the editors of *Echoes of Service* commented that a Muslim ruler would not tolerate "anything like proselytism among his co-religionist".[44] Moore married Mary Langlands, and together they launched a new effort in Malacca. When Muslims showed no interest,[45] they set out for Borneo, where they received permission from Rajah Charles Brooke to work in an isolated Dayak community.[46] But their work ended tragically with the deaths of Mrs Moore and their infant son.[47]

Mr and Mrs Moore undertook work in a remote village in Borneo, but most of the Open Brethren missionaries and Chinese evangelists moved to cities and towns that had increasingly efficient travel connections and communications,

[42] Brief Notes Etc. Canton, *ES* No. 400 (February 1898 Pt. 2): 80.

[43] Moore, Bukit Martajam, 2 August1889, *ES* No. 214 (October 1889): 303; 27 September 1889, *ES* No. 216 (December 1889): 376.

[44] "A Visit to Pahang and Trengganu by Mr. J. W. Moore", n.d., *ES* No. 318 (September 1894 Pt. 2): 222.

[45] Moore, Malacca, 13 January 1896, *ES* No. 354 (March 1896 Pt. 2): 86–7.

[46] Moore, Kuching, Sarawak, 27 February 1900, *ES* No. 452 (April 1900 Pt. 2): 121; Moore, Kuching, Sarawak, 21 June 1900, *ES* No. 460 (August 1900 Pt. 2): 248–9; Moore, Tebekang, Sadong, Sarawak, 10 July 1900, *ES* No. 461 (September 1900 Pt. 1): 264–5.

[47] Moore, Sarawak, 17 May 1902, *ES* No. 506 (July 1902 Pt. 2): 269.

and focused their proselytism on English and Chinese speakers. The Open Brethren missionaries and evangelists also travelled widely in the region, often visiting isolated Christians and small independent gatherings that Christian immigrants had formed.

Although their cross-cultural efforts were focused on Chinese, Brethren attracted English-educated Eurasians and Asians to their English-language meetings in Perak and Selangor. These included Dutch Eurasians from Ceylon (today Sri Lanka) and English-educated Tamils who had migrated from India to work in the colonial administration. From time to time, Eurasian Catholics also joined their English meetings.

By the 18th century, a Eurasian community resulting from the intermarriage of Portuguese, Dutch, Sinhalese, and Tamils had developed in Ceylon. They were called Burghers and included Eurasians who could prove European ancestry (Dutch or Portuguese) through the male line, and who spoke Dutch and belonged to the Dutch Reformed Church, which resembles Presbyterianism in its doctrines and organizational practices. When Ceylon became a British Crown Colony in 1815, the Burghers adopted English and some became Anglicans. Although they were a tiny minority, they formed a privileged upper class elite, "Westernized in race, language, religion and cultural norms and involved in administering British colonial policy" (Jupp 2001: 694; see also Ramerini 1998). Many Burgher immigrants to Malaya remained Anglican, but some joined Brethren assemblies.[48]

When the British expanded their control to the Malay States, English-educated Tamils, most of whom were Catholic or Anglican, also migrated there to work.[49] The evangelical Church Missionary Society had been active in India, but Tamil Christians "did not find a home" in Malaya's Anglican Church, which was connected with officialdom and was formal in its ritual practices (Northcott 1992: 40). Some Tamil Christians joined Brethren gospel halls or became Methodists.

Finally, the Brethren sometimes attracted English-educated Catholics to their assemblies. When Catholics applied to join their gospel halls, the Brethren observed that they did not know the Bible and were unfamiliar with

[48] In Ipoh and Kuala Lumpur, Brethren assemblies included many prominent Burgher members with the surnames Cooke, Foenander, Grenier, Jumeaux, LaBrooey, and Van Langenberg. For this information, I draw on an interview with Harold Cooke.

[49] With support from the Anglican Society for the Propagation of the Gospel, in 1871 a South Asian catechist attached himself to the Anglican Church in Penang. He held services for Tamils in a wooden chapel behind Saint George's Church and did itinerant evangelistic tours of the mainland (Northcott 1992: 39).

extemporaneous prayer. They doubted that they were truly Christian, noting that Chinese Catholics merely substituted the crucifix for the idol on their altars, and describing Catholic rites and ceremonies, incense, and bowing as no different from Chinese "idol worship".

Tongkah, Southern Thailand

Starting in 1884, the Brethren missionaries and Chinese evangelists began to visit Phuket Island in Southern Thailand. Early European visitors called Phuket Junk Ceylon (Malay: Hujong Salang), but Hokkien Chinese called the island Tongkah, a name that also refers to a tin smelting furnace. Macdonald described Tongkah as the Penang mission's northern station, and advertised a Chinese Christian and his church to his readers as a model of the independent, self-supporting primitive church.

Phuket Island was located on the sea highway between India and China 200 miles north of Penang. As early as the 16th century, the island had become a centre for tin mining, and the town of Thalang became a centre for the tin trade for Portuguese, Dutch, English, and French traders. By the 1880s, many Hokkien Chinese had migrated there to work in its tin mines.

In 1884, Macdonald made the 24-hour journey to Tongkah by steamer with Lee Teng Hun. He and Lee did open-air exhortations and tract distribution, then sought out Ong Im (b. 1830), a Chinese Christian whom Macdonald had met when he first arrived in Penang in 1866, but who had left for Tongkah soon after:[50]

> We found that the brother long here, who is called Heem [Ong Im], had of late been preaching the Word pretty much, but his story is not without much sadness; for he long gave way to the vice of gambling. He confesses his sin to any who, hearing him preach, remind him that he was recently a gambler, and he tells them that Satan possessed him.

Macdonald encouraged Ong Im and other Christians to form a primitive church. Later that year, a Christian wrote him to report that a few Chinese met with him in his house for "prayer and edification".[51]

---

[50] Macdonald, Lower Siam, 20 February 1884, *ME* No. 149 (May 1884): 82.

[51] The Christian who wrote Macdonald did not speak Chinese and had no interpreter, and reported that he could only help them by pointing to passages of Scripture. Macdonald, Penang, 15 October 1884, *ME* No. 157 (January 1885): 13.

Macdonald visited again in 1885 to preside over four baptisms and described the small gathering, whose members included an "East Indian of English education" named Jansen (who almost certainly was Dutch Eurasian) and his wife, who had been raised Catholic and could read the Bible in romanized Malay.[52] Even before his baptism, Jansen had tried to assist the Chinese Christians, with a recent Chinese convert interpreting from Malay to Chinese, but this fragile arrangement ended when Jansen and his wife returned to Penang. Consequently, the small group of seven or eight believers had no members who were "well able to expound the Word".[53]

In 1886, Ong Im established his own gospel hall, purchasing a shophouse at 24 Thalang Road that is still a Christian Assembly.[54] The Christians used its upstairs room as a meeting place, and the cake seller dedicated a percentage of his revenues for building materials. Since he could not earn enough money to pay workers, he did the renovation work himself. Ong Im told Hocquard: "When I am gone to be with Christ, for I am now 59 years of age, those who come after me will have a place to meet in."[55]

In June and July of 1886, Hocquard and Sun Liong travelled to Tongkah with a letter of introduction to the island's only European resident, Captain Weber. Hocquard and Sun Liong immediately went in search of Ong Im, whom he found selling his cakes by the roadside. On seeing Hocquard and Sun Liong, the cake seller exclaimed "Praise the Lord! We have been asking God to send us some one to help us, and He has done so."[56] The next day, Hocquard sold Chinese, Thai, Tamil, and Malay gospel portions, while Sun Liong preached. On Sunday they met with seven Chinese Christians in a "little loft over a stable," and read them Ephesians chapter 2, which teaches that "by grace ye are saved," making Christians "fellow citizens with the saints, and of the household of God." Later, Hocquard and Sun Liong preached in an opium shop, and at a marketplace where men left their gambling table to listen to them.

---

[52] Macdonald, Penang, 22 July 1885, *ES* No. 165 (September 1885): 143–4.

[53] Macdonald, Penang, n.d., *ES* No. 177 (September 1886): 140.

[54] "Addresses on Works in Other Lands" at Leominster Conference: Hocquard, Straits Settlements, *ES* No. 201 (September 1888): 262–3. According to the authors of *Turning the World Upside Down* and a recent report, this house is still used by the assembly in Phuket (Stunt et al. 1972: 297; Khoo Salma Nasution, personal communication).

[55] Hocquard, Penang, 22 June 1889, *ES* No. 212 (August 1889): 241–2.

[56] "A Visit to Tongkah, Siam", Hocquard, 28 June–30 July 1886, *ES* No. 179 (November 1886): 171–4.

Hocquard recounted the story of the Chinese cake seller at the 1888 Leominster Conference in Britain, and the editor of *Echoes* summarized his report:[57]

> In Tongkah, a small island belonging to Siam, to the north of the Straits, there was a gathering of Chinese, but only one of them could read. Two years ago he [Hocquard] visited and broke bread with them. Then they felt the need of a place in which to preach the gospel. One of them saved a little money and bought a house. Being asked what he intended to do with it, he replied that the house was not his, it was the Lord's. It was given to the Lord for the preaching of the gospel; and over it four Chinese characters were now written, meaning "Gospel House." Their numbers had increased, and they now had the joy of seeing souls converted to God.

When Hocquard next returned to Tongkah, he reported that they held two meetings daily for a week that was attended by about 20 Chinese. As he described it, the 6 am prayer meetings were especially refreshing, and "the dear brethren prayed one after another without the least restraint, often seven or eight of them pouring out their hearts before God in the most simple way." A few days later they met at 5 o'clock, and he baptized four members of the small group in a small river outside the town.[58]

In 1890, W.D. Ashdown moved to Tongkah. At first he lived with Ong Im, and the two had nightly meetings and did street evangelism together. Ashdown reported that two individuals whom the cake seller "brought to the Lord" through his "testimony" had asked to be baptized.[59] But he also complained that he needed a separate house for preaching, since the cake seller ran his bakery on the ground floor of the shophouse. The editor of *Echoes of Service* reported that Ong Im was unhappy that his "humble gospel hall" would not be used, and they reached a compromise that Ashdown would use another place for preaching the gospel, and Ong Im's gospel hall for other meetings.[60]

Ashdown did not remain long in Tongkah, but Ong Im continued to lead the Chinese assembly. Hocquard visited in 1890, and again observed that at their small prayer meetings, they poured "out their hearts to God one after another in the most simple manner" (SKI 1891: 46). A year later, W.H. Stanes, an estate manager in India who sometimes travelled as an evangelist, visited

---

[57] "Report at Leominster Conference: Hocquard, Straits Settlements", *ES* No. 201 (September 1888): 262–3.

[58] Hocquard, Perak, 9 December 1890, *ES* No. 233 (March 1891 Pt. 1): 64.

[59] Ashdown, Tongkah, Lower Siam, 23 April 1890, *ES* No. 223 (July 1890): 205–7.

[60] Editorial summary, Ashdown, Tongkah, *ES* No. 237 (May 1891 Pt. 1): 112.

them.[61] Fifteen Christians met in the cake seller's upstairs room—an allusion that Brethren would recognize to the upstairs room where early Christians met to break bread, as described in Acts 20: 7–8. Like Hocquard, he noted that Ong Im took every opportunity of preaching the gospel even while he was making his cakes.[62]

Hocquard observed that the island had no modern medical facilities, and sought a medical missionary: "I long for some brother to be settled there, one with a knowledge of medicine would be best, as in the whole island with its 80,000 inhabitants there is not a single medical man, nor a hospital."[63] They recruited Dr Amner, who opened a dispensary in Tongkah in 1892, but he and his wife could not find a place to live, and they returned to Penang, where he set up a dispensary.

When Prince Damrong, the Thai Prime Minister, visited Penang, Dr Amner heard the news that he favoured his doing medical work in conjunction with the royal hospital there, and soon after received permission to build a house in a seaside location outside the town.[64] In 1902 he reported that the government had built a plague hospital and needed someone to manage it; he recommended a China-born nurse who was a member of their assembly, and she and her husband took over managing the new facility.[65] Dr Amner continued to work in Tongkah until 1917, treating opium addicts and offering medical support during epidemics of cholera and plague.[66]

Sumatra

In 1887, Macdonald listed Sumatra together with Singapore, Penang, Larut, and Tongkah, as places where Brethren labourers might work. The Dutch had opened export agricultural production in Sumatra to private investors, and by

[61] Stanes was a member of a large family in India whose members were involved in a variety of enterprises between 1856–1964, including tea and coffee plantations, and who supported evangelical work, including establishing a school for Anglo-Indians in Coimbature (Cousins 2006).

[62] Stanes, Thaipeng, Perak, 9 September 1891, *ES* No. 251 (December 1891 Pt. 1): 287.

[63] Hocquard, Penang, 22 June 1889, *ES* No. 212 (August 1889): 242.

[64] Macdonald, Penang, 31 April 1900, *ES* No. 457 (July 1900 Pt. 1): 200.

[65] "A brave Chinese nurse.—Opium slaves", Amner, Tongkah, 30 June 1902, *ES* No. 510 (September 1902 Pt. 2): 349.

[66] In 1927, a decade after Amner left, a Canadian Presbyterian medical missionary proposed to work at the Brethren mission in Tongkah. Ashdown, Penang, 25 February 1927, *ES* No. 989 (May 1927): 105; Walter B. Toy, 7 February 1928, *ES* No. 1001 (May 1928): 105.

1889, 179 plantations producing cash crops like tobacco existed in Deli (Stoler 1985: 16–7). As was the case in British Malaya, roads, railroads, and ports were developed to facilitate the export of goods to global markets, and migrant workers provided labour at the plantations. British investors were among those who developed plantations, and they recruited European managers from Penang. Chinese from the Straits Settlements also migrated there seeking economic opportunities. In 1890, and again in 1896, Brethren workers and Chinese evangelists visited Sumatra.

In 1896, Alf Green and Ah Siap, a colporteur of the Bible Society, went to Deli, where they stayed with British friends and 'put the gospel' before Chinese coolies and Bataks living on a tobacco estate. Landowners in Penang and Province Wellesley had encouraged Christians to open schools for the children of plantation owners, and perhaps they imagined that they would receive similar support from the Sumatran plantation owners. But after a few days the estate manager ordered them to stop:[67]

> I called on him, and he said the order was from the head administrator, but he himself said, "we look upon our coolies as working machines." I drove over to Rimboen, and had an interview with the administrator, but he would not alter his decision, nor allow any preaching to Chinese, Javanese, Battaks, etc., on the estate. He said that no good could come of these preaching visits; and that they might cause coolies to oppose or get rowdy. If any really became Christians they would come on a footing with Europeans, which would never do. He believed they would be better coolies as heathen, and so on. I endeavoured to reason with him, and also pointed out the solemn responsibility of shutting out the gospel from these large numbers of heathen, but he said he was quite prepared to bear it as he had his responsibility to the Company. I came away sad at heart, and in the evening we had special prayer over the matter.

The Brethren workers and Chinese evangelists in Penang continued to visit Sumatra, hoping to start new work with Chinese immigrants in Medan and the Batak, but established nothing permanent. They reported no indigenous gospel halls like the one in Tongkah, nor primitive European-led churches like the gatherings in Larut.

Evangelical Practices in Penang and Its Network

In Penang and Singapore, the Brethren missionaries and their Chinese partners held weekly meetings and occasionally came together for the

[67] "A Visit to North Sumatra", Alf Green, Medan, Deli, 26 August 1896, *ES* No. 368 (October 1896 Pt. 2): 312.

breaking of bread ceremony for their English and Chinese members. But the missionaries' everyday practices also included visiting private homes, which included long journeys to visit isolated Christians living in remote locations. They also visited hospitals, prisons, and ships, and made frequent journeys by boat to Pulau Jerejak, the so-called leper island, where individuals suffering from the disfiguring disease were confined. They did street evangelism at public sites, including temples where festival events provided opportunities for evangelistic outreach to large crowds, and sometimes visited opium dens, where they found men desperate for cures for their addiction (see DeBernardi 2017).

Although they enjoyed describing arduous journeys by elephant and ox-cart, by the end of the 19th century they could advertise modern amenities to potential missionaries. In 1894, for example, the Editors of *Echoes* summarize a government report showing that far from being a dangerous wilderness, the Malay States, including Perak, where Chinese evangelists had commenced work in 1880 and European missionaries followed in 1889,[68] now had order and prosperity (which they ascribed to British intervention):[69]

> Most of the State [of Perak] is now accessibly by good roads, on which bullock 'busses run; a line or railway will soon traverse the country; the telegraph is carried to all parts; substantial school buildings, hospitals, prisons and all the usual accessories of a well ordered government are everywhere found. Religious liberty prevails, so that the gospel may be freely preached.

The editors conclude that although little work had been done among Malays, "the opportunities of work amongst the Chinese are abundant and bear fruit".

They often reported the number of conversions as evidence of their success and made frequent reports on one of their most prominent converts, Chew Boon Hean. Chew chose to convert while imprisoned in Taiping, and after his release joined the Brethren movement. He built a gospel hall for his Tamil plantation workers in Klang in 1911, but also became a popular evangelist, travelling often with the Brethren missionaries. As I discuss in Chapter 11, in the 1920s and 1930s Chew also made evangelical tours of Indonesia, the Philippines, Hong Kong, and China.

---

[68] In *Turning the World Upside Down*, the authors do not report the early established work in Larut undertaken by the Chinese evangelists, and date the beginning of the Taiping mission to 1889, which is the year in which the Hocquards commenced work there (Stunt et al. 1972: 251).

[69] Editorial Preface to Alf E. Green, Taiping, 6 March 1894, *ES* No. 311 (June 1894 Pt. I): 139.

The Conversion of Chew Boon Hean

Starting in 1892, the government allowed the Brethren missionaries to work in the Taiping prison, where they taught 150 prisoners on Sunday and a class attended by 30 men on Saturday (SKI 1894: 50).[70] As Henry Freeman Marks (1877–1962) described it, prison taught them "obedience, order and cleanliness", but also prevented them from smoking opium. He claimed that they heard the gospel "continually", and that some could read Chinese and owned New Testaments.[71] The missionaries reported frequent conversions, including that of individuals who had been sentenced to death.[72]

The Brethren regarded the conversion of Chew Boon Hean as one of their greatest successes. Chew was a handsome Straits Chinese entrepreneur who had been involved in tin and gold prospecting. The sale of opium and alcohol were government monopolies that wealthy Chinese businessmen typically operated as franchises, and he was also the managing agent for the Klang opium, spirit, gambling, and pawnbroking farms.[73] But in 1904, he was convicted of fraud and sentenced to five years in prison in Taiping.

When Angus and Green first met Chew, he "objected to restraint" and was both skeptical and cynical about Christianity. But they claimed that he "became deeply convicted of sin".[74] After he showed interest in becoming Christian, the Brethren helped secure his early release after serving less than four years of his sentence. He was released in early January 1908 and was baptized on 19 January.

---

[70] Prison visitation was a regular practice in Singapore and Kuala Lumpur, but Mr Macdonald does not mention visiting Penang's prisons after his return in 1874.

[71] He added that most of the inmates had "little conception of what sin is; it is only sin to be found out, they think". H.F. Marks, Taiping, 18 August 1900, *ES* No. 464 (October 1900 Pt. 2): 314.

[72] In the 1860s, John Chapman and Alexander Grant frequently visited Penang's prison to exhort the prisoners and distribute tracts. Access depended on the approval of the prison superintendent and was never certain. But where they found support, the Open Brethren assembled multilingual teams to address the diverse population of inmates. The missionaries often offered the readers of *Echoes* accounts of their efforts to redeem the inmates from sinful lives.

[73] In 1908, he was identified as the managing agent of the Klang Opium and Chandu Farm and Spirit, Gambling and Pawn-broking Farms, but perhaps this information was out-of-date. Since the Brethren opposed opium and alcohol use and gambling, he likely gave up these business interests after his conversion (*Directory and Chronicle for 1908*: 1278).

[74] "Encouragement amongst Prisoners", Green, Kuala Lumpur, 17 July 1907, *ES* No. 630 (September 1907 Pt. 2): 353.

The missionaries reported that "His friends cannot understand the change—the speculating, money-loving, pleasure-loving man now waiting to see God's way for him to earn clean money and live a humble, useful life."[75] On his release, the missionaries reported that he converted his wife and children and kept a Christian home, even covering a clock face that advertised a brand of whisky with a salvation message: "THIS IS A FAITHFUL SAYING, AND WORTHY OF ALL ACCEPTANCE, THAT CHRIST JESUS CAME INTO THE WORLD TO SAVE SINNERS" (Klang Gospel Hall 1991: 27; emphasis in original).

Chew returned to business, investing in a rubber plantation and other commercial enterprises, and attributed his economic successes following his release to God's help. He joined the Penang Gospel Hall, and often accompanied Marks on sweeping tours of the region, paying his own expenses and sometimes those of the British missionary. Together they visited Malaya, Lower Thailand, Lower Burma, and Sumatra, walking, bicycling, and boating (by Marks' estimate) over 10,000 miles (Marks 1953: 21).

Within the Brethren network, Chew was a popular speaker. When he visited Singapore in 1910 to address a meeting of Chinese women, Green reported:[76]

> We have lately had an interesting visit from our dear brother Boon Hean, the ex-convict. . . . The name of Boon Hean is well known; and eighty or more women came to hear him speak. . . . It is most stimulating to hear Boon Hean narrate the way in which the Lord helps him in his business, whilst he gives the first place to the Lord's work, proving Matt. vi. 33.

The verse in the New Testament Gospel of St. Matthew that Green cited promises rewards to those who esteem God above all else, hinting at an interpretation of the Bible today known as the prosperity gospel: "But seek ye first the kingdom of God, and his righteousness; and all these things shall be added unto you."

In 1911 Chew established a meeting place in a shophouse in Klang, which was the royal capital of Selangor but also a centre for tin mining and rubber cultivation. In 1913 he built and furnished a new gospel hall next door to his house for a few friends and their estate workers, and renovated a rubber smokehouse into a mission house for local workers and European missionaries.

---

[75] "Fruit among Lepers and Prisoners", Green, Kuala Lumpur, 16 January 1908, *ES* No. 642 (March 1908 Pt. 2): 112.

[76] "Once Darkness, now Light", Green, Singapore, 18 November 1910, *ES* No. 686 (January 1910 Pt. 2): 31.

He transferred title in the property to the Stewards Co., Bath (the Brethren property trust) in July 1921 (Klang Gospel Hall 1991: 14).

The opening Chinese meeting was "packed out", attended not only by Christians, but also by the local schoolmaster, who was a prominent Confucianist, and other "leading men of the place" whom Chew had invited.[77] Two European Brethren and two Chinese evangelists addressed the meeting in three dialects of Chinese and offered a few days later an English-language service.[78] One of his new converts testified that he had been a "sorcerer" (probably a spirit medium) and had smoked opium for 37 years. But, he noted, "God can save a sinner like me", and he urged others to convert.[79] They regularly held two meetings, one for English-speaking Tamils and one for Hokkien speakers.[80]

Conclusion

In 1912, Brethren author William Hoste, whose brother was the General Director of the China Inland Mission, stopped in Singapore on his return to Britain from Shanghai.[81] He visited Open Brethren assemblies in Kuala Lumpur, Kampar, Ipoh, Taipeng, Province Wellesley, Penang, and Province Kedah, and spoke at meetings in "halls, hospitals, a prison, leper asylums, schools, and the open air, speaking generally by interpretation, but sometimes directly in English". Hoste observed that "Places which I expected to find jungle villages are large, civilized towns, with fine public buildings and offices. British rule, Chinese labour and tin have been the making of the country." He ignored the Malays and Islam, as well as Singapore's 40-odd nationalities when he claimed that British rule, Chinese labour, and tin had made Malaya. But these three

---

[77] "Conversion of a Sorcerer", Ashdown, Penang, 21 April 1913, *ES* No. 768 (June 1913 Pt. 2): 228.

[78] "Opening of a New Hall", Tipson, 22 April 1913, *ES* No. 768 (June 1913 Pt. 2): 228.

[79] "Conversion of a Sorcerer", Ashdown, Penang, 21 April 1913, *ES* No. 768 (June 1913 Pt. 2): 228.

[80] Tipson, Kuala Lumpur, 8 December 1912, *ES* No. 736 (February 1912 Pt. 2): 73.

[81] William Hoste (1860–1938) visited Ceylon and Shanghai, China before returning to Britain by way of the Straits Settlements and Malaya. Hoste trained for ordination at Cambridge before joining the Brethren movement and was involved with the Victoria Institute (Grass 2013: 123). His brother Dixon Edward Hoste was one of the so-called Cambridge Seven who joined the China Inland Mission, and James Hudson Taylor's successor.

elements played a large role in creating the Brethren circuit that he followed on his speaking tour.[82]

As we have seen, many of the Chinese evangelists were recent emigrants from China, and the missionaries depended on them to work with Chinese speakers. As a consequence, the early Chinese gospel halls in Penang and Singapore were as much a creation of the development of Christian missions in Fujian and Guangdong as they were of Brethren efforts. My focus in this chapter has been on Penang and its regional networks. But as the next chapter shows, by the 20th century, travel and communications efficiently linked Penang, Singapore, and the Malay States to both Europe and China.

---

[82] "Visits to Different Places", W. Hoste, *ES* No. 735 (February 1912): 52.

Chapter 10

Alexander Grant and the Boxer Uprising

> Let Europeans imagine a parallel case, of Buddhist or Confucian missionaries working in London or Paris, the Christian Church and all her doctrines condemned as the most baneful creations of the devil, and all the time-honoured customs of the French and English people interdicted! Would anyone guarantee that no mob would rise up against such Mongolian intruders?
>
> Lim Boon Keng, 1901[1]

The Brethren missionaries in the British-ruled Straits Settlements and colonial Malaya continued to seek new workers, but the descendants of the first missionaries chose China over Penang and Singapore. Maria and Burella Dyer were born in Malacca and Penang, but went to Ningpo, where Maria met and married James Hudson Taylor, the founder of the China Inland Mission (CIM). In 1897, Singapore missionary Alexander Grant's daughter Lucy and her husband went to Shanxi Province in North China as missionaries.

In 1900, the editors of *Echoes of Service* saw the judgement of God in plague and famine in India and prolonged war in South Africa. They observed that the unity of the British empire in the face of these challenges was impressive but noted that Britain was overly proud of its power, that its leaders were vain, and that they depended too much on the weapons of war. They predicted that if God was not honoured, "humiliation in some form or other must follow", and proposed that Christians pray.[2]

A few weeks after this essay on "God's Dealings with Nations" appeared in print, China's Empress Dowager deemed foreign powers to be enemies of China, catalyzing violent attacks on European and Chinese Christians

[1] Lim Boon Keng 1901: 325.

[2] "God's Dealings with Nations", W[illiam] H[enry] B[ennet], *ES* No. 455 (June 1900 Pt. I): 161–2.

throughout northern China. Lucy died in 1900 in the event known as the Taiyuan Massacre. At the time of the uprising, her father was in China, visiting Brethren missionaries in Mongolia. They fled to the coast on mules, by train, and by boat with the help of Chinese officials. Grant remained in China for another two years, and in letters to the editors of *Echoes of Service* reflected on what had gone so terribly wrong.

Lucy Lovitt, Alexander Grant, and the Shouyang Mission

When Alexander Grant retired to London in 1885, he and his family returned to Tottenham and the Brook Street Chapel. Grant conducted Bible readings for young people on Saturday nights at Bruce Grove Hall, a lecture hall that the Brethren used as a meeting place. Their eldest daughter Lucy (1868–1900), who had been born in Singapore, taught at the Brook Street Chapel Sunday School.[3] She visited homes and taught Jewish children in a Sabbath School in Whitechapel, an overcrowded slum in London's East End.[4]

For two years Lucy lived in Koslin, a city in Prussian Poland, where she taught English in a German school and studied Yiddish. On her return to London, she entered a nursing programme at the London Hospital, and while working as a private nurse met Dr Arnold E. Lovitt (1869–1900). In 1896, Thomas Wellesley Pigott (1847–1900) visited England and recruited Lovitt to work at a hospital in Taiyuan, the capital of Shanxi province. Lucy Grant and Dr Lovitt married at Bruce Grove Hall in 1897, and a month later they sailed to China to work as medical missionaries (Edwards 1907: 226–7).

Pigott was a wealthy Anglo-Irish aristocrat whose family had opened the doors of their estate to revivalist preachers during an 1862 awakening in Ireland. His family belonged to the Church of Ireland, but Pigott had walked 22 miles every Sunday to attend a Brethren breaking-of-bread ceremony (Pigott 1903: 15). He went to China in 1869 with the China Inland Mission (CIM), and moved to Taiyuan in 1880. There, he worked with Dr Harold Schofield (1851–83), an Oxford graduate and gifted surgeon, to develop a new hospital facility (Kaiser 2016: 35). After Dr Schofield died of typhus, Dr Ebenezer Henry Edwards became the hospital's director. Pigott had paid for the Schofield

---

3 Brook Street Chapel, Tottenham, No. 17, 1839–1964: 15. Christian Brethren Archive, University of Manchester (CBA 13105).

4 Lucy's two sisters published *A Brief Memoir of Lucy Elisabeth Lovitt* (1904), which included her letters to family from Germany and China and a few of her poems. I thank Hazel Andrews for sending me copies of this private publication.

Figure 22 Missionary Helps postcard focused on medical missions. The medical missionaries identified by name include James Hudson Taylor and Harold A. Schofield, whose exhortation to medically trained Christians to take up medical missions is quoted in the bottom centre section of the postcard. This postcard was reproduced in *Links of Help with Other Lands* Vol. IV (1914–15): 70, with a date of 1911. *Echoes of Service* archive.

Memorial Hospital, and his brother-in-law Dr Edwards directed it on behalf of CIM (Austin 2007: 350–1).

Between 1881 and 1895, over 50 missionaries in Shanxi resigned from CIM due to conflict with James Hudson Taylor, whom they found to be overly autocratic (Austin 2007: 268–9). Pigott was among them. As he described it, they regretted severing the "bonds of organization" but still wanted to cooperate with CIM (Edwards 1907: 238). By 1896, the independent Shouyang Mission controlled both the Taiyuan Girls' School and the Schofield Memorial Hospital (Kaiser 2016: 56).

Conflict with Taylor led to a further division in the Taiyuan missionary community. In 1893, Anna Sofie Jakobsen (1860–1911), a CIM female missionary from Norway, had become engaged to a Chinese evangelist, Ch'eng Hsiu-Chi (Cheng Xiuqi). Taylor refused to approve the marriage, and after waiting five years they married in 1898 in the home of Chu, a Christian photographer who was a member of the Shouyang Mission. Taylor reproached Jakobsen in a letter, claiming that apart from Dr and Mrs Edwards, the entire Taiyuan missionary community had identified the union as a "cruel wrong". After Taylor accepted her resignation, Mr and Mrs Edwards gave the couple travel funds, and they moved to Hunan to start 'Anna Cheng's Mission' (Laegreid 2015: 62–86; see also Austin 2007: 390–1).

When Dr Edwards took a leave to visit England in 1899, he left Dr Lovitt in charge, and Lucy looked after routine work with women (Edwards 1907: 226–7). She described opium as "the great curse of this city, both men and women taking it". Opium addiction was a focus for the medical missionaries of CIM and the Shouyang Mission, and Lucy's letters to her family are filled with reports of the drug's ill effects.

In a letter published in *Echoes*, she described the poppy fields of Shouyang:[5]

> We are on a visit to Sheo-Yang, which is much cooler than our city at this time. It has pretty walks round and fields planted with millet, maize, melons, patches of potato, and cucumber, and a few poppy fields, but of the latter there are more between this and T'ai-Yüen. The beautiful colours of the poppy—purple, mauve, pink but principally white, look so pretty, and it is sad to think of the evil those lovely flowers mean. Opium is the curse of this province. Men, women, and sometimes little children smoke it. The result is vice and degredation to a terrible degree.

Her husband's patients included a father who had sold his infant children to buy opium, and in letters to her family she described the deaths of people who

---

[5] Lucy Lovitt, T'ai-Yuen-Fu, n.d., *ES* No. 417 (November 1898 Pt. 1): 329.

had used opium to commit suicide. One young female slave had killed herself by taking a ball of opium to retaliate against her mistress, and a young man who could not repay his gambling debts took opium as a way to end his troubles. In one letter, she exclaimed, "O, this crying sin of England!" (Lovitt 1904: 9, 16, 20, 26).

Brethren philanthropist John Eliot Howard had helped develop quinine into an affordable medical treatment, and his family's company Howard & Sons provided CIM missionaries with free or low cost supplies of quinine, which was used as a palliative for treating recovering opium addicts (West 2016: 6; Austin 2007: 242). But Dr Schofield, who had practised medicine in battlefields in Turkey, is credited with developing an even more effective treatment for opium addiction using a hypodermic needle and injecting doses of morphine that were gradually reduced until only water was being injected, at which point the cure was complete (Austin 2007: 246; Kaiser 2016: 41–2).

Figure 23 Dr and Mrs Lovitt (Edwards 1907: facing p. 226).

Alexander Grant in China, 1899–1902

In 1899, Grant returned to Asia, stopping in India and Southeast Asia before continuing to North China. He visited Taiping, Penang, Tongkah, Kreean, and Parit Buntar on the mainland before going to Kuala Lumpur (SKI 1900: 55), where he and Gan Kui held a week of special meetings. He observed that the Christians were perfunctory in their prayers, advised that: "Strong crying and tears, not mere words spoken, would befit us well."

In Singapore, Grant questioned the rhetorical strategy of shaming Chinese into conversion:[6]

> As to the preaching: it seems better we should preach but little against the idols (at any rate native brethren may be left to do that), and not ridicule idols. We do not forget that Elijah said "cry aloud"; but that was not to raise a laugh. This is easily done with Chinese. One can hardly read ps. cxv. 4–8 without moving their risible faculties; not that they are laughing at God's words, but rather they are interested to find so vivid a setting forth of what they know to be true.
>
> It is not well to work on their self-esteem, and put them to shame. On the other hand we speak wisdom among them that are perfect. . . . Even for a full gospel of salvation, the unpricked heart and the unawakened conscience are not ready.

Psalm 115 is the psalm that describes idols as man-made objects, unable to walk or speak, see or smell, and Christians often cited it when they criticized so-called idol worship.

Welsh Baptist missionary Timothy Richard had published a tract on Daoism "acknowledging what was true in it", which coworkers in Taiyuan regarded as "rank heresy" (Richard 1916: 205). Although his proposals were not as radical as Richard's, Grant suggested that Christians could blend Chinese adages like "Heaven begat us, earth rears us" with Christian teachings. Justifying his recommendations by allusions to a string of New Testament texts, he observed that "their five virtues—benevolence, justice, reverence, wisdom, fidelity; or the proverb, 'Good has a good recompense; evil an evil one'—a familiar phrase with them" would provide good subject matter for public discourse.

Grant reached Taiyuan at the end of 1899. There, he wrote lengthy letters to the editors of *Echoes of Service* in which he expressed doubts about the missionaries' strategies, old and new. He noted that the missionaries in China had built modern schools and hospitals, but objected to New Theology, questioning the effectiveness of imparting Christianity alongside science (see also Maxwell 1991). Grant further proposed that the missionaries should leave the Chinese churches on their own and only revisit them from time to time. He found the model for this method in *Acts of the Apostles*, which described the early missionaries as travelling in small groups of two or three or four, "men knit

[6] Grant, Singapore, 12 May 1899, *ES* No. 435 (August 1899 Pt. 1): 230.

together in love; each desirous to help one another's ministry; each esteeming others better than himself".[7]

In a letter written in Shouyang, Grant exhorted missionaries to seek the "power of the Holy Ghost" to make converts. But he ridiculed "earnest young men" who thought that they could "preach in Chinese, by the gift of tongues without learning the language". He added that in starting a new sect or school of thought, it was not always easy to draw the line between "what is of faith" and what is "unhinging of mind".[8] He praised some missionaries and criticized others as "down-grade", and prayed that the Anglican Church Missionary Society workers "could leave national English notions and practices in the West!"[9]

Grant spent five months in Shanxi, visiting with his daughter and her family in Taiyuan, but also explored nearby areas with Alexander Hoddle, an independent missionary. He and Hoddle covered 800 or 900 miles, stopping for a few days in different places. His fluency in Hokkien was useless in North China, and when he preached, Hoddle interpreted for him into Mandarin.

In April 1900, Grant and Hoddle visited Rev. Archibald E. Glover (1859–1954), an ordained Anglican minister with a degree from Oxford who had left a position at St Paul's Church in Onslow Square, London in 1896 to become a CIM missionary. In China, Glover had joined Stanley P. Smith in Lu'an (now Changzhi). Smith was one of the Cambridge Seven—seven men from elite backgrounds who made CIM famous when they went to China as missionaries in 1885.[10]

In his memoir of the Boxer Uprising, Glover recalled how happy he was to meet Grant, whom he described as a veteran missionary who had worked in Amoy and Singapore:

> How little we dreamed as we met together in happy fellowship what three months hence would have to reveal: Mr. Grant a refugee, barely escaping with his life and only with the loss of his effects. Mr. Hoddle (together with Dr. and Mrs. Lovitt and some forty other foreign workers)

---

[7] Grant, Thai-yuen-fu, North China, December 1899, *ES* No. 450 (March 1900 Pt. 2): 90. See also Grant, Tien-tsin, 28 April 1900, *ES* No. 460 (August 1900 Pt. 2): 251.

[8] Grant, Sheo-yang, Shan-si, 27 February 1900, *ES* No. 454 (May 1900 Pt. 2): 155. The Brethren relationship to Pentecostalism is complicated. They attributed conversions not to their own actions but to the Holy Ghost and sought signs of divine providence, but they rejected claims to Pentecostal gifts like speaking in tongues.

[9] Grant, Sheo-yang, Shan-si, 27 February 1900, *ES* No. 454 (May 1900 Pt. 2): 155.

[10] Smith and his wife had returned to Britain on furlough in 1899, and were not in Lu'an when Grant visited Glover.

> beheaded and in a martyr's grave. Our own station rioted, and ourselves stripped of all and in the hands of the Boxers (Glover 1904: 14).

The Boxer Uprising

Grant next went to Tianjin, where he planned to meet Robert Stephen, the Brethren missionary who had started their mission in Mongolia in 1897. While waiting, Grant wrote a long reflection on what he had seen, concluding that although China had many problems, the country was as well off as many regions of Europe. He observed that "The gospel in London does not prevent misery existing in the East End, nor preclude the possibility of such an event as the South Africa War. What worse could China do?" But Grant also reported rising tensions and hostility, observing that the idea of driving foreigners out was gaining ground.[11]

He knew that Christians had aggravated the tensions: when Chinese Catholics broke the law, they sought protection from the European priests, who interceded with the Mandarins on their behalf. But he also knew of a Protestant missionary who had made a similar intervention. Fearful of getting entangled with the British, on receiving the missionary's card, the Mandarin took no action against the law-breaker. Grant concluded that the growing anti-foreign movement. coupled with anger at Christians, had led directly to the 1899 murder of Mr Brooks of the Society for the Propagation of the Bible in Shandong.

On receiving confirmation by telegram that Mr Grant had arrived in Tianjin, Mr Stephen met him there, and on 2 May they set out by train for Jehol (now Chengde), in an area of North China then called Inner Mongolia (Woodbridge 2019: 77).[12] Mr Grant did Bible readings and went with the missionaries when they visited a village outstation that held a Christian meeting once a month at full moon.[13] Not long after, Edward Eagger—a missionary who had worked in Larut and Selangor with Hakka speakers between 1888 and 1897, but who had moved to North China—wrote:[14]

> I have never known the state of the country so critical; men's hearts are failing them for fear. Mongols are selling land and property to flee from expected danger. The richer Chinese are buying silver to bury and hide

[11] Grant, Tien-tsin, 28 April 1900, *ES* No. 460 (August 1900 Pt. 2): 250.

[12] H.J. Barnett, Pa-kou, Mongolia, 22 April 1900, *ES* No. 457 (July 1900 Pt. 1): 201.

[13] E.A. Stephen, Pa-kou, 27 May 1900, *ES* No. 460 (August 1900 Pt. 2): 251.

[14] Eagger, Pa-kou, 30 May 1900, *ES* No. 460 (August 1900 Pt. 2): 251.

> it from plunderers. It seems as if a little spark would set things into a blaze. The movement is distinctly anti-Christian.

In June 1900 the Militia United in Righteousness (*Yihetuan*) Movement erupted in violent attacks that spread throughout in North China.

In the last week of May, the Boxers destroyed the Tianjin–Beijing railway and cut the telegraph cables of Western companies between Beijing, Tianjin, and Russia. Foreign diplomats could not communicate with their home governments, and relied on warships to carry telegrams as they coordinated their response. The fighters whom the British called Boxers laid siege to Beijing, forcing Europeans and Chinese Christians to take refuge in the Legation Quarter. Unable to communicate with anyone in Beijing, British ministers in other Chinese cities contacted London for news (Knuesel 2007: 528).

The Europeans refused an imperial order to evacuate Beijing, and on 17 June allied Japanese and Western naval forces captured the Dagu forts near Tianjin and started to bring troups on shore. On 21 June the Empress Dowager Cixi (1835–1908) declared war on the foreign powers (Cohen 1997: 44–51). As Joseph Esherick notes, prior to the court's declaration of war, few Europeans had lost their lives, but with "substantial official encouragement and complicity, a major bloodbath would begin" (Esherick 1987: 304).

Soon after, imperial troops, Boxers, and monks from a Tibetan Buddhist temple attacked the foreign legations and the Catholic cathedral in Beijing, and missions throughout North China were assaulted (Clark 2011: 139). In response, Japan, Russia, Britain, France, the United States, Germany, Italy, and Austria-Hungary formed an Eight Nation military alliance. The international force first took control of Tianjin, then marched to Beijing, stealing, killing, burning, and raping as they went. The Empress Dowager and members of the Qing court fled Beijing, and foreign troops occupied the city on 14 August 1900. The soldiers ransacked the Forbidden City, stealing imperial art treasures as trophies of war (Esherick 1987: 309–11).[15]

The telegraph and the telegraphists who decoded the messages played a major role in the unfolding events. The Boxer rebels cut telegraph lines and disrupted railway travel, and for a time little news came of events in Beijing and Shanxi. But everywhere else, news travelled almost instantaneously. The Empress sent imperial orders to the Provincial Governors, the British consul in Shanghai broadcast threats of retaliation, and missionaries sent news home from many locations in China by telegraph.

---

[15] The repercussions of this and other looting events live on in a modern campaign to recover these objects and restore them to Chinese museums.

By 1875, a telegraphic network that some now call the Victorian Internet connected Great Britain to 20,000 cities, towns, and villages worldwide via 1 million kilometres of landline wires and 50,000 kilometres of submarine cables (Huurdeman 2005: 106–7, 136). With the creation of this global telegraphic network, news that once had taken months to arrive now came in hours or minutes. By 1900, the telegraph had become a foundational technology for modern governance, global commerce, and warfare (Baark 1997: 59–60).

By 1870, telegraphic cables linked London to Bombay, and in 1871 a submarine cable was laid from Madras to Malaya, with landing points in Penang, Malacca, and Singapore. Singapore was already connected with Hong Kong, and the telegraphic lines were further expanded to include Batavia and Port Darwin in Australia. The foreign powers also landed underwater cables in the treaty ports in 1871, connecting Hong Kong, Shanghai, and London. The new technology reduced the time it took for a message to travel from China to London from 40 days to a couple of hours, or, in the case of high-priority messages, 53 minutes (Baark 1997: 55, 65, 82). Chinese elites feared the potential of the new technology to undermine the established order (see Richard 1916: 231). But despite political opposition, by 1900 China had an extensive domestic telegraph network, a telegraphic code for Chinese characters, and a corps of trained telegraphists (Baark 1997: 157–77).

Grant was starting to plan his journey home when the missionaries received a telegraph from Tianjin on 10 June warning them that the road to Tangshan was dangerous and that if they travelled, they should go via Jinzhou in Liaoning Province. They learned that fighting had broken out between the foreign powers and China on 17 June, then at 3 pm heard from the telegraph officer that the Dagu forts near Tianjin had been taken, and that the Chinese had retreated.[16] When they decided to leave, the civil and military authorities helped them engage carts to take them to Jinzhou, a seven-day journey. The mandarin also sent two soldiers to protect them. They had four carts and one mule-litter, and the two younger men rode mules.

As they passed through Nanpiao, a coal mining district in what is today Liaoning Province, they learned that three Englishmen in a mining camp sought help to leave. They had already passed the camp, but Mr Stephen went back, and the rest stopped at an inn to wait. Hundreds of people surged in, and they later learned that robbers had planned to attack them at night. The innkeeper had begged the robbers to not attack them at his inn, and they agreed

[16] Eagger, Niu-chang, 1 July 1900, *ES* No. 462 (September 1900 Pt. 2): 280.

to wait for the travellers on the road. Uneasy staying at the inn, they decided to go back to the mining camp, a decision that saved them.

At the camp they met a military mandarin with 200 soldiers who offered them the use of a house and posted soldiers to guard them all night. Later they identified him as Colonel Wei and described him as an old soldier who had served under Li Hongzhang during the Taiping Rebellion.[17] Sure that armed robbers planned to attack them, they stayed several days. In Nanpiao, Grant wrote in his diary: "We have been face to face with the question of departing out of this world to be with Christ. All of us, I believe, have offered up ourselves, if God please so."[18]

They telegraphed to the British consul at the treaty port Niuchuang (Yingkou) to ask for help, and the British miners also sent three telegrams. Colonel Wei also sent a telegram to the chief official at Jinzhou, asking him to assist the travellers to reach Niuchuang. The reply was positive, and they set off:[19]

> the mandarin sent us off with an escort of thirty soldiers with trumpets blowing. We made quite a long procession—eight carts, a mule-litter, thirty horses ridden by soldiers, three by the Englishmen, three by attendants, and Mr Stephen's and my mule. At mid-day we arrived at an inn, and dense crowds collected, but there was no disturbance, and at night we reached Chin-chou [Jinzhou], the trumpets again blowing, so some thought we were prisoners. Through the help and kindness of an English-speaking Chinese gentleman we were comfortable housed at an inn. We heard that our presence caused excitement in the city; some 7,000 workers not receiving their full pay were riotous, and waiting an opportunity to create a disturbance.

The Europeans had already evacuated, and Chinese Christians sent a message that it would be better if they did not visit their gospel hall.[20] They stayed in an inn near the railway station, and in the morning a telegram came from the consul informing them that a train would be sent to Jinzhou to take them to Niuchuang.

On their arrival in that city, they learned of the burning of the mission house, chapel, and other property in Mukden (Shenyang), at a distance of less than 200 kilometres.[21] While waiting to leave for Chefoo (Zhifu, today Yantai),

---

[17] Barnett, T'ang Shan, 15 May 1902, *ES* No. 507 (August 1902 Pt. 1): 291.

[18] Grant, Nan-piao, 26 June–2 July 1900, *ES* No. 462 (September 1900 Pt. 2): 282.

[19] "The Escape of the Pa-Kou Party", Eagger, Niu-chuang, 1 July 1900, *ES* No. 462. (September 1900 Pt. 2): 221.

[20] Grant, Nan-piao, 26 June–2 July 1900, *ES* No. 462 (September 1900 Pt. 2): 282.

[21] "The Escape of the Pa-Kou Party", Eagger, Niu-chuang, 1 July 1900, *ES* No. 462. (September 1900 Pt. 2): 281.

Grant visited William Chalmers Burns' grave and picked flowers: "There is a knot of graves, precious dust awaiting the Lord from heaven in the cemetery."[22]

From Chefoo, Mr Stephen had reported that some Christians were still missing "in Peking, Pao-ting-fu, Tai-yuen-fu, and other places". There was no news of Grant's daughter and her family, and he added "Poor Mr. Grant is in awful suspense now."[23] Hoping for news of those who were missing, Stephen returned to Tianjin. There, he found blackened ruins and empty streets, foreign troops, and Boxer war captives in chains.

He located one refugee Christian from Pa-kou, who told of two Christian refugees who had fled after one found his family slaughtered. As they approached Tianjin, they had asked foreign soldiers for help, but the soldiers tied them together by their queues and threw them into the river. The two managed to untangle their queues, but one could not swim and drowned. The survivor fled to Tangshan, and Stephen sent a messenger for him, hoping to get him across Russian lines. The Brethren rarely mentioned Foxe's *Book of Martyrs*, but Stephen observed that although some Chinese Christians had recanted, others died "witnessing as bold and as heart-stirring confessions as ever did any of their predecessors of whom Foxe wrote".[24]

From Chefoo, Grant and the Eaggers continued to Weihaiwei, a treaty port and naval base that the United Kingdom had leased in Shandong Province.[25] Grant conducted a week of special Bible readings there, but his return ticket was expiring and he had to go south.[26] He went to Shanghai, where he soon met the Brethren missionaries working in Jiangxi Province, who had evacuated there.[27] His daughter, son-in-law, and grandchild were still missing, and he tried to find meaning in the disruptive violent events:[28]

> Many thoughts will arise in the minds of those who would fain see the news that the Son of God is come carried into all the earth, as to what may be the mind of God in this extraordinary outburst. If it be the

---

[22] Grant, Nan-piao, 26 June–2 July 1900, *ES* No. 462 (September 1900 Pt. 2): 282.

[23] R. Stephen, Chefoo, 2 August 1900, *ES* No. 463 (October 1900 Pt. 1): 299.

[24] Stephen, Tientsin 28 August 1900, *ES* No. 466 (November 1900 Pt. 2): 345.

[25] Buxbaum, Wei-hai-wai, 22 June 1900 *ES* No. 462 (September 1900 Pt. 1): 266. Buxbaum wrote that the long-expected "burst up" had come, and that they were preparing for hundreds of refugees; John W. Wilson, Wei-hai-wei, 18 July 1900 and Benjamin Mudditt, 19 July 1900, *ES* No. 463 (October 1900 Pt. 1): 298.

[26] Wilson, Wei-hai-wei, 18 July 1900 and Mudditt, 19 July 1900, *ES* No. 463 (October 1900 Pt. 1): 298.

[27] Edward J. Blandford, Shanghai, 4 August 1900, *ES* No. 463 (October 1900 Pt. 1): 300.

[28] Grant, Shanghai, 6 August 1900, *ES* No. 464 (October 1900 Pt. 2): 316.

> occasion of leading servants of Christ to consider more closely what is the gospel of God, and if it lead them to purge away all teachings that are merely national, local or sectional, and bring in only fundamental and unquestionable matters, it will be well.

Grant also comforted his fellow missionaries, reminding them that "nearly in every place rioting was what followed on souls being saved; also that Paul was over and over again forced to leave his labour and escape for his life; so we need not think this a strange thing".[29]

The Editors of *Echoes* noted in August that although Grant was safe, massacres had been reported at Taiyuen, "where he recently visited his daughter, her husband and child", and they hoped that they had escaped.[30] The news of their deaths reached them in England by telegraph before it reached Mr Grant.[31] In September they printed a report from Blandford:[32]

> News just to hand from T'ai-yuan-fu, Shan-si Province. Thirty-seven foreigners and fifty native Christians beheaded, and their heads hung up on the street. The Governor inquired of the natives whether they had given up the false religion and returned to the true, to which they replied, "Governor, you can draw the sword; do not ask us such a question, please." Thereupon they were beheaded!

By September, the missionaries knew of 91 Protestant missionaries, including children, who had been killed, and over 80 were still not accounted for.

Grant wrote a long letter to the editors of *Echoes,* but only said of his loss that nothing needed to be said, since the news had reached England at the same time as it reached them in China. Apparently trying to read the mind of God, he suggested that if doors opened again for the missionaries, they should do itinerant rather than stationary work, implying that there was a message in the destruction of Christian hospitals, schools, and mission houses.

He also recommended separation from European might: "Let the powers make treaties regarding commerce and such things, and let the gospel labourer be regarded as an unrecognized outlaw, with no passport, entering such doors as might be open to him at his own risk." He concluded, "My own matters are very dark. Our God gives no account of what He does. Do not both evil and good proceed out of the mouth of the Most High. . . . Tears are in some

---

29 Eliza J. Lennox, 31 August 1900, *ES* No. 465 (November 1900 Pt. 1): 333.

30 "China", Editorial note, *ES* No. 460 (August 1900 Pt. 2): 249.

31 Editorial note, *ES* No. 466 (November 1900 Pt. 2): 345.

32 "Wu-Ch'en After the Exodus", Blandford, Shanghai, 24 September 1900, *ES* No. 466 (November 1900 Pt. 2): 347.

measure our portion." Letters and reports from Chinese Christians describing the loss of life and property had started to reach them, and he worried about the Chinese Christians whom he had met on his travels in North China.[33]

A Chinese Christian, Yong Zheng, claimed to have witnessed the mass killings in Taiyuan, and many months later, the editors of *Echoes* cited a newspaper article based on his account. As he described Lucy Lovitt's execution, after a soldier removed her glasses, she spoke to the crowd:

> Mrs. Lovitt held the hand of her little boy, even when she was killed. She said to the people, "We all came to China to bring you the good news of salvation by Jesus Christ; we have done you no harm, only good; why do you treat us so?"

Rumours were many, and a story had circulated that a child had been spared. All hoped that it was Grant's grandson, but Yong Zheng confirmed that all the children had been beheaded.[34]

The Brethren in England raised money from "friends in Glasgow and London" to pay for passage home for their missionaries, but Grant refused to return, hoping that his wife would come to China instead.[35] He next wrote from Amoy, where he continued to question what had gone wrong. He proposed again that instead of looking to "Western science and erudition" to promote Christianity, as the Methodists were doing, they should instead look for "holiness, living in the saints, understanding of the mystery of Christ, manifest conversions, . . . and the upbuilding of God's children."[36]

Some historians have criticized Christian accounts of the Taiyuan Massacre for their hagiographic tone, but for the Brethren, no matter how they died, all who were born again were saints. And in Grant's memorial statement for his son-in-law and daughter, he traced the chain of causality back to the Empress Dowager's edicts and European aggression:

> The advent of a Governor willing to carry out the exterminating edicts of the Empress-Dowager, issued, it is believed, on the taking of the Taku forts, led to the extinction of the band of workers in T'ai Yüan and

[33] Grant, Shanghai, 24 September 1900, *ES* No. 466 (November 1900 Pt. 2): 345.

[34] "Details of Massacres in China", *ES* No. 477 (May 1901 Pt 1): 182. The Swedish missionary who attended a public memorial ceremony at Taiyuan on the first anniversary of the massacre also reported that the story of a child being spared was untrue. Tjader, Tai-yuen-fu, 18 July 1901, *ES* No. 489 (November 1901 Pt. 1): 413.

[35] "China", Editorial note, n.d., *ES* No. 468 (December 1900 Pt 2): 374.

[36] Grant, Amoy, 28 February 1901, *ES* No. 477 (May 1901 Pt. 1): 173.

> elsewhere in Shansi. What is done cannot be undone. . . . Resurrection glory will finally crown all (Edwards 1907: 230).

Although Grant may have looked forward to a reunion with his loved ones at the end of time, he deeply lamented the extinction of the Shouyang Mission.

The Taiyuan Massacre

Dr Edwards had been on leave in England when war broke out, but he returned to China and represented the Shouyang Mission in reparation negotiations with the Chinese government. He embarked on a detailed investigation of the Boxer Uprising, and published translations of letters and interviews reporting on the persecution of Chinese Christians in the *Shanghai Mercury* (1901). Several years later he published an illustrated book-length study focused on Shanxi province (2007).

Anthony E. Clark describes *Fire and Sword in Shansi* as Protestant hagiography, and also claims that Edwards promoted anti-Chinese stereotypes by representing the events as a war of good versus evil (Clark 2015: 43; 2017: 91–3). Edwards wrote this book with passion, and after extensive research concluded that the provincial governor had ordered the massacre, labelling him the butcher of Shanxi. But he also reported on the province's history of drought and famine, and political events that led to an anti-foreign governor's posting to Shanxi.

Historian Roger Thompson (2007) has proposed that Governor Yuxian was unfairly blamed and punished for the massacre in Taiyuan. He claims that the accepted version of the event was based on a single eyewitness, Yong Zheng, whose description of Lucy Lovitt's last words I cite above, and judges his account to be unreliable. He proposes an alternate narrative: that the missionaries went to the *yamen* seeking protection and were killed by an angry mob. But as Andrew T. Kaiser notes, "the simple fact that the accepted account has stood for so long, giving ample opportunities for contradiction, suggests that while details may be questioned—particularly the more maudlin reports of how the various foreigners faced their deaths—the currently accepted narrative as summarized by Edwards remains the most likely" (Kaiser 2016: 94).

Rather than simply glorify his European co-workers and Chinese Christians as martyrs, Edwards interviewed and corresponded with Chinese witnesses of the event, and claimed to have published their accounts "as far as possible in the words of the narrators" (Edwards 1901: 6). He knew that the full story would never be known, but drew on the missionaries' letters and diaries to piece together what details he could of his co-workers' final days (Edwards

1907). Letters from Pigott also survived and were later compiled into a book (Pigott 1903).

Although the Protestant and Catholic missionaries in Taiyuan met with the same fate, their histories have been told separately (see Clark 2011, 2015). Edwards begins *Fire and Sword in Shansi* by listing the names of the 157 European Protestants who died. The China Inland Mission had the highest loss of life, with 63 members killed. The small Shouyang Mission lost 13 men, women, and children, leaving only Edwards. Also among the dead were 15 members of the American Board Mission, 16 members of the English Baptist Missionary Society, 5 members of the British and Foreign Bible Society, 4 members of the Swedish Mongolian Mission, 36 members of the Christian and Missionary Alliance, 5 members of the Scandinavian Alliance Mongolian Mission, and Mr Hoddle, the independent missionary who had travelled in Shanxi with Grant (Edwards 1907: 14–6).

On 21 June, the Empress Dowager declared war on the foreigners. And on 21 or 22 June, the telegraph clerk in Taiyuan told a Baptist missionary that the empress had sent a "secret edict" via telegraph commanding that "all the foreigners were to be killed" (Pigott 1903: 227). Rev. Farling passed on the warning, but none of the Europeans fled. Then on 25 and 26 June, Imperial Decrees were posted at the telegraph office in Taiyuan announcing that war had begun. One of these decrees further stated that "Foreign religions are reckless and oppressive; disrespectful to the gods and oppressive to the people. The righteous people will burn and kill" (Edwards 1907: 48). The missionaries read them but because they had no official seal, they decided to remain in Taiyuan (Edwards 1901: 1).

The Schofield Memorial Hospital where Lucy Lovitt and her husband worked was one of the first targets, destroyed by arson on the night of 27 June. According to Chang Wen Tsui, a teacher in the Taiyuan girls' school, the European missionaries and Chinese Christians first hid, then decided to try to reach Rev. Farthing's house. The missionaries left the mission carrying three revolvers, and as they went through the "boisterous" crowd, one of the male missionaries shot a man who tried to stop them (Pigott 1903: 217).[37]

The two girls could not keep up, and Chang and Miss Coombs fell behind the others. Chang tripped over the body of the man who had been shot, and the crowd dragged Miss Coombs and one of the Chinese girls back. The girl

[37] All other contemporary descriptions I have read of the burning of the hospital omit mention of the shooting. Edwards mentions only that the men "had to use their arms to protect the women and children" (Edwards 1907: 64).

survived, and later reported that the female missionary was struck on the head with a brickbat and they both fell. Miss Coombs begged the rioters to save the girl, and a man grabbed her while others "rushed" Miss Coombs into the fire (Edwards 1907: 207–9; Pigott 1903: 217–9).

The missionaries in Taiyuan took refuge with friends whose houses were guarded by soldiers. But an official informed them that the Governor had commanded them to go to another house for their protection, and they reluctantly agreed. They were taken to a house that they shared with Catholic Bishop, priests, and nuns (Edwards 1907: 70–1; see also Chapter 5 in Clark 2015).[38]

According to Edwards, Governor Yuxian had decided on 9 July that all the foreigners in Taiyuan would be killed. At 2 pm, he rode his horse to the house, accompanied by soldiers who seized the Catholic bishops, priests, and nun, the Protestants, and all Chinese whom they found in their quarters, and marched them to the *yamen* between files of soldiers. Once there, the governor asked each of the Europeans where they came from, and when they responded "England" or "France", he gave the command "kill". From the accounts that he gathered, Edwards was certain that Yuxian had not personally assaulted anyone, but he was also certain that soldiers—not Boxers—had killed them (Edwards 1907: 71–2).

Pigott was working in Shouyang when he learned about the burning of the Schofield Hospital, and received a message from the Shouyang mandarin that he could no longer protect him. At the advice of Chinese Christians, he and his family took refuge in a small cave village. But on 2 July they heard that Boxers were burning homes and killing Chinese Christians in nearby villages, and decided to return to Shouyang and "give themselves up" to the magistrate. They stayed in the *yamen* for three days, possibly as prisoners (Edwards 1907: 76–9).

The magistrate refused to turn them over to the Boxers, but on 6 July again sent word that "in consequence of instructions received from the Governor, he could no longer protect him". This time he offered to send them under escort to the border of his jurisdiction in any direction, and it is not know whether the mandarin sent them to Taiyuan or it it was their choice to go there (Pigott 1903: 234; Edwards 1907: 76–7). The men were transported wearing handcuffs, allegedly so that the Boxers would allow them to continue to the *yamen* without interference. On 9 July they were taken to the *yamen* for

[38] Edwards claimed that two of the four Chinese servants who accompanied them to that house evaded arrest and survived. Grant had hoped for information on how they had spent their final days, and they minutely described the Protestants' activities while under detention to Edwards.

a meeting with Yuxian, where they were first beaten, then taken to the central courtyard for execution.

The bodies of the executed Christians were stripped of their clothing and taken to an empty lot before being thrown outside the city on the execution ground, where their remains were eaten by wolves and dogs (Edwards 1907: 80–2). On learning this, Grant lamented that those executed in Taiyuan had suffered the same fates as Old Testament kings Jereboam and Baasha, who were killed together with their entire families, and Ahab and Jezebel, whose bodies were eaten by dogs.[39]

Chu—the Chinese Christian photographer whose house had provided the venue for Anna Jakobsen and Cheng Xiuqi's 1898 wedding—sent a letter to Edwards in February 1901. He reported that although their bodies could not be identified, in January a deputy of the new governor had coffined and buried the remains of the dead in all the districts. Their names were supplied, and the remains gathered and put in the appropriate number of coffins (Edwards 1907: 111–2).

Chu also reported that in Taigu and Shouyang Chinese Christians had been persecuted during the month following the killings at the *yamen*, and that 170–80 Chinese Christians had died. The day after the missionaries were murdered, his own house had been looted and his family scattered. General Sung Ching's soldiers had also occupied the houses of other Chinese Christians and ruined them by using them as horse stables (Edwards 1907: 114). Chu estimated that more than 4,000 Chinese Christians had lost 8 to 9 tenths of their property, and pled for help (Edwards 1907: 116).

Little had been known about the events in Taiyuan for months, almost certainly because the Empress Dowager had taken refuge in that city after fleeing Beijing in mid-August. She and her court reached Taiyuan in September, and stayed there before continuing their journey to Xi'an on 1 October (Edwards 1907: 111). The mountain passes to Shanxi were closely guarded by Chinese troops who sought to prevent the European troups from following the court but also blocked most cart traffic. Could the court's plan to evacuate through Taiyuan have been a factor in the anti-foreign violence?

When German troops finally broke through Chinese defences, the Shanxi head of the foreign bureau wrote to Timothy Richard and invited him to Shanxi to help settle "the missionary troubles". This, he hoped would also help revive trade, since missionary troubles had resulted in commercial troubles. Richard

[39] "Aims and Methods of Work", Grant, Amoy, 28 March 1901, *Echoes of Service* (June 1901): 213.

went to Beijing, and on 29 May 1901, Richard, Dr Atwood, who represented the American Board, and Dr Edwards met with Qing diplomat Li Hongzhang. Li had been called on to negotiate a settlement with the Eight Nation Alliance, and signed the Boxer Protocol in September 1901 (Edwards 1907: 120–2).

A year after the murders, a delegation of missionaries representing the affected agencies, including Dr Edwards, met with the officials in Taiyuan. They reached an agreement to hold a "public funeral with full Chinese ceremonial, to be attended by the officials and generals". Thirty-two coffins had already been buried in a special graveyard, and the ceremony was held while they were there. The ceremony included banners and a formal address from the government that Edwards translated and published in his memoir.

In Taiyuan, the missionaries asked that the house where those executed had been detained be replaced with a memorial to the dead missionaries:

> It was agreed, too, that the house where the missionaries were kept previous to the massacres should be demolished, a pavilion with tablet and inscription erected on the site, and the ground around made into a garden. Memorial tables were to be placed in a wall close to the scene of massacre, and a large stone erected outside the south gate of the city on the exact spot where the tablet to the infamous Yü Hsien had been put up (Edwards 1907: 132).

The next year, the tablet was erected opposite the pavillion and a memorial service held.[40] This time Richard attended, and construction was begun on a new university whose creation he had proposed for reparation (Richard 1916: 299–304).

The Return Home

Although he had heard that Governor Yuxian had committed suicide, when Grant returned to China from Singapore, he still hoped to meet with the governor's successors and to "have an opportunity of a word with them".[41] He travelled as far as Tangshan in North China, but went instead to Tianjin, and from there to Weihaiwei. He remained through the winter months, teaching at nightly meetings and advising the missionaries on the "work of the Holy

[40] James Hevia observes that the Christians established sacred sites after the uprising, seeking to "inscribe on the land and on the minds of the Chinese a perpetual memory of Christian martyrdom" (Hevia 1992: 124).

[41] Grant, Shanghai, 20 October 1901, *ES* No. 492 (December 1901 Pt. 2): 469. Apparently the rumour of suicide was untrue, and he was executed on 22 February 1901 (Clements 1915: 200).

Spirit".[42] Although he visited the Brethren missionaries in Jiangxi Province in 1902 before returning to Hong Kong via Shanghai, he never returned to Taiyuan.[43] Still, in his memorial to his daughter and her husband, he expressed certainty that the Christians' medical work in the city and region had made a favourable impression, and that "the best of the inhabitants" regarded the massacre with "sorrow and abhorrence" (Edwards 1907: 23). He sailed to Singapore in June, and from there to Java.

While he was still in China, Grant had mentioned that his old friend Gan Kui still worked in Java, praying "the Lord spare him a few years yet—he is eighty—and allow me once more to stand by his side to preach Christ my Lord".[44] In 1902 he went to Batavia for two weeks, to see how the Chinese Christians in Java were doing. On arrival he learned that Gan Kui had died the previous year, and that the businessman Gouw Kho was leading the Chinese Gospel Hall. Grant reported approvingly that the Chinese Christians had the Batavia Gospel Hall "under their own control", and that an evangelical German minister from time to time preached there.[45]

Grant also visited Depok again, where he found two Australian Salvation Army workers and visited some of the people he had met on that earlier visit. He "heard their testimony to the blessing then experienced", noting with satisfaction that "the fruit of those days has remained", but also observed that Apostasy confused all. As he made plans to return home, he wrote that he left the East, especially China, with deep regret. That year, the "Hok-Im-Koan Christians in Batavia" invited Grant's replacement in Singapore, Alfred Thoburn, to visit them, but he never went.[46]

---

[42] J. Norman Case, Wei-hai-wei, 6 January 1902, *ES* No. 498 (March 1902 Pt. 2): 112; Charles H. Buxham, Wei-hai-wei, 3 February 1902, *ES* No. 501 (May 1902 Pt. 1): 170.

[43] "Mr. A. Grant's Account of Wu-chen", Grant, Shanghai, 28 March 1902, *ES* No. 503 (June 1902 Pt. 1): 212–3; "In Memoriam—Alexander Grant", *ES* No. 785 (March 1914 Pt. 1): 85.

[44] Grant, Shanghai, 22 November 1901, *ES* No. 470 (January 1901 Pt. 2): 31–2.

[45] "Visiting the Churches: Between Java and Singapore", Grant, 1 September 1902, *ES* No. 513 (November 1902 Pt. 1): 411.

[46] Thoburn, Singapore, 1 September 1902, *ES* No. 512 (October 1902 Pt. 2): 389. Two years later, a Chinese Christian from Batavia, Gui ngi Hok, whose house Mr Grant had stayed at during his final visit to Batavia, moved to Singapore, where he started a monthly meeting for Malay-speaking women. When he visited the Brethren missionaries, he recalled that years earlier he had sold his interest in a major brewery at a financial loss because Mr Grant advised him that this investment "was opposed to the spirit and the teaching of Scripture" ["Evangelizing Indians and Chinese Women at Singapore", Baird, Singapore, 31 August 1904, *ES* No. 560 (October 1904 Pt. 2): 392].

When he reached Ceylon, Grant observed despondently that many of the lay faith missionaries in China lacked training and that because they had not learned to speak Chinese languages well, they were ineffective preachers. He further noted that their prayer meeting were lifeless and routine, and recommended to the editors of *Echoes of Service* that they should simply encourage many of the missionaries to return home:[47]

> Labourers in the gospel may be divided into three classes. First, those who would be better at home; second, those who would be benefited by a return to the home lands, and some time well spent there, so as to return more fully furnished; and third, those who are vessels unto honour meet for the Master's use.

The editors of *Echoes* added that some missionaries remained only because they would return to an uncertain future.

Singapore and Penang

Only weeks after the Boxer rebels attacked Beijing and attacks on Christians spread throughout China, the conflict had spread to Singapore and Penang. Fearing violence, police and soldiers in Singapore heavily armed themselves. Chinese avoided the evangelists' public preaching stations and would have "very little to do with the native Christians except reviling them".[48]

In July 1900 a missionary reported that "[o]n all sides the native Christians are being told that they will soon lose their heads for believing in and following the foreigner's God".[49] A few months later he observed that many held Christians responsible for the China crisis:[50]

> The feeling here is very hostile against missionaries. . . . Part of the local press is most bitter in its criticism of missionary work, and one of our Straits-born Chinese says that the persecution he experiences day by day is almost beyond endurance. . . .

---

[47] Grant, Colombo, 2 December 1903, *ES* No. 517 (January 1903 Pt. 1): 30–1.

[48] Marks, Taipeng, 18 August 1900, *ES* No. 464 (October 1900 Pt. 2): 314; Thoborn, Singapore, 31 October 1900, *ES* No. 470 (January 1901 Pt. 2): 9–10.

[49] "Brief Notes", Thoburn, Singapore, 5 July 1900 (included in the 1900 volume as endnotes): 32. This note is dated four days before the Taiyuan Massacre, which suggests that the Chinese press had reported the Empress Dowager's 21 June 1900 Imperial Decree declaring war on foreign powers.

[50] Thoburn, Singapore, 12 September 1900, *ES* No. 464 (November 1900 Pt. 2): 330.

Soon after Macdonald wrote from Penang that a Chinese woman who had asked to be baptized had been beaten by a neighbour who reviled her for being a Christian, saying that "all Christians in China were killed, and that she should be put to death as an enemy of China".[51]

When the anti-foreign, anti-Christian Boxer Rebellion broke out in China, English-educated Straits Chinese leader Dr Lim Boon Keng published a series of essays in the *Singapore Free Press* that were reprinted in *The Chinese Crisis from Within* (1901). Dr Lim was a Queen's Scholar who had received his medical training at University of Edinburgh, and was one of two Chinese members of a prestigious Singapore debating club known as the Straits Philosophical Society (1893–1916). The other Chinese member was Tan See Boo's son, Tan Teck Soon, who as a teenager had translated his father's letters to George Müller.

In these essays, Dr Lim Boon Keng concluded that Christianity was not compatible with Chinese identity: "As soon as a man becomes a Christian he really ceases to be a Chinaman, from the native point of view. He literally becomes an outcast of his own choice" (Lim 1901: 202). In a chapter entitled "The White Peril", Lim further observed that the manner in which Europeans imposed the opium trade on China had led Chinese to conclude that Europeans had only one aim—to make money irrespective of rights or morals (Lim 1901: 294). He recognized that missionaries consistently attacked opium trafficking and use, but concluded that the opium trade had led many to discount Christian teachings regarding "unselfishness, benevolence, and virtue" (Lim 1901: 295).[52]

Lim blamed the Qing court and Manchu rule for China's problems. But he also observed that after the Treaty of Tientsin, Christian missionaries had built an *imperium in imperio*—an empire within the empire—in China. He queried his reader:

> Let Europeans imagine a parallel case, of Buddhist or Confucian missionaries working in London or Paris, the Christian Church and all her doctrines condemned as the most baneful creations of the devil, and all the time-honoured customs of the French and English people

[51] Macdonald translated her statement into English and sent it to the Protector of Chinese. Macdonald, Penang, 6 October 1900, *ES* No. 468 (December 1900 Pt. 2): 362.

[52] Lim was the founder of the *Straits Chinese Magazine*, which published the essays and commentaries of authors like Tan who advocated social and political reforms. In his essays, Lim promoted female education, the anti-opium movement, and the revival of a reformed Confucianism.

> interdicted! Would anyone guarantee that no mob would rise up against such Mongolian intruders? (Lim 1901: 325).

Lim agreed with some Christian criticisms of Chinese traditional religious practices, but promoted a reformed Confucianism, first in Singapore, then in China as Xiamen University's second president (1921–37). Although he promoted science and education, he praised traditional forms of ancestor worship as a form of local memory (DeBernardi 1995).

As Stanley J. Tambiah so well described it, modern Asian histories show both the persistence of "historical continuities that modify modernization" and transformations based on tradition (Tambiah 1973: 80). As was the case in India, in China and Southeast Asia Christian influence "hastened the construction (or invention)" of both modern nationalist movements and religious revivalisms (Frykenberg 2005: 107; see also DeBernardi 2009b; Veer 2001).[53] To the rise of modern revivalism and politics in China and Southeast Asia I now turn.

[53] The scholarly literature on modernist religious reform movements is too large to review here, but see the essays in Yoshiko Ashiwa and David L. Wank (2009) for thoughtful insights into the impact of modernity on Chinese religions. My introduction to these reform movements came from the work of Joseph Levenson (1958–65) and Stanley Tambiah (1973), and both are still worth reading.

PART IV
Schism and Continuity

Chapter 11

Chinese Revivalists in Southeast Asia, 1929–41

> Christianity has done away with racial distinction, sexual distinction, and social distinction. Those who believe in the Lord Jesus Christ belong to the same household of faith, and are all the children of God.
>
> Leland Wang[1]

In the 19th century the Open Brethren prayed for revival and spread news about the Second Evangelical Awakening of 1859–60 from North America and Europe to Asia. Although the event is not chronicled in the history of Pentecostalism, when the Brethren organized a week of prayer in Kuala Lumpur in 1905, their meeting room was filled with persons offering spontaneous testimonies, prayer, and praise, including a multilingual Chinese who was "wrought upon by the Holy Spirit".[2] A missionary reported that "quite a revival" had broken out among them and that they had made a number of conversions among students and adults. The new converts, he added, "were full of joy and zeal for the spread of the gospel".[3] The 1905 Kuala Lumpur revival was inspired by reports of the Welsh Revival of 1904, news of which also reached Los Angeles, where the Azusa Street Revival began in 1906, an event that many agree was the starting point for the American Pentecostal movement.[4]

---

[1] Leland Wang n.d.: 11.

[2] "Special Prayer Followed by Rich Blessing", Alfred E. Green, Kuala Lumpur, 14 April 1905, *ES* No. 575 (June 1905 Pt. 1): 210.

[3] "Reviving and Conversions", T.R. Angus, Kuala Lumpur, 13 April 1905, *ES* No. 575 (June 1905 Pt. 1): 210–1.

[4] Evan Roberts, the Methodist leader of the Welsh revival, prayed for guidance from the Holy Spirit, and participants sang and prayed with great fervour at four-hour marathon prayer meetings (Gitre 2004).

In the first three decades of the 20th century, waves of revival continued to reach Christians in Southeast Asia. In those decades, diaspora Chinese also became increasingly involved in China's political struggles. In 1910, Sun Yat-sen (1866–1925) moved the Southeast Asian headquarters of his underground resistance movement, the Tongmenghui, to Penang, where a reading room provided a cover for his revolutionary activities. There he launched a radical newspaper and raised funds from wealthy Chinese businessmen to support the overthrow of the Qing government.[5]

In this chapter, I focus on a new phase of Christian circulations. Starting in 1924, Chinese evangelists visited Penang and Singapore with increasing frequency. Many were from Fuzhou, a treaty port in Fujian that was the site of one of the earliest Protestant missions. In 1901, Huang Naishang led Christian immigrants to found New Fuzhou in Sibu, Sarawak (Barwick 2005–20). Two years later, the Methodist Church and the British government helped hundreds more Fuzhou Christians migrate to Sitiawan, where they formed an agricultural commune in a coastal region of Perak that had been added to the Straits Settlements in 1874.[6] Watchman Nee, John Sung, Leland Wang, and his brother Wilson Wang were all born in or near Fuzhou, and they included Sitiawan on their evangelistic tours of Southeast Asia.

The best known of these revivalist is John Sung (*Song Shangjie* 宋尚節, 1901–44), whose ministry of "signs and wonders" Malaysian Church historian Tan Jin Huat has described as charismatic (Tan 2011: 231). Sung was the son of a Methodist pastor in Putian, Fujian Province. He obtained a doctorate in chemistry in the United States before deciding to study theology at Union Theological Seminary in New York. There he was born again, but when he preached to his fellow students he was deemed to be mentally ill and confined to an asylum. He returned to China without completing his theology degree.

Sung initially did public preaching in Fujian. But a successful 1931 revival event that a Singaporean author calls the Nanchang Pentecost opened the door

---

[5] See the website of the Sun Yat-sen Museum Penang: http://sunyatsenpenang.com/sun-yat-sen/ [accessed 23 February 2016]. One of his fundraisers was a medical doctor from Hainan, whose sons were leaders in promoting modern education and newspapers as well as modernist forms of Buddhism in Penang. His descendants in Ayer Itam were my main sources on Mahayana Buddhism in Penang (see DeBernardi 2004, 2006).

[6] For details on the life of Huang Naishang that focuses on his career in China, see Dunch 2001. Dunch proposes that the Fuzhou Methodists synthesized an ethos of "piety, patriotism, and progress" that helped define a direction for China as a new nation (Dunch 2001: xx).

to a China-wide ministry (Tow 1985: 117). Soon after, he was invited to join the Bethel Worldwide Evangelistic Band in Shanghai and travelled with them for two years. Between 1931 and 1935, this band visited 133 cities and held almost 3,400 revival meetings (Bays 1996: 315–6; Sng 2003: 172–5).

Starting in 1935, Sung held meetings throughout Southeast Asia, including the Philippines, Indonesia, Burma, and Thailand. Singapore was a major transportation hub for the region, and between 1935 and 1939, Sung visited the city seven times (Sng 2003: 175–6). In 1935, he spoke three times a day in the large Methodist church to a packed audience. A Brethren missionary noted that he was "mighty in the Scriptures, fearless in his denouncement of sin" and that he preached a full Gospel, depending on the Holy Spirit "for guidance in all things".[7] He also visited Penang, where the Brethren gospel hall's youth group soon formed an enthusiastic band of tract distributors.[8]

Bible Presbyterian Timothy Tow recalled that on his 1939 visit, Sung went by car to Penang to speak at a union meeting of all the denominations. An elder in a Brethren church had married two sisters, "believing that he was following Jacob's example". Although the Old Testament provides many ensamples of polygyny, Western Christians had established monogamy as normative, leading some non-Western Christians to question whether monogamy was truly Christian or merely a European cultural practice. Whatever the Brethren elder's convictions in this matter may have been, Sung's sermon led him to repent and make a "proper settlement for this double involvement" (Tow 1985: 190).

In the early 20th century, the Brethren assemblies in Penang and Singapore continued to be divided by language into English-speaking and Chinese-speaking services. Hokkien was the unofficial lingua franca for Chinese in Singapore and Penang, and some Chinese churches used the Hokkien translation of the Bible and sang Hokkien hymns. But the population included speakers of other Min topolects, Hakka, and Cantonese.

Chinese reformers promoted the creation of a new, standard national language, Mandarin, an innovation that Chinese Christians evangelists adopted. Bible Presbyterian Timothy Tow recalled that when Sung spoke Mandarin with Hokkien interpretation at the 1935 revival in Singapore, this awakened him "to the important of the Chinese language". He later adopted Mandarin in his work as a Bible Presbyterian pastor (Tow 1993: 18–9).

---

[7] Leslie J. Donaldson, Singapore, 7 November 1935, *ES* No. 1093 (February 1936): 40.

[8] Miss M. Lindsey, Penang, 24 September 1936, *ES* No. 1104 (December 1936): 317.

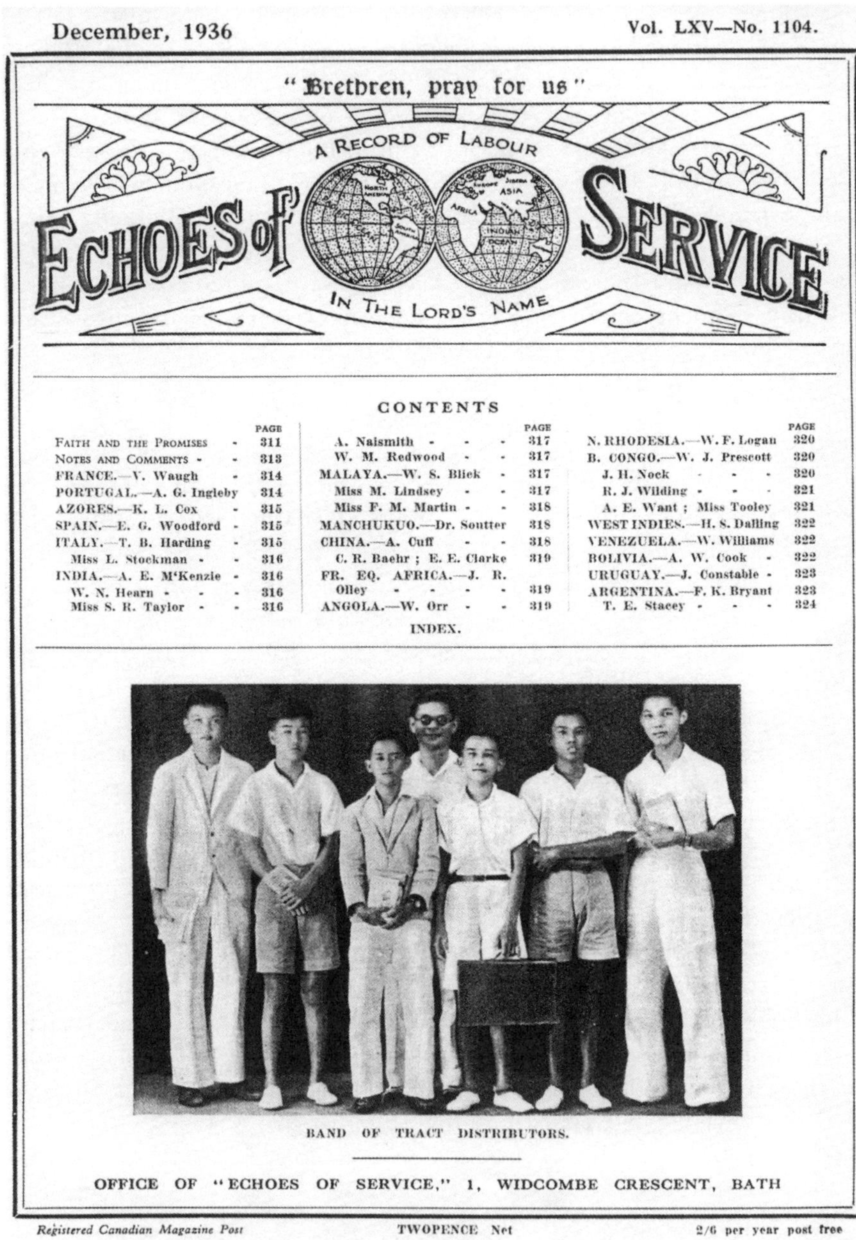

December, 1936 Vol. LXV—No. 1104.

" Brethren, pray for us "

A RECORD OF LABOUR

ECHOES of SERVICE

IN THE LORD'S NAME

CONTENTS

BAND OF TRACT DISTRIBUTORS.

OFFICE OF "ECHOES OF SERVICE," 1, WIDCOMBE CRESCENT, BATH

Registered Canadian Magazine Post TWOPENCE Net 2/6 per year post free

Figure 24 Band of young tract distributors in Penang. *Echoes of Service* December 1936.

Chinese Christians connected to the Christian and Missionary Alliance (C&MA) also conducted revival campaigns in Southeast Asia. These included Leland Wang, the co-founder of the Chinese Foreign Missionary Union (*Zhonghua Guowai Budaotuan* 中華國外佈道團) (CFMU, est. 1928), which sent Asian evangelists to proselytize in Southeast Asia. In the decade after the CFMU was founded, both Leland and Wilson conducted revival campaigns in Singapore and Penang. Like the Open Brethren, these independent evangelists used networked communications and travel to promote their form of Christian practice. And like John Sung, Leland and Wilson Wang spoke Mandarin in their campaigns.[9]

Remarkably, C&MA Chinese evangelists had their first contact with Brethren from Penang and Singapore in Java in 1928. In August 1928, Penang Straits Chinese evangelists Chew Boon Hean (the businessman who was converted in the Taiping prison) travelled in Java, Makassar, and Borneo with Mr Ernest Tipson, a former Brethren missionary who had become the secretary of the British and Foreign Bible Society in Singapore. In Batavia Chew noticed a Chinese church and introduced himself to its German pastor. The pastor took him to the Chinese gospel hall on Patekoan Street that had been built and donated by the Chinese merchant, Gouw Kho [Gohkoe], where Gan Kui had worked. They invited Chew to speak, and he attributed his finding the independent Chinese Church to God's "leading hand". A few days later at a Chinese restaurant, someone asked him what his business was in Batavia. He answered "Gospel Preacher", and on overhearing him, two men introduced themselves. They had been sent to Java by the Christian and Missionary Alliance in Wuzhou to "reconnoitre", and one claimed to have heard of Chew. Together they sang "Halleluja" in the busy restaurant and supplied diners with tracts and Gospel booklets.[10]

Civil War and the New Life Movement in Nanchang

In 1933, the Guomindang government launched the New Life Movement in Nanchang. The proponents of the New Life Movement called it a "revival" (*fuxing* 復興), and Madame Chiang Kai-shek invited Christians to help

---

[9] In my discussion of Leland and Wilson Wang, I take some details from a 2010 book posted on a blog. The author Dr Huang Mingming was a professor at University of California at Davis who after retirement wrote a book about the "Fujian Twelve" and the "Fuzhou Seven", including the Wang brothers (Huang 2010).

[10] "Borneo (Extracts from a Tour)", Chew Boon Hean, *Links of Help* Vol. 18, No. 212 (February 1929): 28–9.

them promote it (Ferlanti 2010: 963; 972–7). The Brethren missionaries in Nanchang and Leland Wang were among those she called upon to support the new movement.

With support from overseas Chinese, Sun Yat-sen had formed a revolutionary coalition that forced the Qing government to abdicate. In December 1911 he was elected the first provisional president of the Republic of China. But Sun was unable to unify China, which splintered into large territories controlled by regional armies and militias. Chiang Kai-shek, Sun's successor as leader of the China Nationalist Party (*Guomindang,* often written *Kuomintang*) sought to restore order, forming an alliance with the Communists to fight the Northern warlords.

In 1927, Chiang embarked on a purge of Communists, expelling them from the Nationalist party, suppressing labor unions, and attacking them in Shanghai, a event described as the Shanghai massacre of 12 April 1927. The GMD army stationed in Nanchang was supposed to launch a peasant uprising, but instead some left-wing leaders rebelled and staged the event known as the Nanchang Uprising on 1 August 1927.[11] Days later Chiang Kai-shek's army launched a counter-attack and recaptured the city (Elleman 2009: 4–5, 122). Some regard this as the first military engagement of the Chinese Civil War.

Working in the Red Cross Hospital in Nanchang, Brethren medical missionary Alfred Cuff observed that the Southern Army officers whom he met there had been radicalized to varying degrees depending on their training. Officers who had been trained in the Whampoa Military Academy in Canton believed that Russia would help them deliver China from the Northern Warlords and from foreign oppression, but also endorsed Sun Yat-sen's "Three Principles"—nationalism, democracy, and the livelihood of the people. But those who had been Moscow-trained aspired to destroy the existing social order and launch worldwide revolution.[12] Cuff reported that "in the trail of the Southern army we find desecrated chapels, looted Mission houses, closed schools and hospitals, and in the area under Southern control all white people, be they missionaries or merchants, have found it impossible to live".[13]

[11] The date of the uprising, 1 August 1927, is now celebrated as the founding date of the People's Liberation Army.

[12] "A Little Light on the Situation in China, part II", A. Cuff, *Links of Help* Vol. XVI (April 1928): 251.

[13] "A Little Light on the Situation in China, part III", *Links of Help* Vol. XVI (May 1928): 266.

The Open Brethren had established a mission in Nanchang in 1896, building the Gracie Kingham Memorial School in 1913 to memorialize a child who had died together with her parents in a violent 1906 attack on foreign missionaries. In 1927, the Brethren missionaries were forced to evacuate Nanchang, but a Chinese principal remained and continued to run the school even after GMD soldiers had appropriated their buildings.[14]

The Communists retreated to a mountainous and remote area, where with Russian support Mao Zedong and Zhude established an unrecognized state, the Jiangxi Soviet (est. 1931).[15] In 1931 the GMD army used Nanchang as a base from which to wage encirclement and suppression campaigns against them, and in 1934 the fifth of these overcame the Communists. By 1935, the GMD had restored the old regime in the countryside (Opper 2018: 57–61).

As Chiang Kai-shek explained it, the fifth campaign was "three parts military, seven parts political", including the use of education and propaganda (Opper 2018: 47). The Communists had lost popular support in the wake of a radical programme of land redistribution followed by the mass executions of civilians who were suspected of sympathy for the advancing GMD. The GMD victory was decisive, and the Communists retreated to Shaanxi in the event now called the Long March.

Nanchang became the Field Headquarters for the GMD, which became the effective government centre for Jiangxi, Fujian, Hunan, Hubei, and Guangdong provinces (Ven 2003: 140). When the Brethren missionaries returned to Nanchang, they announced that religious freedom had been restored, the troops were vacating the mission property, and their students were only expected to bow before the portrait of Sun Yat-sen once a week.[16]

After driving out the Communists, the GMD leaders invented a novel ideology to compete with Communism that blended neo-Confucian precepts, New Testament Christianity, and YMCA-style social activism (Li 2006: 102). Chiang's nationalist government called this programme of moral reform the New Life Movement (NLM), and launched it in Nanchang on 19 February 1933.[17]

---

[14] Delia Hu, Nanchang, 9 May 1927, *ES* No. 992 (August 1927): 181. The school remained open until the Japanese invasion in 1937 (Stunt et al. 1972: 509–12).

[15] They adopted the ideology and tactics of Vladimir Lenin (1870–1924) and Joseph Stalin (1878–1953), and Moscow dispatched advisers and provided financial support (Wittfogel 1951; Elleman 2009).

[16] Fannie L. Bergin, Nanchang, 30 December 1928, *ES* No. 1011 (March 1929): 61; F.J. and E.A. Hopkins, Nanchang, 12 November 1928, *ES* No. 1012 (April 1929): 85.

[17] Leland Wang identifies this as the movement's founding date. "I Continue", Leland Wang, *The Pioneer*, Vol. 19, No. 47 (August 1947): 29.

In May 1933, Leland Wang visited Nanchang and held a ten-day campaign. A Brethren missionary reported that many chose to "accept Christ" at Wang's gospel services, including "nurses, older students, younger scholars, soldiers, workmen, husbands and sons, mothers and daughters, and others".[18] While Wang was still there, the Brethren missionaries met Madame Chiang Kai-shek. They were satisfied that she was a "true believer" and reported that she had remarked, "People say I am always talking about the gospel, and so I am, I want everyone to be a Christian." She secured them passes to visit wounded soldiers in the military hospital, who likely had been injured in the Third Encirclement Campaign against the Jiangxi Soviet. Wang accompanied them on their first visit to the military hospital.[19]

In autumn 1933, Madame Chiang invited Nanchang's missionaries and members of the YMCA to meetings with Chiang Kai-shek and other founders of the New Life Movement. About 30 missionaries and representatives of missionary schools and hospitals were guests at a tea party where she "explained the NLM and emphasized the similarities between the principles endorsed by the movement and Christian values and the ways which the Christian community could contribute in spreading the movement in Nanchang" (Ferlanti 2010: 973). The methods she proposed resembled those of evangelical Christians, including visiting hospitals and prisons, public proselytism, and distributing propaganda.

In promoting the New Life Movement, GMD leaders sought to establish local control in a country overrun by conflict and violence. European fascism inspired some of the NLM initiatives, and not all Christians agreed to sponsor it (Ferlanti 2010: 975). But evangelical Christianity and its social programmes provided a model for the unity of a shared ethos, for the regeneration of the individual, and for methods of proselytism.[20]

Leland and Wilson Wang

Leland Wang (Wang Zai 王栽, 1898–1975) was a frequent visitor to Penang and Singapore starting in 1929. Wang had been an officer in the Chinese navy before being converted by his Christian wife. In 1921 he gave up his commission to become a full-time worker and lived by faith, "being influenced

18 F.J. and E.A. Hopkins, Nanchang, June 1933, *ES* No. 1065 (September 1933): 203.
19 Ibid.: 203–4.
20 Liu Wennan concludes that the New Life Movement was primarily a top-down political programme with the goal of transforming China into a modern state (Liu 2013: 31–2).

Figure 25 1936 Map of the Nanyang ("South Seas"), including insets of Malaya, Java, and the Pacific and showing the web of travel routes by air and sea (Li and Shi 1936?). Library of Congress.

to do this through reading the Life of George Müller".[21] He also had an indirect connection with the Brethren in Malaya, since the "brother" who baptized him had been converted and baptized by Henry Freeman Marks, a Brethen missionary in Taiping. On Wong's first evangelical tour of Malaya he visited Marks, and when Mr and Mrs Marks visited Hong Kong in 1933, they stayed in a building where Wong had a flat and a large meeting room.[22]

In a famous tract entitled "No Bible no Breakfast", Wang described himself as Chinese by birth and Christian by rebirth, Chinese by race and Christian by grace. In 1921, he recalled, he had started to do open-air evangelism, then rented a hall in Fuzhou "that later became known as the Christian Assembly". He was joined there by Watchman Nee, his younger brother Wilson (Wang Zhi/Wang Tse 王峙, 1903–2011), Simon Meek (Miao Shaoxun 繆紹訓), who later worked in Manila, Faithful Luke [Luk] (Lu Zhongxin 陆忠信), who later worked in Singapore and Indonesia, and John Wang.[23] This, he added, was the start of a "vital Christian evangelical movement in China" (Wang n.d.). Although Watchman Nee separated from Leland Wang, their networks continued to overlap both in China and in Southeast Asia.

Wang soon became famous in Christian circles for leading a 1925 revival in Shanghai together with A. Paget Wilkes, a cofounder of the Japan Evangelistic Band, Jesse Blackburn Thornton, and Dora Yu. The meeting was organized by Grace and Henry Woods, who in 1924 had launched a Worldwide Revival Prayer Movement. They had invited Wilkes to speak at a missionary convention in Kuling, but after British troops suppressed student protestors, an anti-foreign and anti-Christian movement spread nationwide. Since travel was unsafe, they invited Wilkes to speak instead in Shanghai, and booked rooms at the Union Church. They decided to invite Chinese to the event and sought an interpreter. By chance Leland Wang was visiting Dora Yu, and he agreed to participate. Wang's role became that of co-revivalist at an event that Grace Woods called the Shanghai Revival of 1925, whose significance she compared to the 1857–58 revival in New York that had followed "a sudden and fearful convulsion in

[21] F.J. and E.A. Hopkins, Nanchang, June 1933, *ES* No. 1065 (September 1933): 203–4. China Inland Mission missionary Frederick William Baller (1852–1922) had translated Müller's biography into Mandarin (Austin 2007: 232).

[22] H.F. Marks, Hong Kong, 22 March 1933; *ES* No. 1062 (June 1933): 132. I have not been able to locate the name of the person who baptized Leland Wang.

[23] In his biography of Watchman Nee, Kinnear identified Meek, Luke, Leland Wang, and John Wang as being associated with the Little Flock movement (Kinnear 1973: xi–xii).

the commercial world" (Woods 1927: 19; see Carpenter 1997: 120).[24] The missionary conference lasted three weeks, and Chinese meetings continued for another six weeks (Woods 1927: 74–92).

At the 1925 Shanghai Revival, a large group of young people decided to become Christian, including Andrew Gih (Ji Zhiwen 計志文), who formed the Bethel Worldwide Evangelistic Band with John Sung in 1931 (Yu 2000). Gih requested that Wang baptize him, and Wang also baptized Jennie Hughes and Ruth Bell, the daughter of a missionary, who later married Billy Graham (Li 2005–18; Lian 2010: 162).[25]

In 1928, Wang began to formally cooperate with Canadian missionary Robert A. Jaffray (1873–1945). Jaffray was the son of a Scottish immigrant who had become a wealthy publisher in Toronto, Canada. His family attended a Presbyterian church, but a Sunday School teacher introduced him to the teachings of Albert Benjamin Simpson. He joined the Christian and Missionary Alliance (est. 1887), an undenominational parachurch group that Simpson had founded, and studied at the C&MA Missionary Training Institute (est. 1882) in Nyack, New York. Jaffray arrived in Guangxi Province in 1896 and established a Bible school in Wuzhou.

In 1907 Jaffray and other missionaries at the Wuzhou mission experienced baptism of the Holy Spirit, and Jaffray spoke in tongues. He wrote to North American Alliance Christians claiming that these Pentecostal manifestations in South China fulfilled Old Testament "latter rain" prophecies, and proposed that spiritual awakening would not occur in China unless the church claimed the "old Pentecostal power and gifts promised so long ago, but lost for [many] centuries" (Nienkirchen 2010: 125). Christian historian Charles Nienkirchen concludes that "his life contained all the supernatural dimension held dear by Pentecostals—tongues speaking, healings, signs and wonders, dreams and visions, numerous instances of direct divine guidance, and a commitment

---

[24] Lian Xi attributes the success of the 1925 revival to Wilkes (Lian 2004: 875–6), but an eyewitness account by a Chinese Christian who was among those converted at the event emphasized the important of Leland Wang's role (Yu 2000). Other speakers at the event included J.B. Thornton, an American missionary based in Kobe, who spoke by interpretation during the first week at the missionary conference due to Wilkes' ill health, and Rev. J. Russell Howden, Deputy Director of the China Inland Mission in England, who spoke to a "great cosmopolitan audience" (Woods 1927: 83, 90).

[25] As of 1951, Gih's Evangelize China Fellowship engaged in outreach in Taiwan, Hong Kong, Johore, Malaya, Singapore, and Java (Gih 1961: 53–4). In the early 1950s, the Brethren missionaries in Singapore and Malaya described the activities of Wilson Wang and Charles Lee, but did not mention Gih.

to training Spirit-baptized church leaders" (Nienkirchen 2010: 128). Like Simpson, Jaffray emphasized divine healing, and often published reports of events where he claimed that healing had followed prayer (Green 2013: 1–3).

In 1928, Jaffray visited the Dutch East Indies and decided to launch a new Alliance Mission from a base in Celebes (South Sulawesi). A number of independent Chinese Christian Churches already existed in the region, and Jaffray recognized that Chinese Christian evangelists could work independently of foreign missionaries. In 1928, he and Leland Wang co-founded the Chinese Foreign Missionary Union (CFMU) in Hong Kong with Wang as president and Jaffray as vice-president. The CFMU sent Chinese missionaries to work in French Indo-China and the Dutch East Indies, and Jaffray claimed that the were "the first 'foreign missionaries' sent out from the Chinese Christian Church".[26] Wang became the face of the Chinese Foreign Missionary Union, which later claimed a membership of 5,000 in Southeast Asia (Lian 2010: 188; see also Fiedler 1995: 288).[27]

Concurrently, Jaffray launched a C&MA mission in Borneo. In 1930 he and his family relocated to Makassar (now Ujung Padang) in South Sulawesi. In 1913 he had begun publishing a Chinese *Bible Magazine* (*Shengjing Bao*). In 1931 he launched a Malay edition of this publication, the *Kalam Hideop* (*Living Word*), whose readers included Malay-speaking *nyonya / baba* Chinese.[28] The Alliance missionaries also established a Bible School in 1932 and built a Gospel Tabernacle, where they held monthly healing services.[29] These services were open to all, and Jaffray described a Makassar Bible school student praying for a non-Christian to be delivered of a demon. He viewed himself as waging battles against oppressive powers, and healing services as a struggle between the Spirit and the kingdom of darkness (Green 2013: 3).

---

[26] "An Evangelistic Tour in the Dutch East Indies", Leland Wang, *The Pioneer* Vol. II, Nos. 7&8 (December 1931): 12–7.

[27] Because the CFMU was not affiliated with any denomination, Daniel Bays views Leland Wang's work as evidence that after the anti-imperialist May Fourth student movement of 1919, Chinese Christians were working with increasing independence from foreign missions (Bays 1996: 314). But the CFMU cooperated with Jaffray, CIM missionaries (Lian 2010: 162), and Brethren missionaries in Penang, Taiping, and Singapore, who sometimes travelled with them to proselytize.

[28] "Report for 1931 The Dutch East Indies Mission of the Christian and Missionary Alliance", R.A. Jaffray, Makassar, DEI, pp. 11–2.

[29] "It All Began in Makassar", Richard K. Smith, *The Pioneer 50th Anniversary Edition*, 1978: 3–5.

As Jaffrey explained it to the readers of *The Pioneer*, a magazine publicizing the work of the Alliance Mission in the Dutch East Indies, the C&MA missionaries worked in "close association" with Wang and the CFMU. As Jaffray explained their financial arrangements, the Alliance missionaries were supported by the Alliance Treasury in New York, but the Chinese missionaries in Southeast Asia were entirely supported by voluntary contributions. About half of CFMU's funds were supplied by World-wide Christian Couriers in Chicago, with the balance made up of individual offerings.[30]

The founder of the World-wide Christian Couriers was Daniel Paul Rader (1879–1938), whom Joel Carpenter describes as "one of the most innovative and broadly influential of the fundamentalist revivalists" (Carpenter 1997: 127; see also Rogers 2013). Rader was born into a Methodist household but joined the C&MA, and accepted a post at a C&MA Tabernacle in Pittsburgh. He was appointed pastor of Moody Church in 1915, and in 1919 succeeded Simpson as president of the C&MA, a position that he held for only four years.

In 1921 he resigned from Moody Church and launched the Chicago Gospel Tabernacle (Hangen 2002: 38–41). The Tabernacle had no permanent membership but featured evangelists, musicians, and renowned urban pastors in a format that Joel Carpenter has compared to a theatre or vaudeville circuit. To the displeasure of Chicago's fundamentalist establishment, Rader's Tabernacle also hosted Pentecostal revivalists like Aimee Semple McPherson. Rader struck a deal to broadcast programmes over a new radio station owned by Chicago's mayor, and by 1925 had launched the National Radio Chapel, an all-day radio programme whose audience extended to the East Coast and Western Canada (Carpenter 1997: 127–8).

In 1926 Rader proposed to form Bible study groups composed of what he called World-wide Christian Couriers. The groups were intended to be local and small-scale, and concurrently he founded a new Chicago-based Christian newsletter the *World-Wide Christian Courier* and a foreign missionary society with the same name (Carpenter 1997: 127; Hangen 2002: 51). The resemblance to the Open Brethren movement, which also combined autonomous local churches with a newsletter and missionary society, is striking, although Rader added Christian radio into the mix.

Rader and Wang had met in 1929, when well-known revivalist and "evangelical celebrity" Jonathan Goforth arranged for them to hold a few weeks of revival meetings in Manchuria (Bays 1993: 165; Lian 2010: 88). That

---

30 "A Statement concerning the Dutch East Indies Mission", R.A. Jaffray, *The Pioneer* Vol. 4, No. 15 (August 1933): 6–9.

year, Rader's *World-Wide Christian Courier* featured a photograph of Leland Wang on a list of the faith missionaries they supported. Rader was not able to accompany Wang and Jaffray to the Dutch East Indies in 1929, but the World-wide Christian Couriers donated funds to pay for a launch used for travel in Borneo.

Figure 26 Leland Wang's photograph, given as a gift to Chicago fundamentalist revivalist Paul Rader (1879–1938). Paul Rader Ephemera Collection. Courtesy of the Billy Graham Center Archives, Wheaton College (Illinois).

When Rader returned to Asia in 1932, he spoke at a combined conference of C&MA and CFMU missions in Makassar, after which he and Jaffray embarked on a ten-day evangelical tour of Java accompanied by Rev. P.H. Pouw, who translated for Rader. Pouw had been the pastor of a Chinese Church in Batavia and also chairman of the All-Java Chinese Christian Association, which promoted "self-governing, self-propagating, and self-supporting" Christian churches that were local in style. In Makassar, he translated and wrote for the *Kalam Hideop*.[31]

Some have described Leland Wang as the "Moody of China", comparing him to Dwight L. Moody, the famous 19th-century revivalist who worked with gospel singer Ira Sankey in his evangelical campaigns (Bays 1996: 314). His C&MA coworkers undoubtedly influenced his use of music at revival meetings. In Wuzhou, Jaffray had used gospel songs to attract listeners when he did street corner evangelism and his publications included hymn books (Tozer 1948). Rader was also well known for his use of American gospel music, which he promoted through his radio ministry in Chicago.

Although Hong Kong became his main base, Wang made several evangelical tours in Southeast Asia. He first visited Macassar in 1929 on an exploratory trip, and that year held revival meetings in Penang, Taiping, Ipoh, Klang, and Singapore.[32] In Penang Wang spoke for four nights, and Chew Boon Hean reported that 27 persons had come forward "to confess the Lord". Wang also visited Marks in Taiping.

Not long after Leland's revival campaign, Chew visited Hong Kong. His 1930 evangelical tour was descibed in the *Malaya Tribune*, which reported that while in Hong Kong, the "Chinese Evangelist of Penang" had travelled to Manila on the "Empress of Japan" and preached to a congregation consisting of "Europeans, Americans, Filipinos and Chinese". On his return to Hong Kong, Chew made a tour of churches in China.[33] Marks also visited Hong Kong and Shanghai that year on his way to Canada. Hong Kong was Leland's base, and almost certainly Chew and Marks sought contact with him and members of the CFMU.

---

[31] "The Lord's Way is Best", Mr P.H. Pouw, Makassar, *The Pioneer* Vol. 3, No. 9 (April 1932): 28–34; "Introducing N.E.I. Friends", R.A. Jaffray, *The Pioneer* Vol. 7, No. 28 (October 1936): 8–9.

[32] "Arise and Go......South" (Acts 8: 26), Leland Wang, *The Pioneer* Vol. 9, No. 33 (January 1938): 34. Chew Boon Hean, Penang, 23 January 1929, *ES* No. 1012 (April 1929): 84; Donaldson, Singapore, 18 March 1929, *ES* No. 1014 (June 1929): 131.

[33] Untitled, *Malaya Tribune*, 19 December 1930: 10. I have found no mention of Chew's visit to Hong Kong, Manila, or China in *Echoes of Service.*

KIANGSI WORKERS AND FRIENDS, KULING, JULY 18th, 1934.
At back—Messrs. Chew Boon-Hean, Hopkins, Vines, Melville, Duff, Jones, Lester.
Remainder standing—Mrs. Lim, Miss Gale, Mrs. Outerbridge, Miss Hu, Miss Loggia, Miss Hulbert, Mrs. Melville, Mrs. Duff, Miss Pollock, Mrs. Jones, Mrs. Keith, Miss Hunter, Miss Foden, Mrs. Price, Miss Mooney, Mrs. Gillan, Miss Lee, Mrs. Alderson, Mrs. Whipple, Mr. Alderson.
Seated—Mrs. Hopkins, Miss Dunphy, Mrs. Buckley, Miss Norman, Mrs. Gulston, Mrs. Lester, Miss Dawson, Miss Bergin, Mrs. Pownall, Miss Ridley.
On ground—Harold Buckley, Mr. James, Miss Richards, Miss Madill, Mr. Phillips.

Figure 27 Chew Boon Hean returned to China in 1934, where he joined the Jiangxi Brethren missionaries at a conference in the hill station Kuling. Chew Boon Hean is standing in the back at the left; Mr Phillips, who moved to Malaya in 1948, is seated on the ground at the bottom right. *Echoes of Service* archive.

In 1931 Wang made a tour to visit Chinese Christian churches in Celebes, Borneo, and Java with Rev. Pouw, then visited Singapore. There, they stayed with Brethren missionaries, Mr and Mrs Leslie J. Donaldson. Wang held six nights of meetings in the Brethren Chinese town assembly to a packed house. The missionary reported 20 converts, noting that wherever he went he preached to large crowds and aimed at conversions.[34]

That year, the first Christian radio station XMHD went on the air in Shanghai as a nondenominational Christian broadcasting station. Its signal reached all of China, but also East Asia and the western Pacific (Krysko 2011: 126–34). When Leland Wang spoke at the Keswick Convention in Britain in 1939, he reported on the CFMU's 21 Chinese missionaries in Southeast Asia, but also that many government leaders and educated people were receptive to the Christian message, and that they had a radio broadcasting station in

[34] Donaldson, Singapore, 27 July 1931, *ES* No. 1043 (October 1931): 227.

Shanghai "where the Gospel was preached day and night" (*The Keswick Convention* 1939: 246).[35]

Wilson Wang and the Bible Magazine

In 1913, Jaffray began publishing a bimonthly Chinese *Bible Magazine* (*Shengjing Bao* 圣经报).[36] In 1932 he moved the editorial offices from Wuzhou to Shanghai, and also shifted the style from literary Chinese to Mandarin. Jaffray invited Leland's brother Wilson to join the editorial board, and by 1936 he had become co-editor.

The *Shengjing Bao* brought together original articles written by Jaffray and Wang with the writings of well-known evangelical Christians, many of whom were undenominational in their practice. The most frequently translated author was A.B. Simpson, but after the editorial offices moved to Shanghai, they also translated the writings of well-known British, American, Canadian, and New Zealand Christian authors, including George Müller.[37] The *Shengjing Bao* also included translations of biographies and memoirs, including *The Life of A.B.*

[35] According to the Far Eastern Broadcasting Corporation's International Archive, Wang helped make broadcasts in Shanghai prior to 1949, and later did so in Hong Kong and the Philippines.

[36] A 2006 reprint of the *Shengjing Bao* includes two magazines from 1918, and incomplete volumes between 1936 and 1941. The magazine ceased publication in 1941 and resumed in 1947, and the reprint includes what appears to be a complete set of issues between 1947 and 1951, and a single issue from 1954. The Christian and Missionary Alliance's archive holds an incomplete set at the A.B. Simpson Historical Library in Robert Jaffray Papers, 1896–ca. 1925. According to the managing archivist, Ms Kristin Rollins, the archive holds scattered copies of the *Bible Magazine* from 1913–33, and has no copies for the period between 1933 and 1947. They are missing issues from 1958–60, but have a 1962 copy of the magazine in which Wilson Wang is no longer identified as the co-editor. Although the editors of the 2006 reprint series claims that the magazine ceased publication in 1951, their own reprint includes one issue from 1954.

[37] These included Oswald J. Smith, the founder of the independent People's Church in Toronto; Henry W. Frost, CIM's North American director (who like Simpson believed in spiritual healing); Arthur Tappan Pierson, the so-called Father of Fundamentalism, whose 1899 biography of George Müller had been translated into Chinese; New Zealand Open Brethren Robert A. Laidlaw; the famous British pastor Charles Haddon Spurgeon; the British editor of *The Dawn* magazine, D.M. Panton; Cyrus I. Scofield, the editor of the *Scofield Reference Bible*; Dwight L. Moody; and R.A. Torrey.

Simpson (which Faithful Luke translated) and *Hudson Taylor's Spiritual Secret*. Popular topics included revival, prophecy, and spiritual healing.[38]

The magazine also published Bible expositions, teachings, and testimonies from Chinese Christian evangelists, including Faithful Luke and Simon Meek, both of whom were associated with Watchman Nee's local church movement. They also published essays by Calvin Chao, the founder of the Inter-varsity Christian Fellowship in China, who later founded the Singapore Bible College (est. 1952); Shanghai preacher Timothy (S.K.) Chao (aka Timothy Dzao, Zhao Shiguang 趙世光), founder of the Ling Liang church (est. 1942); Teh Phai Lian of the Burmah Road Gospel Hall in Penang; and Leland and Wilson Wang.

The Japanese Occupation and World War II

In 1937, Japan invaded China, launching the Second Sino-Japanese War. The Japanese military captured Shanghai and Nanjing, and soon attacked southeastern China, seizing Amoy in 1939, and bombing Canton, Shantou, and Hainan (Turnbull 2009: 158). When Japan occupied Nanjing, Chiang moved his capital to Chongqing. The Japanese troops massacred up to 300,000 of Nanjing's residents, and the so-called Rape of Nanjing marked the end of the decade of Nationalist control.

After the Japanese attacks, many refugees fled from China to to Singapore, where a Brethren missionary reported them to be "willing to hear the gospel". Leland's brother Wilson moved to Singapore, and in 1938, held nine days of special meetings in the Chinese Town Assembly in Singapore, preaching in Mandarin with Hokkien interpretation. As Donaldson described it:[39]

> From the first the meetings were packed; we borrowed every available chair and stool and they we could not find room for all who came; many stood outside the door and listened. Over 500 heard the gospel each evening. One the Thursday ten professed conversion, on Friday twenty-three, on Sunday twenty-seven, and on Tuesday ten.

[38] Ernest Tipson, who had been a Brethren missionary in Penang and Kuala Lumpur, but who had moved to Singapore to become the Secretary for the British and Foreign Bible Society for Malaya, offered a 400-year history of the English Bible written in Chinese.

[39] Donaldson, Singapore, 15 June 1938, *ES* No. 1125 (September 1938): 237.

He reported that because of the war, the refugees' hearts were "humbled", viewing the nine-day event as "days of wonderful opportunities here among the Chinese".[40]

The Brethren in Penang moved to a new gospel hall on Burmah Road in May 1938. *Echoes of Service* published a photograph of an elegant stone building in a large compound, and the missionaries reported that attendance had increased at both the Chinese and English meetings.[41] By then, Sidney S. Adams, who had been commended by Cholmeley Evangelical Church, Highgate, London in 1921, was Penang's full-time missionary. When Wilson Wang conducted revival meetings in the new gospel hall, Adams described him as "very spiritual, and overflowing with genuine joy in the Lord", adding that "Numbers increased nightly, until our new hall was packed out." Wang accompanied Adams to Jerejak Island to visit lepers and spoke on the theme of "Blessed Hope".[42] The next year he travelled with Marks and Donaldson to visit a new independent hall in a village 65 miles south of Taiping.[43]

But in 1941, the Japanese Occupation disrupted travel and communications for more than three years. Leland Wang remained in Java, while his brother Wilson moved to Penang.

[40] Donaldson, Singapore, n.d., *ES* No. 1126 (October 1938): 263.

[41] "New Hall, 164 Burmah Road, Penang", Photo caption, *ES* No. 1123 (July 1938): 177; Sidney S. Adams, 11 July 1938, *ES* No. 1125 (September 1938): 237.

[42] S.S. Adams, Penang, 1 March 1939, *ES* No. 1133 (May 1939): 123.

[43] H.F. Marks, Taiping. 28 Mar 1940, *ES* No. 1146 (June 1940): 108. The missionary described this as an outreach of an existing hall, possibly the Little Flock local church in Sitiawan.

Chapter 12

Wilson Wang and Teh Phai Lian

The Japanese occupied Penang on 17 December 1941. Singapore fell on 15 February 1942, and the Japanese occupied the Dutch East Indies in March. The British evacuated Penang, and the Brethren missionaries moved to Singapore. Some returned to Europe, but two months later those who had stayed, including Sidney Adams, were interned in Changi Prison, where the missionaries remained for three years and eight months (Adams n.d.: 11–13). Robert Jaffray was also interned in Celebes (now South Sulawesi), and in 1945 died in a Japanese camp.

In 1941, Leland Wang had sent his daughter Amy to study at Wheaton College in the United States, a school attended by the children of many prominent evangelicals, but he and his wife had returned to Java with their son. They remained there throughout the war, unable to send more than a postcard or to travel. Wilson Wang was with him in Java, but because his wife and six children were in Singapore, he returned there just as the Japanese Occupation began. Six months later, he and his family moved to Penang.

In Penang, the Mission House on Farquhar Street became the headquarters of the Japanese Military Police, and other buildings were used as police barracks and a petrol store. But the Asian Christians convinced the Japanese that the Burmah Road Gospel Hall was their property and that the European missionaries had only helped them in their work.[1] They continued meeting with Wilson Wang as their full-time worker.

Wilson recalled his experiences during the war in a two-part article published in 1949 in the *Shengjing Bao* that was also reprinted as a bilingual tract in Mandarin and English (Wang 1949a; 1949b; 1949c). The title was translated as "God's Deliverance in the Day of Trouble", and he recalled that six months after the fall of Singapore, Christians in Penang invited him there to

[1] "Malaya", n.d., *ES* Vol. 75, No. 2113 (January 1946): 4, 16.

"serve the Lord". He and his family went to Penang by train, and he began to work there in September 1942. The Burmah Road Gospel Hall was registered in his name, and he acted as marriage registrar in 1943 and 1944 (Wang 1949b: 85–6; 1949c: 54, 56). During the war years, he organized worship services, Sunday School, a young people's choir, Bible study classes, and a musical band on their behalf (Wang 1949c: 58).

On 15 October 1942, the Japanese arrested the son of Chinese elder Teh Phai Lian, declaring him to be a "bad man" (Wang 1949c: 58). According to family members, he had written and staged Hokkien street theatre with an anti-Japanese message that had been performed on the flatbed of a lorry. As the group's leader, he was arrested. Three weeks later, the Japanese arrested two other church members—Oh Lock Heng, who had been a pilot and had flown reconnaisance missions for the British, and Tye Poh Sun, a friend of his who had also aided the British military. For a time the two communicated through a small hole in the wall between their cells, but the soldier guarding them prohibited them from speaking. Tye helped Oh relearn Morse code, a skill they had learned as boy scouts (Wang 1949c: 64, 66).

Using this code, Oh taught him how to pray and "gave him a spiritual revival" (Wang 1949c: 66). The two prisoners were released the day after Wang had spoken at the Bible Hall on the text "Sanctify yourself: for tomorrow the Lord will do wonders among you" (Joshua 3:5) (Adams n.d.: 16; Wang 1949c: 62). Soon after, Tye's entire family chose to be baptized (Wang 1949c: 66).

The day after Oh's release, the church held a thanksgiving service that Teh Phai Lian attended, but he wept loudly because his son was still imprisoned. Wang prophesied that his son would return the next week. "I was not making a prophecy out of boldness, but I was really led by the Spirit and had burden and determination in my heart to pray unceasingly until my prayer was answered." He had been visiting Teh daily at his home and his office, and on 15 January 1943 reached the door of his business just as Teh's son arrived in a rickshaw after three months of imprisonment. They hired a car and took him home (Wang 1949c: 63–4).

According to his niece, the Japanese had tortured Teh's son, using a hose to fill his stomach to bursting point. They pronounced him dead and threw his body out. His family was well-to-do, and a trishaw man recognized him and took him to his father's office. He was "mad already" and would not allow anyone to touch him except for his cousin, who fed him and washed him.[2] He married her on 25 December 1943 at a ceremony that Wang witnessed.

---

[2] 1999 interview with Teh Chiew Oo's niece, Ch'ng Oon Hooi.

Wang observed that during his imprisonment, Teh had "repented of his sins and was reborn", and that after his release he was "much help in the Lord's work in the church" (Wang 1949c: 66). Teh Phai Lian renamed him *Qiuyu* (秋雨, Hokkien: Chiew Oo, "Autumn Rain"), an allusion to a Biblical passage known as the latter rain scripture, which compares grace and the outpouring of the Holy Spirit to rain falling near the end of the growing season and preparing the crop for harvest.[3]

Teh Phai Lian

Today, Teh Phai Lian (Mandarin: Zheng Peiran 鄭沛然, 1901–87) is best known among Malaysian and Singapore Christians for his role in leading a schism in the Brethren assemblies in 1963 and for promoting the charismatic movement against strong opposition from the Brethren and Christians in mainline denominations. Teh's life story suggests the many social forces shaping the development of a fully indigenous Chinese Christianity first in Fujian, where he was born again, then in Penang, where Wilson Wang described him as a close friend whom he visited almost daily.

Teh was born in Tong'an, an economically vibrant city north of Xiamen. William Chalmers Burns first visited Tong'an in 1853, and the Amoy Mission established an outstation there in 1867. They baptized their first converts in 1870, eventually building a church, a hospital, and schools (Pitcher 1893: 122).[4] Teh attended a school run by the Tong-An Church, but quit at the age of 13 to help his father in his dentistry business. Although he had met a non-Christian girl whom he wanted to marry, his Christian mother insisted on his marrying a Christian, and he finally agreed to the match (Teh 1958 [1961]: 509–11).

He recalled that he became a born-again Christian as the result of the influence of an evangelist named Wang. Wang had asked to do open-air evangelism outside Teh's dental shop. Likely influenced by the anti-imperialist, anti-religious rhetoric of the May Fourth Movement, Teh loudly accused Wang of being superstitious and Westernized and refused his request. To his surprise, Wang returned a few days later and gave him four books. He accepted the gift.

[3] I thank Ch'ng Oon Hooi for information about Teh Chiew Oo's renaming. I base the interpretation of the meaning of "Autumn Rain" on commentaries on Zechariah 10:1, as translated in the King James Bible.

[4] As I note in Chapter 7, the Amoy Mission established a new station in Tong'an after a revival that resulted in conversions (Band 1948: 225). It also built a church there in 1871 (Pitcher 1893: 122; De Jong 1992: 92). They soon built a hospital and schools, including the Christian school that Teh likely attended as a child.

Figure 28 Teh Phai Lian (seated, sixth from the right) and his family, including his sisters and their families, at the Burmah Road Gospel Hall, c. 1945. His son Teh Chiew Oo is seated fourth from the right. Photograph courtesy of Ch'ng Oon Hooi and Radiance Chuang.

China was in a state of crisis, and when relatives in Penang offered to help him start a business there, he planned to emigrate. But six months before he was due to go, he injured his foot and could not walk (Teh 1958 [1961]: 512–3).[5] Confined to his bed, he picked up *Study of Divinity* (神道学, *Shen Daoxue*) and read it.

The book was written by Jia Yuming (贾玉铭), a theologian who proposed that "Christianity could learn from and improve Chinese culture and that Confucian thought and Christianity could work together on the issue of morality" (Kwok 2014: 150; see also Kwok 2017). To that end, Jia blended China's traditional moral culture with Christianity and mysticism. Before reading the books, Teh recalled that he thought Christianity was merely a laughable superstition or a Western doctrine. But on reading them, Teh decided to attend Wang's services (Teh 1961: 512).

[5] I draw some details of Teh Phai Lian's life from interviews with Ch'ng Oon Hooi and Goh Ewe Kheng. The identity of his wife's former church is unclear, but Teh Phai Lian reports that in the 1960s her brother attended a Little Flock Assembly, and that he objected to speaking in tongues (Teh 1976b: 12).

When he visited Wang's church, the text for the day was John 3:16: "For God so loves the world that He gave his only Son, that whoever believes in Him should not perish but have eternal life." After the sermon, Wang insisted that everyone learn this verse by heart. But then, he asked to them to change the verse, inserting the pronouns "I" and "we": "For God so loved me that He gave his only Son to me, that I who believe in Him should not perish but have eternal life." They recited this again and again, and in the process, according to Teh, his heart was moved by the Holy Spirit and filled with the love of God. He recalled the experience of being born as life-changing: he gave up smoking and gambling, and was less bad-tempered (Teh 1958 [1961]: 512–3).

Not long after, he and his wife moved to Penang. In an essay entitled "How to Succeed in Business (A Personal Testimony)", Teh recalled that on their arrival in 1925, he found that the relative who had encouraged them to emigrate was unable to help them start a business. They sold his wife's jewellery and opened a dental and photographic business that they called the Hokkien Photo Studio. He later adopted Tithes as the company's English name.[6] He joined the Chinese Gospel Hall, and soon was travelling "all over Malaysia and Singapore to preach the Bible" (Teh 1976b: 2).[7] As Teh described it, when he was not extracting a tooth, developing a negative, or travelling to and from work, he read the Bible, and he attributed his business success to his Christian commitments (Teh 1958 [1961]: 514; Teh 1980b).

When she explained feng shui (geomancy) to me in 1979, my former research assistant Ch'ng Oon Hooi observed that the Tithes shophouses in Penang and Singapore both faced casket shops. Feng shui experts deemed the location to be bad, predicting that a business facing a casket shop would not prosper. But, she observed, her uncle prayed to God, and everything turned out fine. She later observed that because he was not afraid of the consequences of breaking this taboo, he paid a low rent and realized higher profits.[8]

During the Japanese Occupation, Teh Phai Lian had obtained a formula for Western-style fluoride toothpaste from Japan chemists that he manufactured and sold. After 1945, he experimented with the formula and developed Raiya

[6] A 3 June 1960 article in the *Singapore Free Press* imprecisely gives the founding date of Tithes as 40 years earlier, which would be 1920. The date when he rented the shophouse on Carnarvon Street is uncertain but 193 Carnarvon Street was given as his family's address in 1938.

[7] A Penang missionary described an outreach effort where Teh "told the gospel, with the help of pictures, to quite an attentive crowd, many of whom had never heard the Good News before". Lindsey, Penang, n.d., *ES* No. 1092 (December 1935): 317. He does not describe how he became recruited to do evangelical outreach.

[8] Ch'ng Oon Hooi, November 1979; personal communication.

Figure 29 Tithes Camera store and Raiya toothpaste outlet on Carnarvon Street, Penang. Photograph: Jean DeBernardi.

toothpaste, a locally popular product whose red-and-white packaging and mint flavour resembled a major American brand.[9] After the war, Tithes also became the sole importers of Yashica cameras and transister radio sets, and also represented the Fuji Photo Film Company, selling their cameras and black-and-white film (*Singapore Free Press* 1960: 8).[10] The Teh family expanded their business, opening a branch of Tithes in Singapore in 1948, and a third shop in Kuala Lumpur. Teh Chiew Oo became the company's managing director.

Postwar China and the Communist Revolution

As soon as they could do so after the war ended, Leland and Wilson returned to Shanghai. In 1947 Leland began a series of broadcasts on the Chinese Christian Broadcasting Station, and visited the Baptist Church, Bethel Mission, and the C&MA Church. Publication of the *Shengjing Bao* had been suspended in 1937, and Wilson had already returned to relaunch it. The brothers met in Shanghai, then went to Nanjing, where they held meetings in hospitals, universities, and Bible schools.

Generalissimo and Madame Chiang Kai-shek invited Leland to dinner in their home, then the government invited him to preach at the Officers' Moral Endeavor Association from 19–21 February. Attendees included Generalissimo and Madame Chiang, but also ministers, generals, admirals, high officials, and professors. He observed that this was the first time an evangelist had been invited to preach the gospel to "our high officials" and took as his theme "New Birth", since 19 February was the 13th anniversary of the New Life Movement. He concluded that "China is open to the Gospel as never before."[11]

Wilson also addressed the elite gathering, and afterwards Generalissimo Chiang personally thanked them both.[12] When he returned to Malaya, he was invited to speak in the English and Chinese gospel halls, and the Chinese Hall in Taiping "was filled to capacity several times". Marks also arranged for him to speak at the independent Chinese Church in Sitiawan that the Fuzhou evangelists often visited. He commented that Wilson was fluent in a number of Chinese dialects and English, and had "a vast field in which to witness and preach the gospel".[13]

---

[9] In 1990 Tithes sold Raiya to another company, which was soon embattled in trademark violation litigation. Ch'ng Oon Hooi provided me with information on this history of Tithes' involvement in toothpaste manufacturing.

[10] "Fujifilm Corporation History in Singapore", http://www.fujifilm.com.sg/about/history/singapore_history/ [accessed 2 September 2016].

[11] "I Continue", Leland Wang, *The Pioneer* Vol. 19, No. 47 (August 1947): 29.

[12] Marks, Taipeng, *ES* Vol. 77, No. 2142 (June 1948): 68–9.

[13] Ibid.

Figure 30 Leland Wang and students from the Central University Christian Fellowship, Shanghai, who helped provide music for national radio programmes, March, 1947. FEBC International Archive. https://febcintl.org/photos/picture.php?/152/category/53.

But that "vast field" soon did not include mainland China. The Chinese Civil War continued, and after a series of military victories, Mao Zedong declared victory and founded the People's Republic of China on 1 October 1949. Chiang Kai-shek moved the Guomindang government and troups to Taiwan, and declared Taibei to be the new temporary capital of the Republic of China. When the Communists gained control of China in 1949, some prominent Chinese Christian leaders including Watchman Nee remained in China, but many fled to Taiwan, Southeast Asia, and North America. Among those joining this exodus were Leland and Wilson Wang.

Starting in 1948, Teh regularly published articles on gospel exposition and exhortation in the Bible magazine that Wilson Wang edited, the *Shengjing Bao* (Teh 1948, 1950, 1954, 1957). The magazine had resumed publication in Shanghai in 1947 with Paul Bartel (1904–2001) as the new co-editor. But in 1949 Bartel moved the Alliance Press to Hong Kong, and Wilson Wang returned to Penang. The Alliance Press had distribution centres in Penang,

Singapore, Surabaya, and Taibei, and the editors claimed to have over 10,000 subscribers in Southeast Asia alone (*Shengjing Bao* 1949: 4927).

Wang remained in Penang for a decade as the Burmah Road Gospel Hall's "international evangelist" (Ung 2005). During those years, Wang frequently visited Brethren assemblies in Malaya and Singapore as a speaker, taught at youth camps, and travelled widely with Henry Freeman Marks.[14] In 1949 he spent a year in Rochester, New York (Huang 2016), and on his return in 1950 the missionary in Kuala Kangsar reported that Wang had shown a Moody Bible Institute film "The God of Creation: A Sermon From Science" (c. 1945) to an audience of over 50 Chinese, Indians, Malays, and Europeans.[15]

Starting in 1950, Teh Phai Lian and another Brethren, Yeoh Kiam Hiong, co-edited and published an annual magazine in Penang that they called *The Way, Truth, and Life* (*Daolu, Zhenli, Shengming* 道路, 真理, 生命). It was published by the Burmah Road Gospel Hall and distributed by Tithes Dental and Photo Supply in Kuala Lumpur and Singapore. In 1958, a Brethren missionary reported to the editors of *Echoes of Service* that "[a] gifted brother in business, Mr. Teh Phai Jian, together with a fellow worker, Mr. Yeo [Kiam Hiong], continue the issuing of their magazine in Chinese". He described it as "full of good matter and of an excellent standard", adding that Mr Teh had spent hundreds of pounds in the "spread of the truths of the gospel".[16]

In 1957, Teh published a book of essays entitled *A New Explanation of Old Stories* (*Gushi Xinjiang* 故事新講). Teh cited few sources, but the title evokes that of Lu Xun's 1936 book of short stories *Old Tales Retold* (*Gushi Xinbian* 故事新編).[17] Teh printed and distributed 7,000 copies of the first edition in 1957, and in the preface to the book's second edition, he mentions that Chinese Christians had so appreciated it that he had added a second volume of essays. In 1958 he published 8,000 copies of a 517-page second edition, and the book was reprinted in 1961 (Teh 1958 [1961]: 1–2). In 1962 he added a fifth volume that was printed and distributed in Hong Kong (Teh 1962). Not until 1980 did he publish a two-volume English translation of the second edition with the title *Ancient Chinese Stories with a Modern Message* (Teh 1980a; 1980b).

14 H.F. Marks, Taipeng, 27 February 1948, *ES* No. 2131 (May 1948): 57.

15 T.A.S. Watt, Kuala Kangsar, 18 September 1950, *ES* No. 2172 (December 1950): 138. This film is still available on DVD.

16 E. Phillips, Penang, 4 December 1958, *ES* No. 1370 (February 1959): 22. Ch'ng Oon Hooi recalled that the magazine was assembled in Penang and sent to Hong Kong to be printed.

17 Like the magazine, the book was published by the Burmah Road Gospel Hall and distributed by Tithes. I thank Ch'ng Oon Hooi for giving me paperback and hardbound copies of the 1961 reprint of the second edition.

Figure 31 Cover of Wilson Wang's 1956 *Salvation Sermons* (*Jiu En Jiang Tai* 救恩講台), written in 1952 in Penang and published by the Alliance Press in Hong Kong. The drawing shows a strong arm identified as Jesus reaching down from heaven to rescue a man who is "sinking in evil"(*zuien chenlun)*. From the library at the Charismatic Church of Penang.

In these essays, Teh retold classical Chinese ethical tales from the writings of Mencius, Confucius, the *Romance of the Three Kingdoms*, and the biography of Sun Yat-sen (among others), as a vehicle for teaching Bible truths. In the preface to the second edition, Teh describes the book as a "morality book" (*shanshu*), a term that evokes the merit-making distribution of moral literature of both Chinese Daoists and Buddhists. The essays are models of Christian contextualization.

One essay tells of an event in the early life of Sun Yat-sen, the founding father of the Republic of China, whom Teh described as a "juvenile revolutionist" and a "pioneer in China's war against superstition".[18] Sun later became Christian, and Teh claims that the success of the 1911 revolution was closely bound up with "his serving the real God instead of idols" (Teh 1958 [1961]: 130–4; 1980a: 8–13).

According to Teh, when Sun was 12 [c. 1878], he and his father visited their ancestral tombs during the Clear Bright Festival (*Qingming*). On their return home, they walked past a temple filled with devotees "burning incense, kowtowing, and praying to the idol for preservation from danger" (Teh 1958 [1961]: 8–9). Sun wondered why people were bowing down to lifeless clay images and entered the temple, where he boldly broke off the arm of a statue of the Northern Emperor (*Beidi*). When the devotees accused him of harming the god, he responded, "The idol did not even wince in pain or rise up to defend itself when I broke its arm. And these clearly show it is not a god. You are worshipping it in vain as it can neither bless nor curse you."

In an account that echoes James Legge's 1880 study of *The Religions of China*, Teh also claimed that China had always been a monotheistic nation that recognized the existence of the "heavenly true god Shangdi" (*Tianshangde Zhenshen Shangdi* 天上的真神上帝). He contrasted veneration of *Shangdi*—the "Emperor above"—with the polytheistic veneration of *shen*, or saints, which emerged only began after Buddhism and Daoism gained popularity. He further noted that a number of *shen*, including the Jade Emperor, the God of Literature, Taishang Laojun (the deified Laozi), and the God of War, were merely humans whom emperors had honored as deities as a consequence of their service to the country (Teh 1958 [1961]: 133).

The Postwar Chinese Christian Diaspora

Sun Yat-sen's conversion had encouraged Chinese Christians to hope that China would soon be a Christian nation. But after the Chinese Communist

[18] Different versions of this story exist; I rely here on Teh's account.

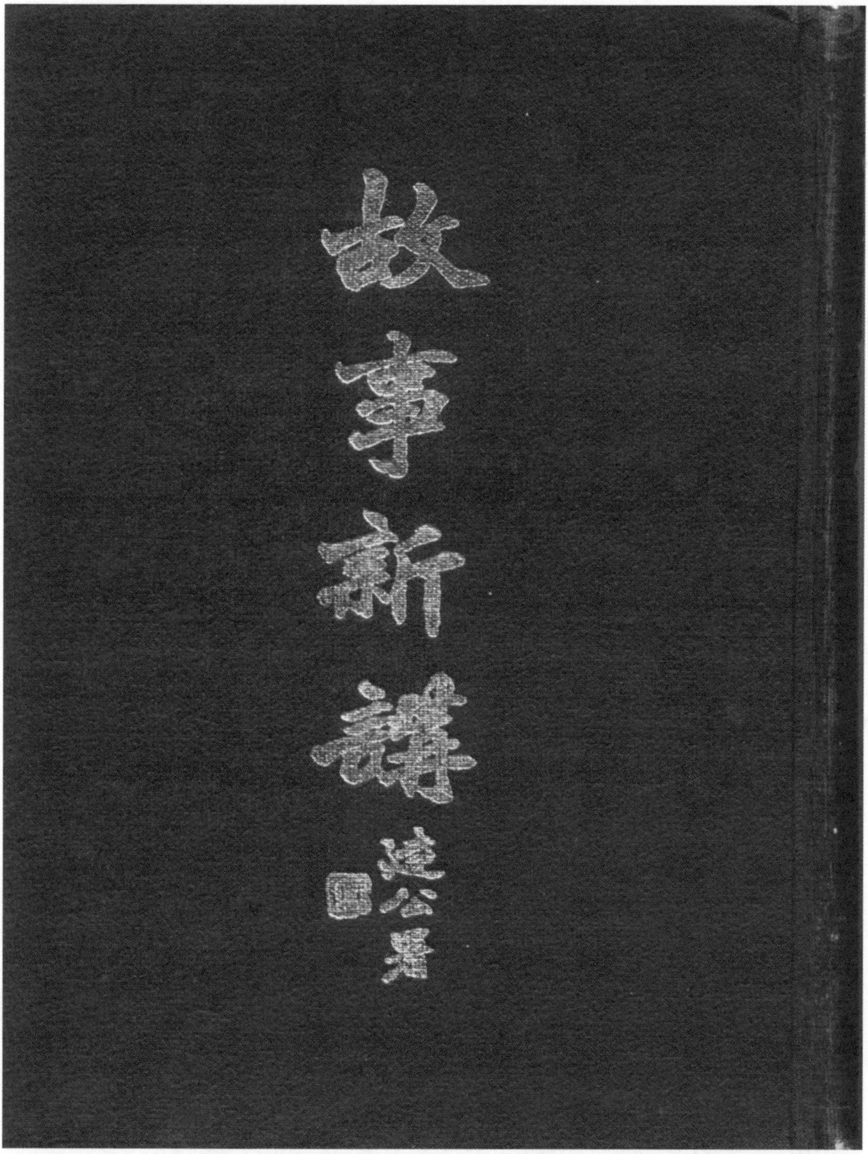

Figure 32 The Chinese edition of *Ancient Chinese Stories with a Modern Message* (1958 [1961]), which was printed with both a buckram cover with a gilt title and a paper cover. Well-known Hong Kong artist Au Kin Kung (區建公) (1887–1971), who provided the characters for many Hong Kong shop signs and public institutions, wrote the characters for the title.

Figure 33 Cover of the 1980 English translation of parts I and II of Teh Phai Lian's book of essays *Gushi Xinjiang* 故事新講, translated as *Ancient Chinese Stories with a Modern Message*.

Revolution of 1949 succeeded and the Guomindang fled to Taiwan, Chinese Christian leaders faced precarious futures in both Communist China and postcolonial Southeast Asia. Many Chinese Christians migrated to North America, including a number of prominent Christian leaders. Teh's son Teh Chiew Oo remained in Penang to run Tithes, but sent his wife and children to Vancouver, Canada.

By the 1960s, many of the Chinese evangelists who had once worked in Southeast Asia had moved to North America. Leland Wang continued to work with the CFMU in Hong Kong, Taiwan, and Southeast Asia, but shifted his evangelical campaigns to the United States, Canada, Europe, and the Middle East (Wong 2000).[19] His American-born Hakka son-in-law Hong Sit (1921–2014, Xue Chuntong 薛春桐) succeeded him as president of the Chinese Foreign Missionary Union, and from their base in Houston, Hong and Leland's daughter Amy Wang Sit (1926–2008) established churches in Tahiti, Taiwan, Singapore, Malaysia, Indonesia, Australia, and Hong Kong.[20]

Between 1949 and 1969, Wilson Wang worked in Penang, Singapore, the United States, and Australia before retiring to Boston. In 1949, his son enrolled in Wheaton College and his daughter at Northwestern Schools in Minneapolis, whose president was Billy Graham (News at a Glance 1949). He spent that year at the Rochester Missionary Society in New York, then returned to Penang for a decade, which is likely the longest period he was allowed to stay in Malaysia as an international evangelist under new immigration policies. In 1960 he worked for a year in the Detroit Chinese Bible Church, which supported one of two large para-church organizations in the US, the Chinese Christian Mission (CCM) (Early History 2018; Tseng 2004–06: 146). He returned to Southeast Asia the next year as the Singapore Bible College's second principal (About Us 2018).

[19] In 1949 he received an honorary Doctor of Divinity degree from Wheaton College, which two of his children attended (Willard 1950: 197). *Bulletin of Wheaton College* N.S. Vol. 27, No. 4 (April 1950): 115.

[20] According to an obituary in the *Houston Chronicle*, Hong Sit was president of the Chinese Full Gospel Fellowship International and also of the Chinese Foreign Missionary Union ("Dr. Hong Sit" 2014), and Joel Osteen identified him as a major personal influence (1978). After Leland visited Tahiti in 1961, Hong Sit followed up the next year, introducing speaking in tongues and miraculous healing to Chinese immigrants and launching a Hakka reawakening (Fer and Black 2005: 52–3). The Hakka church that Hong and his wife helped found divided in 1981 after some members adopted the doctrines of the New Testament church founded by Kong Duen Yee and founded the Church of Tahiti (Fer and Black 2005: 55–6). On Kong's influence in Penang and Singapore, see Chapter 14.

In 1963, the Sydney Chinese Christian Association was founded with help from Leland Wang, who recommended first Hong Sit, then Wilson to them. Wilson went to Australia in 1965 on a short-term visa, and was offered a position as the first pastor of a newly formed independent Chinese Christian Church (CCC). He returned to Penang while awaiting a visa, then worked at the CCC until his retirement in 1969 (Huang 2016). In 1970 he moved to the United States and lived in Boston, where he preached regularly at a church formed in 1961 by recent Chinese immigrants (BCEC 2011: 86).[21] Chinese Christians in Penang, Singapore, Detroit, Sydney, and Boston still recall Wilson Wang in anniversary publications and newsletters.

Before the war, the Christians in Southeast Asia had increasing contact with leaders and revivalists like John Sung, Leland Wang, and Wilson Wang. Chinese magazines, tracts, and books, including both translations and original compositions, circulated widely, finding a place in the personal libraries of Chinese elders like Teh Phai Lian. Just as the Brethren had used travel and publications to create a global movement and revival, the Chinese Christian evangelists used revival campaigns and the printed word to strengthen their relationships with Chinese Christians in China, Hong Kong, and throughout Southeast Asia. When the outcome of World War II resulted in a global diaspora of Chinese, Christian evangelists followed them to Tahiti and Australia, Canada and the United States.[22]

Because the network of independent Chinese Christian Churches that Wilson and Leland Wang helped form is uncentralized and global in its scope, their role in modern Chinese Christian history has not yet been fully documented by historians. I have told their story from the perspective of Chinese Christians in Penang and Singapore, but many more chapters could be added to this account.

Postscript

In 2019 I visited the Charismatic Church of Penang and took inventory of the Chinese books in their library, which his great niece Ch'ng Oon Hooi identified as having belonged to Teh. He owned many Chinese translations of Christian works, including three that the Brethren would have readily accepted:

[21] See http://www.cbcdetroit.org/aboutCBC/history.php [accessed 29 July 2018].

[22] In North America, Chinese Christian Churches remained separate from both mainline Protestants and Chinese American political groups, using evangelicalism as a way to construct an alternative Chinese identity unconnected to national and political commitments (Tseng 2004–06: 122).

Scofield Bible Study Course (1950), published by the Alliance Press, Harry A. Ironside's *Except Ye Repent*, and H. Holmquist's *Life of Martin Luther* (1937). But many more of the Chinese books in his collection were those popular with independent Chinese evangelists, including Dr Yu Chenghua's 1938 translation of Madame Guyon's *Sweet Smelling Myrrh*, T. Austin Sparks' *In Touch with the Throne* (1953) and Canadian independent church founder Oswald J. Smith's *The Enduement of Power*.

Teh's Chinese library included a few issues of the *Shengjing Bao* and publications of the Alliance Press, including a Chinese translation of Paul Bunyan's *Holy War* (*Sheng Jan* 聖戰) and books by Wilson Wang (see Fig. 31). But his library also held books and tracts by Chinese Christian leaders Andrew Gih, Timothy Dzao, Calvin Lee, Charles Lee, and Wu Enpu. The collection also included popular modern books on Buddhism, Confucianism, and Chinese history.

The Charismatic Church of Penang's library collection also includes Teh's own books and tracts. Up until 1963, the Burmah Road Gospel Hall published Teh's tracts and books, which he produced and funded, without seeking to translate them into English. The Chinese-speaking and English-speaking Christians at the Burmah Road Gospel Hall cooperated as a single oversight to manage the gospel hall and its events. But Teh's library suggests that Chinese- and English-speaking elders studied Christianity through the lens of overlapping literatures that both joined them to global Christianity and divided them into different imagined Christian communities.

Chapter 13

A New Local Church Movement and Living Waters

> Frankly, we have doubts about your present method of receiving others. Is the Holy Spirit the Head in every matter, or is man doing the receiving? Your practice of receiving others may have been living in the beginning, but through years of habit it may have become a set of rules.
>
> 1935 letter from Shanghai Christians to Exclusive Brethren in London[1]

One of the most famous Chinese Christian leaders of the 20th century is Ni Tuosheng (倪柝聲, 1903–72), who came to be known as Watchman Nee. Nee promoted forming independent churches free of European control, and the local church movement that he led soon spread China-wide (Bays 1996; Woodbridge 2016, 2019). He had early success in Malaya, where he claimed to have established the first local church in Sitiawan on a speaking tour in 1925. Nee visited Penang and Singapore on the sea journey to Europe, and his coworker Faithful Luke moved to Singapore in 1937, where he worked with both the Brethren and with a newly-formed independent Christian Assembly whose founder had seceded from the Brethren.

Watchman Nee and Faithful Luke were closely networked with Fuzhou revivalists Leland and Wilson Wang and the evangelists of the Chinese Foreign Missionary Union. The CFMU evangelists maintained a close relationship with Robert Jaffray and the Christian and Missionary Alliance missionaries; Nee praised the C&MA but promoted the formation of indigenous local churches independent of any denominational or missionary organization.

[1] "A Reply to a Meeting in London", July 1935 (Nee 1993b: 424). The letter's authors included Watchman Nee, Witness Lee, and four others, representing members of two churches in Shanghai.

The Brethren promoted the model of the primitive local church and described themselves as undenominational Christians. Watchman Nee ensampled the ideals of Brethren founders while questioning whether the modern Brethren were any different than missionary-led denominational churches. European missionaries had been working in Asia for over a century, and many of the Asian and Eurasian Brethren in Singapore and Penang were second- or third-generation Christians. Some British Christians also questioned why missionaries still remained in these cities.

In the 1950s, the Brethren missionaries in Singapore, Penang, and British Malaya distanced themselves from Watchman Nee and his local church movement while promoting an independent evangelist Charles Lee. Like Nee, Lee cooperated for a time with the Brethren missionaries, but finally separated from them, using his influence with Chinese Christians to form a new local church in Singapore.

Watchman Nee

Watchman Nee was raised Methodist in Fuzhou and attended Anglican-run Trinity College. He observed that the missionaries enjoyed a comfortable standard of living, but that their Chinese assistants were poorly paid, and decided against becoming an evangelist (Kaung n.d.).[2] He participated in revival meetings led by Dora Yu, who introduced him to Margaret E. Barber (1866–1929), a former Anglican missionary who had become independent. In 1921, he and his mother and one brother were baptized by immersion. The next year, he joined Leland Wang and other Chinese Christians when they started to meet in Fuzhou, and he and other family members formally withdrew from the Methodist Church.[3]

In 1924 Nee's mother was invited to Malaya to preach, and she invited him to accompany her. They visited Sitiawan, and when Nee and his mother met with a tepid reception from the Methodist pastor, they began to hold meeting in private homes. Nee later claimed to have founded the first local church in

[2] This set of three audiotapes was available through the library at Wilkie Terrace Christian Assembly. Similar lectures by Stephen Kaung are now available on YouTube.

[3] Many Chinese evangelists who visited Southeast Asia were from Fuzhou, where Christian elites had allied with progressive reformists to propose new directions for China (see Dunch 2001).

Southeast Asia, which is still called the Church of Sitiawan and takes 1925 as its date of establishment (Kinnear 1973: 62–3; Lee 1989: 21).[4]

In Fuzhou, Barber had an extensive library of British Christian publications, and she encouraged Nee to read the writings of John Nelson Darby, George Müller, and a contemporary British author T. Austin-Sparks. He began to exchange letters with and purchase books from Brethren in England. In 1932, a small group of Exclusive Brethren from England and America in the Ravenite faction visited China and accepted Nee and other independent Chinese Christians in Shanghai into fellowship.

In 1933 they invited Nee to visit assemblies in London, Vancouver, and New York. But when his hosts limited his lectures to Exclusive Brethren groups, Nee secretly met with non-Brethren at Honor Oak Christian Fellowship Centre in London. While in New York, he also visited a Presbyterian medical missionary and his wife who were on leave in New Haven, and broke bread with them in their home (Kinnear 1973: 92–3; see also Lian 2010: 173–4).

On learning of these meetings, the Exclusive Brethren objected, demanding that Nee and his followers take "the same attitude and stand" as them (Nee 1993b: 419). Much like the Open Brethren who refused to obey Darby in 1848, the Chinese Christians responded by insisting on local autonomy. In the letter that I cite in this chapter's epigraph, Watchman Nee, Witness Lee, and their coauthors stated, "Frankly, we have doubts about your present method of receiving others." They further implied that the Exclusive Brethren's strictness and desire to regulate others was evidence that they were no longer led by the Holy Spirit (Nee 1993b: 424–6). In 1935, their relationship with the Exclusives ceased (Lee 1991: 203; Roberts 2005: 25).

Although they had separated from the Exclusives, their shared principles could still have provided them with a basis for cooperation with the Open Brethren. Watchman Nee had read George Müller's writings, and his coworker Witness Lee (Li Changshou 李常受, 1905–97) had joined an assembly in Chefoo led by an "old British brother" who had been taught by Benjamin Wills Newton (1807–99) in Plymouth. Newton had been at the centre of the events leading to the 1848 division between Exclusive and Open Brethren. Darby had deemed Newton's teachings to be heretical, and when other Brethren refused to follow him in excluding Newton and those associated with him from their meetings on Darby's say-so, he broke relations with them.

---

[4] Faithful Luke and Wilson Wang later visited Sitiawan frequently, and this church joined the network of charismatic local churches formed after Kong Duen Yee's 1963 tour.

The "old British brother", Mr Burnett, had worked with the China Inland Mission, but left it to establish an independent Brethren assembly in Chefoo, where his ability to expound the Scripture attracted followers. Witness Lee met with this group for more than seven years, but left when he found that the assembly was not growing. Later he offered this experience as an example of a case in which the leader's insistence on control had impaired growth and multiplication (Lee 2004: 154). At the same time, he could claim to have studied with a skilled Bible teacher who himself had been discipled by one of the British Brethren's most famous leaders and founders. Witness Lee joined Watchman Nee's movement, and in 1934 moved to Shanghai to become the editor of Nee's magazine *The Christian*.

Like the Open Brethren, members of the new local church movement avoided taking a name since they did not want to become a denomination. And like the Open Brethren, they found that others named them. Some refer to their churches as Christian Assemblies or local churches, but the missionaries called them "Little Flock" Christians. Watchman Nee had translated some hymns from an Exclusive Brethren hymn book, which he published under the title *Little Flock Hymns* (*Xiaoqun Shige* 小群詩歌).[5] For that reason, others nicknamed them the "Little Flock", a name that members rejected. As one member explained it in 1934, the expression "little flock" referred to all believers—past, present, and future, Chinese and foreign—and should not be used to name their gatherings. As he described it, they simply called themselves "brothers in the Lord" who met in a particular location. The author also rejected the notion that Watchman Nee was their chairman, claiming that they were led by "the Lord Jesus Himself" (Nee 1993a: 172–4).

In the 1930s, Nee published newsletters (1933–35) and a bimonthly magazine *The Open Door* (1937–39) that was distributed in China and Southeast Asia. *The Open Door* was a digest of letters and reports from Watchman Nee and his coworkers, which like *Echoes of Service* described their travels and conversations. Just as *The Revival* had done in 1859, the new publications promoted awareness of how quickly and widely their movement had spread.

Nee could have made common cause with the Open Brethren, but he questioned whether the Brethren still followed the same principles as their founders. In 1934, he laid out his argument that despite their claims to the contrary, the Open Brethren were no different from other denominations. He

[5] This hymnal had been compiled by George V. Wigram in 1856 and revised by John N. Darby in 1881.

did so in a published response to a letter from Singaporean Christian Wong Kai Seng (1888–1977), who had emigrated to Singapore from Fuzhou in 1916.

According to his daughter, Wong was an Anglican lay minister who had formal theological training (probably in Fuzhou). But when the Anglicans decided to write to England to request money for a project, he proposed that they should pray instead. He was advised that if he disagreed with their approach to managing church affairs, he should leave. He did so, and joined Bethesda.[6]

Wong started an informal prayer meeting in his home in 1932 with recent emigrants from China, including some who were followers of Watchman Nee. When Nee visited Singapore on the way to England in 1933, the two met and spoke at length. The next year, Wong wrote to Nee that the "Western brothers" in Singapore had become aware that his faith was not the same as theirs, and that they had attended closely to his and another Chinese elder's teachings. They corrected the two Chinese elders, rejecting their counter-arguments, and would no longer permit them to teach. Both stopped attending meetings at the gospel hall. In 1934 Wong wrote to Nee, asking for evidence that the Brethren were a denomination so that they could meet with them again and "prove their many errors" (Nee 1993b: 306–7).

In his published "Answer to Brother Wang Kai Sen [*sic*]", Nee proclaimed that despite their early history and their claims to being an undenominational New Testament church, the Open Brethren had become a denomination. Nee had corresponded with G.H. Lang (1874–1958)[7] and may have been fortified in his arguments by reading Lang's 1925 book *Departure*, in which Lang had come to the same conclusion.[8]

Like Lang, Nee observed that the Open Brethren had a mission board named Christian Missions in Many Lands, and a central organization in Bath, England

---

[6] He went into business, but his business apparently failed in the 1930s; his daughter Ruth Hie King Wong (1918–82) received a PhD from Harvard University and became well known as a leading educator in Singapore and Malaysia (Ho 2003). I interviewed one of his daughters at Wilkie Terrace Christian Assembly on 17 March 1999.

[7] Nee had asked Lang for advice as conflict with the Exclusive Brethren unfolded, and Lang, whose parents had been Exclusive Brethren but who was known as an independent thinker, had supported him in his decision to reject their demands.

[8] In 1939, Lang wrote biographies of independent Tamil evangelist John Christian Arulappan (1939) and Anthony Norris Groves (1949 [1939]). As the subtitle of the biography of Groves described it, the book was also a study of the "*Original Principles and Practices of THE BRETHREN with Applications to Present Conditions*". In both books, Lang held up the method of rapid indigenization as exemplary for contemporary Brethren.

that transmitted donations to the Western workers. Their Chinese workers, he observed, received their salaries from the Western missionaries, just like the other denominations. He also claimed that the Brethren had a hierarchy, and that the Western missionaries took an elevated position at meetings. Finally he observed that the Brethren had established new gatherings in places where he and his followers had already started meetings (Nee 1993a: 252–3).

Nee's published proclamation was immediately followed by a letter from a former worker in the Brethren mission in Jehol, who had met Nee in Shanghai, and was encouraged to find that his movement was already nationwide. As he described it, the new movement had begun by "calling a group of God's children out of the denominations to practice the principles and examples in the New Testament". He regretted leaving the Brethren, but expressed his desire to participate in work led by the Holy Spirit (Nee 1993a: 256–7).

In 1935, Wong announced to Watchman Nee that he and two other former Brethren elders had formally separated from the Brethren in Singapore. He described his confusion, since the Brethren too had announced that denominations were not in accordance with the Bible. But he finally reasoned that although they were "the best denomination among denominations", they nonetheless had become an "invisible denomination" (Nee 1993b: 341–2). As his daughter described it, they simply called themselves Christians, and only took the name "Christian Assembly" because the government required them to have a name in order to register.

The Local Church and the Invisible Denomination

The Japanese Occupation in 1937 forced many of Watchman Nee's associates to move from the coastal provinces of China to its interior. In Hankow (today part of Wuhan), they launched a magazine *The Open Door* that, like *Echoes of Service* and *China's Million*, was a digest of letters. The newsletter allowed the scattered members of their movement to stay in contact with each other during this period of disruption.[9] *The Open Door* published reports on Overcomer's conferences, events whose name was derived from a term

[9] In the first issue, Nee wrote an "Open Letter" in which he described the purpose of *The Open Door* as the publishing of: (1) Articles concerning the principles of the work; (2) News of gospel preaching in all the localities; (3) The addresses of the workers (the apostles) on the move; (4) The addresses of the meeting halls of the local churches so that the brothers who are escaping the war might know where to meet; (5) The whereabouts of the brothers (the disciples) in the Lord at every place in order that comfort might be given to those who are concerned for them (Nee 1993c: 1–2).

in the Book of Revelation that Austin-Sparks took up to represent "God's inner company", who would be raptured at the second coming (Austin-Sparks 1945). The newsletter also included accounts of the travels of Watchman Nee and itinerant workers, and letters from all parts of China and from Penang, Singapore, and Ipoh.

In 1937, Nee visited Manila, Singapore, Penang, and Sitiawan.[10] He also met with "a brother (an Englishman) in Tai-ping" (almost certainly Brethren missionary Henry Freeman Marks). The Brethren missionary convinced Nee that the phrase "Christian Missions in Many Lands" did not represent a mission board, since the word "missions" was plural and the word "in" was used, not "of".

In 1938 *The Open Door* published "An Announcement by Brother Watchman Nee", in which he reminded his readers that four years earlier he had publically stated his conclusion that the Open Brethren were a denomination. Nee admitted that although many people considered the Brethren to be an organization and abbreviated their name as C.M.M.L, he had been mistaken on this point, and that the Brethren had no missionary board. He further observed that since all churches in the Bible were local, there was no need to say who was and was not a denomination. He concluded, "We cannot say whether the Brethren in a certain place are a denomination or not. We should determine this by the condition in that locality." Nee asked "the brothers" to forgive his inaccuracy, and invited them to read his book when it was published, referring to his plans to translate his new book into English so that the missionaries could read it (Nee 1993c: 218–9).

Because of their commonalities and despite their differences, Nee and his followers sought a relationship with well-established Brethren gospel halls in the Straits Settlements and Malaya. Although Wong and a few others had left Bethesda in Singapore, members of other Chinese gospel halls remained with the Brethren. Watchman Nee's admission that the Open Brethren were not necessarily a denomination was a concession that opened the door to cooperation with them.

In 1938, Nee travelled from Shanghai to Europe, stopping in Hong Kong, Singapore, and Penang to hold meetings. Soon after his visit, a member of the "assembly in Penang" wrote to the editors of *The Open Door* to thank them for Nos. 1–6, and reported that they had "learned with much rejoicing about the

---

[10] One Penang missionary reported in 1937 that "[t]here is a movement among the Chinese", and that they were starting a series of Chinese gospel meetings in the Chinese quarter of Penang (A. Hardwidge, Penang, n.d., *ES* No. 1112 (August 1937: 206). But he makes no mention of Watchman Nee's visit to Penang.

meetings, the work, and the situations of the brothers and sisters in all these places!" Chang Ke-shu also described the recent visits from Faithful Luke and Watchman Nee:

> In January Brother Faithful Luk came and conducted an evangelistic revival meeting. We witnessed an abundant blessing from the Lord. On April 1 Brother Watchman Nee passed through on his way to Europe, and through him we again received the Lord's grace. He stayed with us for a few days and spoke to us about the truth. All the children of the Lord received much edification.

He reported that their church had about 40 members and 30 breaking bread together (Nee 1993d: 375).[11]

Watchman Nee had published his new book *Rethinking our Work* (*The Normal Christian Church Life*) (*Gongzuo de Zai Si* 工作的再思) in Shanghai in January 1938. According to Chang, the Penang Christians had all read the new book and wished to "act according to the principle of the Bible". He enclosed a donation to support "apostolic work in the pioneering endeavor in remote regions" together with a letter from a few members, including Teh Phai Lian (Nee 1993d: 374–5).[12]

On his arrival in Europe in 1938, Nee attended the Keswick Convention, where an American Presbyterian pastor and radio preacher recommended that Christians pray for missionaries and national Christian leaders as they read news from around the world—for Wang Ming Tao (Wang Mingdao) when they read of Beijing; for John Sung and Watchman Nee when they received news of Shanghai; and for Leland Wang as they read about events in Hong Kong. In what was described as a "crowning moment of vision", the chairman of the convention invited Nee to lead conference participants in a prayer for China and Japan (Keswick Convention 1938: 209, 246). The next year, Leland Wang attended the convention as an invited speaker and also led a Methodist service (Keswick Convention 1939: 241, 246, 273).

Nee also visited Austin-Sparks' convention and training centre at Honor Oak, where he met his future biographer, Angus Kinnear (1912–2002). He

---

[11] The Brethren in Penang opened a new gospel hall on Burmah Road on 25 May 1938. The fact that the Brethren had well-established meeting places may also have been a factor in members' continued loyalty to the Brethren.

[12] The letter was signed by "Tseng Pei-ran", a Mandarin romanization of his name (pinyin: Zheng Peiran). Because they described themselves as the "assembly in Penang", and because he was among the donors, I am confident that the group writing to Nee were members of the Burmah Road Gospel Hall in Penang.

was invited to Denmark, where he gave a series of ten lectures that he entitled "The Normal Christian Life". From there he visited Paris, where he met up with China Inland Mission missionary and revivalist Elizabeth Fischbacher and Phyllis Deck, who worked with him to translate *Rethinking Our Work* into English (Kinnear 1973: 113).

He returned to England for four months, and in February 1939 wrote to his followers to describe Honor Oak, claiming that "the testimony, the revelation, and the knowledge of the self and the natural man are here" (Nee 1993d: 521). Before he left England, Austin-Sparks published the new translation as a book entitled *Concerning our Missions* (1939) (Kinnear 1973: 114).[13]

In this influential book, which has been reprinted many times, Nee laid out the basic principles of the local church. As he described it, each church should be autonomous and led by its elders, much like the Brethren. He described the elders as being chosen by God as "overseers" who had been "appointed for church governance". But unlike the Brethren, he contrasted the role of elders with that of apostles, who were gifted as prophets, teachers, and evangelists. Brethren missionaries and Chinese evangelists both depended on Christians to donate so that they could live by faith, and Nee also called on local church members to support their workers (Nee 1982).

While Nee was in Europe, Faithful Luke (Lu Zhongxin 陸忠心, 1900–73) moved to Singapore, and Stephen Kaung (Jiang Shoudao 江守道, b. 1915) also visited.[14] In 1938 Leslie J. Donaldson reported in *Echoes of Service* that he and "Mr. Luk" had "some splendid open air meetings" in the Dutch-controlled island of Karimon, where he spoke in Hokkien and Luk interpreted into Mandarin. He added that "I have an excellent companion in Liok Tiong Sin who not only has a passion for souls, but is able to speak four Chinese languages well besides English. He gives his whole time to the Lord's work and looks to him for his daily needs."[15]

Faithful Luke cooperated with the Brethren, but he also worked at the Singapore Christian Assembly (*Xinjianpo jidu tu juhui suo* 新加坡基督徒聚會所) that former Brethren elder Wong Kai Seng had founded. Because their numbers increased to over 50 people, in 1938 they had moved to a rented meeting place on Wilkie Road that became Faithful Luke's home (Anon 1966–67: 5; Nee 1993d: 187). In Singapore, he and Wilson Wang conducted

[13] Between 1939 and 1942, Austin-Sparks also published the translated lectures in his magazine *A Witness and Testimony*.

[14] The Wilkie Terrace Christian Assembly remained in Kaung's network after he moved to New York.

[15] Donaldson, Singapore, n.d., *ES* No. 1126 (October 1938): 263.

meetings together, and a recent history of the Brethren in Singapore identifies Faithful Luke and Wilson Wang as their two evangelists in the prewar years (Nee 1993d: 350; Tong 2014: 44).

Nee returned to Shanghai by way of India and Singapore in May of 1939 (Lee 1991: 203–5). But in China as in Southeast Asia, the Second World War interrupted the flow of persons and publications. Faithful Luke and his family escaped Singapore to a small village in Johore, and Kaung fled to India, where he met Lady Ogle, a missionary in India who was associated with T. Austin Sparks and Honor Oak (Kaung n.d.: 6–7).

During the war Nee remained in Shanghai and ran a pharmaceutical company, and the church in Shanghai ceased meeting. The church was relaunched in 1948, but in 1952 Nee was arrested and spent the rest of his life in jail. The centre of their local church movement for a time shifted to Taiwan, where Witness Lee had moved in 1949. In 1952, Kaung joined a local church in New York, and in 1961 Witness Lee moved to Anaheim, California, which is still the base for Living Stream Ministry.[16]

For a time Witness Lee cooperated with Kaung, but they disagreed on the question of whether there could be more than one local church in a location, a principle that Witness Lee called the "ground of locality" (Lee 1991: 105–6). In North America, Lee and Kaung separately promoted the local church movement through the translation of Nee's publications into English, but only Kaung continued to work closely with Austin-Sparks. Faithful Luke remained in Singapore, and the Christian Assembly bought a former Japanese Buddhist temple at Wilkie Terrace. They continued to maintain links with local churches in Hong Kong, Taiwan, and the Philippines, as well as with Kaung.[17]

The Local Church in Singapore and Penang

Although they had initially worked with him, when Faithful Luke went to England in 1950, Penang missionary Sidney S. Adams wrote to the British Brethren to advise them to "keep him out" since he was "Faithful only to Watchman Nee and his ideals". The missionaries also expressed concern about a new local church movement in India led by Bakht Singh (1903–2000). Bakht

[16] Living Stream has published the complete collected works of Watchman Nee and Witness Lee in English. For a complete listing of their publications, see https://www.ministrybooks.org/index.cfm [accessed 3 November 2018].

[17] I first learned of Stephen Kaung when I visited the Wilkie Terrace Christian Assembly library, which held an extensive collection of his books, translations, and tape recordings. So far as I am aware, this Christian Assembly had no relationship with Witness Lee.

Singh sometimes visited Singapore's Christian Assembly, and Faithful Luke had visited him in India on his way to England. Adams dismissed him as "another free lance chap linked up with Lady Ogle's group (Overcomers)".

Adams added that Bakh Singh and Faithful Luke both claimed to be apostles and laid hands on people, including senior elders.[18] Albert E. Phillips, a missionary who had worked in China but moved to Malaya after the war, observed, "Without doubt these groups set a good example of knowing and asserting what they believe, and it is a privilege to know many of them, and this makes the problem more acute." He recommended that Bakht Singh not be given further opportunities to exercise influence within the assemblies.[19]

From the perspective of the Brethren missionaries, several practices and teachings defined their differences. "Little Flock" members insisted on using unleavened bread for the breaking of bread ceremony, and they would seek to convince Brethren to do so.[20] The missionaries preferred to continue using leavened bread, arguing that if individual assemblies changed their practices, then the network of assemblies on the Malay Peninsula would no longer share a single ritual form.[21] One missionary feared that if they gave way on the issue of unleavened bread, the Chinese-speaking Brethren would embrace "the many things connected with the teachings of the LITTLE FLOCK",[22] including the doctrine of the Partial Rapture, an interpretation of Biblical prophecy that the Brethren rejected.[23]

The two groups also differed in the role women took in meetings. Phillips observed that although "Little Flock" women covered their heads at meetings, they were "allowed to take part at the Table as well as other meetings".[24] Phillips argued against changing the role of women in assemblies on the basis that to change practices that "had been taught otherwise" would put into doubt all other teaching and would discredit former teachers.[25]

---

[18] Adams, Penang, 5 June 1950 (ES/IC).

[19] Phillips (Bury St. Edmunds, Suffolk) to *ES* editors, 25 November 1952 (ES/IC).

[20] One of the missionaries mentioned "Honor Oak" in connection with the insistence on using unleavened bread, which suggests that they were aware of the practices of Austin-Sparks's non-denominational local church.

[21] Angus (Kuala Lumpur) to Stunt, 21 March 1956 (ES/IC).

[22] Regler (Malacca) to Pulleng, 5 March 1956 (ES/IC).

[23] Watchman Nee's mentor Barber had been influenced by British pastor David Morrieson Panton, who promoted the partial rapture through his magazine *The Dawn*.

[24] Phillips (Bury St. Edmunds, Suffolk) to the editors, 25 November 1952 (ES/IC).

[25] Phillips (Suffolk) to *ES* editors, 25 November 1952 (ES/IC).

Charles S. Lee

Although the missionaries distanced themselves from Watchman Nee's local church movement after World War II, Phillips highly recommended another independent Chinese evangelist, Charles S. Lee, whose Chinese name was Li Jisheng (李继圣) (1902–61) (Seow 1997: 35). Lee was from Chefoo (today Yantai), a city on the north coast of Shandong province, where the China Inland Mission had established a large Christian boarding school. Converted by John Sung in 1933, he worked for the Bethel Mission in Shandong. Although many of his practices resembled those of Watchman Nee's local church movement, Lee worked independently of them and cooperated closely with Open Brethren missionaries first in China, then in Singapore and Malaya.

Albert E. Phillips (born 1902) had come to Jiangxi in 1934, but in 1939, the Japanese took Nanchang, disrupting the Brethren mission (Stunt et al. 1972: 512). He and his wife returned to Nanchang in 1946, and by 1948, Charles Lee was cooperating with him. Phillips described him as a gifted coworker, and he and Lee were the main speakers at a special convention at the hill station Kuling (today, Lushan).[26]

When the Communists assumed control of the mainland in 1949, Phillips and Lee both left China for Taiwan, where they continued to work together, holding meetings in a medical college, in the University, and among the military and refugee students. Their young members tracted often at train stations wearing cloth sashes "with suitable texts".[27] In 1950 Phillips reported that Madame Chiang Kai-shek had heard of Lee from Mrs Wu, the wife of the former mayor of Shanghai, and had invited him to speak to a small circle of elite Christians.[28]

All news from China suggested the hopelessness of the situation for foreign missionaries, but Phillips also anticipated being unwelcome in Taiwan after the British government recognized the People's Republic of China in 1950.[29] He and his wife moved from Taiwan to Penang, and at his invitation Lee visited Singapore and Malaysia for three months in 1952. Lee held seven weeks of nightly meetings in Singapore, where he packed the assembly hall every night with 800 to 1,000 people. He next held meetings

[26] Phillips, Nanchang, 1 August 1948. *ES* No. 2146 (October 1948): 118.

[27] Phillips (Taiwan) to *ES* editors, 1 November 1949 (ES/IC).

[28] Phillips (Singapore) to *ES* editors, 9 May 1950 (ES/IC). The editors requested that Phillips pass on a gift to Charles Lee.

[29] Phillips (Singapore) to *ES* editors, 9 May 1950; Phillips (Taiwan) to *ES* editors, 16 November 1949 (ES/IC).

in Kuala Lumpur and Malacca.[30] A missionary commented, "They will accept truth and act upon it from Mr. Lee, whereas they are slow to accept it from us foreigners."[31] Lee visited New York in 1954, and went from there to London on the *Queen Mary*. Phillips recommended him to the editors of *Echoes*, hoping that they would arrange for him to visit assemblies in the London area and elsewhere to help "break down barriers (real and supposed) between Eastern & Western believers".[32]

(These photos were sent to us by Mr. Teh Chiew Oo of Penang. The one shows Mr. Charles Lee dressed in the " sin " clothes, apparently giving an object-lesson. The other shows the entrance to Burmah Road Hall, Penang, taken on Oct. 17th, the 3rd Anniversary of the Young People's Group, when about 500 young people were present. Much wisdom is needed by the leaders of this thriving work.

Figure 34 Photograph of Chinese evangelist Charles Lee at the Burmah Road Gospel Hall. Teh Chiew Oo, n.d., *ES* No. 1308 (January 1954): 12.

In 1954 *Echoes of Service* published a photograph sent by Teh Chiew Oo, showing Lee at the Burmah Road Gospel Hall wearing long white robes covered

[30] Phillips (Penang) to *ES* editors, 2 April 1952; Phillips (Taiping) to *ES* editors, 7 October 1953 (ES/IC).

[31] R.A. Vines, Malacca, 16 July 1952, *ES* No. 2193 (September 1952): 100.

[32] Phillips (Taiping) to *ES* editors, 25 October 1954 (ES/IC).

with Chinese characters on which the Chinese character for 'sin' was centrally written.[33] When I gave her a copy of her uncle's photograph, my former research assistant observed that Lee was wearing 'gospel robes' like those worn by "Little Flock" evangelists. Despite the similarity of style, all evidence points to Lee working independently of Watchman Nee, Witness Lee, and the local church movement that they led.[34]

Followers of Watchman Nee criticized continued European control of churches, and this issue concerned Asian members of the Brethren assemblies. In 1953, Teh Phai Lian's son Teh Chiew Oo wrote to the editors of *Echoes of Service* to ask why Chinese worker's names were not included in the Brethren prayer list, asking the editor William Lewis to "plainly say whether colour prejudice is to be tolerated in God's work".

Before responding to him, Lewis wrote to Adams to inquire about Teh's character. Adams praised him as a "very worthy brother and not a mere critic", but suggested that members of Watchman Nee's "Little Flock" groups had "pointed to the prayer list as evidence of our 'centralized' system which they say is totally 'whitefaced'".[35] Adams recommended to *Echoes'* editor that he reply that he had published the words of Charles Lee "for you hold him in honour for his work's sake".[36]

Teh's nephew Goh Ewe Kheng Goh also wrote to the editors of *Echoes of Service* from Singapore. Goh was one of Bethesda Gospel Hall's leaders, and after the war he was one of three elders overseeing their youth fellowship service (Tong 2014: 44–5). Mr Stunt replied by sending him a letter and a booklet, "Whose Faith Follows". Phillips wrote Stunt to attest that both Teh Chiew Oo and Goh Ewe Kheng were "excellent brethren and esteemed by many", and passed along payment from Teh to cover the cost of airmail postage.[37]

Lee visited Singapore in 1955 to speak at the opening of a new meeting place for the Chinese speaking assembly in the Geylang district, an event

---

[33] "Idolatry in Malaya", A.E. Phillips, Taiping, 7 October 1954, *ES* No. 1308 (1954): 12.

[34] I sent an inquiry about Charles Lee's relationship to the Watchman Nee's local church movement to Living Stream Ministry in Anaheim, California. Witness Lee's grandson Samuel Lee contacted me to confirm that Charles Lee had no known relationship to their movement.

[35] Adams (P&O Canton) to Lewis, 7 May 1953 (ES/IC).

[36] Adams to *ES* editors, 7 May 1953 (ES/IC).

[37] Phillips (Bury St. Edmunds) to Stunt, 15 March 1953 (ES/IC). On receiving copies of this correspondence from me, his niece Ch'ng Oon Hooi commented that this attention to detail was typical of her uncle.

that drew visitors from throughout Malaya.[38] Lee moved freely between the Hokkien-speaking Brethren and the "Little Flock"until 1957, when he abruptly announced at the end of a Bible reading that there was to be another meeting. He did not return to the Chinese Hokkien Assemblies, keeping to the groups he had "taken over". Adams reported that the Brethren had felt deceived and regretted that the issue of leavened versus unleavened bread had led to division.[39]

Goh Ewe Kheng and other Chinese Brethren elders in Singapore wrote a letter to the editors of *Echoes of Service* to declare that Charles Lee had "set up a table for the Lord's supper at 37, Jalan Besar Singapore without first notifying any of the local assemblies gathered in the name of the Lord". They also declared that they did not have anything to do with this secession. One of the editors wrote a comment on their statement, querying "Why should he? How far away is it?"

The comment highlights the paradox of the Brethren situation. Chinese evangelists like Faithful Luke and Charles Lee ensampled their form of Christian practice on the New Testament primitive church, just as the Brethren did, and the Brethren themselves had long fostered indigenous leadership. Despite that, the European missionaries remained as full-time workers, living in mission houses and taking charge of the English services. The editors of *Echoes* sometimes questioned why cities with well-established Brethren assemblies still needed missionaries. But for the Open Brethren, who had no ordained ministers, becoming a lay missionary was one of the few avenues to full-time Christian work.

Not only in Singapore but also in Kuala Lumpur and Ipoh, in the 1950s the Brethren lost members to new local churches. The Penang Chinese Gospel Hall was not affected, and Adams asked Teh Phai Lian to speak with "Brother Charles" while visiting Singapore on business, hoping that these two "leading brethren can be in happy friendship as before".[40] Although the issue ostensibly was that Lee had insisted on the importance of using unleavened bread, the covert issue may well have been that which Teh's son, Teh Chiew Oo, had

---

[38] W.G. Stott, 18 May 1955, *ES* No. 1327 (July 1955): 99; T.G. Scott, 14 July 1955, *ES* No. 1329 (September 1955): 125. He also took the youth group to Johore on Sundays, and when the new Geylang Gospel Hall was completed in 1955, apparently the youth did not join it.

[39] Adams to Stunt, 6 May 1957 (ES/IC). On his final reported visit, Lee rented a hall at a Hong Kong Trade Fair and led a number of Chinese Brethren in Singapore to conduct meetings that attracted large crowds. T.G. Scott, Singapore, 4 September 1957, *ES* No. 1355 (November 1957): 168.

[40] Adams to Stunt, 6 May 1957 (ES/IC).

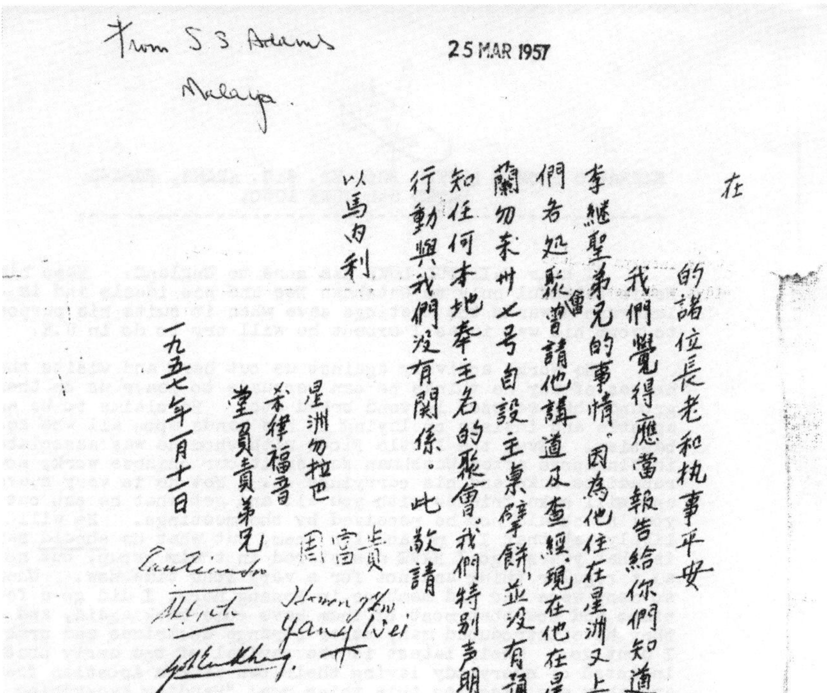

From S S Adams
Malaya

25 MAR 1957

在
的諸位長老和執事平安
我們覺得應當報告給你們知道關於
李継聖弟兄的事情，因為他住在星洲又上次我
們各処聚會曾請他講道及查經，現在他在星洲惹
蘭勿末卅七号自設主桌擘餅，並沒有預先通
知任何本地奉主名的聚會，我們特別声明他的
行動與我們沒有関係。此啟請
以馬内利

星洲勿拉巴
沙律福音
堂負責弟兄
一九五七年一月十一日

English Translation:-

We feel that it is our duty to inform you concerning brother Charles S. Lee, because he is staying in Singapore and also because he had been invited by all of us to speak and to conduct Bible studies before in each of our assemblies. He had set up a table for the Lord's supper at 37, Jalan Besar Singapore without first notifying any of the local assemblies gathered in the name of the Lord. We announce most emphatically that we have nothing to do with his action.

Signed by the reponsible brethren
of Chinese Hokkien Assembly,
Bras Basah Road, S'pore.
dated 11th Jan., 1957

Why should he?
How far away is it?

Figure 35 Letter from the elders of the Chinese Hokkien Assembly in Singapore to the editors of *Echoes of Service* in Bath, with translation and handwritten comments, 11 January 1957.

approached so bluntly when he wrote to the editor of *Echoes of Service*: the issue of whether the Brethren was no different from the other denominations in offering a centralized system controlled by the European missionaries.[41] Throughout these disruptions, Teh Phai Lian and his family remained within the Brethren network. But as I discuss in the next chapter, they too soon chose the path of separation and independence.

Not long after Watchman Nee was baptized by immersion in Fuzhou, the editors of *Echoes of Service* had published a summary report of a 1922 Brethren conference held in London. Much as Alexander Grant had proposed as he returned from China after the Boxer Uprising, the participants had concluded that the missionary should be an itinerant evangelist and not assume the role of pastor or minister, and that he should avoid being tied down by mission buildings and meetings. They further observed, "The cry to-day of Asia for the Asiatics, Africa for the Africans, should be no argument against allowing full liberty to brethren amongst these nationalities to take responsibility but rather the reverse, for it they were induced to think that saints could be led only be Englishmen or Americans it would be a grievous thing." The author concluded, "There is nothing national or racial in the Church of God."[42] But for the Open Brethren missionaries, the goal of motivating Christians to form primitive, local churches existed in dialectical tension with the paradoxical desire to remain in Asia as full-time workers.

[41] Although the Malacca Assembly also did not report a division, when the missionary requested the Chinese secretary to call a meeting of the Oversight, the secretary retorted that the missionary was an advisor not an elder, and that they could manage the affairs of the assembly without his help. Regler (Malacca) to Pulleng, 5 March 1956 (ES/ICO). The local Brethren also protested collectively to the *Echoes of Service* office when the missionaries set a meeting to form a property trust for the Brethren properties in Malaysia to which they invited all the European missionaries, but only a few Asian Brethren.

[42] "A Summary of a Conference of Brethren at Kinsway Hall, London, October 1921". Editorial, *ES* No. 936 (December 1922): 267–8.

Chapter 14

Schism and Continuity

> The Christian Assembly believes in covering the sisters' heads with a veil. Without a veil, women are not allowed to preach or to pray. But God had done something great and new—a woman encompasses a man! Great was the company of women who proclaim the glad tidings.
>
> Kong Duen Yee[1]

When the British returned to Southeast Asia after World War II, Singapore became a separate Crown colony and Penang joined the Malayan Union. The Malayan Union was reformed as the Federation of Malaya in 1946 and granted independence within the British Commonwealth in 1957. In 1963 Singapore declared independence and merged with Malaya, North Borneo (Sabah), and Sarawak to form the Federation of Malaysia. Penang remained one of Malaysia's 13 states, but as the consequence of nationalist politics Singapore was expelled from the new Federation and became an autonomous nation state in 1965.

In September and October of 1963, the Assemblies of God sponsored a former actress from Hong Kong, Kong Duen Yee, to make an evangelical tour of the newly independent Federation of Malaysia.[2] Soon after, Chinese-speaking Christians withdrew from their gospel halls and churches to form ten new independent churches (Sng 2003: 274). In Singapore and Penang, former Brethren elders Teh Phai Lian (1901–87) formed a new Church of

[1] Kong alludes to the Old Testament Book of the Prophet Jeremiah Chapter 31 verse 22: "…for the LORD hath created a new thing in the earth, A woman shall compass a man". Kong 1995: 12.

[2] I will refer the reader to the Internet, where photographs of Mui Yee are available on Hong Kong cinema websites.

Penang (*Bincheng Jiaohui* 槟城教会), and his nephew (and son-in-law) Goh Ewe Kheng founded the Church of Singapore (*Xinjiapo Jiaohui* 新加坡教會).

"A Woman Encompasses a Man!": Division within the Chinese Assemblies

Kong Due Yee (Jiang Duan Yi, 江端仪1923–66) was an actress who made her first movie in Hong Kong at the age of 14. She made about 140 movies under the stage name Mui Yee (Mei Qi 梅绮) but retired in 1960 after a diagnosis of tongue cancer. She was known to millions in China and Southeast Asia through her films, and is one of the earliest Asian evangelists to have capitalized on mass media exposure in her campaigns.

Converted by actress Zi Luolian (Tsi Lo-lin), Kong Duen Yee enrolled in Bible study courses at Pei Ling College (培灵学院) and gave testimony at Hong Kong churches. A foreign evangelist visiting Hong Kong pointed at her and prophesied that God would make Kong a prophet of her time. Not long after, she declared herself to be the leader of the New Testament Church, and demanded that all speak in tongues as evidence of the Holy Spirit (Wu 1981: 124–5). Kong publicized her experience as a born-again Christian through personal testimony at Hong Kong churches, and later in a 1968 book entitled *A Living Testimony to the Truth,* which was reprinted in 1996 with the subtitle *The Powerful Testimony of a Hong Kong Movie Star Mui Yee Chosen and Raised and Used by God in the East.*

She does not identify her influences, but American Chinese charismatic evangelist Hong Sit (Xue Chuntong 薛春桐, 1921–2014) and his wife Amy spent six months in Hong Kong between November 1962 and May 1963. During their six-month stay in Hong Kong, they held revival campaigns sponsored by a network of churches that described themselves as New Testament Full Gospel churches. In his memoir, Hong claimed that Kong sent her followers to record his services and that she had adopted his teachings. He added, though, that she "went to extremes" (Hong 1999: 72).[3]

Hong Sit was an American-born Chinese Christian who had worked in China with the China Inland Mission and the China Intervarsity Fellowship briefly before returning to the United States in 1947. His wife Amy Wang Sit

[3] At his home church in Houston, Hong Sit had promoted speaking and singing in tongues, and Joel Osteen described Hong as instrumental in initiating him into charismatic Christian experience in the early 1960s, including speaking in tongues with interpretation (Sinitiere 2015: 32). Hong's claim that she ensampled his teachings and practices is entirely plausible.

(1925–2008) was Leland Wang's youngest daughter. Born in Fuzhou, she was only 14 when she moved to the United States to study music at the Curtis Institute. She and Hong Sit met at Wheaton College (where she attended a "Plymouth Brethren" assembly), and Wilson Wang—Amy's uncle—presided over their marriage in 1949 (Hong 1999: 50–1).

In Houston Hong worked at a Baptist Church, but resigned to found an independent New Testament church and live by faith. Hong adopted charismatic practices, and in his memoir reported that his in-laws Leland and Ada Wang both experienced baptism of the Holy Spirit at his church (Hong 1999: 146). Hong followed Leland Wang in becoming an international revivalist, and in the early 1960s wrote articles describing charismatic revivals that he led in Hong Kong, Tahiti, Japan, and Hawaii. Joel Osteen, whose Lakewood church was also in Houston, published these reports in *Praise* magazine (1962–65) (Sinitiere 2015: 32, 241).[4]

On 9 June 1963—the month after Hong and Amy Sit finished their six–month charismatic campaign in Hong Kong—Kong Duen Yee and her entourage flew from Hong Kong to Singapore for a 55-night gospel campaign. She recalled her campaign in Singapore and Malaysia in a book entitled *Acts of the Holy Spirit* (1979).[5] At four different Assembly of God chapels, her hosts set up a large tent where she exhorted people to repent, then encouraged them to speak in tongues, which she described as the Baptism of the Holy Spirit (Kong 1979: 24–9). Almost immediately she converted young men who were involved in the youth gangs known as black societies, whose members often practised black magic and other occult activities. These new converts testified at the later meetings, and a female "witch" (probably a spirit medium) also "repented and received the Savior Jesus". The Christians collected her temple's idols from Johore Bahru in a truck and brought them to Singapore to be burned in a massive bonfire at the final night of her Singapore gospel campaign (Kong 1979: 36–54).

[4] According to Osteen, when he first started practising Baptism in the Spirit, a man whom he had invited onto the platform had yelled "Shawndi! Shawndi! Shawndi!" Hong Sit later proposed that he was saying "Sheang Dai", which he interpreted to mean "Most High God" in Cantonese. Osteen claimed that when he spoke in tongues, others recognized his words as Chinese, Spanish, Hebrew, Arabic (Osteen 1978: 16–7, 42–3).

[5] I thank members of the New Testament Church Grace of God Jesus Crusade in Mount Zion, Taiwan, for supplying me with copies of Kong Duen Yee's publications.

In August 1963, she continued the Grace of Jesus Christ Crusade in Malaysia, starting in Kuala Lumpur and Ipoh.[6] From there, she went to Penang on 6 September, then to Sitiawan. To the distress of her AOG sponsors, on her return to Ipoh in October, she exhorted Chinese Christians to leave their denominations and form autonomous New Testament Churches.

She recalled that the Holy Spirit moved her to sing and interpret in tongues and provided a paraphrase of the message:

> *God wants to establish the sheepfold in Singapore and Malaysia. This sheepfold—the local Church is not a man-made organization such as X X Hall or X X Assembly. She is the New Testament Church. She is free from the obstruction of human ideologies, for the Holy Spirit shall move and work freely in her. God announced, The Church of Ipoh is established. God wants to forsake the house of Saul which is dominated by human will* (denominations which are under man's control) *and establish the house of David which is after his heart* (New Testament Church which is dominated by the Holy Spirit) . . . *God has sent his servants and handmaidens* (Grace of Jesus Christ Crusade) *to Singapore and Malaysia to accomplish this work. . . . Children of God must fight courageously for the truth because the day of the Lord's return is at hand! Blessed are those who obey the will of God !* (Kong 1979: 153; italics in original).

After the prayer, she claimed that the Holy Spirit moved her to announce the establishment of the Church in Ipoh. And as the meeting concluded, visitors from Sitiawan told her that "God told them that the New Testament Church in Sitiawan, Penang, and other places had been declared established" (Kong 1979: 154).

She claimed that during her campaign in Singapore and Malaysia, 10,000 people were baptized in the Holy Spirit, and that despite persecution 1,000 came out to form New Testament Churches, including "the cream of the

[6] Kong founded Taiwan's New Testament Church (which is still known as the "Grace of Jesus Christ Crusade") in 1963, but died of tongue cancer in 1966. First her daughter, then Elijah Hong, a former elder in Watchman Nee's Christian Assembly, assumed leadership of the independent Church. At present, the New Testament Church is based on a mountaintop in Taiwan that they call Mount Zion, and has branches in Malaysia, Australia, New Zealand, Tahiti, Germany, England, the USA, and Canada. They continue to propagate Kong Duen Yee's and Elijah Wong's teachings through evangelism campaigns, but also on a multilingual website that includes books, pamphlets, and gospel posters available for free download (Grace of Jesus Christ Campaign 2018; see also DeBernardi 2009a; Rubinstein 1994).

organizations of Christian Assembly, the Brethren, Methodist, Presbyterian and other denominations" (Kong 1978a: 26–7).

A year after the campaign, a Brethren missionary in Ipoh reflected on Kong's impact:[7]

> There has been a move since a converted actress had meetings and preached tongues etc. In Penang there was a large group that went out from the meetings, and joined up with others from other Churches, to form a new meeting. Here in Ipoh, the few who left the meeting have returned, but the Methodist Chinese Church has suffered. So it has been right through the country. Some are sincere in their search for more spiritual power, and think they have found the answer. Others have been carried along by the glamour of the thing. In two places the police were called in to control the meetings!! No wonder they say our meetings are tame.

The New Testament Church

Kong Duen Yee and her successor, Elijah Hong, rarely cite the works of other Christians, but their influences included the Brethren movement, Watchman Nee's local church movement, and T. Austin-Sparks, the British Christian evangelist with whom Watchman Nee had stayed in London. Austin-Sparks taught that the history of Christianity was a "history of prisons" that sought to bring the movement of the Spirit into bondage (Austin-Sparks n.d.). He concluded that Christians needed to reject "succession and continuation" in favour of a rebellious, spirit-filled life.

A Grace of Jesus Christ Crusade tract that the Charismatic Church of Penang still distributed in 1981 echoed Sparks' critique of Christian denominations, describing them as "man-made organizations ... reeking with the traditional theologies and fallacious teachings of the Truth which lead believers away from the Will of God". Kong claimed that only her New Testament Church offered the "full gospel" of "blood, water, and the Holy Spirit". Blood referred to "confession, repentance, and being born-again", water to full-immersion water baptism to signify the individual's "death, burial, and resurrection with Christ", and the Holy Spirit referred to "accepting spirit baptism and being constantly filled with the Holy Spirit" (Kong 1996: 157). The tract further explained that "Blood, Water, and the Holy Spirit is the Full Truth received by the disciples of the early Church and this is what every believer of today ought to receive" (GJCC n.d.: 2).

---

7 Phillis Wilson (Ipoh) to Mr Pulleng, 10 January 1964 (ES/IC).

Kong was aware of the similarities between her own New Testament Church and Watchman Nee's and the Open Brethren's local churches. But she claimed that her charismatic New Testament Church had something new to offer:

> Though the Christian Assembly and the Brethren also teach the truth concerning building the church, they unfortunately lack the reality of the Holy Spirit. Their preachings come from human ideas. It is just like a person who has never seen an apple trying to describe one by his imagination. However, we are those who have tasted the "apples" given by God. So we understand every aspect of this apple: its shape, color, taste, fragrance, skin, contents and texture. We have even tasted rotten apples. Hence, we are able to tell others what an apple is really like. We will not only introduce the apples to others, but also let them taste it for themselves (Kong 1978b: 13).[8]

She insisted that all Christians must speak in tongues, but also noted that some (including herself) also had the gift of teaching in tongues, accompanied by an interpreter who could discern God's message. Kong's message that Christians could take their spiritual experiences to new heights captivated many Chinese Christians in Singapore and Malaysia.

The Open Brethren had accepted women evangelists after the 1859–60 revival, and Miss O'Callaghan and Miss Kidner both did public outreach. But Open Brethren leaders later set strict limits on women's public leadership roles (Dickson 1993). By the time of Kong's campaign, the Brethren did not allow women to be elders, to teach men, or to pray out loud in assemblies.[9] Although women took a more active role at Little Flock meetings, Kong recalled that she was disappointed when the Christian Assembly in Singapore invited her to speak, then sent her to a small room to address the women's service. Because the group was too large for this room, they were allowed to use the main meeting room, which she interpreted as a providential intervention (Kong 1979: 46–7).

In a message presented during a 1965 convention at the Church of Hong Kong, Kong proclaimed that women would be used by God, and that God had confirmed his choice of female apostles and prophetesses with "signs, wonders and miracles":

> The Christian Assembly believes in covering the sisters' heads with a veil. Without a veil, women are not allowed to preach or to pray. But

[8] This translation differs slightly from that printed in *The Golden Lampstand Volume 1* (1978: 17); although the pamphlet is not easily obtained, I prefer this translation.

[9] Both the Brethren and Christian Assemblies required women to cover their heads with a veil or hat at their breaking of bread ceremony (see Wee 1997).

> God had done something great and new–a woman encompasses a man! Great was the company of women who proclaim the glad tidings (*see* Ps. 68: 11). When the Lord was on earth, Mary Magdalene was the one who reported the good news of Christ's resurrection. *Today, God also has entrusted me to preach this good news–the full truth of Blood, Water, and Holy Spirit, and the law of building the church* (Kong 1995: 12 [emphasis in original]).

Her successor Elijah Hong later described her as the "great prophetess of all nations" (Hong 1995: iv).[10]

The Grace of Jesus Christ Campaign in Penang

On 6 September, Kong went to Penang to hold a 16-night open-air gospel campaign. She claimed that many "pagans and heathens" came to hear her and gave up their idols, but also that "many people who were formerly possessed by the evil spirits (the demon of cigarettes, wine, opium, gambling, lust, etc.) were all released by the mighty Holy Spirit of the Lord Jesus Christ". As she had done in Singapore, she concluded her Penang campaign with a bonfire of wooden idols, charms, and "evil religious books" (Kong 1979: 100–2).

A Christian in Singapore had written Teh Phai Lian a letter introducing Kong, and soon after she arrived she spent six hours meeting with him in his home. She knew that as a Brethren elder, he "disagreed with women preaching", but she laid hands on him and also advised him to get rid of his radio and statues and paintings. The Brethren had concluded that the gift of tongues and healing were confined to the apostolic age, and rejected the teaching that they were still operative as "divisive and erroneous" (Lineham 1982: 36). Over the objections of other elders, he invited her daughter and the daughter's Hokkien interpreter to address the youth at the gospel hall. Afterwards, the elders criticized them, concluding that their "loud prayer, sermon and interpretation of tongues came from evil spirits" (Kong 1979: 104).

---

[10] In the postwar period, Chinese Seventh Day Adventists translated the writings of Ellen Gould White, an America Adventist who claimed to be a prophetess, and discreetly published these works in Hong Kong. The translation of White's book *The Great Controversy* interpreted history as ongoing spiritual warfare between good and evil, and was circulated widely in China (Chow 2017). Although it seems likely that Kong modelled her role as prophetess on White, whose translated works were available in Hong Kong at the time of Kong's conversion, neither she nor Elijah Hong mention White or the Seventh Day Adventists in their publications.

Figure 36 Mui Yee (Kong Duen Yee) on the cover of *International Screen* magazine (Hong Kong), promoting her 1958 film *Over My Dead Body* (殺妻案). Private collection of author.

Figure 37 Kong Duen Yee (wearing a dark dress) seated with members of the newly-formed Church of Penang at Teh's home in 1963. Teh Phai Lian (wearing a dark shirt) is standing in the second row. Photograph published with permission of Ch'ng Oon Hooi.

On 23 September, 49 people were baptized, including elder Teh, his sister, and their families. Because the elders at the Burmah Road Gospel Hall questioned the legitimacy of their claims to charismatic experiences and did not accept them, they left the Burmah Road Gospel Hall. Those whom I interviewed commented that the separation was mutual since the elders at the gospel hall did not want them to remain. But they also recalled that the elders' wives had urged their husbands to leave.[11]

Soon after Kong's campaign, Teh led 40 or so followers to form the new Church of Penang.[12] Initially they met at a basketball court at Union Primary School, where one of Teh's sisters was headmistress. But they soon moved to Teh's large seaside bungalow on Northam Road, which he rented from a Malay prince. He knocked down the walls to make a hall large enough for the group to assemble and moved their residential space upstairs. A few years later they

[11] In 2013, the CCOP celebrated their 50th anniversary and reviewed the details of this history in their anniversary volume (Ebenezer 2013).

[12] One prominent Singaporean elder recalled that when Teh left Burmah Road, he "took half the pews". I assume that his meaning was metaphorical not literal.

changed their name to the Charismatic Church of Penang (*Bincheng Ling'en Jiaohui* 槟城灵恩教会) to distinguish themselves from another local church, but they continued to meet in Teh's home for 29 years.

In her memoir of the campaign, Kong recalled that soon after the new church formed, she met with Teh in Singapore and they "fought a small spiritual battle". He had received a few thousand copies of books published in Hong Kong that he wanted to distribute during services—likely the final issue of the magazine that he co-edited, *The Way, Truth, and Life* (*Daolu, Zhenli, Shengming* 道路, 真理, 生命 1963). Most of the essays in the magazine had been written by Teh, but it also included essays by other preachers, some of whom opposed charismatic teachings.[13] Although he tore out pages written by those authors, she directed him to stop distributing all publications he had written before receiving the Baptism of the Holy Spirit. Teh argued that it would be a great loss to not distribute these books, which had cost him a large sum of money to print, but finally agreed to withhold them. As the self-identified Prophetess of all Nations, she deemed herself to speak for God, and she praised Teh for submitting to God's will despite his wealth and status (Kong 1979: 228–9). Teh's books and articles had contributed to his status in Christian circles, and her refusal to allow him to distribute these publications must have been troubling.

Figure 38 Teh Phai Lian and his interpreter, together with a Mandarin/English bilingual chart, at the Charismatic Church of Penang, 1981. Photograph: Jean DeBernardi.

[13] The library at the Charismatic Church of Penang includes multiple copies of the 1963 edition of this magazine, which likely was never distributed.

Figure 39 The Charismatic Church of Penang, No. 49 Northam Road, celebrating their sixth anniversary on 12 October 1969. Photograph courtesy of the CCOP.

In 1964, Teh wrote a 64-page Mandarin pamphlet *Praying in the Spirit, in Tongues: What I have Experienced* (*Fangyan Lingdao: Wosuo Jinglide* 放言灵祷我所经历的). Kong printed 10,000 copies of this tract and one that she wrote entitled "The Great Work of the Holy Spirit on Triple April 18" and announced her plans to distribute them to Singapore and the nine new churches in Malaysia (Kong 1964: 13).

In his pamphlet Teh described extraordinary feelings of joy and heat when he was "led by the Holy Spirit" to speak in tongues. He claimed that others had been transformed from being tepid Christians, experiencing a new rebirth, and that the weak had been strengthened and had led their family members to God. He also cited the headmaster of a middle school who testified: "to be bathed in the Holy Spirit and to speak in tongues bring so many benefits to followers, but some even called it an 'evil spirit'. If such an 'evil spirit' could make one have a warm heart, to love God and serve God, to pray and read the bible, and to leave all sins, I would like to accept it" (Teh 1964b: 2).[14]

---

[14] This tract is not dated, but in a 1976 lecture published as a tract, he mentioned that he had distributed 10,000 copies of *Fangyan Lingdao (Praying in the Spirit, in Tongues)* 12 years earlier (Teh 1976b: 2). Since Wu's 1964 book comments on it, this date seems likely to be correct.

But when Teh published this defence of speaking in tongues, he met with strong opposition:

> I wrote one book entitled "Praying in the Spirit, in Tongues" twelve years ago and ten thousand copies were printed. When all of these were distributed, many Chinese Churches in other countries were affected and were shaken and very soon, we received seven books sent by some of them which were published against me. The authors all objected to "speaking in tongues" (they say that it is a special gift to certain people only) and they quoted many verses from the ordinary Chinese Bibles. The most deadly of them was Pastor Wu who alone published three books to criticize me. His books were very popular and they sold very well. My books were distributed free to the people. In those days, I wept nearly every day and I said to myself that if speaking in tongues is wrong then I will have to confess to all the churches and accept their criticisms as correct (Teh 1976b: 2–3).

Pastor Wu was Wu Enpu (吳恩溥), who had been "repented, revived, and dedicated" at a meeting led by John Sung in the Chaoshan area (Wu 1981: Chapter 1). Wu was living in Hong Kong when Kong Duen Yee launched her charismatic movement, and had sternly criticized her and her followers. He had previously collaborated with Teh on publication projects, but also harshly attacked him.

Soon after Teh published his defence of "praying in the spirit", Wu published a 117-page book entitled *A Critique of Today's Charismatic Movement* (*Ping Jinr de Fangyan Yundong* 評今日的方言運動) (Wu 1964). The book had two parts. The first was a refutation of Kong Duen Yee, the second a refutation of Teh Phai Lian. In this and subsequent publications, Wu proposed that Christians needed to discriminate between the work of the Holy Spirit and the work of evil spirits pretending to be the Holy Spirit. If the devil only appeared in the form of an evil spirit or a dragon, he observed, people would not be deceived, but Satan also could assume the form of a bright angel (Wu 1964: 91).

The controversial practice of speaking in tongues refers back to the New Testament account of the event known as the Day of Pentecost. As the editor of *Echoes of Service* explained it:

> At Pentecost the Holy Ghost came as a "rushing mighty *wind*," and also with "*cloven tongues* as of fire". . . . The scattered Israel nation were themselves at that time a Babel as to speech, even as they still are, and at their own annual feasts could not understand each other; but the Spirit came to minister to them that grace which had been so dearly bought at Gethsemane and Calvary, and gave unlettered Galileans ability to speak in the many languages of those present. We do not find this "GIFT of

> tongues" amongst us now, but the same Holy Ghost is with us, and happy are they who do not allow even difficulty of language to hinder them from seeking to give the gospel of Christ its full spread over earth.[15]

The New Testament is clear that when the Holy Spirit "gave them utterance ... every man heard them speak in his own languages" (Acts 2: 6). The Open Brethren missionaries in Penang and Singapore found Hokkien difficult to master, and often lamented that the gift of tongues was withheld from them.

The practice that charismatic Christians call speaking in tongues is in fact glossolalia—uttering unintelligible syllables that Pastor Wu called "dede, dada, zhizhi dada". Charismatic Christians claimed that although these utterances they made while speaking in tongues were in no known language, some individuals had the gift of interpretation and could understand them.[16] Pastor Wu asked if babies were speaking in tongues when they babbled and concluded that glossolalia had nothing to do with the Pentecost (Wu 1964: 89–98). He dismissed Teh's arguments in support of speaking in tongues one by one, and also the Penang schoolmaster's testimony, describing them as laughable.

As Kong described it, almost all Christians in Hong Kong had read Wu's critique of the charismatic movement, causing them to reject "the Spirit of grace, thinking that it is an evil spirit". Wu's attack on her and Teh Phai Lian was widely distributed, and she was sure that "believers and theological students in Thailand, Vietnam, Singapore, Malaysia, Taiwan, and America" had also been "poisoned" (Kong 1964: 144). Kong lamented the attacks, but also reported that her followers in Singapore and Malaysia had written a book entitled *For the Defense of the Truth*, in which they exposed "the wiles of Satan" (Kong 1964: 81).[17]

Teh Phai Lian was the book's primary author, and it appeared in November 1964, the same year as Pastor Wu's critique. The cover featured a drawing of an armed warrior, standing steadfast and vigilant, and the title *Justifying the Truth: A Refutation of "A Critique of Today's Charismatic Movement"* identified Wu's essay as the warrior's opponent. Teh printed 10,000 copies of this book, which was distributed through the network of new local churches in Penang,

---

15 H.D., "'Abba, Father'", *ME* (April 1882): 48.

16 In an interesting parallel, Chinese spirit mediums in Penang were said to speak the 'deep language' of the gods and relied on interpreters to translate their speech into comprehensible messages for their devotees and clients. See DeBernardi 2006.

17 Elijah Hong published a book with a similar title that identifies the "fallacies" in articles published in Chinese newspapers that are critical of him and Kong, but this book dates to 1993 and does not appear to contain content from the 1964 book (Hong 1993).

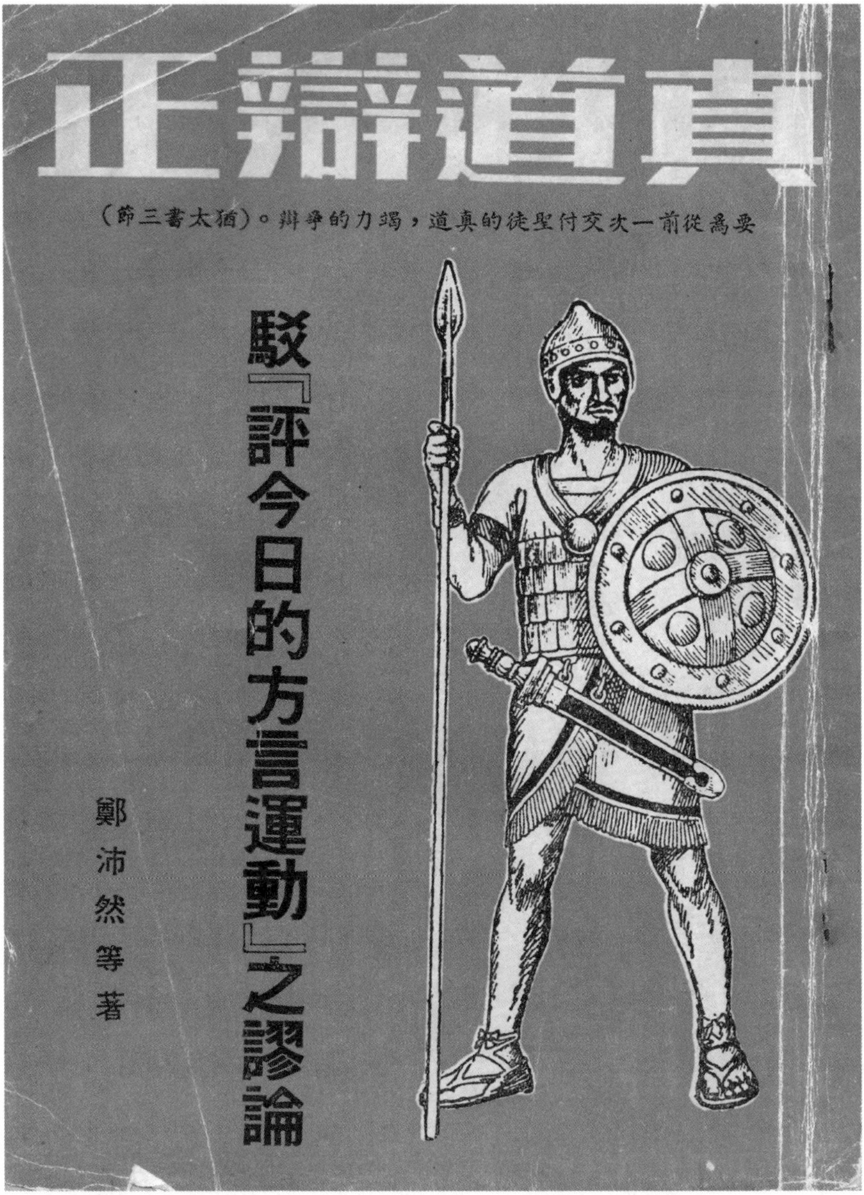

Figure 40 Cover of Teh Phai Lian's 1964 response to Wu Enpu's critique of Kong Duen Yee and the movement to speak in tongues (Teh 1964a). Library, Charismatic Church of Penang.

Singapore, Petaling Jaya, Johore, Sitiawan, Taiping, and Kong's church in Hong Kong. In the preface, Teh expressed his wish that his book would convince readers to reject "false dao/doctrine" (*jia dao* 假道) and to return to "true principles" (*zhen li* 真理) (Teh 1964a).

Seeking to answer Wu and other critics, Teh also enlisted his son and two grandsons to help him to research different versions of the Bible. True to his Brethren roots, in a 1965 tract "Milk and Honey, Flames of Fire" (*Naimi Huoyan* 奶蜜火焰), Teh sought to develop a Biblical foundation for speaking in tongues, focusing on analyzing the Greek term *pneuma hagion*, which is translated into English as Holy Spirit.

In a revised photocopied edition of "Milk and Honey, Flames of Fire", Teh also cited his personal experiences and the success of their new church as evidence of the correctness of their understanding and practices. Teh noted that their unnamed critics and opponents had labelled speaking in tongues not as a gift of the Holy Spirit but rather as possession by evil spirits (*xieling*), and asked him, "Why do you promote speaking in tongues? This kind of language is something that not everyone [10,000] can do!" But, he observed, "People who speak like this have not yet experienced the flavor, and therefore think that tongues is something you can have or not have. But we have seen the proof, we have experienced it, and we have certainly seen it. Above all we do not overestimate speaking in tongues (we do not belong to that faction that every day only speaks in tongues)" (Teh n.d.: 2–3).

He also claimed that Kong had convinced people to repent of their sins and transform their lives. Because they were filled with the Holy Spirit, opium smokers, gamblers, and movie-goers gave up their bad habits (although a former actress herself, Kong had preached against attending all films), and people were able to reform all manner of evil habits. Initially they were small, but soon the new Church of Penang had over 200 people attending their Sunday service, 180 members in their youth group, and a strong, regular attendance at their prayer meetings, even, Teh added, when it rained (Teh n.d.: 2).

Teh also included letters he had exchanged with He Xiaodong (何曉東), a well-known Christian lawyer and writer from Shanghai who had moved first to Taiwan, then to the United States after 1949. He Xiaodong had been baptized by Witness Li in Taiwan and for a time belonged to the Church of Cleveland. After the schism, Teh had published letters in *Triumph Newspaper* (勝利報) defending his viewpoint. He Xiaodong wrote to Teh to say that he had believed that Teh had gone astray and had stopped reading his publications. But after the editor of the newspaper wrote him to explain Teh's "actual situation", he had read Teh's works and decided he agreed with him. He Xiaodong noted that he also had connections with a Brethren assembly in Illinois for many years, and that he had fiercely argued with the elders on the question of spiritual gifts. He concluded (as Watchman Nee had done in 1934) that Brethren practices had formerly been close to the Bible, but that they had gone down the path of becoming an organization.

In his response, Teh explained that he had conducted extensive research on the Holy Spirit in books and magazines from Europe and America, and also prayed; as a consequence he and his church's over 200 members had been revived. He concluded that those who rejected gifts of the Holy Spirit became "stranded, pitiful, poor, blind, naked, and shameful". But he also defended himself against the charge of extremism, claiming to have sought a "middle way" (Teh n.d.: 43–6).

In 1975 Teh again presented his arguments in a lecture in Hokkien. A member of the Charismatic Church of Penang transcribed a tape of the lecture and published it in both Mandarin and English (Teh 1976a, 1976b). Teh described his 30 years of evangelical work prior to "being filled by the Holy Spirit":

> When I was twenty-eight years old, I was travelling all over Malaysia and Singapore to preach the Gospel. It was only after thirty odd years that I began to preach this truth about the baptism of the Holy Spirit. I wrote a few books and printed over a hundred thousand of them for free distribution. There were many great preachers who knew me, as a very hard working Christian who at the same time worked for his own living, and they were surprised, when at the age of 62, I was filled with the Holy Spirit and spoke in tongues (1976b: 2).

Teh had a close relationship to Wilson Wang, but his and Leland's revivalism apparently did not include speaking in tongues, nor did Watchman Nee's followers practise it.[18] The experience Teh described as joy from the "filling of the Holy Spirit" was something new and exhilarating for the former Brethren elder (Teh 1976b: 8–9).

In his lecture, he traced the meaning of the Greek term *pneuma hagion*, which he translated as the Holy Spirit, but also as "power from on high" (Teh 1976b: 3), concluding that the Greek New Testament offered sure proof that

[18] Teh mentioned that his brother-in-law attended a "Little Flock" local church, and that he opposed speaking in tongues (Teh 1976b: 12). There are reports of Watchman Nee speaking in tongues, but the practice apparently was not widely adopted (see for example Kinnear 1973: 104–5). Leland and Ada Wang's son-in-law Hong Sit claimed that both received "baptism of the Spirit" in his church in Houston (Hong 1999: 146).

both speaking in tongues and the performance of miracles were biblically correct practices. At the same time, he offered testimonies of miraculous healings to demonstrate the power that the Holy Spirit could confer on those who spoke in tongues (Teh 1976b: 9–11). He concluded: “Therefore those that believe shall receive the Holy Spirit (*pneuma hagion*) and speak with new tongues” (Teh 1976b: 27).

Goh Ewe Kheng and the Church of Singapore

When I first met the Teh family in 1980, Teh's son, Teh Chiew Oo (郑秋雨, 1923–95) was managing the Penang branch of Tithes and Teh's nephew Goh Ewe Kheng (1924–2014) managed the Singapore branch. Teh Chiew Oo led the Charismatic Church of Penang, and Goh Ewe Kheng the Church of Singapore. In a 1999 interview with me and also in a volume celebrating the Church of Singapore's 25th anniversary, Goh described the events that led to the schism and the establishment of the Church of Singapore and the Charismatic Church of Penang.[19]

At Kong's evangelistic meetings in Singapore, Goh recalled, many were baptized in the Holy Spirit, and after praying, people who had suffered strokes got up and walked. Some gangsters also were slain in the spirit (Church of Singapore 1988). As Goh described it to me:

> Someone asked me to go. She taught the Gospel–that the blood of Jesus Christ, the Holy Spirit, had come to heal us, empower us. It was all Biblical. I saw things happening; people were slain on the floor. I had a hunger to have this experience.
>
> At that time, the Brethren warned people “don't go.” They were against a sister preaching, laying hands on people, with manifestation of gifts, speaking in tongues, prophesy, healing. They said that this had happened in the early stage, in Apostle times, the Holy Spirit healed, had manifestations. But after the person [of Jesus] the main thing was preaching the gospel. God does heal, [but they advised us] not to emphasize this, and to oppose the sister.
>
> I went and listened, and then I went back to share with the elders. They asked me, “Do you believe a sister can preach? Take the pulpit?” I told them, “This is the work of the Holy Spirit.” [They argued that] a sister should not take authority over brother, a sister can not prophesize and pray. I left at this.

[19] The Church of Sitiawan for many years maintained a relationship with the Charismatic Church of Penang; at one time its founder, a friend of Teh Phai Lian, drove up on alternate weeks.

> She went to Malaysia, to Penang. My father-in-law in Penang invited her to his house also. He left the Brethren there. Teh Phai Lian left.
>
> She made a second visit to Singapore. She had one week free–there were no meetings planned. Two elders from Wilkie Terrace invited me to come listen. They invited her to have meetings. It was too short notice to rent a place, so I offered, "Use our compound!" They rented chairs and a PA system, and announced the meetings. One week every evening there was a meeting, there were many converts, many were baptized in the Holy Spirit, some were healed. I phoned the Brethren church, and told them that I had to take care of the new converts. I left them.

An elder from the Wilkie Terrace Christian Assembly joined him in leading the new group, as did a member of the Church of Johore Bahru.

Initially 70 to 80 people attended meetings at Goh's house. But soon the new group had more than 100 members, including former Baptists, Anglicans, Methodists, Brethren, and members of the Wilkie Terrace Christian Assembly.[20] The new group welcomed to their meetings everyone who sought a church. They offered them communion, and (according to Elder Goh) they "didn't forbid the sisters to pray". Goh commented that the group was very intimate, and that after the Sunday meeting, they would prepare porridge (congee), then go out tracting and testifying together.[21]

After Goh, Teh, and their followers seceeded from their assemblies and churches, Kong instructed them to call themselves the "Church of Singapore" and the "Church of Penang" and they registered the new churches under those names. But Kong soon demanded obedience and unity of all. As her successor in Taiwan, Elijah Hong, described it in an 1968 message on "The Way God Works":

> When Sis. Kong came, the way to live in the body [of Christ] appeared, for she was the apostle raised up by God. She was not just an apostle, she was the chief among the apostles. God revealed to her the secrets of the blueprint for building the church. If we do as the Bible tells us, and **give ourselves first to the Lord and then to the apostles (be like-minded with Sis. Kong) the testimony of unity will appear.**

---

[20] As Kong described it, the new members included former Roman Catholics, Seventh Day Adventists, True Jesus Church followers, as well as former members of the Christian Assembly, Brethren, and Evangelical Mission (Kong 1979: 229).

[21] In 1999 one of its younger members described the Church of Singapore to me as a 'family church', despite the fact that it meets for its main services in a large auditorium-style room that holds over 800 people, and has space to convene 10 events simultaneously.

> Sis Kong said, "All of you ought to be of the same mind, and co-work and co-ordinate with me." She also said, "The Bible states that you must let them return to you; you must not return to them." In other words, everything must go to Sis. Kong, and she and her co-workers must not go to others. Initially, I was very annoyed by her words. I said, "Sis. Kong is too arrogant. I have never seen anyone exalt himself as highly as she does. So you are the only one who has the truth, and everyone has to listen to you? Are you not being very subjective. God is omnipresent He is not only with you, Sis. Kong. To achieve unity, and to attain peace, we must love each other. Give me one step and I'll give you one step. Only then can we talk!"
>
> Then someone said to me, "Sis. Kong is God's vessel of the era. The flow of the Holy Spirit starts from her." That annoyed me even more… Later I realized that the body of Christ is built through the apostles. So if you don't abide by the apostle's teachings, you are not built into the body. But if you respect the ministry of the apostles and obey their teachings, you will be in the flow of the Holy Spirit, and on the path of unity. Therefore, **the practical way to be in the flow of the Holy Spirit is to submit to the apostles' leading** (Hong 1995: 36 [emphasis in original]).

Elijah Hong finally assented to Kong's authority, as did Elder Teh when he withheld his books from distribution. But Goh Ewe Kheng soon objected to her demand for control, and Teh also insisted on the independence and autonomy of the local church.

Initially, two of Kong's followers had stayed back and the new Church of Singapore supported them. The two men monitored the selection of visiting speakers on her behalf, and when Goh invited a charismatic preacher to the Church, they knew that he had not written to her for permission. Afterwards they berated Goh. As he described it, one spoke in tongues, and the other interpreted the sounds to be a message from God, saying "You must repent!" Goh later asked him, "Why didn't you talk to me?" He responded, "The spirit moved me."

Very likely the unapproved visitor was Hong Sit, Leland Wong's son-in-law. He and Amy Sit had been holding evangelistic meetings throughout Taiwan when they received an "urgent invitation" to hold meetings in Malaysia. In December 1963 they flew to Kuala Lumpur, then travelled to Penang, Ipoh, Sitiawan, Johore Bahru, and Singapore to visit the newly independent assemblies. Hong Sit recalled that they told him, "You've come at just the right time, neither too early nor too late. Surely, God has sent you." Hong "had fellowship" with Teh in Penang and Goh in Singapore, praising both for their strong leadership, and influenced another family member, Jerry Yeoh, to become a full-time worker. But he also described the new charismatic churches as lacking "foundation and balance" (Hong 1999: 80).

In addition to objecting to Kong's demand to control the selection of speakers, Goh also recalled that when she published gospel tracts, she placed both her Hong Kong address and the address of the Church of Singapore, which he also opposed. He began to have doubts:

> I began to discover error, wrong teachings. Speak in tongues is a real gift. But people . . . tell lies. They offend the holy gift, they pretend. So I wrote articles. [They claimed that] speaking in tongues is a supernatural gift, 'if you want to lay hands, you must speak in tongues...brr... you should not doubt.' They forced me to accept it. But I did see real things happen. There must be something real!

Goh concluded that while God had prepared Kong to establish a New Testament Church, she had shown evidence of pride and a spirit of deception after she left Singapore.

She claimed that "God had covenanted with her", and that she was the woman spoken of in Revelation 12: "And there appeared a great wonder in heaven; a woman clothed with the sun, and the moon under her feet, and upon her head a crown of twelve stars" (Rev. 12: 1) (Church of Singapore 1988: 12). Goh challenged her, writing her letters that he circulated to all the churches in Singapore in which he argued that "the relationship is not fulfilled in you. Man who has rod of iron to rule earth is Jesus Christ, how can you make yourself so great?" In response, he reported, "She cursed me."[22]

Teh also cut off his relationship with Kong. According to Wu, Teh had given her several thousand yuan a month, but separated from her after she demanded control over the Church of Penang and the Church of Singapore.[23] I have found no letters or tracts in Teh's publications explaining his decision. But Wu reported that Teh was clear that local people should be responsible for the local church, and that as a lay person she had no right to control them. Not long after she sent Teh and Goh a letter cursing them, her cancer recurred and

---

[22] Among the New Testament Church's more controversial practices is that of cursing their enemies. For example, they apparently distributed a leaflet entitled "Lee Hsien-loong [Lee Kuan Yew's son] will not get well but will surely die!" Elijah Hong explained that they had cursed Lee Kuan Yew and his family because "[t]he regime of Lee Kuan-yew opposes Christ and persecutes the church of the living God" (Hong 1993: 3).

[23] In a 1981 book *Distinguishing the Holy Spirit from Evil Spirits* (*Bianbie Shengling yu Xieling*), Wu described his campaign against her and observed that she had failed. He gave two reasons: first, her death from cancer, and second, her loss of financial support from Teh Phai Lian.

in 1966 Kong died. She had predicted her own resurrection, but her followers waited in vain for this event (Wu 1981: 127–8).[24]

The Church of Singapore

After the Church of Singapore broke relations with Kong's New Testament Church in 1965, 50–60 of their members left them to form a new church—Christ Church of Singapore—which remained in her network (Church of Singapore 1988: 12).[25] The Church of Singapore (COS) first met in Goh's home, then rented a building in Marine Parade that they bought in 1988. There, they built a modern multistorey building that was opened in 1992. The Church of Singapore is an undenominational local church with a network of independent branch churches. In their large auditorium-style meeting room, they convene English and bilingual English/Mandarin services on Sunday morning. Smaller rooms hold Mandarin, Cantonese, and Hokkien services, but also Filipino and Burmese services for Singapore's guest workers (primarily maids, to whom many churches provide outreach), and an evening China ministry.[26]

In an interview Goh Ewe Kheng recalled that "During the early years, there were hardly any independent churches. Almost all Pentecostal churches were the Assembly of God. It was quite lonely. Most of the established churches kept away from us because we spoke in tongues." He noted that even members of the interdenominational Scripture Union and Gideons avoided him, although gradually the other denominations became friendlier. But when the Anglican bishop and archbishop and other Christian leaders embraced the charismatic movement, Goh once again became a respected church leader. By the mid-1990s the Church of Singapore had become one of the largest independent Charismatic churches in Singapore. Goh also chaired the Evangelical Fellowship of Singapore, "indicating the respectability and acceptability that the Church of Singapore has among the Singaporean churches" (Tan 2011: 233).

---

[24] The New Testament Church divided, and one branch continued in Taiwan under the leadership of Elijah Hong. I visited "Mount Zion" in Taiwan in 2008, and found it to be a mountaintop commune in Hsiaolin, Kaohsiung that members celebrate as a utopian "lost Eden" on earth (DeBernardi 2009a).

[25] In a 1999–2000 church directory, Christ Church of Singapore gives 1969 as their foundation date (National Council of Churches of Singapore 1998).

[26] In addition, the Church offered three Sunday school meetings, Youth Services, meetings and fellowships, prayer meetings, and prayer and fellowship groups. https://www.cos.org.sg/sunday-services/ [accessed 20 July 2018].

Many point to the Anglican turn towards the charismatic movement as a defining moment in Singapore's church history. In retrospective articles, Anglican Canon James Wong recalled that he had avoided contact with charismatic Christians. But after his bishop counselled him that no one was sure of salvation, he found himself spontaneously speaking in tongues while praying. He soon learned that Bishop Chiu had experienced a similar "encounter with the Holy Spirit" at a 1973 World Council of Churches conference on "Salvation Today" in Bangkok (Wong 2002 Pt. 2).

In 1973 Goh introduced Canon Wong to Brian Bailey, who worked in the Philippines with a small evangelical Christian group known as Zion Ministries. Bailey was associated with a new American organization called World MAP (Missionary Assistance Plan) that had been founded to train indigenous pastors. In an article on "The Great Crisis in World Evangelism", World MAP's founder Ralph Mahoney recalled that at a 1969 conference in Santa Cruz, the Holy Spirit had revealed to him that the Third World did not need missionaries, but advanced leadership training for local leaders:

> We didn't need to continue the largely fruitless and very expensive effort of deploying a few hundred Western workers to 3rd-World nations. Tens of thousands of potential workers were already there–waiting to be raised from their spiritual death to life and power in the Holy Spirit (Mahoney 1998: 3).

In 1973 Bailey was "moved by the Holy Spirit" to visit Singapore, and Wong invited Bailey to speak to a youth group in Good Shepherd Church.

While in Singapore, Bailey "laid hands" on the Anglican bishop, who was "baptized in the Holy Spirit" (Mahoney 1998: 5). For seven years, the group returned to Singapore to offer Singapore's Christian leaders World MAP Spiritual Renewal Training Seminars. Mahoney recalled that "thousands of Catholic and Protestant leaders who were not born again were birthed into the life of Christ. Thousands more were also baptized in the Holy Spirit" (Mahoney 1998: 5). By the 1990s the Anglican Church were leaders in introducing Third Wave charismatic activities and events in Singapore (see DeBernardi 2008a).

The Los Angeles-based Full Gospel Business Men's Fellowship International (FGBMFI) (est. 1951) also promoted the charismatic movement in Singapore. Their president, Demos Shakarian, had proposed that the Pentecostal experience could be integrated into mainline Protestant and Catholic Churches, and their lay Christian fellowship was soon global in its scope and influence. The group organized undenominational meetings in convention centres and hotels that focused on leadership and success. But their events also offered participants the opportunity to experience charismatic practices in the neutral setting of hotel ballroom luncheons.

In Singapore, the Full Gospel Businessmen's Fellowship established a fellowship in 1972. They held a series of Spiritual Renewal Fellowship meetings, first in 1974 for Pentecostal and charismatic Christians, then in 1975 for professionals (see Lim 2015). In 1978, one of the prominent speakers at a Singapore Spiritual Renewal seminar was "Mr. Pentecost"—David du Plessis—an Assemblies of God leader who, like them, promoted the Charismatic movement within the mainline denominations. That year, together with Anglican Canon James Wong, Goh Ewe Kheng helped establish the Tung Ling Bible School (*Dongling Shengjing Xueyuan* 東嶺聖經學院), an interdenominational charismatic Bible school.

In the 1980s and 1990s, Hong Sit and his wife Amy continued to visit Singapore and Malaysia frequently. In addition to becoming the North American leader of the Chinese Foreign Missionary Union that Leland Wang had co-founded, Hong was also president of the Chinese Full Gospel Fellowship International Limited (*Shijie Huaren Quanbei Fuyin Lian Hui Youxian Gongsi* 世界華人全 備福音聯會有限公司), an interdenominational fellowship for Chinese charismatic churches that he had helped found in Hong Kong (Hong 1999: 141).[27]

Starting in 1984, the CFGF organized a series of world conferences for Chinese charismatic Christian leaders that were held in Hong Kong, Singapore, Taiwan, Kuala Lumpur, Vancouver, and Los Angeles. In the 1980s and 1990s, Hong also taught courses at Zion Bible College and Christ International Theological Seminary in Los Angeles and Singapore's Tung Ling Bible School (Hong 1999: 144–5).

Although many aspects of the charismatic movement came to be widely accepted, Christian leaders continued to question others. When I interviewed him in 1999, Goh Ewe Kheng expressed doubts about the practices of speaking in tongues and spiritual healing. Regarding speaking in tongues, he had concluded that there were two kinds: while one was a supernatural gift, the other was nothing more than "a praying language, something not real". He also noted that at the Charismatic Church of Penang, people were "singing in tongues", which he found awkward since there was no melody to the hymns, which they termed a "new song" or "singing in the spirit".

[27] The FGBF sponsored a lecture in the Singapore Cultural Theatre in 1981, and Hong Sit spoke in the DBS auditorium in Singapore's financial district in 1983. Advertisements, *Nanyang Siang Pau*, 2 August 1981; *Lianhe Zaobao*, 9 October 1983. http://eresources.nlb.gov.sg/newspapers/ [accessed 28 November 2018].

He shared with me a letter he had written to the COS elders and two short essays in which he criticized speaking in tongues as repetitive and lacking in creativity. In the letter to the elders, he cautioned against the danger that people would idolize the gift and "make it like 'a charm' " (Goh 1999: 3). He concluded that "Our common sense should also be sanctified to discern that repetition of tongues is not the real supernatural gift" (Goh 1999: 7).

In another essay, he noted that the "gift of tongues" was a "gift speaking to God" and should therefore be used in private, not in public, adding that if a person spoke in tongues at a meeting, an interpreter should be present to interpret the language spoken (Goh n.d.[b]: 2). He also observed that far from being evidence of charismatic gifts, the routinized, mechanical practice of speaking in tongues was not a real gift, concluding that when "believers make tongues a test of fellowship or spirituality", this "shows very clearly that it is not from God" (n.d.[b]: 16). Finally, he noted that since gifts belong to the Holy Spirit, they cannot become the possession of the individual, reasoning logically that otherwise someone with the gift of healing could empty the hospital wards (Goh n.d.[a]: 1, 4). He noted even more bluntly that although charismatic Christians were able to heal, sometimes they also cheated, adding "the truth still is very important".[28]

Conclusion: A Twin Sister?

Allan Anderson has proposed an inclusive definition of Pentecostalism that includes all movements and churches that emphasize "an ecstatic *experience of the Spirit* and a tangible *practice of spiritual gifts*", including "prophecy, healing, exorcism, speaking in tongues, and revelations through dreams and visions" (Anderson 2013: 8). He recognizes that the modern Pentecostal movement is polycentric, with new centres of influence in the global south.[29] Whatever the influence of American-style Pentecostalism may have been on global Pentecostalism, the "Pentecostal message" has been contextualized in different cultures and nations, giving the movement local character (Anderson 2013: 47).

[28] He gave as an example a pastor from Taiwan who claimed that he could heal "long and short legs". Goh observed that the minister was cheating, since "if you move, you see the leg 'grow'". He added that after spiritual healing, some people claim that even though they were deaf in one ear, they could now hear. But he noted skeptically that if you clap in their ear after praying, they actually hear the sound in their good ear.

[29] In his *Introduction to Pentecostalism* (2014), Anderson conveys the globality of Pentecostalism by offering a series of regional and local histories.

Figure 41 Church of Singapore. Photograph: Jean DeBernardi.

Charismatic Christians often observe that the ministries of exorcism and spiritual healing have found a receptive audience among "unreached peoples" in Africa and elsewhere (Pousson 1992: 141). With respect to China, Allan Anderson and other scholars have proposed that "Pentecostalism with its emphasis on the supernatural was in sync with Chinese folk religion" (Anderson 2007: 136).[30] But in Malaysia and Singapore, new charismatic churches were formed in 1963 not as the result of outreach to "unreached peoples", but rather as the outcome of so-called sheep stealing from long-established mainstream churches.

Moreover, the similarities between Pentecostalism and folk religion did not always promote acceptance. A prominent Malaysian Brethren elder in Kuala Lumpur whom I interviewed practised demonic exorcism, also known as the ministry of deliverance. But precisely because of its similarity to spirit

[30] Bays explains the practices of the Pentecostal True Jesus Church in light of the "heritage of Chinese sectarian folk religion" (Bays 1996: 313), and Murray Rubinstein has proposed that some Pentecostal practices found acceptance among Taiwanese members of this church precisely because they resembled Chinese popular religious practices like spirit possession (Rubinstein 1996b: 362; see also DeBernardi 1999).

possession, influential Christian leaders like Wu Enpu argued that speaking in tongues was a deceptive demonic manifestation (see DeBernardi 2020).

The Brethren have long claimed to be Spirit-led, but since the 1960s have been divided on the question of what experiences should be counted as truly charismatic.[31] Canadian Plymouth Brethren author Ernest Tatham, co-founder of Emmaus Bible College and author of *Gifts of the Holy Spirit*, initially taught the cessationist doctrine, concluding that spiritual gifts like speaking in tongues had ended when the last Apostle died. But after Tatham had a charismatic experience in the 1970s, he became convinced that spiritual gifts were still operating in the modern world.

He described himself as recoiling from narrow zealots who condemned Pentecostalism as heretical. And he noted that many viewed the newcomer as "Old Pentecostalism in fresh clothing", perhaps a twin sister or an attractive cousin, or maybe even a family member who lives in your home (Tatham 1976: 68–9). But like the Malaysian Brethren, Tatham rejected the charismatic theology that proposed that speaking in tongues was necessary evidence of spirit baptism. He published a book with a much-cited subtitle on the cover: "for all who want God's gifts, but are unable to accept mainstream Charismatic theology" (Tatham 1976; Lineham 1982: 43).

[31] Peter Lineham notes that diverse healing missions attracted attention in New Zealand after World War I, and that the Brethren were open to the possibility that miracles could occur. But in the 1930s, Brethren authors criticized the so-called Tongues Movement as "dangerous, divisive and influenced by Spiritualism" (Lineham 1982: 12–3). In 1962, the attitudes of New Zealand Brethren leaders hardened against the Charismatic movement, and they declared it not just unsound but as an "instrument of Satan himself" (Lineham 1982: 27).

Chapter 15

The Full Gospel Assemblies and the Charismatic Church of Penang

> What a happy mixed bunch we were! You could say that the church in its early days was Methodically Baptizing many into the Pentecostal experience whilst governing in the Brethren way! Four streams were merging into one river.
>
> Website, Full Gospel Assembly in Penang[1]

In 1980, about 200 persons attended the Charismatic Church of Penang's Chinese New Year celebration, which was held outdoors in the church's spacious compound. Members of the church youth group staged skits for the guests:

> A child is ill, and the parents are distraught. They ask each other in Hokkien, "What spirit medium do we go to? Should we pray to this Datuk Gong spirit, or another one? Or visit a Malay herbalist (*dukun*)? Or maybe we should get him adopted by the Goddess of Mercy?" "But we've already done that three times!" "Maybe the Monkey God will adopt him!" But then the Christian lays hands on the child, who is instantly healed.

In the next vignette they dramatised Christian salvation:

> A man wanders in a graveyard, stabbing himself. He is blind, but then he sees the cross and is saved. He takes off his sarong and bloodstained shirt, and now he is wearing modern dress.

The second sketch depicted the conversion of a man wearing a sarong—typical dress for Malays—as a passage from death to life, blindness to sight. The change of clothes from a blood-stained sarong to clean modern dress visually identified Christianity as the religion of modernity.

---

1 Full Gospel Assembly (FGA). History of FGA, Part 1: 4. http://www.fgacentre.com/ [accessed 15 December 2002]. This website is no longer active.

The youth performed a poem in English that was translated into literary Hokkien. But they also sang a song in Malay, Malaysia's national language. As Ch'ng Oon Hooi explained, "[N]ext time everyone will speak Malay, so we start to teach it in Sunday School."[2] But only two years later, the Charismatic Church of Penang lost 120 members to the Full Gospel movement. Those who left included most of their youth, many of whom were related to the Teh family.

In the 1970s and 1980s, a new wave of the charismatic movement reached Singapore and Malaysia. After the elders at one Brethren assembly in Kuala Lumpur decisively announced that their members should distance themselves from the Charismatic and neo-Pentecostal movements, two dissenting elders founded a new charismatic church. Joining them were other Brethren secessors, but also individuals whose mainline churches had expelled them when they returned to their churches after attending rallies or special meetings with reports of charismatic experiences (Lim 2015: 129). As the new movement gained momentum, the Church of Singapore moved from the margins to the centre, the Charismatic Church of Penang lost most of its younger members, and Brethren assemblies again divided.

Schism in the Brethren Assemblies

In 1978, Dr David [Paul] Yong-yi Cho (born 1936), founder and pastor of South Korea's Yoido Full Gospel Church, had held healing and evangelistic rallies at Stadium Negara in Kuala Lumpur. He returned in 1979, and that year the Full Gospel Business Men's Fellowship, together with other interdenominational Protestant charismatic organizations, also invited the World MAP American evangelists to hold a revival meeting in a large hotel in Kuala Lumpur. When those organizing the 1979 World MAP Spiritual Renewal Seminar obtained visas for the American evangelists, the chair of the organizing committee declared it to be a miracle (Ackerman 1984: 48). Anglicans, Baptists, Brethren, Lutherans, Methodists, Roman Catholics, and denominational Pentecostals attended, and the seminar was the scene of "many Spirit Baptists, exorcisms, healings, and conversions" (Ackerman 1984: 41).

After the first of Cho's rallies, eight young women living in a hostel met with a prominent Brethren elder and his wife. Two had attended the rally and reported that Cho claimed to have had a vision in which he visited heaven. Cho asserted that those worshipping God in heaven did so in the manner of present-

[2] Personal communication, 17 February 1980.

day Pentecostalist Christians. The Brethren elder observed that the implications were both obvious and disturbing. The residents of the hostel also reported that another Christian had urged them to destroy T-shirts with images related to idol worship and also a water jar in their bathroom that had a dragon image engraved on it. One of the residents refused to destroy her property and the rest feared possible adverse effects (see DeBernardi 1999).

After extensive research and discussion, the elders of one assembly in Kuala Lumpur decided to take action. In April 1979 they publically stated that because of the incompatibility of the teachings and practices of the Charismatic Renewal or Neo-Pentecostal Movement with those of the Brethren Assemblies, especially with respect to the ministries of healing, tongues, and deliverance, they discouraged their members from attending meetings of this movement. They advised those who could not agree with their conclusions to seek fellowship elsewhere.

Lawyer Ang Chui Lai (1928–2016) had already withdrawn from the Brethren in 1978; in April 1979 his brother-in-law Dr Koh Eng Kian also withdrew, and they began to hold Pentecostal meetings in Dr Koh's home. By August of 1979, 50–5 members of one assembly, including many young people, had joined the new gathering. The two former elders helped found an independent Full Gospel Assembly in Kuala Lumpur in 1981 that later affiliated with the Full Gospel Business Men Fellowship International (Lim 2015: 129).

The elders who withdrew had criticized both churches and Brethren assemblies for not proclaiming the Full Gospel, and for omitting to teach and practise "healing, tongues, and deliverance".[3] They described themselves as seeking relief from "dryness, powerlessness, and fruitlessness". In response, Brethren elders observed that they had been reluctant to pursue these exciting new experiences because (like critic Wu Enpu) they feared that in manifestations of power, the genuine was "easily camouflaged by the counterfeit". They also criticized the shift of emphasis from the Word of God to the individual's experience of spiritual gifts.

The leaders of the movement next introduced the mega church as an aspirational goal. In 1981 in Singapore, the Full Gospel Business Men's Fellowship, together with over 100 churches, organized a Bible Rally featuring David Yonggi Cho. The organizers trained 10,000 counsellors, 1,500 ushers,

---

[3] I draw here on unpublished correspondence in Harold Cooke's private archive. For a detailed consideration of later developments in the Pentecostal-Charismatic movement in Kuala Lumpur, see Cheong and Tong (2017).

and a 2,000-person choir; 40,000 persons per night attended the five-day event at Singapore's National Stadium (Sng 2003: 296). Yoido Church in Korea claims the distinction of having the world's largest congregation, and in 1982 Yonggi Cho returned to Singapore and conducted a church growth seminar.[4] Malaysian Assembly of God leaders who attended began to envision mega churches, and thousand-member churches were soon formed in the Klang Valley (Lim 2015: 129).

Schism in the Charismatic Church of Penang

Tan Jin Huat notes that unlike the Church of Singapore, the Charismatic Church of Penang did not win acceptance from the mainline churches in Malaysia and failed to grow (Tan 2011: 288–9). But the changing political and religious field of practice promoted different fates for the two churches. After World War II, Christian groups that could no longer base themselves in mainland China moved their headquarters to Hong Kong and Singapore. Consequently, Singapore became a centre for evangelical Christianity in Asia, and many now call Singapore the Antioch of Asia (see DeBernardi 2008a, 2008b).

By contrast with Singapore, in postcolonial Malaysia, Christians found themselves increasingly limited in their activities and influence. At independence, Malaysia had adopted a nationalist agenda, including identification of Islam as Malaysia's official religion in the Malaysian constitution and the adoption of Malay as the national language. A controversial programme of affirmative action for the Malay Muslim majority has ensured that most leadership positions are held by Malays. In Malaysia, Christians form a minority of 9%,[5] and membership in a Christian church confers no social advantages.

Faced with dimishing opportunities, many members of minority populations chose to emigrate or encouraged their children to do so. Teh Phai Lian's son, Teh Chiew Oo, remained in Penang to run Tithes, but his wife and children emigrated to Vancouver, Canada. Some of James Gawthorne's descendants stayed in Penang after the war, but most moved to Canada and Perth, Australia; many Brethren Eurasian Burghers migrated to Australia.

---

4 "Last Year in Malaysia", *Brethren Evangelist*, March 1983.

5 For summary details of the 2010 Population and Housing Census, see https://web.archive.org/web/20150301154300/http://www.statistics.gov.my/portal/download_Population/files/census2010/Taburan_Penduduk_dan_Ciri-ciri_Asas_Demografi.pdf [accessed 19 February 2020].

Malays cannot be evangelized, and the Malaysian government used immigration regulations to set limits to visits and longer stays of non-Malaysian Christian workers. In post-colonial Malaysia, the government also strictly limits the construction of non-Muslim religious buildings.[6] Although the founders of the Charismatic Church of Penang had the financial means to build a new church, for almost two decades they were unable to grow beyond being a house church.

A wave of secessions followed Yong-yi Cho's 1981 and 1982 visits. In 1983, two-thirds of the English-speaking Brethren Assembly in Taiping left to form a "full gospel fellowship",[7] and in Penang 120 members seceded from the Charismatic Church of Penang, joining with former Baptists, Methodists, and Anglicans to form a new church. And in 1986 in Singapore a former Methodist who had been the International Director and Vice-President of the Full Gospel Business Men's Fellowship formed a Full Gospel Assembly.

The 1983 schism within the Charismatic Church of Penang did not result from disagreements over the gifts of the Holy Spirit. The CCOP not only engaged in charismatic practices, but distributed copies of the *Full Gospel Business Men's Voice*, and identified themselves in their address stamp as a "FULL GOSPEL CHURCH". Rather, conflict had arisen within the group over personal and administrative matters, including stalled plans for church growth, the issue of control over Church finances, and issues of authority.

One of the leaders of the secession noted that they had pushed for a new church for five years, comparing their decision to leave to that of Teh Phai Lian when he left the Burmah Road Gospel Hall in 1963. A few of those who had remained with Teh and the CCOP observed that a power struggle was at the root of the division, and that some of the youth group leaders who left had wanted to be elders. Moreover, the new generation of members were largely English-educated, while the CCOP's leader Teh Phai Lian taught in Chinese. Goh Ewe Kheng arranged to have *Ancient Chinese Stories with a Modern Message* translated into English, and the first of two volumes was published in 1980. But the English-educated youth leaders were drawn to the Full Gospel Movement and the new trend to form mega churches with cell groups.

---

[6] Harold Cooke lamented in 1999 that although they had at one time convened Keswick-style meetings in Malaysia, it had become difficult to arrange permits for visiting speakers, and that they had not organized such an event since the late 1980s.

[7] Bill and Gwen Stott (Taiping) to editors of *ES*, 11 September 1986 (ES/IC).

Because Penang had rent control for many years, Teh paid only 106 Malaysian ringgit (about US$48) to rent the bungalow on Northam Road that he transformed into a house church.[8] Church members had raised funds to build a church and had bought land on York Road opposite Union High School. But when they applied for a permit to build a church there in 1978, the government rejected their application. Some questioned the delay, and as the church grew, newcomers observed that Mrs Teh was the treasurer, and that the church finances were merged with Teh's business, Tithes. They proposed that a committee should be formed with a new treasurer who was not a member of the Teh family.

Moreover, some church members found Teh Phai Lian and Teh Chiew Oo to be conservative and over-controlling not only in their administration of the house church, but also in their teachings. They had adopted practices like speaking in tongues and healing, but continued to maintain Brethren teachings on End Times prophecy. Teh Chiew Oo had declared one visiting pastor's teachings on the millennium to be wrong since he did not endorse the doctrine of the rapture. Some members favoured a more relativistic interpretation of the Bible, and were offended when he would correct them.

Finally, not long before the schism Teh Phai Lian's former critic Wu Enpu (aka Elisha Wu) had spoken at a 1982 Bible rally in Penang to over 4,000 people (Ingrahim 1983: 11). Wu had moved to Canada, but returned to Asia for a speaking tour not long after publishing a new book entitled *Distinguishing the Holy Spirit from Evil Spirits* (Wu 1981). Although Teh had published his self-defence in English and Mandarin a few years earlier (Teh 1976a, 1976b), Wu's 1981 book circulated his critique of Kong and Teh to a new generation of Chinese Christians.

The seceders from the CCOP joined together with former members of Baptist, Methodist, and Anglican congregations to form an independent charismatic church that met in a hotel dance hall. They called it Springtide Chapel, named for the hotel in which they met.

> What a happy mixed bunch we were! You could say that the church in its early days was Methodically Baptizing many into the Pentecostal experience whilst governing in the Brethren way! Four streams were merging into one river (History of FGA, Part 1: 4).

---

[8] He rented the house from the nephew of the Sultan of Kedah. The church faced the Sultan's residence, Kedah House, and church members believed that it would not be redeveloped since the Sultan would not want a tall building facing his residence. But after it was sold, the bungalow was replaced by a high-rise building.

They followed David Yong-yi Cho's cell church model,[9] but also improvised a new form of governance in which they employed full-time pastors who were accountable to their elders and deacons, and separated financial accounting from spiritual leadership.[10] In 1986, the Springtide Chapel changed their name to Full Gospel Ministries and formally registered as a branch of Kuala Lumpur's Full Gospel Assembly Bhd.[11]

In a 1995 interview, the FGA's Executive Pastor, Lim Heok Hooi, a former member of the CCOP and a founding member of the Penang Full Gospel Assembly, noted that they engaged in "power ministry" and prophecy.[12] He listed among their influences Bob Mumford, who early in his career was a speaker for the Full Business Men's International Fellowship and who also participated in the World MAP training seminars for Third World religious leaders. Lim also mentioned as an influence former Assemblies of God minister and charismatic author Judson Cornwall.

FGA leaders whom I interviewed in Penang and Taiping stressed that they had fellowship with a number of charismatic groups including Assemblies of God Churches. Bernard Teh, the pastor at the Full Gospel Assembly in Taiping, observed that when members of all the different denominations joined together in a stadium for an event, they could see that they all worshipped in the same way, concluding that "nowadays it doesn't matter what church you came from, there is an explosion of praise and worship".[13] But he contrasted different forms of leadership, noting that his church practised a five-fold ministry that included apostles, prophets, evangelists, pastors, and teachers.

Coincidently (or not?), three men from the Logos ship visited Pastor Teh's storefront church when I visited Taiping to interview him. The Logos ship is a programme run by Operation Mobilization that takes an ever-changing group

---

[9] While the Singapore Brethren did not experience a major division in this period, a Brethren Sunday school teacher who was drawn to charismatic practices separated from the Frankel Estate Brethren Assembly, and had a vision to build Bethesda Cathedral (est. 1992).

[10] This pastor also noted that the Full Gospel Assembly in Kuala Lumpur, the group's elders (two former Brethren elders), supervised its pastors.

[11] In 2002 they called themselves the FGA Centre BHD and state on their website that "FGA now stands for Fruitfulness, Growth, and Abundance" (2002: 1). A 2016 version of their website includes a timeline history of their church. http://fgacentre.org/wordpress/fga-centre/history-of-fga-centre/ [accessed 24 September 2016].

[12] In the interview, Lim identified the author of books critical of Teh Phai Lian as Wu Enpu but did not discuss his writings with me in any detail.

[13] Bernard Teh, personal communication, 1995.

of Christians from port to port to do evangelical outreach. Teh noted that the Logos ship stopped in Korea so that its multi-denominational passengers could worship at the Yoido Full Gospel Church in Seoul, and that he had visited the church himself.

Rebuilding the Charismatic Church of Penang

For a few years after the 1983 schism, only 30 or so members remained in the CCOP, most of them Teh's relatives (including my former research assistant, Ch'ng Oon Hooi and her children). After Teh's death in 1987, his son Teh Chiew Oo took over as the CCOP's chief elder. In 1993 they lost to urban redevelopment the seaside bungalow that they had rented from the Sultan of Kedah's nephew since the war. For three years they used another house for their services while they built a modern-style church in a new housing estate. Those who had remained felt that their elders had been vindicated of the allegations of financial impropriety.

In 1978 Teh Phai Lian had applied to the Penang Development Corporation for a piece of land, but received no response. Teh Chiew Oo then bought the land on York Road that they were not allowed to develop. When a new housing development was planned in Bayan Baru, some land was zoned for religious use, and the CCOP's elders competed with leaders of major denominations to purchase the land at a fraction of the market value. Teh Chiew Oo had kept copies of the earlier correspondence, and in 1992 their application succeeded since they were deemed to have applied first (CCOP 1998: 18). The CCOP elders sold the land that they had previously bought, which had appreciated in value, and planned the new church.

A few weeks after the 1995 groundbreaking ceremony, Teh Chiew Oo gave a message at a service on Chinese New Year. He proposed benevolence as a means to prosperity, explaining that Christians should help others in order to receive blessings, stressing that charitable donation was the foundation of Christian practice.

He opened his message by considering the meaning of the Year of the Pig (although explaining that he was not "using the Chinese horoscope to preach"), explaining that the character for 'house' (*jia* 家) was comprised of radicals meaning 'roof' and 'pig', a combined meaning suggesting abundance and productivity in "working and reaping for the Lord". He juxtaposed this with four Chinese translations of a Bible verse; the English translation of his message supplied three additional versions from widely used English Bibles:

> Prov. 11:25 The Liberal man shall be rich by watering others, he waters himself. (Living Bible)

> Be generous and you will be prosperous. Help others and you will be helped (Good News Bible).
>
> A liberal man will be enriched and one who waters will himself be watered (Harper Study Bible Revised Standard Edition).

The Chinese texts used the Chinese term *fu* (福, wealth, prosperity) to translate the term that the English translations give as "rich", but which Chinese Christians also translate as "blessing." He explained:

> Brothers and sisters, do you want God to bless you? First you must water others and help others. By it you are lending help to the Lord Himself. May God bless His word and may God bless every one of us that in this year, we will help and encourage one another in the Lord (*Ebenezer* 1995: 5).

He exhorted members that life was full of hardships but that Jesus offered them eternal hope. But he also admitted that he was not feeling well, and soon after collapsed, dying of heart failure.

Most accounts of the Chinese Christian diaspora focus on immigrants from mainland China. But when faced with political, economic, and educational disadvantages in Malaysia, many ethnic Chinese also left Malaysia for North America. Members of the Teh family were among those joining the postwar Chinese diaspora.[14]

After Teh Chiew Oo's sudden death in 1995, Teh's eldest son returned to Malaysia from Vancouver, Canada to manage the family business. He had completed an MBA degree in Canada and ran the business on a Western business model, taking little interest in church activities.[15] But one of Teh Phai Lian's daughters and her husband (Teh Phai Lian's nephew, whom Leland Wong's son-in-law Hong Sit had encouraged to leave business to do Christian work) together took over as ministers of this church. They had lived in Vancouver,

---

[14] Despite earlier conflict with Teh Phai Lian, when Wu Enpu (aka Elisha Wu) launched *Steering Magazine* (*Daoxiang* 導向) in 1985, the CCOP distributed it to its members (Ch'ng Oon Hooi, personal communication, 12 November 2018). The publisher was the Overseas Evangelical Mission (OEM), which had bases in California and Canada, and Rev. Wu was the organization's General Director. In 1982, he had observed that immigrant Chinese in North American struggled as they confronted an "alien culture", and launched *Steering* to guide and encourage them (Rev. George Chu, personal communication, 22 November 2018). OEM has published digitized back issues of the magazine. http://www.steering.org/index.html [accessed 13 November 2018].

[15] My former research assistant had started working at Tithes in 1980 mixing toothpaste and took on increasing responsibilities in the company, but resigned to take up full-time work at the CCOP.

British Columbia for many years, where they were active in Amazing Grace Christian Fellowship (*Jia'en Jidu Jiaohui* 佳恩基督教會), a cell church involved in outreach to recent immigrants to Canada from China. Members modelled the new Charismatic Church of Penang and its modern sound system on the Canadian church.[16] They came for the dedication of the church, then moved back to Penang to become the CCOP's pastors.

The new church is located in a row of religious structures that include a Hindu temple and a traditional Chinese temple known locally as the Snake Temple dedicated to the Clear Water Patriarch (*Qingshui Zushi Gong* 清水祖師公), a popular destination for tourists. Influenced by Peter Wagner, for a time the new minister led spiritual warfare prayers against the Snake Temple and the Clear Water Patriarch every morning at 6 am. Perhaps because of the early hour, the programme proved unpopular with church members. At one Sunday service, Teh's nephew compared the CCOP's members unfavourably to fervent Christians he had visited in China, leaving many members in tears.

Figure 42 The new Charismatic Church of Penang. Photograph: Jean DeBernardi.

[16] By 2002 the CCOP had joined the Pentecostal Assemblies of Malaysia.

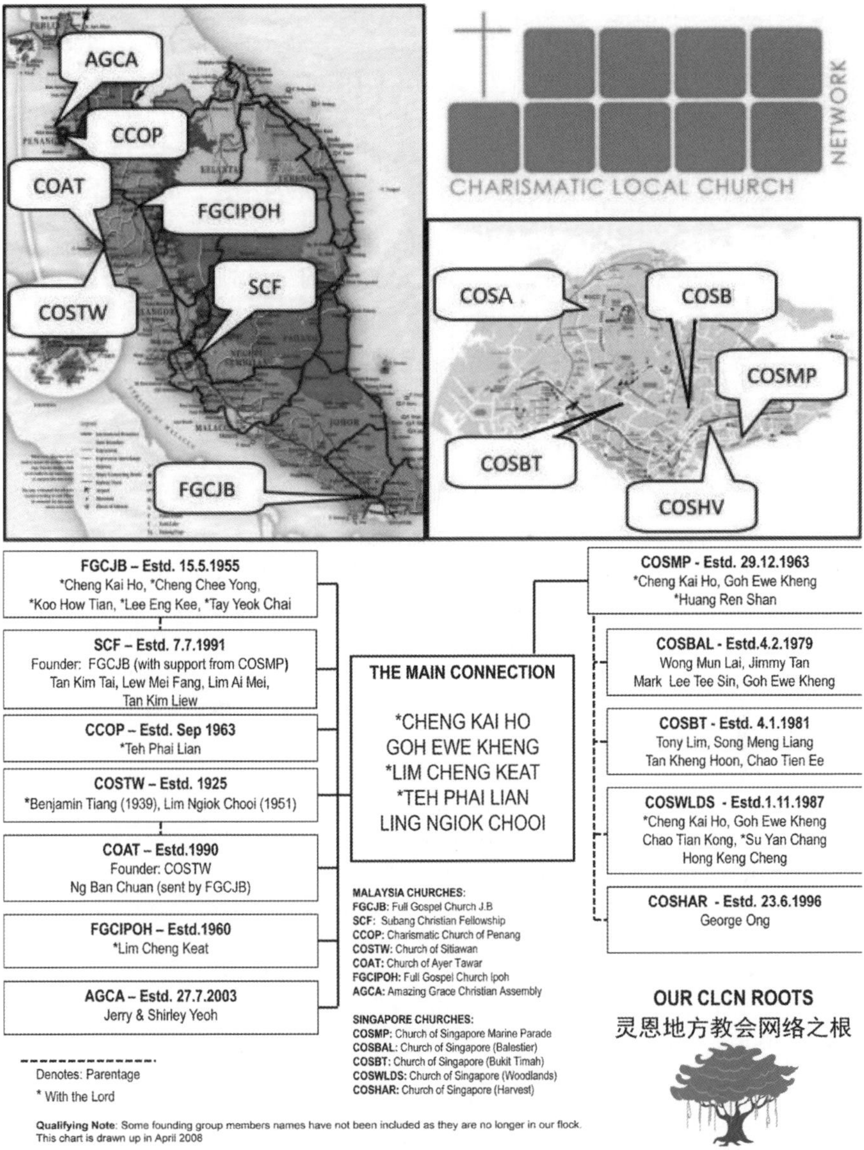

Figure 43 Maps (above) and schematic diagram (below) of the Charismatic Local Church Network, showing the names of founding members and the dates of founding. Website, Church of Singapore. http://www.cos.org.sg/our-ministries/clcn/ [accessed 7 October 2018]. Used with permission of the Church of Singapore Church Board.

Not long after, Mr and Mrs Yeoh notified the CCOP elders of their intention to resign, and in 2003 they founded Amazing Grace Christian Assembly with some of CCOP's former members. Both Amazing Grace Christian Assembly and the CCOP are members of the Charismatic Local Church Network (est. 2002), which also includes the Church of Singapore, the Church of Sitiawan, which was formed under Watchman Nee's influence (est. 1925), and Full Gospel churches in Ipoh and Johore Bahru (see Fig. 43).[17]

The CCOP is well-networked with charismatic and Pentecostal Christians, and they regularly host Christian training seminars and other large-scale inter-denominational events at their church. The Brethren pattern of lay leadership continued while Teh Phai Lian and his son still led them, but they now hire trained full-time ministers. Few members of the CCOP can recall the church's Brethren roots.[18]

Conclusion

In an interview, a popular Singaporean Christian speaker observed that churches have a developmental cycle from revival to routinization. As he described it, "The first generation gets a cup of water, and passes it on to the next half full, the third generation only gets the cup, no water, the following generation sells the cup as an antique." He observed, for example, that the once vibrant Christian Assembly established in 1935 under Watchman Nee's influence could no longer compete with newer independent Churches, in part due to a conservatism instilled by the continued authority of senior members. He observed that schisms occurred since "rebellion is wrong in the context of Chinese culture". Consequently, when faced with internal conflict, there is no recourse other than to split or withdraw.

Grant Wacker has observed that Pentecostals have sought to "capture lightning in a bottle and, more important, to keep it there, decade after decade, without stilling the fire or cracking the bottle" (Wacker 2001: 10). The Full Gospel schisms reveal a similar pattern to earlier ones: people from diverse Christian groups found spiritual renewal in breaking out of old structures to create new

---

[17] http://www.cos.org.sg/our-ministries/clcn/ [accessed 20 July 2018].

[18] One cost of schism is the loss of the "unique histories" and heritage of religious groups (Finke and Scheitle 2009: 23). When I received copies of the marriage records for the Burmah Road Gospel Hall, for example, I made copies for Ch'ng Oon Hooi and her family, since the senior generation of her family had all married there and were recorded in this register. She noted that many of their family photographs prior to the mid-1960s had been taken at the gospel hall.

ones. The young members of the CCOP wanted to build a new Christian community based on modern principles, replacing their intimate family-based local church in its seaside bungalow with the large-scale urban cell church. But they too will face the problem of passing on their spiritual experiences to a new generation, who learn their Christian practices as routine, and who may themselves some day seek revival in new forms of spiritual expression.

Conclusion

The Brethren Movement and Its Modern Fate

> It is early evening, and I am strolling around Little India with a young Chinese Singaporean. He came directly here from work, still smartly dressed in office attire. Tonight we have a special assignment for our missions course: we must introduce ourselves to some of the Indian migrant workers who are thronging the streets to enjoy the evening air and ask them to teach us a few words of their language. Most willingly agree, and I have filled a few pages in my small notebook with Tamil words scrawled in International Phonetic Alphabet. I reflect out loud that one hundred years earlier, Chinese migrant workers might have filled the same streets at night. The would-be missionary retorts, "Singaporeans were never migrant workers!"[1]

The first Singaporean Brethren whom I interviewed was Dr Ernest Chew, a Cambridge-educated historian who at that time was Dean of the Faculty of Arts and Sciences at the National University of Singapore. Dean Chew noted that because they did not believe in denominations, the Brethren could not be described as a mainline denomination, but that they were well represented in mainline evangelical organizations and events. He described the Brethren practice of open communion and their rejection of a restricted priesthood, noting that around the world the Brethren had promoted indigenous leadership. He also asserted that because of their moral commitments, Christians had superior lives to non-Christians.

[1] This mission course was held at the Church of Singapore. COS is not Brethren, but this Chinese Singaporean had worked in India as an undenominational faith missionary and explained the practice of living by faith to his students, noting that it was hard for Singaporeans to give up their luxurious lives and become cross-cultural missionaries.

I soon discovered that Dean Chew's father, Dr Benjamin Chew (1907–94), epitomized the Brethren movement to many Singaporeans. Dr Benjamin Chew's Straits Chinese mother and grandparents had become Methodists in Malacca in 1904, and his father Chew Cheng Yong had been baptized at Bethesda in 1910.[2] As a child, Benjamin had read Christian books in his father's library, including two by George Müller reporting on the Ashley Down orphanages in Bristol (Talib 1991: 46). He was baptized in 1921 at the age of 14, then studied medicine in Singapore, graduating in 1929. In 1948 he was appointed an elder in a new Brethren assembly, Bethesda Katong Church.

Dr Benjamin Chew was one of the first Asian Directors for the Overseas Missionary Fellowship (OMF, formerly the China Inland Mission), and President of the Board for Singapore Youth for Christ, which was founded in 1957 at a time when secret society activity and youth gangsterism was a pressing social issue in Singapore (Talib 1991: 114, 121–6). Singapore's Christians elected him chair of the Billy Graham Evangelical Crusade, which brought together most of Singapore's churches in the 50,000-seat National Stadium (Talib 1991: 117). His two sons Jim and Ernest Chew also served on the executive committee for this event.[3] Dr Chew's children and grandchildren are fourth- and fifth-generation Christians, and part of Singapore's English-educated elite.

The Brethren in Modern Singapore

In Singapore, Methodists and Presbyterians still own centrally located churches, and the white Anglican Cathedral with its large compound testifies to Singapore's British colonial heritage. Singapore's oldest gospel hall once stood nearby the Cathedral, but was demolished to make way for redevelopment. Its congregation moved to a new multistorey building surrounded by high-rise residential flats that makes no architectual reference to the simple bungalow style of the British gospel hall. The Brethren may have lost their central location in Singapore's business district, but as Singapore's urban lifestyle was transformed from low-

[2] I based this section on a locally published biography that describes Benjamin Chew's life (Talib 1991) and an obituary published in the *Singapore Medical Journal* (Khoo 1995).

[3] At the time Jim was a full-time Christian worker who worked for The Navigators, an interdenominational faith ministry based in Colorado Springs but with outreach in over 100 countries. For information on The Navigators, see http://www.navigators.org/us/aboutus/. Dr Ernest Chew was professor of history at the National University of Singapore.

rise neighbourhoods to high-rise apartment living, the Brethren in Singapore founded new evangelical organizations, supported American-style evangelical events, and promoted church growth, mentoring younger members to lead new assemblies.

In the postwar period, many new denominations and independent churches entered the religious field in Singapore and Malaysia. But the "big four" Protestant churches—Anglican, Methodist, Brethren, and Presbyterian—are religions of heritage for many of Singapore's English-educated elite. Singaporeans observe that Christians have great influence within government and educational circles, and some ministers quietly speculate that the cultural cachet of being Christian rather than spiritual convictions draw new members to their churches.[4]

For many, the image of Christians in Asia or Africa is of new Christians seeking help in churches that offer the promise of wealth and success in exchange for prayers and donations. Indeed, Jean and John Comaroff have quipped that for neo-Pentecostal Christians (including those who preach the so-called Prosperity Gospel), "the Second Coming evokes not a Jesus who saves, but one who pays dividends" (Comaroff and Comaroff 2000: 315). Neo-Pentecostalism, with its charismatic global evangelists, mega churches, and media empires, has captured the imagination of many Western observers as the representation of something profound about our current era. Nonetheless, we should resist turning the image of the naïve convert praying for airline tickets into an icon of the contemporary Asian or African Christian.[5]

In many parts of the world, Christians are aligned with minority groups and demands for socio-political change, but in Asian cities like Singapore and Penang, Christianity is a long-established tradition. The three main centres of evangelical Christianity in Asia—Hong Kong, Singapore, and Korea—are commercial centres with modern economies and communication systems. In those cities, evangelical Christians promoted education, social welfare and reform, and medical care. In colonial Singapore, English-educated Christians accumulated cultural and social capital that in post-colonial Singapore still

[4] In the 1980s, a government-sponsored programme of moral education may have spurred a wave of religious revivalism, but with the ending of this programme and restrictions on the organization of religious-sponsored groups and events in schools, the level of interest has not been sustained. Although Christian leaders frankly admit that most local church growth is a matter of sheep stealing (or as one person put it, moving fish from tank to tank), the percentage of Christians continues to grow.

[5] Anthropological research on Pentecostal and Charismatic Christians has increased greatly in recent decades; a full review is beyond the scope of this work but see Rosalind Hackett and Simon Coleman's 2015 edited volume (Hackett and Coleman 2015).

translates into economic success. Today, Singapore, and Hong Kong are centres for international evangelical organizations, but are also linked to Christian diasporic groups throughout the world (Goh 2005: 832, 841).

Nineteen Singaporean and 60 Malaysian churches, chapels, and gospel halls identify themselves as Brethren or Christian Brethren (Tong 2014: 8).[6] Well-designed websites now advertise Brethren distinctives, which include baptism by immersion, the weekly breaking of bread ceremony, and lay leadership. Although the website of Bethesda (Ang Mo Kio) describes their elders and deacons as male,[7] another proposes that "every believer has the right and privilege to come before God through Jesus Christ, to engage in prayer, praise, and worship, without any humanly appointed mediator or priest".[8] The Bethesda Frankel Estate Church website further explains that their form of Christian practice is authentically charismatic: "we seek to practice a daily dependence on God's Spirit to enable us to do what is right. In doing this, we become truly charismatic (move in the gifts of the Spirit)."[9]

Travelling international evangelists visit Brethren assemblies in Singapore and Malaysia as guest speakers, bringing greetings from afar, but the era of the full-time resident foreign missionary has ended. Some assemblies are named gospel halls (in Mandarin, *Fuyin Tang,* Good News Halls), but most identify themselves as churches, chapels, or centres, and some assemblies have full-time pastors and workers.

In this chapter, I explore modern developments in the Brethren movement. These include the loss of leaders to new parachurch groups, which I investigate with a vignette of the career of Tamil evangelist G.D. James; the introduction of Emmaus Correspondence courses, and with them a renewed emphasis on the theological system of John Nelson Darby; and the postwar shift to developing institutional supports for Asian missionaries and so-called tentmakers, who informally proselytize non-Christians while volunteering or working overseas. As a final colloquy of difference, I close with an account of the struggles that ensued when "Exclusive" Brethren from Northern Ireland gained influence among a small circle of Asian Brethren in postwar Malaysia and Singapore.

---

[6] For information on Malaysian Brethren churches, see http://www.cbsm.com.my/index.php/assembly-directory [accessed 7 August 2017]. These include six on Penang Island and one in Butterworth, six in Perak, thirteen in Selangor, and six in Kuala Lumpur. http://www.malaysian-Brethren.org/ [accessed 4 August 2017].

[7] https://www.bethesdahall.com/beliefs [accessed 30 December 2018].

[8] Yio Chu Kang Chapel website. http://www.yckc.org.sg/about-us/statement-of-faith-menu.html [accessed 5 August 2017].

[9] http://www.bfec.org.sg/about-us/doctrines-practices.html [accessed 5 August 2017].

The Billy Graham of Asia

As we have seen, in the 1960s the introduction of American-style Pentecostalism precipitated schisms in Brethren assemblies in Penang and Singapore. In the postwar period, American-style evangelical and fundamentalist Christianity also came to Asia in the person of Billy Graham (1918–2018), a Baptist minister and international Christian celebrity. Graham conducted 417 crusades in 185 countries, including the week-long mass revival event held in Singapore in 1978 chaired by Dr Benjamin Chew.[10]

Another Brethren elder, Dr G.D. James, came to be known as the Billy Graham of Asia. Although most recent histories of Christianity in the region focus on the introduction of Pentecostalism to Asia, James founded a new organization, the Asia Evangelistic Fellowship, and conducted crusades throughout Asia. As his life history shows, in the postwar period, Asian Brethren leaders were well positioned to promote innovative forms of evangelicalism, including the use of Gospel recordings, radio evangelism, and the translation of Emmaus Correspondence courses into Asian languages.[11]

During a 1995 pilot study for a project on Chinese Christian syncretism, I searched Singapore bookstores for publications by Asian Christians. Most sold Christian books from North America and Britain, but I found one entitled *The Great Deception* (1994), a critique of New Age practices, by a Singaporean author. Jonathan D. James was the International Director of the Asia Evangelistic Fellowship, and answered the phone when I called their Singapore office. He was planning to return to Australia, but advised me to contact his sister, Dr Violet James.

Dr James holds a BA and MA from Wheaton College and a doctorate from the University of Aberdeen. She teaches church history and Asian religions at the Singapore Bible College, and is a member of the pastoral staff at Yio Chu Kang Chapel (est. 1953). When we met, I learned that she and Jonathan were the children of well-known Tamil evangelist G.D. James.

While visiting Dr James at the Singapore Bible College, I explored the library, where I found her father's book *Missionary Ventures in Malaysia* (1961

---

[10] "Profile, William (Billy) F. Graham, Jr." https://billygraham.org/about/biographies/billy-graham/ [accessed 17 November 2017].

[11] Bobby Sng observes that the Brethren had promoted the indigenization of leadership long before the Japanese Occupation made it a practical necessity. Only after World War II ended did Anglicans, Methodists, and Presbyterians recognize the need to train greater numbers of local leaders and cooperate to establish Trinity Theological College (est. 1948) (Sng 2002: 200).

[1984]). Included in the book is an excerpt from a review in the *Malayan Evangelical Beacon* declaring the author to be the "first Asian missionary to contribute to the rare series called 'Missionary Adventure' ". Like the missionary letters published in *Echoes of Service*, James' book reports his work itinerating through the Malayan peninsula, doing roadside evangelism, and distributing tracts. He travelled with Brethren missionaries, and together they performed a multilingual tour de force that attracted onlookers. Christian music was also part of the performance: sometimes in small towns he played gospel recordings, and he often travelled with a popular men's choir from Singapore.

James was born into a Hindu family in Tamil Nadu in 1920 and was converted while studying in a Christian school. An English missionary baptized him in 1937, and in 1940 he became convinced that he had a call to full-time ministry, despite the fact that he had not read a single missionary biography or attended any missionary conference. But like Watchman Nee, James was discouraged by the poor pay that "local preachers and pastors received as a hand-out from English missionaries", which he found to be both pathetic and demeaning (James 1991: 8).

His father opposed his becoming Christian, and gave him enough money to travel to Malaya, where he and James' stepmother had emigrated. He arranged for James to work as assistant manager on a rubber plantation and to marry a Hindu girl with a handsome dowry. James refused both offers, and instead gathered his relatives and friends at his father's house to preach the gospel. Within six months, he claimed "no fewer than thirty relatives", including his father, had become Christian. He studied the Bible and pursued academic studies by correspondence (James 1991: 8).

When James moved to Malaya in 1941, he joined the Klang Gospel Hall, the Brethren assembly that Straits Chinese entrepreneur Chew Boon Hean had founded in 1913. The resident missionaries Mr and Mrs Brewerton invited him to be a full-time worker with Tamil plantation workers. When the Japanese occupied Malaya, some missionaries fled while others were interned. But the Japanese authorities allowed local members of the Klang Gospel Hall to retain their property and hold meetings. James continued his work with Tamil speakers working on nearby rubber plantations and villages, and also took over the English-speaking services, which he claims to have been unprecedented in a Brethren assembly (Abraham and Moyes 2002: 7).

In 1949, James moved to Singapore, where he began to launch evangelistic campaigns using recordings supplied by an American group, Gospel Recordings Inc. Joy Ridderhof, a missionary who could no longer work, had observed that short taped Christian messages in diverse languages could be a useful accessory to evangelism. She founded the Gospel Recordings ministry in Los Angeles in 1939 to produce and distribute records through a global network of missionaries (Thompson 1960; 1978). By the 1950s, Gospel Recordings Inc. offered missionaries free records that they could distribute much as they did tracts.[12]

During World War II, the Japanese military had driven out the British and occupied Singapore and Malaya. When the British returned after the Japanese defeat, they faced armed resistance from the Malayan Races Liberation Army, a guerilla force created by the Malayan Communist Party that was dominated by ethnic Chinese. British troops were deployed to Malaya to suppress the anti-colonial resistance movement known as the Emergency (1948–60). Highly-trained British commandoes fought Chinese youth who had retreated to the jungle to fight a war using terrorist tactics.[13]

As one strategy to defeat them, the government declared a state of emergency and moved people living in remote areas into 614 settlements known as "New Villages". Some of these were in Southern Malaysia not far from Singapore, and Christians formed Bethesda Evangelistic Teams that regularly visited ten villages. Members included James, Goh Ewe Kheng, Peter Yap, and other young Brethren leaders. James also travelled often with coworkers to visit rubber estates and tea plantations, where most of the workers were Tamil (James 1984: 21–60).

After Teh Chiew Oo wrote to the editors of *Echoes* to complain that Chinese worker's names were not included in their prayer list, they published Teh's photographs of evangelistic campaigns in Penang. The caption to one of these photographs described a 1954 evangelistic meeting in Penang: "On

---

[12] With recordings in over 6,000 languages, the ministry continues to be an active form of outreach. Gospel Recordings is popular for use in areas that have limited technological resources, and they supply missionaries not only with tapes but also with inexpensive hand-wound cassette players. The organization still provides cassette tapes of stories and songs that they describe as "culturally appropriate ways to communicate God's word", which they produced for evangelical outreach to people who speak minority languages and cannot read. They offer for translation into new languages a number of simple scripts with titles like "Medicine from God", "The New Birth", "Power over Evil Spirits" and "Are You Afraid?" See their website: http://globalrecordings.net/en/ [accessed 26 March 2017].

[13] In a curious coincidence, the Chinese communist leader known as Chin Peng (Ong Boon Hua, 1924–2013) was born and raised in Sitiawan (Shih 2004: 260–72), which was settled by Christians from Fuzhou and where Watchman Nee helped form a local church in 1925.

this occasion, Mr. G.D. James, a Tamil, preached in English, which Mr. A.E. Phillips interpreted into Mandarin. Then Mr. Phillips spoke in Mandarin, and Mr. Teh Phai Lian interpreted into Hokkien."[14]

In England we find it difficult to imagine the need for interpreters! On this occasion, Mr. G. D. James, a Tamil, preached in English while Mr. A. E. Phillips interpreted into Mandarin. Then Mr. Phillips spoke in Mandarin, and Mr. Teh Phai Lian interpreted into Hokkien.—Eds.)

Figure 44 1954 photograph of the Burmah Road Gospel Hall taken by Teh Chiew Oo. *ES* No. 1308 (January 1954): 12.

In the 1950s, the editors of *Echoes* also began to regularly publish letters from James. In 1960 he reported in *Echoes of Service* that he had completed a three-month gospel tour of Malaya, during which he and his two coworkers had distributed 100,000 gospel tracts, together with 3,000 gospel portions and "scores of Gospel records" in English, Chinese, Tamil, Malayalam, and Hindi.[15] They took along a small gramophone and played gospel music to attract the crowd; later they added a loudspeaker system with even better results. When

[14] A.E. Phillips, Taiping, "Idolatry in Malaya", 7 October 1954, *ES* No. 1308 (January 1954): 12.

[15] "Tamil Evangelistic Campaign in Malaya", G.D. James, *ES* No. 1378 (October 1959): 143; Singapore, 4 November 1959, *ES* No. 1381 (January 1960): 4.

the crowd gathered, they preached, but they also distributed free copies of records. On subsequent visits, they were gratified to see that because people (including some restaurant owners) had played gospel music records over and over, they had learned the lyrics by heart. James commented that although some would dismiss this as "mechanical preaching", he found the gospel records to be effective tools for evangelical outreach (James 1984: 51–2).

The Brethren have a rich hymnody and the *Believers Hymn Book*, first published in 1884, is still in print and used (Andrews 1958). But after World War II, American-style gospel music became widely popular with Open Brethren in Singapore and Malaysia. A study of Brethren hymnody through time would almost certainly reveal that new music accompanied revivals, and that each revival had its own "soundtrack" (Vaters 2014). Gospel music was the soundtrack for the 1978 Billy Graham campaign, but long before Graham came to Singapore, many Christians likely had already heard American gospel music on the radio or had obtained recordings.[16]

James worked with the Brethren missionaries to launch an Emmaus Bible School Depot in Singapore. But after he had a heart attack in 1960, he decided to found the Malaysia Evangelical Fellowship. Dr Violet James observed that her father had done so because he was unable to support his wife and six children by "love gifts" alone. Like other Christians faced with the "uncertain certainty" of living by faith, he sought opportunities to earn a living doing Christian work. The MEF established Tamil Bible training centres as well as Asian-wide evangelical outreach, and in 1980 he renamed it the Asia Evangelistic Fellowship.

Because the Singapore government limited the amount of overseas work the AEF could do, he moved the AEF to Australia. In the decades that followed, James conducted citywide evangelical crusades throughout Asia, visiting Java and Sumatra in Indonesia, and Kerala and Gujerat in India. James also preached and/or held gospel campaigns in Korea, Vietnam, Laos, Hong Kong, and Australia (James 1991: 10–1; see also Abraham and Moyes 2002).

G.D. James' son Jonathan succeeded him as the AEF's International Executive Director. The AEF website describes the organization as an "indigenous and interdenominational faith mission" that trains "national workers to carry out pioneer missionary work in their own countries in Asia". They claim to have more than 200 national missionaries working in India, China, Singapore, Malaysia, Indonesia, Myanmar, the Philippines, Cambodia,

[16] A Brethren full-time worker observed that many of the hymns that the older members considered to be traditional were introduced at the Billy Graham Crusade.

Vietnam, and the Solomon Islands.[17] Thus the AEF represents a broader trend in Asia in which evangelism at home has replaced cross-cultural missions, and indigenous missionaries have replaced Europeans.

John Nelson Darby and American Fundamentalism

In the postwar period the theological teachings of John Nelson Darby had renewed influence in Singapore and the new Federation of Malaysia. That influence reached Singapore and Penang by way of a new North American institution, the Emmaus Bible College and its correspondence courses, which were as important for the postwar development of the Brethren movement in Singapore and Malaysia as *Echoes of Service* and other magazines had been in the colonial period.

The 1848 division between Open and Exclusive Brethren had diminished Darby's influence on the Open Brethren, who identified Anthony Norris Groves and George Müller as their main founders. But with the introduction of the Emmaus courses, Open Brethren in Singapore and Malaysia began to study the details of Darby's end-times theology. Because of Darby's prominence in the big story of 20th-century Christianity, many were proud to claim the association.

As Donald Akenson observes, although Darby and his followers were not enthusiasts of foreign missions or of programmes of social amelioration like those promoted by George Müller, they nonetheless decided to find a new continent to conquer. James Hudson Taylor had claimed China as his territory; Darby and his followers chose North America (Akenson 2018: 430).

Darby made seven trips to North America between 1862 and 1867. He initially focused on Canada, which was a Dominion of the British Empire until after World War II. The Brethren movement had already spread by migration to Canada, where Brethren formed eight varieties of assemblies according to the degree of exclusivism (Sawatsky 2006). Darby travelled extensively in Ontario, attending annual Brethren meetings in Guelph and prophetic Bible conferences at Niagara-on-the-Lake.

In later trips, Darby focused on the United States, visiting Chicago, New York, Boston, and Philadelphia (Akenson 2018: 434). Even those who disagreed with Exclusive Brethren principles found the virtuosity of his Bible readings and Darby's rich doctrinal system compelling. The form of American evangelicalism known as Fundamentalism owes much to Darby's theological

[17] Asia Evangelistic Fellowship. https://aefi.asia/about-us/who-we-are/ [accessed 22 June 2018].

tenets, including the doctrine of the rapture and his apocalyptic millenialism (Akenson 2018: 437–8).

Although some doubt its relevance, many Brethren assemblies teach their members a version of the premillennial dispensational theology that Darby promoted throughout the world through his writings, lectures, and the Brethren movement itself (Baylis 1997). Most Christian theologies include some interpretation of end-time prophecies concerning the second coming of Christ, but liberal theologians tend to relate to these prophecies as non-literal or metaphorical, and to see the Bible as a historical document. By contrast, the premillennial view is that the Bible should be seen as a document that must be literally understood and believed, and that many of God's prophecies are as yet unfulfilled. The prophetic dimension of the Bible provides a framework for understanding that I heard discussed repeatedly in conversation, teachings, and Bible studies classes in Singapore and Malaysia, especially in 1999 as the year 2000 and a new millennium approached (see DeBernardi 2001).

According to this reading of the Bible, God's chosen people were the Jews, and many of the prophecies regard the Jewish people. When many Jews refused to accept their messiah, however, God's grace was extended to the Gentiles, and here is where the period of church history begins. The figure of Christ is central to this history—Christ is the head, and the Church is the body. Christ and his church join come together in the communion ceremony but will only be permanently reunited when the Church is "raptured" into heaven. Christians anticipate this rapture (a term invented by Darby in the 19th century that has no exact equivalent in the Bible) as a mystical climax to Christian history.

Darby taught that at the rapture Christ will return to meet his church in the air and non-Christians will remain on the earth to suffer a seven-year period of tribulation, after which Christ will return to earth and reign for a thousand years (Ryrie 1953: 12). At this time, history will focus once again on the Jewish people, and God's final prophecies to the Jews will be fulfilled. At the end of history, Christ and his saints (meaning all born-again believers) sit in judgment on the rest of the human race, separating the sheep from the goats, the saved from the unsaved (see also Kyle 1998; Ryrie 1996).

In North America, the so-called rapture doctrine spread through annual Bible conferences, popular books, and *The Scofield Reference Bible* (1909). Darby's interpretation of the Bible was also taught in Bible colleges and institutes, including the Moody Bible Institute and Dallas Theological Seminary. The Emmaus Bible College also made Darby's theology the foundation for Bible courses and textbooks that they translated and distributed globally in the postwar period.

The Emmaus Bible College

During World War II, three Brethren in Toronto, Canada, developed a Christian correspondence school for prisoners of war and men and women serving in the military. One of these three was Ed Harlow (1908–2003), a missionary who had returned to Canada from the Congo when World War II broke out. Darby's theology as interpreted by North American fundamentalist Christians directly shaped Harlow's understanding of Christianity, and formed the foundation for the Emmaus courses that he and his coworkers wrote.

When he was a teenager Harlow had met Henry Allen Ironside (1876–1951), a Toronto-born Brethren who popularized Darby's premillennial dispensational theology in North America through lecture tours, publications, and later in his role as pastor of Moody Church, a nondenominational evangelical church in Chicago. Harlow was impressed by him, and also by the Bible teachers whom he encountered at his assembly, one of whom (a visitor from New Jersey) sent him a copy of Darby's synopsis of the Bible. At the age of 20 he decided to be baptized.

He had dropped out of high school, but took classes at the Toronto Bible College while continuing to work at the post office. He then entered the University of Toronto as a full-time student in 1931, graduating in 1934. In 1935, he and his wife began work as faith missionaries in the Congo, then a Belgian colony, where Ed established a Bible School for Boys and his wife a school for girls (Letkeman 2000: 58).

When the Congo was drawn into World War II, they returned to Canada, and Ed began working with John Smart and Ernest Tatham to establish the Emmaus Bible School in Toronto (est. 1941). They gave evening courses, but decided that they could reach more people if they turned these into correspondence courses. Among their early students were those serving in the military, who were offered courses for free, and prisoners of war, who received their courses through the Red Cross (Letkeman 2000: 136–7). In 1946 they also started an Emmaus Day School, and in 1947 an Emmaus Bible School in Chicago that by 1953 had become their main base.

In 1948 Harlow completed a doctorate in the Department of Educational Theory at the University of Toronto, although he had feared failure since the chairman of his oral examination was known to be "anti-Biblical and anti-Christian" (Letkeman 2000: 165). From his study of educational testing, he adopted the practice of so-called objective testing through true/false or multiple choice answers, which also standardized the evaluation process for those grading the examinations. To give but one example from lesson 11 of their course on Book of Revelation:

Question 4 The first resurrection

a. takes place completely at the rapture of the Church
b. took place at the resurrection of Christ
c. takes place when the tribulation saints are raised
d. takes place in stages and embraces all the above events [the correct answer] (MacDonald 1973b: 105).

By 1949, 4,030 students had enrolled in one or more of the 16 correspondence courses offered.

In 1949 he crossed Canada by train, visiting major Canadian cities, but he saw potential in expanding internationally. Between 1951 and 1953, he and his wife visited 38 countries, including England, where they met with Brethren assembly leaders. On their 2-year tour they also met with 350 missionaries and recruited translators, and Emmaus soon had courses available in 35 languages (Letkeman 2000:165–6, 190). By 1965 Emmaus had translated their courses into 80 languages and distributed 3 million courses worldwide.

Harlow and his associates moved Emmaus Bible School to Chicago in 1947 and recruited William [Bill] MacDonald (1917–2007) as a teacher. MacDonald had received a BA from Tufts College (1938) and an MBA from Harvard University in 1940, before enlisting in the Navy in 1942. MacDonald became the Bible College's president in 1959 and one of Emmaus' most popular authors and speakers.[18] The college was renamed the Emmaus Bible College and moved to Dubuque, Iowa in 1984.

Emmaus in Asia

As part of their postwar efforts at global promotion, in 1950 the Emmaus Bible School sent a copy of the Emmaus course to American Brethren missionaries in the Philippines. Cyril and Anna Brooks decided to use it as a foundation for a new Bible School of the Air that broadcast short Bible lessons, and offered the full printed course for free to anyone who requested it. They soon had the text translated into Tagalog, and eventually the Bible School of the Air provided Emmaus courses in English, Chinese, Indonesian, and five Filipino languages.

The practice of using radio as a tool for evangelical outreach became common practice in the 1950s, in part due to the influence of a new radio

[18] In the 1990s Singaporean and Malaysian Brethren Assemblies used his book *Christ Loved the Church* (1973a) to instruct new members. "William MacDonald Personal Information", Online Library of Brethren Writers. http://www.plymouthbrethren.org/user/6 [accessed 21 June 2018].

ministry, the Far Eastern Broadcasting Company (FEBC). Two Americans based in Los Angeles had established FEBC in 1945, inspired by Voice of America, which had been launched in 1942 under the auspices of the Office of War Information to broadcast programmes to countries occupied by Nazi Germany. As I discuss in Chapter 11, Chinese Christians had launched a Christian radio in Shanghai in 1931. After World War II, the new FEBC radio ministry broadcast its first programme from Shanghai in 1947, with Leland Wang as a regular preacher.

In 1948 FEBC moved its based of operation to the Philippines and commenced broadcasting to China and most of Southeast Asia from Manila. Mr and Mrs Brooks publicized this work in letters published in *Echoes of Service* and articles in the *Echoes Quarterly Review* reporting remarkable growth.[19] The early Philippine radio broadcasts could be heard in Singapore and Malaya, and the missionaries in Kuala Lumpur and Penang soon started their own local radio broadcasts. In 1953, the Penang-based missionary S.S. Adams broadcast short English gospel meetings monthly on Radio Malaya.[20] In 1954 missionaries in Sri Lanka purchased time on Radio Ceylon planning to broadcast *What the Bible Teaches* in English and also a variety of Indian languages.[21] In 1956, FEBC interviewed Billy Graham on air and publicized his Manila crusade, which was one of many stops during Graham's first tour of Asia.[22]

The Brethren missionaries in the Straits Settlements and Malaya adopted the correspondence courses and assisted in their translation. By July of 1951, a missionary, Albert E. Phillips, who had relocated from China to Malaya after World War II, had completed a translation of the courses into Chinese in collaboration with a Hong Kong-based missionary, and reported an enrolment

---

[19] See, for example, "The Bible School of the Air", Cyril H. Brooks, *Echoes' Quarterly Review* Vol. 7, No. 3 (July–September 1955): 2–6.

[20] S.S. Adams, Penang, 2 April 1954, *ES* No. 1314 (June 1954): 86.

[21] "Broadcasting in India", H. McGregor, 17 September 1953, *ES* No. 1308 (January 1954): 11.

[22] They continued to expand by forming a number of regional Far Eastern Broadcasting Associates (FEBA), including one in Singapore, which began operations in 1962 as a recording studio, and in 2003 FEBC established an International Office in Singapore. Today, FEBC broadcasts on AM and FM radio stations, by shortwave from the Philippines, and also via satellite and on the Internet, including in countries where Christian radio is banned. They broadcast programmes in over 130 languages worldwide, which in China include Mandarin, Cantonese, and seven minority languages. FEBC/Christ to the World by Radio https://www.febc.org [accessed 2 September 2016].

of over 500 students in the Chinese course in Penang, including a number of students from Buddhist homes. They also had 800 students enrolled in their English course.[23] A few months later the number of those using the courses in Penang had climbed to nearly 3,000, and the Hong Kong missionary also reported strong enrolments.[24]

In 1954, G.D. James announced that he and missionary Matt Finlay were launching an Emmaus Bible School Depot in Singapore. By the next year 80 students had signed up for the Emmaus Bible Courses in Tamil. James reported that three Hindu students had requested images of Christ to worship, but that he had sent them copies of the Tamil Bible instead.[25] The same year, a Singapore-based missionary reported that they were spending "all available time" translating the courses into Malay.[26] Missionaries from Thailand to Fiji reported to the editors of *Echoes of Service* that they were translating courses and by 1965 Emmaus was distributing courses in over 80 languages.[27]

In the postwar period, Canadian and American Christians blended new forms of educational practice with innovative business models, repackaging Darby's teachings for export. By the end of the 20th century, the Emmaus Correspondence School books were widely available in Brethren bookstores in Singapore and Malaysia and also for sale at individual assemblies for use in Bible study classes.[28]

From Evangelized to Evangelists

What then of the Open Brethren missionary movement? As the *Echoes of Service* history of Brethren missions observed in 1972, "For the future it seems clear that the Lord will look to Malaysian nationals for His workers, as the position becomes increasingly difficult for the admission of workers from

---

23 A.E. Phillips, Penang, 18 July 1951, *ES* No. 2182 (October 1951): 113; 5 October 1951, *ES* No. 2184 (December 1951): 137.

24 W. Elliott, Hong Kong, 2 May 1952, *ES* No. 2191 (July 1952): 76.

25 G.D. James, Singapore, 4 March 1954, *ES* No. 1310 (May 1954): 69; 24 March 1955, *ES* No. 1326 (June 1955): 85.

26 M.H. Finlay, Singapore, 23 December 1953, *ES* No. 1311 (April 1954): 53.

27 In 2016 they claimed to have distributed over 40 million courses. http://ecsministries.org/pages/about [accessed 22 June 2016].

28 When I interviewed Bethesda elder Dr Peter Wee Huat Lee, he recommended the writings of William MacDonald, whose book *Christ Loved the Church* (1973a) was used to instruct new members, and identified the 1967 edition of the Scofield Bible as the "most acceptible" version, commenting that it was based on Darby. Interview with Dr Peter Wee, May 1999.

overseas" (Stunt et al. 1972: 262). The postwar European Brethren missionaries' encounters with nationalism and resurgent Buddhism, Hinduism, and Islam, and their gradual withdrawal from Asia, could be the subject of another book-length study.

Much like the mid-19th century Open Brethren, who promoted the idea that every church could be a missionary-sending society, individual Brethren assemblies in Singapore and Malaysia now support cross-cultural evangelical projects. One of the newer Singapore assemblies, for example, provided financial support for development projects in a tribal minority village in China, including building a new school. In the 1990s they regularly organized so-called vision trips to the village with assembly members; several members who made the trip described the living conditions as difficult and did not plan to return. They hired as a teacher a divorced Singaporean who had health issues and had lost her job. She testified in an informal interview that after she began teaching in this village school, her health improved and she was able to support herself again. Although she was not allowed to teach Christianity to her students, she noted that she had given copies of Chinese Bibles to local officials, and that they had accepted them without question.

Singapore offers aspiring cross-cultural missionaries the possibility of studying for bachelor's or master's degrees at Trinity Theological College (est. 1948) or Singapore Bible College (est. 1952), and of taking short-term courses at Tung Ling Bible School (est. 1978) or at the Asia Cross-Cultural Training Institute (ACTI, est. 1985). Many Singaporean churches also offer informal missions courses taught by former missionaries, including one that I took at the Church of Singapore, the source of the vignette at the start of this chapter. Many Singaporeans work for global corporations and may travel or work abroad. They take these courses to prepare themselves to proselytize informally, a practice known as tentmaking. Most Christians in Singapore are ethnic Chinese, and many of their formal and informal outreach efforts focus on China.

When I enrolled in a Mandarin course at a mainline church in downtown Singapore, for example, I discovered that many of the students were medically trained Christians, including one Brethren doctor who planned to visit China to offer free medical care. The instructor was a multilingual court translater and used as his textbook *Good News Reader* (*Xinyang Duben* 信仰讀本 n.d.).

The lessons were written in pinyin and simplified characters, and composed in the colloquial style spoken in the People's Republic of China. The scripted textbook dialogues presented hypothetical encounters between a Christian evangelist and his or her Chinese interlocutor, together with detailed commentary in English, including the analysis of competing ideologies like socialism, Maoism, scientism, and atheism. Each lesson concluded with a short verse from the Bible that the student was encouraged to memorize.

In the Introduction, the textbook's anonymous authors explained that their main goal was to prepare Christians for "long-term witness through friendship". The authors commented that the text did not offer a systematic analysis of doctrine, and contained, no lessons on the second coming of Christ, baptism, or gifts of the Holy Spirit (信仰讀本 n.d.: 1), all potentially divisive topics.

In their first lesson, "The Existence of God" (*Shangdi de Cunzai*), they addressed an old debate, drawing their students' attention to the fact that they have chosen to translate "God" with the Chinese term *Shangdi* and not *shen*. They explained that they chose to use *Shangdi* as a translation for God because the non-Christian Chinese will "immediately think of the One Supreme God, and especially the "Christian God", whereas *Shen* (a god, a spirit, a divinity) has a much vaguer meaning" (信仰讀本 n.d.: 9).

The next two lessons explained who God is, distinguishing him from the Jade Emperor, and describing him as the creator and architect of the universe, limitless and great. Lesson Four offered the script of a testimony describing how God had changed the speaker's life. Subsequent lessons offered scripts that explain Christian ideas concerning sin and redemption, and possible responses to objections from Marxist, evolutionist, and secularist perspectives. As I mention in the Introduction, the authors paid special attention to explicating Marxist ideology, observing that Communist and Christian ideals are similar, and that some even regard Marxism as an atheist sect of Christianity. They concluded, however, that Christianity and Marx's theory are opposed: "God's way of changing society is to change individual hearts (from the grassroots), Marx' way is to change the economic and political system (from the top)" (信仰讀本 n.d.: 134).

Asia Cross-Cultural Training Institute

Singapore is now the headquarters of OMF International, an inter-denominational Protestant missionary society with historic roots in the China Inland Mission. CIM left mainland China in 1953 and relocated to Singapore, and was renamed the Overseas Missionary Fellowship (OMF) in 1964. At that time, the OMF was reorganized to allow non-Western Christians to become full members and to organize councils in their own countries. Brethren elder Benjamin Chew became Director and Chairman of the newly formed Singapore Home Council (Talib 1991:114–5). Like George Müller, whose fundraising practices CIM founder James Hudson Taylor adopted, OMF International communicates information about their activities and funds to their supporters, but does not directly solicit funds, making it unique among major evangelical organizations (Austin 2000: 234).

In 1985 OMF organized the Asia Cross-Cultural Training Institute (ACTI) to provide a short pre-field training course for cross-cultural Christian workers in Asia.[29] OMF invited other mission agencies to join the ACTI Board of Directors, which in 2017 included representatives from 12 organizations: the OMF, CRU Singapore (formerly the Singapore Campus Crusade for Christ), Operation Mobilization (OM) Singapore, Pioneers in Asia, SIM East Asia,[30] World Evangelization Crusade (WEC) Singapore, Asia Gateway, OC [One Challenge] International, The Navigators Singapore, the Perspectives on the World Christian Movement course, and FOMOS (Fellowship of Missional Organisations of Singapore).

In a 2004 analysis of ACTI graduates, Rev. Kim Chong Pae observed that for 200 years the mission movement had been the monopoly of Western churches and mission agencies, but that the movement was declining in the West. By contrast, Asian churches were no longer mission fields; rather many countries including Singapore and Malaysia were now cross-cultural missionary-sending countries. Moreover, countries like Nepal, Myanmar, and Thailand were now sending students to ACTI for training for cross-cultural ministry in their own countries. Kim emphasized the importance of cross-cultural training for this emerging Asian mission movement, but also suggested that Asian perspectives would yield new strategies for the Asian mission field and might even "revive the declining Western churches" (Kim 2004: 11). According to Kim, Korea was the first missionary-sending country in Asia, and by 2004 had dispatched 12,000 missionaries worldwide.[31] Singapore also sends out a high number in proportion to the country's population (Kim 2004: 10).

As of March 2017 ACTI had trained more than 355 cross-cultural missionaries, the majority of whom were from South Korea (30%), Singapore (20%), and Hong Kong (11%). Smaller numbers of students came from Taiwan, Nagaland (whose population is 90% Christian), Japan, Malaysia, Indonesia, the Philippines, India, Myanmar, Thailand, and Nepal. Twenty-five Westerners

---

[29] The OMF is the successor to the China Inland Mission (CIM) that James Hudson Taylor founded in 1865 on Brethren principles.

[30] SIM is an acronym for Serving in Mission but includes another well-known SIM, the Sudan Interior Mission, which was established on principles similar to those of the China Inland Mission.

[31] The Chinese Foreign Missionary Union (est. 1928) sent Chinese missionaries to Southeast Asia before World War II, so this claim likely could be challenged.

(7%) from the United States, United Kingdom, New Zealand, Norway, and Australia have also completed the course.[32]

In 1999 I attended classes at the Asia Cross-Cultural Training Institute taught by Melville Szto, who worked as the Dean of ACTI from 1995–2001. Szto was a Singaporean Brethren who, together with his wife, had studied at Adelaide Bible Institute in Australia, then worked in Japan as a missionary. He observed in an interview that the Brethren had a "wider vision for cooperation with other groups and organizations" and noted that members of his Singaporean Brethren assembly were full-time workers in Youth for Christ, Campus Crusade for Christ, The Navigators,[33] the Intervarsity Fellowship (IVF), the Overseas Missionary Fellowship (OMF), the New Tribes Mission (NTM), the World Evangelization Crusade (WEC), and Wycliffe.

The group of ten students—from Singapore, Korea, and the Philippines—met for morning and afternoon sessions in a small seminar room. The students read selected pages from American Bible Society linguist Eugene Nida's 1954 book *Customs and Cultures: Anthropology for Christian Missions*, a more recent Christian textbook, *Cultural Anthropology* (Grunlan and Mayers 1988), and C. Peter Wagner's *Praying Through the 100 Gateway Cities of the 10 – 40 Window* (1995).

When the discussion turned to marriage and family, Szto explicated a series of terms relating to kinship: endogamy, exogamy, incest taboo, levirate, sororate, monogamy, and polygamy. He observed that Solomon had 600 wives and 1,000 concubines, and that he married with the political goal of sealing alliances. But he also added that his grandfather was a wealthy businessman who had had six wives and concubines. His mother was Christian and had married a Christian, but she had grown up as one of 30 children living together in a house in a large compound. He and the students concluded that many practices regarded as Christian were cultural.

He then turned the discussion to the question of contextualization, and handed out an exercise entitled "Separating our worldview from the message of the Gospel—Contextualisation". The exercise listed 18 cultural norms, and he invited the students to decide whether they should ignore them or seek to change them, and then rank them by importance. The cultural norms included a range

---

[32] http://acti-singapore.org/ [accessed 27 March 2017].

[33] The Navigators is an interdenominational youth ministry that uses access to schools to engage in diverse forms of evangelical outreach. I interviewed an unmarried woman in her 20s who was involved in The Navigators and who had worked with youth in schools in the Philippines. Melville's sister Lyndis Szto and Jim Chew, one of Dr Benjamin Chew's sons, also worked with The Navigators.

of social behaviours: lying, fornication (e.g. premarital sex), adultery (a note added that "Christians often fall in this area"), polygamy as a sign of high status, tobacco use by children, opium use, betel nut use, hygiene and unclean water sources, poor nutrition, lack of discipline in child rearing, lack of punctuality and procrastination, demeaning attitudes to women, use of divination, magical forms of curing, initiation, working daily including Sunday, sporadic church attendance, and cursing. The students were also asked to provide a strategy for changing the cultural norm, together with Biblical principles and references.

Szto noted that contextualization required that they promote a Christian life. But if the culture regards liars as clever, or their kinship system allows polygamy, he asked the students, how does the Christian change this? "You can speak out against it", he cautioned them, "but if the practice is a part of the culture, then it may be very difficult to speak out and condemn it." He next discussed adultery and polygamy, and they agreed that with adultery the Biblical teachings were clear; with polygamy they were not so clear, a conclusion that the textbook authors also implied. As Szto noted, the Old Testament is filled with examples of polygamy, and Abraham, David, and Solomon all had plural wives.

He observed that missionaries in Africa had forced Christian men to divorce their wives, some of whom then became prostitutes, noting that sometimes polygamy was a good custom. In some cases, for example, when a man's brother died he would marry his widow and provide for her family. He advised his students that it might be better to wait for change more slowly, generation by generation, rather than demand that a man legally married to multiple wives divorce them on conversion. The class went down the list item by item, deciding that tobacco addiction was not urgent, but opium and betel nut addictions should be changed. Evangelical Christianity is no longer a European-led effort, but the question of how a Christian goes about becoming an agent of change in another society is one that still baffles and challenges Christians.

On Exclusivist Open Brethren

In a recent history of Brethren assemblies in Malaysia and Singapore, Samuel T.W. Wee observes that a majority of "Brethren" assemblies (the quotation marks are his) had embraced change, including adopting ideas flowing from parachurch organizations, the Charismatic movement, and the wider society. He further noted that the growth of mega churches had inspired some Brethren to seek larger numbers, to adopt the use of musical instruments at meetings, and to employ paid pastors and workers with theological training.

But some Brethren, he noted, were still convinced that "continuity should take place without change", a perspective that he endorsed (Wee 2014: 9–10). Singapore's informal Brethren Network Fellowship includes at least one charismatic Brethren assembly, Living Sanctuary Brethren Church. But when that assembly was allowed to join the network, Bethesda (Ang Mo Kio) withdrew.

The person most often identified as the catalyst for a conservative turn in the Brethren assemblies in Singapore and Malaysia was Thomas (Tom) Bentley, who arrived in Malaysia in 1957. Bentley was a member of Ebenezer Assembly in Belfast, Ireland, which belonged to a wing of the Open Brethren sometimes described as being as narrow and separatist. Bentley taught Bible studies at Venning Road Gospel Chapel in Kuala Lumpur and was popular with students. But he taught that being Brethren meant strict separation from other denominations, and an English Brethren critic labelled his approach both "cultic" and too tightly bound with the religious and political situation of Northern Ireland (Bentley 2012: 69). Adding to the discord, in a period in which feminism was on the rise, Bentley and his first wife insisted that women wear head coverings at all assembly gatherings, a practice that some rejected as a Western custom (Bentley 2012: 86–7).

As this study shows, as undenominational Christians, the Open Brethren had long cooperated with other evangelical Christians, including Presbyterians, Methodists, Baptists, and evangelical Anglicans. During World War II the interned Brethren missionaries had become close to other interned Christian leaders, and the sense of amity persisted after the war (Bentley 2012: 89). And in the postcolonial period Brethren leaders founded or led a wide range of parachurch groups.

The editors of *Echoes of Service* agreed to collect and transfer donations to Bentley even though they described his home assembly in Belfast as not agreeing with the existence of *Echoes of Service* as "having any scriptural warrant".[34] But as complaints against Bentley mounted, the editors advised him to ask his supporters to send him funds directly (Bentley 2012: 119). The assemblies in Malaysia and Singapore banned him from teaching, and in 1963, 13 young people who had been influenced by him separated from their assembly. With the help of Bentley and Jim Allen, another well-respected Bible expositor from Northern Ireland (see Allen 1997), they formed a new meeting on Peel Road in Kuala Lumpur that eventually moved to Petaling Jaya (Bentley 2012: 129; Wee 2015: 251).

[34] Alexander Pulleng (Bath) to S.S. Adams (Penang), 10 January 1957 (ES/IC).

With respect to the role of women, assemblies used to require women to wear a head covering at their weekly meeting. But by the time of my 1999 research, Singapore's Bethesda Hall was the only one to insist on this. In defence of the practice, in 1983 Dr Wee, while still an elder at Bethesda Katong, had published a controversial tract "Women's Head Covering—And the Glory of God", which was reprinted, translated, and widely distributed in Singapore, Malaysia, Hong Kong, India, Australia, the United States, and Canada. In this densely-argued 50-page essay, Dr Wee argued that the practice of covering a woman's hair was not an outmoded practice whose adoption should be a matter of personal choice.

In support of this view, Wee cited 1 Corinthians 11:1–16, which indicates that a man should have short hair and leave his head uncovered since "he is the image and glory of God", but that the woman should leave her hair long but cover it since she is the "glory of the man", was created for him, and should have his "authority on her head". Dr Wee concluded that the practice of wearing a head covering remained an important New Testament truth and practice (Wee 1997: 43–4). Dr Wee's son, Samuel, supported his father's views, adding that women's expectation to take public roles in assemblies was the product of the women's liberation movement, and that accepting them as equals would be a rejection of the authority of the New Testament (Wee 2014: 65–8).

But other Brethren elders whom I interviewed disagreed. Melville Szto cited a Bible passage which showed that Priscilla and Aquila taught Appolos in Ephesus, and identified other New Testament ensamples of women who took leading roles. He noted that Frankel Estate Church had invited women to preach, including Dr Violet James. And although she did not teach men, one of their female members led a Sunday morning service for guest workers from the Philippines. She administered the bread and wine to the women, who likely had been baptized as Catholics rather than by adult immersion baptism.

Many Brethren whom I interviewed claimed that the practice of having a group of unordained, lay leaders—a committee of elders or Oversight—ensured their conservatism. Some critically noted that assemblies were not democratic and were often dominated by senior male elders. In an interview, a prominent scientist-inventor who is a popular speaker in Singapore assemblies observed that because rebellion was wrong in the context of Chinese culture, there was no room for discussion, and that when there was conflict, there was no recourse other than to split.[35]

As we have seen, disagreements among elders over practice or Biblical interpretations often resulted in the decision that dissenting viewpoints could

[35] Interview with Prof. Freddy Boey, 13 March 1999.

not be taught. Those who disagreed with the prevailing judgement had no recourse but to seek or found a church more compatible with their beliefs, as was the case when Teh Phai Lian and Goh Ewe Kheng left Brethren assemblies to found the Church of Penang and the Church of Singapore, and when Tom Bentley helped found the Peel Road Gospel Hall in Kuala Lumpur.[36]

Conclusion

In this monograph, I draw on the Brethren archive to write a history of the globalization of Christianity and the local church. This history encompasses Europe, Asia, and North America, but I write that history from the perspective of individuals in Penang and Singapore, investigating their activities, relationships, and influences. As George Simmel has proposed, society is nothing more than individuals connected by interaction. Looked at closely, we see unique individuals, but as we increase our distance, the picture of society emerges with its own "forms and colors" (Simmel 1950: 8). As I noted in the Introduction, Simmel also compares society to "an event: it is the function of receiving and effecting the fate and development of one individual by the other" (Simmel 1950: 11). He added that the production of social life occurs as the product of interacting individuals, but also as the succession of generations, since humans as social beings inherit their traditions (Simmel 1950: 13). Although people inherit their traditions, each new generation of individuals reinvents itself under new circumstances not of its making.

The Brethren missionaries who came to Penang and Singapore in the 1860s were revivalists, and theirs was just the first wave of Christian revival to wash through those two cities. Starting in the 1920s, revival came not from Europe but from China, and with it came demands for independence from European control. The schisms that followed were often framed as conflicts over speaking in tongues, or the correct interpretation of end-time prophecies, or whether or not the breaking of bread ceremony should be celebrated using leavened or unleavened bread. But these diagnostic events and social dramas also revealed conflict between generations over musical styles, debates about gender roles, and the desire to embrace the modern, however it was understood.

[36] In 2004, another secession followed in Singapore's Bethesda Hall. The seceders were branded as "exclusive" when they objected to collaboration with more liberal assemblies at a 2001 Festival of Celebration and insisted that women wear head coverings at meetings. The seceders formed ADELPHIA Joo Chiat Gospel Hall, and soon invited Bentley, who had been banned from Singapore assemblies for decades, to visit them as a guest speaker (Wee 2018: 251–5).

The individuals whose life histories I trace in this monograph moved from place to place, from one religious organization to another, sometimes joining new social networks and adopting new projects. Their stories are a colloquy of differences rather than a simple narrative history. Christians ensample the New Testament, memoirs, and the lives of other Christians, seeking connection and meaning. But Open and Separatist Brethren assemblies, the Charismatic Local Church Network in Singapore and Malaysia, and independent local churches all claim to be New Testament Churches while seeking separation and distinction from one another.

This study of discontinuous continuities in Singapore and Penang reveal that as political, economic, and social fields of practice changed, doors opened and closed, shaping the fates of those who lived in those two cities. And the history of institutions shows that evangelical Christianity as ideology and practice has deep continuities and fractures. For many Brethren, it is a matter of proud heritage to have generations of family history enmeshed with assembly history, but the history of evangelical Christianity in Singapore and Penang is also a history of schism and mutual forgetting.

Chinese Glossary

Names of Persons and Organizations

(*name in Pinyin Romanization/name in parentheses in Hokkien or other topolect/ traditional characters/English name*)

Bincheng Jiaohui 檳城教會 Church of Penang
Bincheng Ling'en Jiaohui 檳城靈恩教會 Charismatic Church of Penang
Chen Shiwu (*Tan See Boo*) 陳時武
Daoxiang 導向 *Steering* magazine
Guangfu Gong (*Kong Hok [Hock] Keong*) 廣福宮 Penang Guanyin Temple
Guanyin Ting (*Koanim Teng*) 觀音亭 Penang Guanyin Temple
He Xiaodong 何曉東
Hong Kang Qing (*Ang Kang Kin or King*) 洪 or 汪康慶
Jia Yu Ming 賈玉銘
Jia'en Jidu Jiaohui 佳恩基督教會 Amazing Grace Christian Fellowship
Jiang Duan Yi (*Kong Duen Yee*) 江端仪
Jiang Shoudao 江守道 Stephen Kaung
Lu Zhongxin (*Liok Tiong Sin*) 陸忠信 Faithful Luk/Luke
Mei Qi (*Mui Yee*) 梅绮 Kong Duen Yee's film name
Miao Shanxun 繆紹訓 Simon Meek
Ni Tuosheng 倪柝聲 Watchman Nee
Song Shangjie 宋尚節 John Sung
Wang Zai 王載 Leland Wang
Wang Zhi (*Wang Tse*) 王峙 Wilson Wang
Wu Enpu 吳恩溥 Elisha Wu
Wu Youqing (*Goh Ewe Kheng*) 吳有慶
Xiaoqun 小群 Little Flock
Xinjianpo Jidu tu Juhui suo 新加坡基督徒聚會所 Singapore Christian Assembly

Xue Chuntong (*Hong Sit*) 薛春桐

Zheng Peiran (*Teh Phai Lian*, aka *T.P. Jean*, *Cheng Pei Jan*, and *T.P. Lian*) 鄭沛然

Zheng Qiuyu (*Teh Chiew Oo*) 鄭秋雨

Zhonghua Guowai Budaotuan 中華國外佈道團 Chinese Foreign Missionary Union

Chinese Terms

(*Pinyin/Hokkien term in missionary Romanization in parentheses/traditional characters/English meaning*)

angkong (Hokkien term; no agreed upon character equivalent) deity

baoen 報恩 repay a debt of gratitude

dao (*to*) 道 literally 'path' or 'way' but also refers to a philosophical tradition

diyu (*tekek*) 地獄 hell

fu (*hok*) 福 prosperity or blessings

Fuxing 福興 revival

Fuyin Tang (*Hok Im Tng*) 福音堂 gospel hall

huigai 悔改 repentance

jia dao 假道 false *dao*/doctrine

jidujiao (*kitok kau*) 基督教 Protestant Christianity ("Christ Teachings")

jin shen (*kim sin*) 金身 god image ("golden body")

jiushizhu 救世主 saviour

Jiuzhu (*Kiu-chu*) 救主 Saviour, Jesus Christ

Linghun (*lenghun*) 靈魂 spirit or soul

Mazu (*Ma Cho*) 媽祖

ouxiang (*ngo siong*) 偶像 idol (Christian term used to refer to deity images)

qingjie (*chhengkhi*) 清潔 pure, clean

Qingshui Zushi Gong 清水祖師公 Clear Water Patriarch

Shangdi (*Siongde*) 上帝 God

Shangdi Gong (*Siongde Kong*) 上帝公 Hokkien name for Emperor of the Dark Heavens

Shen (*sin*) 神 Deity or spirit

Shengling 聖靈 Holy Spirit

shu 贖 redemption

Tiangong (*Tikong*) 天公 Lord of Heaven, Hokkien name for the Jade Emperor

Tianhou (*Thian Ho*) 天后 Queen or Empress of Heaven

Tianshangde Zhenshen Shangdi 天上的真神上帝 heavenly true god Shangdi
Tiantang 天堂 heaven
Tianzhu 天主 God, literally Heaven's ruler
Tianzhujiao 天主教 Catholicism
Xuantian Shangdi (*Hian Thian Siong Tè*) 玄天上帝 Emperor of the Dark Heavens
zhen li 真理 true principles
zui (*choe*) 罪 sin

Archival Sources

British and Foreign Bible Society (BFBS)

The British and Foreign Bible Society's archival collection is housed at Cambridge University Library and includes the annual *Report of the British and Foreign Bible Society* and *Monthly Extracts from the Correspondence of the British and Foreign Bible Society* (1817–58).

Chinese Evangelization Society (CES)

Chinese Evangelization Society publications are held in the archives of the Council for World Mission at the School of Oriental and African Studies, University of London (SOAS CWML 0190). Their publications included *The Gleaner in the Missionary Field* (*GMF*, 1850–51), *The Chinese and General Missionary Gleaner* (*CGMG*, 1851–53), and *The Chinese Missionary Gleaner* (*CMG*, 1853–55, 1856–59). The latter two publications are also available through Nineteenth Century Collections Online.

Christian and Missionary Alliance (C&MA)

The C&MA archive in Colorado Springs holds copies of the *Shengjing Bao* (*Bible Magazine*) for 1913–33, 1947–58, 1960–62. Issues of the magazine for 1918, 1936–41, 1947–51, and 1954 are also available as a reprint (*Shengjing Bao* 2006). The C&MA website includes digitized issues of *The Pioneer* for 1929–41, 1946–58, and 1964–95.

The Missionary Echo (ME) and Echoes of Service (ES)

Echoes of Service in Bath has transferred their historical records, which include correspondence, visual material, and journals, to the Christian Brethren Archive at the University of Manchester John Rylands Library. Digital versions of some visual materials and early publications can be accessed through their guide to Christian Brethren digitised materials. See https://

www.library.manchester.ac.uk/search-resources/special-collections/guide-to-special-collections/christian-brethren-collections/digitised-material/. I refer to unpublished correspondence as Echoes of Service/incoming correspondence, abbreviated to ES/IC.

London Missionary Society (LMS)

Incoming letters to the London Missionary Society directors from Penang missionaries are held in the archives of the Council for World Mission at the School of Oriental and African Studies, University of London (SOAS CWM/LMS/14/02/02 Ultra Ganges, Incoming Correspondence: Penang, abbreviated as LMS/IC). I also refer to the file on property deeds of the Ultra Ganges Mission (CWM/LMS/01/07/1/5/ Property Deeds: Ultra Ganges c. 1818–72, abbreviated to LMS/PD). J.G. Bausum's 1851/52 and J. Chapman's 1861/62 and 1863/64 reports on the Penang Mission Schools are held in the Main Library CWML O15, bound together in a volume entitled *Report of the Protestant Mission School in Pinang*.

The Missionary Reporter

The Missionary Reporter (1853–58) is held in the British Library.

Assembly Record Book, 1865–1934

The record book is held in the private archive of Bethesda Hall (Ang Mo Kio) in Singapore.

Scriptural Knowledge Institution (SKI)

The annual reports of the Scriptural Knowledge Institute are held at Müller House in Bristol.

Society for Promoting Female Education in the East (FES)

The records of the Society for Promoting Female Education in the East, including General and Finance Committee minutes, annual reports, and copies of their magazine the *Female Missionary Intelligencer*, are held at the University of Birmingham, Cadbury Research Library, Special Collections (GB 150 FES). The society is often called the Female Education Society, abbreviated to FES.

Bibliography

"About Us". 2018. Singapore Bible College. https://www.sbc.edu.sg/about/sbc/ [accessed 1 December 2018].

Abraham, P. and Gordon Moyes. 2002. *G.D.: A Legend in our Times. A brief sketch on the life of G.D. James*. Mumbai, India: Light of Life Books.

Ackerman, Susan E. 1984. "Experimentation and Renewal among Malaysian Christians: The Charismatic Movement in Kuala Lumpur and Petaling Jaya". *Southeast Asian Journal of Social Science* 12, 1: 35–48.

Adams, Sidney S. n.d. " 'Malayan Magazine': A Survey by S.S. Adams". Reprinted from *Echoes' Quarterly Review*. 27 pp.

Adamson, John William. 1971. *Pioneers of Modern Education in the Seventeenth Century*. New York: Teachers College Press.

Akenson, Donald Harman. 2016. *Discovering the End of Time: Irish Evangelicals in the Age of Daniel O'Connell*. Montreal & Kingston: McGill-Queen's University Press.

________. 2018. *Exporting the Rapture: John Nelson Darby and the Victorian Conquest of North American Evangelicalism*. Princeton: Princeton University Press.

Allen, Jim. 1997. *What the Bible Teaches: Revelation (Volume 10)*. Kilmarnock: John Ritchie Limited.

American Board of Commissioners for Foreign Missions (ABCFM). 1837. "Mission to Singapore". In *Twenty-Eighth Annual Report of the American Board of Commissioners for Foreign Missions* (September 1837), pp. 89–90, 122–4. Boston: Crocker & Brewster.

Anderson, Allan. 2003. "The Contribution of David Yonggi Cho to a Contextual Theology in Korea". *Journal of Pentecostal Theology* 12, 1 (2003): 85–105.

________. 2007. *Spreading Fires: The Missionary Nature of Early Pentecostalism*. Maryknoll: Orbis Books.

________. 2009. "Pentecostalism in India and China in the Early Twentieth Century and Inter-Religious Relations". In *Global Pentecostalism: Encounters with Other Religious Traditions*, ed. David Westerlund, pp. 117–35. New York: I.B. Taurus.

________. 2013. *To the Ends of the Earth: Pentecostalism and the Transformation of World Christianity*. New York: Oxford University Press.

________. 2014. *An Introduction to Pentecostalism: Global Charismatic Christianity*. 2nd ed. Cambridge: Cambridge University Press.

Anderson, Benedict. 1983. *Imagined Communities: Reflections on the Origin and Spread of Nationalism*. London: Verso.

Anderson, Kevin B. 2010. *Marx at the Margins: On Nationalism, Ethnicity, and Non-Western Societies*. Chicago: University of Chicago Press.

Andrews, John S. 1958. "Brethren Hymnology". *The Evangelical Quarterly* 28 (October–December 1856): 208–29.

Anon. 1966–67. "History of Our Sunday School". *Wilkie Terrace Sunday School Magazine, 1966–1967*. Singapore: Wilkie Terrace Christian Assembly.

Ariel, Yaakov. 2013. *An Unusual Relationship: Evangelical Christians and Jews*. New York: New York University Press.

Aritonang, Jan Sihar and Karel Steenbrink, eds. 2008. *A History of Christianity in Indonesia*. Leiden and Boston: Brill.

Arndt, Johann. 1979. *True Christianity*. Translation and Introduction by Peter Erb. [Vol. 1 originally published in 1605; Vols 2–4 in 1606–10.] New York: Paulist Press.

Arnot, Frederick Stanley. 1884. *From the Zambesi to Benguella*. London: James E. Hawkins.

________. 1887. *Six Months More Among the Garenganze, Letters from September, 1886 to March, 1887*. London: James E. Hawkins.

________. 1889. *Garenganze, or Seven Years Pioneer Mission Work in Central Africa*. London: James E. Hawkins.

________. 1893. *Bihé and Garenganze, or Four Years Further Work and Travel in Central Africa*. London: James E. Hawkins.

________. 1914. *Missionary Travels in Central Africa*. Bath: Echoes of Service.

Arnot, Frederick Stanley, in conjunction with the editors of *Echoes of Service*. 1896. *Across the Seas: A Selection of Missionary Incidents for Young People*. Glasgow: Pickering & Inglis.

________. 1897–1901. *Across the Seas: A Selection of Missionary Incidents for Young People*. Second series. Glasgow: Pickering & Inglis.

Ashiwa, Yoshio and David L. Wank, eds. 2009. *Making Religion Making the State*. Stanford: Stanford University Press.

Asia Evangelistic Fellowship (AEF). 2003. "International Evangelist and Statesman Called Home". Media release 25 July 2003. http://www.aefi.org.au/Announcement.htm.

Assembly Record Book. 1865–1934. Singapore: Bethesda Hall, Ang Mo Kio.

Assmann, Jan. 1998. *Moses the Egyptian: The Memory of Egypt in Western Monotheism*. Rev. ed. Harvard: Harvard University Press.

________. 2011. *Cultural Memory and Early Civilization: Writing, Remembrance, and Political Imagination*. Cambridge: Cambridge University Press.

Augustin, James F. 1970. *Bygone Eurasia: The Life-Story of the Eurasians of Malaya*. Kuala Lumpur: Rajiv Printers.

Austin, Alyvn. 2000. "No Solicitation: The China Inland Mission and Money". In *More Money, More Ministry: Money and Evangelicals in Recent North American History*, ed. Larry Eskridge and Mark A. Noll, pp. 207–34. Grand Rapids: Eerdmans.

________. 2007. *China's Millions: The China Inland Mission and Late Qing Society, 1832–1905*. Grand Rapids/Cambridge: William G. Eerdmans Publishing Company.

Austin-Sparks, T. (Theodore). n.d. "Have We Fettered and Imprisoned the Spirit of Revival?" Austin-Sparks Net. http://www.austin-sparks.net/english/000520.html [accessed 2 February 2007].

Baark, Erik. 1997. *Lightning Wires: The Telegraph and China's Technological Modernization, 1860–1890*. Westport: Greenwood Press.

Band, Edward. 1948. *Working His Purpose Out: The History of the English Presbyterian Mission, 1847–1947*. Reprint. Taipei: Ch'eng Wen Pub. Co., 1972.

Bao Zhongjie (Pao Chung Chieh). 2005–18. "Paul Henry Bartel, 1904–2001". Biographical Dictionary of Chinese Christianity. http://bdcconline.net/en/stories/bartel-paul-henry [accessed 13 November 2018].

Barker, John. 2007. "Comment on "Continuity Thinking and the Problem of Christian Culture: Belief, Time, and the Anthropology of Christianity by Joel Robbins". *Current Anthropology* 48, 1 (February 2007): 18.

Barter, Shane Joshua. 2016. *Explaining the Genetic Footprints of Catholic and Protestant Colonizers*. New York: Palgrave MacMillan.

Barwick, John. 2005–20. "Huang Naisheng". *Biographical Dictionary of Chinese Christianity*. http://bdcconline.net/en/stories/huang-naishang [accessed 18 February 2020].

Bausum, John George. 1852. *Report of the Protestant Mission School in Pinang*. Penang. SOAS CWML O15.

Baylis, Robert H. 1997. *My People: The History of Those Christians Sometimes Called the Plymouth Brethren*. Rev. ed. Wheaton: Harold Shaw Publishers.

Bays, Daniel. 1985a. "Christianity and Chinese Sects: Religious Tracts in the late Nineteenth Century". In *Christianity in China: Early Protestant Missionary Writings*, ed. Suzanne Wilson Barnett and John King Fairbank, pp. 121–34. Cambridge: Harvard University Press.

________. 1985b. "Christian Tracts: The Two Friends". In *Christianity in China: Early Protestant Missionary Writings*, ed. Suzanne Wilson Barnett and John King Fairbank, pp. 19–34. Cambridge: Harvard University Press.

________. 1993. "Christian Revival in China, 1900–1937". In *Modern Christian Revivals*, ed. Edith Blumhofer and Randall Balmer, pp. 161–79. Urbana and Chicago: University of Illinois Press.

________. 1996. "The Growth of Independent Christianity in China, 1900–1937". In *Christianity in China from the Eighteenth Century to the Present*, ed. Daniel H. Bays, pp. 307–16. Stanford: Stanford University Press.

________. 2012. *A New History of Christianity in China*. Chichester, West Sussex: Wiley-Blackwell.

BCEC. 2011. "1961–2011 Celebrating 50 Years". Rev. 2013. Boston: Boston Chinese Evangelical Church http://www.bcec.net/wp-content/uploads/2013/08/BCEC_50th_Anniversary_web1.pdf (accessed 29 July 2018).

Bebbington, David. 1972. "The Life of Baptist Noel: Its Setting and Significance". *Baptist Quarterly* XXIV, 8 (October 1972): 389–411.

________. 1989. *Evangelicalism in Modern Britain: A History from the 1730s to the 1980s*. London and New York: Routledge.

________. 2006. "The Growth of Voluntary Religion". In *The Cambridge History of Christianity World Christianities c. 1815–c. 1914*, Vol. 8, ed. Sheridan Gilley and Brian Stanley, pp. 53–69. Cambridge: Cambridge University Press.

Beighton, John T. 1888. *Betel-Nut Island: Adventures in the Eastern Tropics*. London: The Religious Tract Society.

Bentley, Grace. 2012. *A Biography on Thomas Bentley*. Newtonards, Co. Down: Crimond House Publications.

Beyer, Peter. 2006. *Religions in Global Society*. London and New York: Routledge.

Bhabha, Homi K. 1994 [2004]. *The Location of Culture*. London and New York: Routledge.

Bible Society, British and Foreign. 1817–58. *Monthly Extracts from the Correspondence of the British and Foreign Bible Society.* London.

________. 1854. "The Million Testament Fund for China". *Fiftieth Report of the British and Foreign Bible Society,* Appendix II. London.

________. 1857. *Fifty-third Report of the British and Foreign Bible Society*. London.

Binfield, Clyde. 1977. *So Down to Prayers: Studies in English Nonconformity 1780–1920*. London: J.M. Dent & Sons Ltd.

Bonar, Rev. Andrew A. 1845. *Memoir and Remains of the Rev. Robert Murray M'Cheyne, Minister of St. Peter's Church, Dundee*. Dundee: William Middleton.

Bourdieu, Pierre. 1977. *Outline of a Theory of Practice*. Translated by Richard Nice. Cambridge: Cambridge University Press.

________. 1984. *Distinction: A Social Critique of the Judgement of Taste*. Translated by Richard Nice. Cambridge: Harvard University Press.

________. 1990 [1980]. *The Logic of Practice*. Translated by Richard Nice. Stanford: Stanford University Press.

________. 1998. *Practical Reason: On the Theory of Action*. Stanford: Stanford University Press.

Bourne, Henry Richard Fox. 1866. *English Merchants: Memoirs in Illustration of the Progress of British Commerce*. Vol. 2. London: Richard Bentley.

Bowman, Marilyn Laura. 2016. *James Legge and the Chinese Classics: A Brilliant Scot in the Turmoil of Colonial Hong Kong*. Victoria, B.C.: FriesenPress.

Braddell, Roland St. J. 1921. "Law and the Lawyers". In *One Hundred Years of Singapore*, Vol. I., ed. Walter Makepeace, Dr Gilbert E. Brook, and Roland St. J. Braddell, pp. 160–244. Reprint. Singapore: Oxford University Press, 1991.

Broadbent, E.H. (Edmund Hamer). 1931 [1999]. *The Pilgrim Church: Tracing the Pathway of the Forgotten Saints from Pentecost to the Twentieth Century*. Grand Rapids, Michigan: Gospel Folio Press.

Brock, Peter. 1984. "The Peace Testimony of the Early Plymouth Brethren". *Church History* 53, 1 (March 1984): 30–45.

Brook Street Chapel, Tottenham No. 17. 1965. *Anniversary Issue, 1839–1964* (May/June). London. 20 pp.

Brown, Callum G. 1987. *The Social History of Religion in Scotland since 1730*. London: Methuen.

Brown, Ford K.1961. *Fathers of the Victorians: The Age of Wilberforce*. Cambridge: Cambridge University Press.

Browne, Rev. George. 1859. *The History of the British and Foreign Bible Society, From Its Institution in 1804, to the Close of Its Jubilee in 1854*. Two vols. London: The Society's House.

Buchanan, Colin. 2015. *Historical Dictionary of Anglicanism*. 2nd ed. Lanhan, Maryland: Rowman and Littlefield Publishers.

Buckley, Charles Burton. 1902 [1984]. *An Anecdotal History of Old Times in Singapore*. Two vols. Reprint. Oxford: Oxford University Press.

Bunyan, John. 1984. *Pilgrim's Progress*. Edited with an Introduction by N.H. Keeble. Oxford: Oxford University Press.

Burness, Ian. 2016. "Frederick Stanley Arnot (1858–1914): Reassessing His Impact on African Mission". In *The Brethren and Mission: Essays in Honour of Timothy C.F. Stunt*, ed. Neil T.R. Dickson and T.J. Marinello, pp. 183–96. Glasgow: Brethren Archivists and Historians Network.

Burns, Rev. Islay. 1870 [1975]. *Memoir of the Rev. Wm. [William] C. [Chalmers] Burns: Missionary to China from the English Presbyterian Church*. Reprint. San Francisco: Chinese Materials Center, Inc.

Burrell, J. 1853. *Memoir of the Rev. Thomas Lewis, of Islington, With Extracts from His Diary and Correspondence*. London: Ward and Co.

Caldwell, John R. 1895. "The Ministry of Women". In *The Witness: An Unfettered Monthly Journal of Biblical Literature, Expository Papers, Notes of Addresses, Conference Reports, Questions and Answers, Intelligence, Poetry, Correspondence, &c.*, NS Vol. 5, ed. John R. Caldwell, pp. 141–3, 158–60, 165–7, 185–7. Glasgow: Pickering & Inglis.

Canton, William. 1904. *The Story of the Bible Society*. London: J. Murray.

Cantor, G.N. 2005. *Quakers, Jews and Science: Religious Responses to Modernity and the Sciences in Britain, 1650–1900*. Oxford: Oxford University Press.

Carey, W.H. 1850. "Beighton, Thomas". In *Oriental Christianity Biography containing Biographical Sketches or Distinguished Christians who have Lived and Died in the East* Vol. II, pp. 431–7. Calcutta: J. Thomas, Baptist Mission Press.

Carpenter, Joel A. 1997. *Revive Us Again: The Reawakening of American Fundamentalism*. New York: Oxford University Press.

Carson, Penelope. 2012. *The East India Company and Religion, 1698–1858*. Woodbridge: The Boydell Press.

Chapman, John. 1862. *Second Annual Report of the Income and Expenditure of the Protestant Mission School*. 11 February 1862. Penang. SOAS CWML O15.

________. 1865. *Report of the Mission Schools and some other particulars in connection with the Mission at Penang for 1863–64*. 11 February 1865. Penang: Argus Press. SOAS CWML O15.

Charismatic Church of Penang. 1998. *Dedication 10-10-1998: The Glory of God Fills His Temple*. Penang: Bayan Lepas.

Charter, Vernon and Jean DeBernardi. 1998. "Towards a Chinese Christian Hymnody: Processes of Musical and Cultural Synthesis". *Asian Music* 29, 2: 83–113.

Chen I-Hsin. 2016. "From God's Chinese Names to a Cross-Cutural Universal God: James Legge's Intertextual Theology in his Translation of Tian, Di and Shangdi". *Translation Studies* 9, 3: 268–81.

Cheung, David (Chen Yiqiang). 2004. *Christianity in Modern China: The Making of the First Native Protestant Church*. Leiden: Brill.

Chinese Evangelization Society. 1851–59. *Report of the Chinese Evangelization Society*. London: Nisbet & Co. SOAS CWML O15.

Chinese and General Missionary Gleaner, The (*CGMG*). 1851–53. London: Chinese Evangelization Society.

Chinese Missionary Gleaner, The (*CMG*). 1853–55, 1856–59. London: Chinese Evangelization Society.

Cheong Weng Kit and Joy K.C. Tong. 2017. "The Localization of Charismatic Christianity among the Chinese in Malaysia: A Study of Full Gospel Tabernacle". In *Global Chinese Pentecostal and Charismatic Christianity*, ed. Yang Fenggang, Joy K.C. Tong, and Allan H. Anderson, pp. 309–28. Leiden/Boston: Brill.

Chong, Terence and Daniel P.S. Goh. 2014. "Asian Pentecostalism: Revivals, Mega-churches, and Social Engagement". In *Routledge Handbook of Religion in Asia*, ed. Bryan S. Turner and Oscar Salemink, pp. 402–17. London: Routledge.

Chow, Christie Chui-Shan. 2017. "Indigenizing the Prophetess: Toward a Chinese Denominational Practice". In *China's Christianity: From Missionary to Indigenous Church*, ed. Anthony E. Clark, pp. 219–46. Leiden: Brill.

Church of Singapore. 1988. *Church of Singapore 25th Anniversary November 1963–November 1988*. Singapore.

Clark, Anthony E. 2011. *China's Saints: Catholic Martyrdom during the Qing (1644–1911)*. Bethlehem: Lehigh University Press.

________. 2015. *Heaven in Conflict: Franciscans and the Boxer Uprising in Shanxi*. Seattle: University of Washington Press.

________. 2016. "Local Magistrates and Foreign Mendicants: Chinese Views of Shanxi's Franciscan Mission during the Late Qing". In *Reshaping the Boundaries: The Christian Intersection of China and the West in the Modern Era*, ed. Song Gang, pp. 91–105. Hong Kong: Hong Kong University Press.

Clements, Paul Henry. 1915. "The Boxer Rebellion: A Political and Diplomatic Review". PhD thesis, Department of Political Science, Columbia University.

Coad, F. Roy. 1968. *A History of the Brethren Movement: Its Origins, its Worldwide Development and its Significance for the Present Day*. Wm. B. Eerdmans: Grand Rapids.

Cohen, Abner. 1981. *The Politics of Elite Culture: Explorations in the Dramaturgy of Power in a Modern African Society*. Berkeley: University of California Press.

Cohen, Paul. 1997. *History in Three Keys; The Boxers as Event, Experience, and Myth*. New York: Columbia University Press.

Cohn-Sherbok, Lavinia. 1998. "Darby, John Nelson (1800–82)". In *Who's Who in Christianity*, p. 68. Routledge: London and New York.

Coleman, Simon. 2009. *The Globalisation of Charismatic Christianity*. Cambridge: Cambridge University Press.

Comaroff, John L. and Jean Comaroff. 1991. *Of Revelation and Revolution: Christianity, Colonialism and Consciousness in South Africa*. Vol. I. Chicago: University of Chicago Press.

________. 2000. "Millennial Capitalism: First Thoughts on a Second Coming". In a special issue of *Public Culture* on the theme of "Millennial Capitalism and the Culture of Neoliberalism" 12, 2: 291–343.

Connell, Rev. A. 1915. "William Chalmers Burns". *Presbyterian Messenger* (April 1915): 117–26.

Connerton, Paul. 1989. *How Societies Remember*. Cambridge: Cambridge University Press.

Coppel, Charles A. 1997. "Revisiting Furnivall's 'plural society': Colonial Java as a Mestizo Society?" *Ethnic and Racial Studies* 20, 3 (July 1997): 562–79.

Cousins, Peter. 2006. "Robert Stanes (1841–1932): A Merchant 'Son' of George Muller". *Brethren Archivists and Historians Network (BAHN)* 3: 48–57.

Daily, Christopher A. 2013. *Robert Morrison and the Protestant Plan for China*. Hong Kong: Hong Kong University Press.

Dann, Robert Bernard. 2004. *Father of Faith Missions: The Life and Times of Anthony Norris Groves*. Waynesboro, Georgia: Paternoster/Authentic Media.

Darby, J.N. (John Nelson). 1828. "Considerations on the Nature and Unity of the Church of Christ". Dublin. http://www.stempublishing.com/authors/darby/ECCLESIA/01002E.html [accessed 28 August 2017].

________. 1985 [1857–59]. Letter to Prof. Tholuck, reprinted as Appendix A "J.N. Darby's Own Account of the Origin of the Movement". In *A Historical Sketch of the Brethren Movement*, H.A. Ironside, pp. 181–7. Neptune, New Jersey: Loizeaux Brothers.

Daoxiang 導向 (*Steering*). 1985–2004. Huntington Beach, Vancouver, and Taiwan: Overseas Evangelical Mission. http://www.steering.org/index.html.

Daughrity, Dyron B. 2008. *Bishop Stephen Neill: From Edinburgh to South India*. New York: Peter Lang.

Davies, Evan. 1846. *The Memoir of Samuel Dyer: Sixteen Years Missionary to the Chinese*. London: John Snow.

DeBernardi, Jean. 1991. "Linguistic Nationalism: The Case of Southern Min". In *Sino-Platonic Papers 25*, ed. Victor Mair. Philadelphia: Department of Oriental Studies, University of Pennsylvania.

________. 1995. "Lim Boon Keng and the Invention of Cosmopolitanism in the Straits Settlements". In *Managing Change in Southeast Asia: Local Identities, Global Connections*, ed. Jean DeBernardi, Gregory Forth, and Sandra Niessen. Proceedings of the 21st Annual Conference of the Canadian Council for Southeast Asian Studies, pp. 173–87. Edmonton: CCSEAS.

________. 1999. "Spiritual Warfare and Territorial Spirits: The Globalization and Localization of a 'Practical Theology'". *Religious Studies and Theology* 18, 2: 66–96.

________. 2001. "If the Lord Be Not Come. . . .: End-Time Teachings and Evangelical Practice in the Brethren Movement in Singapore". *Journal of Ritual Studies* 15, 1: 4–16.

________. 2004. *Rites of Belonging: Memory, Modernity, and Identity in a Malaysian Chinese Community*. Stanford: Stanford University Press.

________. 2005. "Christianity and Chinese Religious Culture in Singapore: Anthropological Perspectives". In *Facing Faiths, Crossing Cultures: Key Trends and Issues in a Multicultural World. Dialogues with Chandra Muzaffar, Ibrahim Abu-Rabi' and Jean DeBernardi*, ed. Lai Ah Eng, pp. 178–225. Singapore: Institute of Policy Studies and SNP Reference.

________. 2006. *The Way that Lives in the Heart: Chinese Popular Religion and Spirit Mediums in Penang, Malaysia*. Stanford: Stanford University Press.

________. 2008a. "Asia's Antioch: Prayer and Proselytism in Singapore". In *Proselytization Revisited: Rights Talk, Free Markets, and Culture Wars*, ed. Rosalind Hackett, pp. 155–84. London: Equinox Publishers.

________. 2008b. "Global Christian Culture and the Antioch of Asia". In *Religious Diversity and Harmony in Singapore*, ed. Lai Ah Eng, pp. 116–41. Singapore: Institute of Southeast Asian Studies.

________. 2009a. "Wudang Mountain and Mount Zion in Taiwan: Syncretic Processes in Space, Ritual Performance, and Imagination". *Asian Journal of Social Science*, special issue on religious syncretism, ed. Daniel Goh, 37 (2009): 138–62.

________. 2009b. "'Ascend to Heaven and Stand on a Cloud': Daoist Teachings and Practice at Penang's Taishang Laojun Temple". In *The People and the Dao: New Studies of Chinese Religions in Honour of Prof. Daniel L. Overmyer*, ed. Philip Clart and Paul Crowe, pp. 143–84. Sankt Augustin, Germany: Institut Monumenta Serica.

________. 2010. "On Women and Chinese Festival Foods in Penang, Malaysia and Singapore". *Journal of Chinese Ritual, Theatre and Folklore*, special issue on "Women and Chinese Religion", ed. Daniel Overmyer, 168 (June 2010): 179–223.

________. 2011. "Moses' Rod: The Bible as a Commodity in Southeast Asia and China". In *Chinese Circulations: Capital, Commodities and Networks in Southeast Asia*, ed. Eric Tagliacozzo and Wen-chin Chang, pp. 380–404. Durham, North Carolina: Duke University Press.

________. 2015. "The Brethren Movement and Evangelical Christianity in Singapore and Penang, Malaysia". In *The Anthropology of Global Pentecostalism and Evangelicalism*, ed. Rosalind Hackett and Simon Coleman, pp. 72–94. New York: New York University.

________. 2017. "Emplacing a Network Religion in a World in Motion: Evangelical Christianity and the Brethren Movement in Penang". In *Penang and Its Networks of Knowledge*, ed. Peter Zabielskis, Yeoh Seng Guan, and Kat Fatland, pp. 82–114. Penang: Areca Press.

________. 2020. "Startling, Stubborn Things: Prayer and the Ministry of Deliverance in China and Southeast Asia". In *The Brethren and the Church*, ed. Neil Dickson and T. J. Marinello, forthcoming. Glasgow: BAHN.

De Jong, Gerald Francis. 1987. *History of the Mission to Borneo*. Historical Society of the Reformed Church in America Occasional Papers No. 1. New Brunswick, New Jersey: Historical Society of the Reformed Church in America.

________. 1992. *The Reformed Church in China 1842–1951*. Grand Rapids: Wm. B. Eerdmans Publishing Co.

Dickson, Neil T.R. 1990. "Brethren and Baptists in Scotland". *Baptist Quarterly* 33: 372–87.

________. 1993. "Modern Prophetesses: Women Preachers in the Nineteenth Century Scottish Brethren". *Records of the Scottish Church History Society* XXV, 1: 89–117.

________. 2002. *Brethren in Scotland 1838–2000: A Social Study of an Evangelical Movement.* Carlisle, Cumbria: Paternoster Press.

Dickson, Neil T.R. and T.J. Marinello. 2016. *The Brethren and Mission: Essays in Honour of Timothy C.F. Stunt.* Glasgow: Brethren Archivists and Historians Network.

Directory and Chronicle for China, Japan, Corea, Indo-China, Straits Settlements, Malay States, Siam, Netherlands India, Borneo, the Philippines, &c. for the year 1908. Hong Kong and London: Hongkong Daily Press Office.

Doran, Christine. 2006. "Bright Celestial: Progress in the Political Thought of Tan Teck Soon". *Sojourn: Journal of Social Issues in Southeast Asia* 21, 1 (2006): 46–67.

"Dr. Hong Sit". 2014. *Houston Chronicle*, 29 October 2014.

Dunch, Ryan. 2001. *Fuzhou Protestants and the Making of a Modern China, 1857–1927.* New Haven: Yale University Press.

Early History. 2018. Detroit Chinese Bible Church. http://www.cbcdetroit.org/aboutCBC/history.phphttp://www.cbcdetroit.org/aboutCBC/history.php [accessed 1 December 2018].

Ebenezer. 1995. Issue 16 (April 1995). Penang: The Charismatic Church of Penang.

________. 2013. *50th Anniversary.* Penang: The Charismatic Church of Penang.

Echoes of Service. 1885–present. Bath: Echoes of Service.

Echoes Quarterly Review. 1948–78. London: Published for Echoes of Service by Paternoster Press.

Edwards, David L. 1984. *Christian England (Vol. 3) From the 18th Century to the First World War.* Grand Rapids: William B. Eerdmans Publishing.

Edwards, Ebenezer Henry, ed. 1901. *The Reign of Terror in the Western Hills, or Stories of the Persecution of Chinese Christians in Shansi in 1900.* Reprinted from the "Shanghai Mercury". Shanghai.

________. 1907. *Fire and Sword in Shansi: The Story of the Martyrdom of Foreigners and Chinese Christians.* Rev. ed. Edinburgh and London: Oliphant Anderson & Ferrier.

Eisenstadt, Schmuel N. and Wolfgang Schluchter. 1998. "Introduction: Paths to Early Modernities—A Comparative View". *Daedalus* 127, 3: 1–18.

Elleman, Bruce. 2009. *Moscow and the Emergence of Communist Power in China, 1925–30: The Nanchang Uprising and the Birth of the Red Army.* London: Routledge.

Emerson, Ralph Waldo. 1856 [2008]. "Religion". In *The Collected Works of Ralph Waldo Emerson*, ed. Alfred R. Ferguson, Jean Ferguson Carr, and Douglas Emory Wilson, p. 131. Introductions and notes by Robert E. Spiller et al. Cambridge, MA: The Belknap Press of Harvard University Press. Electronic edition [print edition 1971–2007] [accessed 4 January 2020].

End, Thomas van den. 1999. "Anthing, F(rederik) L(odewijk)". In *Biographical Dictionary of Christian Missions*, ed. Gerald H. Anderson, p. 24. Grand Rapids, Michigan: William B. Eerdmans Publishing Company.

Erb, Peter. 1979. "Introduction" to *True Christianity*, by Johann Arndt. Translation and Introduction by Peter Erb, pp. 1–17. New York: Paulist Press.

Esherick, Joseph W. 1987. *The Origins of the Boxer Uprising*. Berkeley: University of California Press.

The Evangelical Beacon. 1931–50. Minneapolis, Minnesota: Evangelical Free Church of America.

Evangelical Magazine and Missionary Chronicle (EMMC). 1813–1904. London.

Fagg, Rev. John Gerardus. 1894. *Forty Years in South China: The Life of Rev. John Van Nest Talmage, D.D.* New York: A.D.F. Randolph & Co.

Female Education Society (FES), also known as the Society for Promoting Female Education in China, India, and the East. 1847. *History of the Society for Promoting Female Education in the East: Established in the Year 1834*, with a preface by Baptist Wriothesley Noel. London: E. Suter.

Female Missionary Intelligencer and Record of the Proceedings of the Society for the Promotion of Female Education in China, Africa, and the East. 1853–99. London and Dublin: Society for Promoting Female Education in the East.

Fenger, Johannes Ferdinand. 1906. *History of the Tranquebar Mission: Worked Out from the Original Papers*. Published in Danish and translated into English from the German of Emil Francke, 2nd (bicentenary) ed. Madras: M.E. Press.

Fer, Yannick and Michael Black. 2005. "The Growth of Pentecostalism in French Polynesia: A Hakka History. Migration, Cultural Identity and Christianity". *China Perspectives* 57 (January–February 2005): 50–7.

Ferlanti, Federica. 2010. "The New Life Movement in Jiangxi Province, 1934–1938". *Modern Asian Studies* 44, 5 (2010): 961–1000.

Fernandis, Gerard. 2003. "The Portuguese Community at the Periphery: A Report on the Portuguese Quest for *Bumiputera* Status". *Kajian Malaysia* XXI, 1&2: 285–301.

FES. *See* Society for Promoting Female Education in China, India, and the East (London) [Female Education Society or FES].

Feuchtwang, Stephan. 2001. *Popular Religion in China: The Imperial Metaphor*. Richmond, Surrey: Curzon.

Fiedler, Klaus. 1995. *The Story of Faith Missions: From Hudson Taylor to Present Day Africa*. Eugene, Oregon: Wipf and Stock Publishers.

Finke, Roger and Christopher P. Scheitle. 2009. "Understanding Schism: Theoretical Explanations for their Origins". In *Sacred Schisms: How Religions Divide*, ed. James R. Lewis and Sarah M. Lewis. Cambridge: Cambridge University Press.

Finlay, M.H. 1964. *1864–1964: The Story of ONE HUNDRED YEARS of the Lord's Blessing*. Singapore: Bethesda Gospel Hall.

Fitzgerald, Frances. 2017. *The Evangelicals: The Struggle to Shape America*. New York: Simon and Schuster.

Forrest, J.W. 1971. "The Missionary Reporter". *Journal of the Christian Brethren Research Fellowship* 21 (1971): 24–42.

Francke, August Hermann. 1787. *The Footsteps of Divine Providence: or, The Bountiful Hand of Heaven Defraying the Expenses of Faith*. Translation of *Segenvolle Fusstapfen des noch lebenden, waltenden, liebreichen and getreuen Gotte*. London: W. Justins.

Frykenberg, Robert Eric. 2005. "Christian Missions and the Raj". In *Missions and Empire*, ed. Norman Etherington, pp. 107–31. Oxford: Oxford University Press.

________. 2008. *Christianity in India: From the Beginnings to the Present*. Oxford: Oxford University Press.

Full Gospel Assembly [FGA]. N.d. History. http://www.fgacentre.com/ [accessed 15 December 2002].

Full Gospel Businessmen's Voice. 1953–present. Lake Forest: Full Gospel Business Men's Fellowship International.

Furnivall, John Sydenham. 1948. *Colonial Policy and Practice: A Comparative Study of Burma and Netherlands India*. Cambridge: Cambridge University Press.

Gawthorne, Jeff. 2014. *The Gawthornes of Penang*. Privately published.

Geertz, Clifford. 1973. *The Interpretation of Cultures*. New York: Basic Books.

Gibbs, Jenna, ed. 2020. *Global Protestant Missions: Polities, Reform, and Communication, 1730s–1930s*. Milton Park, Abingdon and New York: Routledge.

Gierl, Martin. 2015. "Pietism, Enlightenment, and Modernity". In *A Companion to German Pietism, 1660–1800*, ed. Douglas H. Shantz, pp. 348–92. Leiden, The Netherlands: Brill.

Gih, Rev. Andrew. 1961. *The Church Behind the Bamboo Curtain*. Greenwood, N.C.: The Attic Press.

Girardot, Norman J. 2002. *The Victorian Translation of China: James Legge's Oriental Pilgrimage*. Berkeley: University of California Press.

Gitre, Edward J. 2004. "The 1904–05 Welsh Revival: Modernization, Technologies, and Techniques of the Self". *Church History* 73, 4 (December 2004): 792–827.

Gleaner in the Missionary Field, The. 1850–51. London: Chinese Evangelization Society.

Glover, Archibald E. 1904. *A Thousand Miles of Miracle in China: A Personal Record of God's Delivering Power from the Hands of the Imperial Boxers of Shan-si*. London: Hodder and Stoughton.

Goh Ewe Kheng. 1999. "Evaluation on Speaking in Tongues". Letter to Church of Singapore Elders, 25 February 1999.

________. n.d.[a]. "Excellent Way of Using Spiritual Gifts". Unpublished essay.

________. n.d.[b]. "The Wisdom of Operating Spiritual Gift of Tongue in the Church". Pamphlet.

Goh, Robbie. 2003. *Sparks of Grace: The Story of Methodism in Asia*. Singapore: Methodist Church in Singapore.

________. 2005. *Christianity in Southeast Asia*. Singapore: Institute of Southeast Asian Studies.

Gospel Recordings. n.d. *Gospel Recordings Script Manual.* 157 page typescript.

Gosse, Edmund. 1907. *Father and Son: A Study of Two Temperaments*. Reprint. London and New York: Oxford University Press, 1974.

Grace of Jesus Christ Crusade (GJCC). N.d. "The Holy Spirit has Rebuilt the New Testament Church!" Pamphlet.

Grass, Tim. 2006. *Gathering to His Name: The Story of the Open Brethren in Britain and Ireland*. Milton Keynes and Gainsborough, Georgia: Paternoster Press.

________. 2013. "How Fundamentalist were British Brethren during the 1920s?" In *Evangelicalism & Fundamentalism in the United Kingdom during the Twentieth Century*, ed. David W. Bebbington and David Ceri Jones, pp. 115–31. Oxford: Oxford University Press.

Green, Louise. 2013. "Robert Jaffray: Man of Spirit; Man of Power". *Canadian Missiological Resources* 1, 2: 1–7.

Greer, Robert M. 1959. *A History of the Presbyterian Church in Singapore*. Singapore: Malaya Publishing House.

Groves, Anthony Norris. 1828 [1825]. *Christian Devotedness, or The Consideration of Our Saviour's Precept, "Lay not up for yourselves treasures upon earth"*. 2nd ed. London: James Nisbet.

________. 1832. *Journal of a Residence at Bagdad during the years 1830 and 1831*. London: James Nisbet.

________. 1833. *On the Nature of Christian Influence* [abridged]. Originally published by the American Mission Press Bombay. Reprint. Sacramento: Assembly Bookshelf, 2008.

________. 1835. *A Brief Account of the Circumstances of the Tinnevelly Mission*. Sidmouth: J. Harvey and London: J. Nisbet & Co.

Groves, Edward Kennaway. 1906. *George Müller and his Successors*. Bristol.

Groves, Harriet Baynes. 1869. *Memoir of the Late Anthony Norris Groves*. 3rd ed. London: James Nisbet.

Grundmann, Christoffer H. 2005. *Sent to Heal! Emergence and Development of Medical Missions*. Lanham: University Press of America.

Grunlan, Stephen and Marvin K. Mayers. 1988. *Cultural Anthropology: A Christian Perspective*. 2nd ed. Grand Rapids, Michigan: Zondervan Publishing House Academic Books.

Guericke, Heinrich Ernst Ferdinand. 1847. *The Life of A.H. Francke*. Originally published in German in 1827 and translated by Samuel Jackson. London: Henry Bohn.

Guest, Kenneth. 2003. *God in Chinatown: Religion and Survival in New York's Evolving Immigrant Community*. New York: NYU Press.

Gützlaff. Charles [Karl Friedrich August]. 1834. *Journal of Three Voyages Along the Coast of China in 1831, 1832, and 1833 with notices of Siam, Corea, and the Loo-Choo Islands*. London: Frederick Westley and A.H. Davis.

Gützlaff, Karl Friedrich August and Huang, Shijian. 1833–38. 東西洋考每月統記傳 (*Dongxiyang Kao Meiyue Tongji, Zhuan Eastern Western Monthly Magazine*). Reprint, 1997. Beijing. 北京：中華書局 新華書店北京發行所發行.

Hackett, Rosalind and Simon Coleman, ed. 2015. *The Anthropology of Global Pentecostalism and Evangelicalism*. New York: New York University.

Haines, J. Harry. 1962. "A History of Protestant Missions in Malaya during the Nineteenth Century, 1815–1881". Th.D., Princeton Theological Seminary. Ann Arbor, Michigan: University Microfilms Inc.

________. 1965. *Chinese of the Diaspora*. Published for the World Council of Churches, Commission on World Mission and Evangelism. London: Edinburgh House Press.

Hamberg, Theodore. 1854. *The Visions of Hung-siu-tshuen, and the Origin of the Kwang-si Insurrection*. Hong Kong: China Mail Office.

Hanan, Patrick. 2004. *Chinese Fiction of the Nineteenth and Early Twentieth Centuries: Essays by Patrick Hanan*. New York: Columbia University Press.

Hangen, Tona J. 2002. *Redeeming the Dial: Radio, Religion & Popular Culture in America*. Chapel Hill: University of North Carolina Press.

Hannerz, Ulf. 1992. *Cultural Complexity: Studies in the Social Organization of Meaning*. New York: Columbia University Press.

________. 1996. "Kokoschka's Return". In *Transnational Connections: Culture, People, Places*, pp. 65–78. London and New York: Routledge.

Harrison, Brian. 1979. *Waiting for China: The Anglo-Chinese College at Malacca, 1818–1843, and Early Nineteenth-Century Missions*. Hong Kong: Hong Kong University Press.

Hassé, Evelyn R. 1911. *The Moravians*. London: National Council of Evangelical Churches.

Hee En Ming. 2009. "Tan Teck Soon". Singapore Infopedia. Singapore: National Library Board. http://eresources.nlb.gov.sg/infopedia/articles/SIP_1364_2009-02-12.html?s=tan%20teck.

Hefner, Robert W. 2017. "Christians, Conflict, and Citizenship in Muslim Majority Indonesia". *Review of Faith & International Affairs* 15, 1 (March 2017): 91–101.

Herppich, Birgit. 2016. *Pitfalls of Trained Incapacity: The Unintended Effects of Integral Missionary Training in the Basel Mission (1828–1840)*. Cambridge: James Clarker & Co.

Herzog, Frederick. 2003. *European Pietism Reviewed*. Eugene, Oregon: Pickwick Publications.

Hevia, James. 1992. "Leaving a Brand on China: Missionary Discourse in the Wake of the Boxer Movement". *Modern China* 18, 3: 304–32.

Hill, Christopher. 1984. *Turning the World Upside Down: Radical Ideas during the English Revolution.* Harmondsworth: Penguin Books.

Hirono, Miwa. 2008. *Civilizing Missions: International Religious Agencies in China*. New York: Palgrave Macmillan.

Ho Wa Kim. 2003. "Wong, Ruth Hie King". In *Biographical Dictionary of Chinese Women: Twentieth Century 1912–2000*, ed. Lily Xiao Hong Lee, pp. 547–9. Reprint. Abingdon and New York: Routledge, 2015.

Hofmeyr, Isabel. 2004. *The Portable Bunyan: A Transnational History of The Pilgrim's Progress*. Princeton: Princeton University Press.

The Holy Bible, King James Version, containing the Old and New Testaments. 1983. Grand Rapids, Michigan: Zondervan. Printed in Great Britain by Cambridge University Press.

Hong, Elijah [Hong San-chi]. 1993. *Defending the Truth*. Mount Zion: Grace of Jesus Christ Crusade. https://ziongjcc.org/zion/english/index3.htm [accessed 16 October 2018].

________. 1994. "Vessels Who Bring the Dawn of Salvation". Mount Carmel Global Co-worker's Convention, October 1994. https://ziongjcc.org/zion/english/index3.htm [accessed 16 October 2018].

________. 1995. *Building the Church*. Holy Mount Zion: Grace of Jesus Christ Crusade. https://ziongjcc.org/zion/english/index3.htm [accessed 16 October 2018].

Hong Sit. 1999. *My View from a Bridge: The Autobiography of Hong Sit*. Houston, Texas: Blessing Books.

Hopkins, Steven P. 2011. "Patterns from Particularities". *Harvard Divinity Bulletin* 39, 1 & 2. https://bulletin.hds.harvard.edu/articles/winterspring2011/patterns-particularities.

Howard, Maria Crewdson. 1885. *Memorials of John Eliot Howard of Lords Meade*. Tottenman: Ballantyne, Hanson & Co.

Howsam, Leslie. 1991. *Cheap Bibles: Nineteenth-Century Publishing and the British and Foreign Bible Society*. Cambridge: Cambridge University Press.

Huang Jianhui (黃建輝). 2016. "佳美腳蹤： 盡心遵 勉力傳—記王載、王峙" (*Jiamei Jiao zong: Jinxin Zun Mianli Chuan—Ji Wang Zai, Wang Zhi, Beautiful Footsteps: Do Your Best to Follow Them. Remembering Wang Zai, Wang Zhi*). 各期號角 (*Herald Monthly*). 基督教角聲佈道團 (Chinese Christian Herald Centre Australia). August 2016. http://cchc-herald.org/au/?page_id=13473 [accessed 30 November 2018].

Huang Mingming (黃明明). 2010. 福建十二杰 (*Fujian Shi'er Jie, The Fujian Twelve*). Chapter 5, posted 2014-1-6. Blog: *Christian Information*, 基督徒資訊 (*Jidu Tu Zixun*). http://zx.lrcn.org/default.asp?page=187 [accessed 30 November 2018].

Hughes, J.R.T. 1956. "The Commercial Crisis of 1857". *Oxford Economic Papers* New Series 8, 1 (June 1956): 194–222.

Hunt, Robert, Lee Kam Hing, and John Roxborogh, eds. 1992. *Christianity in Malaysia: A Denominational History*. Petaling Jaya: Pelanduk Press.

Hutchison, James. 1986. *Weavers, Miners and the Open Book: A History of Kilsyth*. Cumbernauld, Scotland: Kelvinprint.

Huurdeman, Anton A. 2005. *The Worldwide History of Telecommunications*. Hoboken: Wiley-IEEE Press.

Indian Watchman, and Journal of Biblical Enquiry, and of Religious Intelligence, The. 1860–64. 4 vols. Madras.

Ingrahim, Rev. M. Virgil. 1983. "Last Year in Malaysia". *Brethren Evangelist* 105, 3 (March 1983): 10–1.

Inouye, Melissa Wei-Tsing. 2016. "A Religious Rhetoric of Competing Modernities: Christian Print Culture in Late Qing China". In *Reshaping the Boundaries: The Christian Intersection of China and the West in the Modern Era*, ed. Song Gang, pp. 106–22. Hong Kong: Hong Kong University Press.

________. 2019. *China and the True Jesus: Charisma and Organization in a Chinese Christian Church*. Oxford: Oxford University Press.

Ironside, Henry Allan. 1985. *A Historical Sketch of the Brethren Movement*. Rev. ed. Neptune, New Jersey: Loizeaux Brothers.

James, G.D. 1984. *Missionary Ventures in Malaysia*. 2nd ed. Epping, New South Wales: G.D. James Multi-Media Ltd.

________. 1991. "The Compelling Call to Evangelise". In *Klang Gospel Hall 80th Anniversary Publication*, pp. 8–11. Klang, Malaysia.

Jenkins, Paul. 1982. "Mission History—A Manifesto". *Missiology: An International Review* 10, 2: 199–210.

________. 2000. "The CMS and Basel Mission". In *The Church Mission Society and World Christianity, 1799–1999*, ed. Kevin Ward and Brian Stanley, pp. 43–65. Grand Rapids and Cambridge, UK: William B. Eerdmans Publishing Company.

Jenkins, Philip. 2007. *The Next Christendom: The Coming of Global Christianity*. Oxford: Oxford University Press.

Jenner, Thomas. 1911. *The Nanking Monument of the Beatitutes*. London: William Clower & Sons.

Jia Yuming (贾玉铭). 1921. 神道学 *Shen Dao Xue* (*Study of Divinity*). Three vols. Nanjing: Ling Guan Baoshe

Johnston, Rev. James. 1860. *Glimpses of Missionary Work in China,* Illustrated by engravings from Chinese Pilgrim's Progress w. Introduction. Edinburgh: William P. Kennedy.

Jones, William. 1850. *The Jubilee Memorial of the Religious Tract Society Containing a Record of Its Origin, Proceedings, and Results, A.D. 1799 to A.D. 1849*. London: The Religious Tract Society.

Jupp, James, ed. 2001. "Sri Lanka—Dutch Burghers". In *The Australian People: An Encyclopedia of the Nations, Its People and Their Origins*, pp. 694–5. Cambridge: Cambridge University Press.

Kaiser, Andrew T. 2016. *The Rushing on of the Purposes of God: Christian Missions in Shanxi since 1876*. Eugene, Oregon: Pickwick Publications.

Kaung, Stephen. n.d. "Life of Watchman Nee". Three audiotapes. Singapore: Great Joy Media Centre.

________. n.d. "God's Eternal Purpose and the Overcomers" (1). PDF file. www.westcoastchristianconference.com/2000/transcript/WCCC2000_SKaung1.pdf [accessed 4 November 2018].

Keswick Convention. 1938. *Notes of the Addresses Revised by the Speakers and Published by Authority of the Trustees.* London and Glasgow: Pickering & Inglis Ltd.

________. 1939. *Notes of the Addresses Revised by the Speakers and Published by Authority of the Trustees.* London and Glasgow: Pickering & Inglis Ltd.

Khoo Oon Teik. 1995. "Obituary: Dr. Benjamin Chew 1907–1994". *Singapore Medical Journal* 36 (1995): 112.

Khoo Salma Nasution. 2006. *More than Merchants: A History of the German-speaking Community in Penang.* Penang: Areca Books.

Kim Chong Pae. 2004. "Trends in Cross-cultural Training in Asia: An Analysis of ACTI Graduates 1985–2004". *Asian Mission* October 2004: 10–2.

Kinnear, Angus I. 1973. *Against the Tide: The Story of Watchman Nee.* Eastbourne, Sussex: Kingsway Publications.

Klang Gospel Hall 80th Anniversary 1911–1991. 1991. Klang, Malaysia.

Knuesel, Arianne. 2007. "British Diplomacy and the Telegraph in Nineteenth-Century China". *Diplomacy & Statecraft* 18, 3 (2007): 517–37.

Kong Duen Yee [Mui Yee]. 1964. *The Golden Lampstand.* Vol. 1.

________. 1978a. "The New Testament Church In Accordance with God's Will" (An Epistle to the Churches in Singapore and Malaysia, 5 July 1964). Excerpt from *The Golden Lampstand* Vol. I (pp. 16–22 in the original; retranslated and issued as a booklet). Taipei: Grace of Jesus Christ Crusade, 19 pp.

________. 1978b. "The Re-establishment of the New Testament Church is Entirely the Accomplishment of the Holy Spirit" (Letter to Preacher in Taiwan, 8 October 1964). *The Golden Candlestick.* Vol. I, pp. 23–9. Taipei: Grace of Jesus Christ Crusade.

________. 1979. *Acts of the Holy Spirit: Sequel to a Life to Testify the Full Gospel of Jesus Christ* Vol. I. Taipei: Grace of Jesus Christ Crusade.

________. 1995. "Christ and the Church". Message presented during the 1965 Convention at the Church of Hong Kong. Reprinted in *Building the Church*, by Elijah Hong, pp. 3–18. Mount Zion, Kaohsiung, Taiwan: Grace of Jesus Christ Crusade.

________. 1996. A *Living Testimony to the Truth: The Powerful Testimony of a Hong Kong Movie Star Mui Yee Chosen and Raised and Used by God in the East.* 1968. 3rd ed. Mount Zion, Kaohsiung, Taiwan: Grace of Jesus Christ Crusade.

Koschorke, Klaus. 2014. "New Maps of the History of World Christianity: Current Challenges and Future Perspectives". *Theology Today* 71, 2: 178–91.

Krapohl, Robert H. 1997. Review of Robert Baylis. "My People: The History of Those Christians Sometimes Called Plymouth Brethren". *Church History: Studies in Christianity and Culture* 66: 397–8.

Kratke, Michael R. 2008. "Marx's 'books of crisis' of 1857–8". In *Karl Marx's Grundrisse: Foundations of the Critique of Political Economy 150 years later*, ed. Marcello Musto, pp. 169–75. Abingdon and New York: Routledge

Krysko, Michael A. 2011. *American Radio in China: International Encounters with Technology and Communications, 1919–41*. New York: Palgrave Macmillan.

Kverndal, Roald. 2004. "Sowing by Sea: Empowering Seafarers with the Gospel". In *Sowing the Word: The Cultural Impact of the British and Foreign Bible Society*, ed. Stephen Batalden, Kathleen Cann, and John Dean. Sheffield: Sheffield Phoenix Press.

Kwok Wai Luan. 2014. "The Christ-human and Jia Yuming's Doctrine of Sanctification: A Case Study in the Confucianisation of Chinese Fundamentalist Christianity". *Studies in World Christianity* 20, 2: 145–65.

________. 2017. "Christ-Human and Jia Yuming's Doctrine of Sanctification". In *Sinicizing Christianity*, ed. Zheng Yangwen, pp. 109–37. Leiden/Boston: Brill.

Kyle, Richard. 1998. *Awaiting the Millennium: A History of End-time Thinking.* Leicester: Inter-varsity Press.

Lai Ah Eng, ed. 2005. *Facing Faiths, Crossing Cultures: Key Trends and Issues in a Multicultural World. Dialogues with Chandra Muzaffar, Ibrahim Abu-Rabi' and Jean DeBernardi*. Singapore: Institute of Policy Studies and SNP-reference.

________, ed. 2008. *Religious Diversity and Harmony in Singapore*. Singapore: Institute of Southeast Asian Studies.

Laegreid, Marte Dronen. 2015. "Missions, Families and the Life Course of Anna Sofie Jakobsen Cheng (1860–1911)". MA Thesis in History Department of AHKR, University of Bergen.

Lang, George Henry. 1925. *Departure: A Warning and an Appeal Addressed by one of Themselves Mainly to Christians Known as Open Brethren*. London.

________. 1939. *The History and Diaries of an Indian Christian (J.C. Aroolappen)*. Reprint. Miami Springs, Florida: Scheottle Publishing Co, 1988.

________. 1949. *Anthony Norris Groves: Saint and Pioneer. A Combined study of a Man of God and of the Original Principles and Practices of THE BRETHREN with Applications to Present Conditions*. 2nd ed. London: Wyman & Sons.

Langdon, Marcus. 2017. *Epitaph: The Northam Road Protestant Cemetery, George Town, Penang* (2 vols). Penang: George Town World Heritage Inc.

Larsen, Timothy. 1998. "'Living by Faith': A History of Brethren Practice". *Brethren Archivists and Historians Network Review (BAHNR)* 1: 67–102.

Latimer, Robert Sloan. 1907. *Dr. Baedeker: And His Apostolic Work in Russia*. London: Morgan and Scott.

Latourette, Kenneth Scott. 1929. *A History of Christian Missions in China*. Reprint. New York: Russell & Russell, 1967.

________. 1953. *A History of Christianity*. New York: Harper and Row.

Lau, Earnest. 2008. *From Mission to Church: The Evolution of the Methodist Church in Singapore: 1885–1976*. Singapore: Genesis Books.

Lee Hwee Hoon. 2010. "Tan See Boo". Singapore Infopedia. Singapore: National Library Board. http://eresources.nlb.gov.sg/infopedia/articles/SIP_1404_2009-01-05.html [accessed 29 May 2018].

Lee Kam Hing. 1992. "The Christian Brethren". In *Christianity in Malaysia: A Denominational History*, ed. Robert Hunt, Lee Kam Hing, and John Roxborogh, pp. 107–41. Petaling Jaya: Pelanduk Press.

Lee Ken Ang. 1989. "Watchman Nee: A Study of His Major Theological Themes". PhD thesis, Westminster Theological Seminary.

Lee, Witness. 1991. *Watchman Nee—A Seer of the Divine Revelation in the Present Age*. Anaheim, CA: Living Stream Ministry.

________. 2004. *Crucial Words of Leading in the Lord's Recovery, Book 1: The Vision and Definite Steps for the Practice of the New Way*. Anaheim, CA: Living Stream Ministry.

Legge, James. 1880. *The Religions of China*. London: Hoddern and Stoughton.

Lenin, Vladimir Il'ich. 1965 [1908]. "Leo Tolstoy as the Mirror of the Russian Revolution". In *Lenin Collected Works*, Vol. 15, pp. 202–9. Moscow: Progress Publishers.

Letkeman, Della. 2000. *No Time to Quit: The Biography of R.E. Harlow*. Scarborough, Ontario: Everyday Publications.

Leung, Philip Yuen-Sang. 2002. "Mission History versus Church History". In *Enlarging the Story: Perspectives on Writing World Christian History*, ed. Wilbert R. Shenk, pp. 54–74. Maryknoll: Orbis Books.

Levenson, Joseph R. 1972 [1958, 1964, 1965]. *Confucian China and Its Modern Fate: A Trilogy*. Berkeley: University of California Press.

Lewis, Donald M. 1986. *Lighten Their Darkness: The Evangelical Mission to Working-Class London, 1828–1860*. New York: Greenwood Press.

________. 2009. *The Origins of Christian Zionism: Lord Shaftesbury and Evangelical Support for a Jewish Homeland*. Cambridge: Cambridge University Press.

Lewis, Su Lin. 2016. *Cities in Motion: Urban Life and Cosmopolitanism in Southeast Asia, 1920–1940*. Cambridge: Cambridge University Press.

Lewis, Thomas. 1818. *All for Christ and the Good of Souls: A Sermon occasioned by the Death of Mrs. Mead, wife of the Rev. Charles Mead, Missionary, delivered on Sunday the 24th of May, 1818, at Chichester*. London: Baynes and Hamilton.

Li Changchuan and Zhonghua Shi. 1936. 南洋群島現勢圖 (*Nanyang Qundao xian shi tu*). Shanghai, China: Shanghai shijie yu dixue she: Ge fu shi jie shu ju. Map. https://www.loc.gov/item/2006626412/.

Li Laura Tyson. 2006. *Madame Chiang Kai-shek: China's Eternal First Lady*. New York: Grove Press.

Li Yading. 2005–18. "1901–1985 Andrew Gih Ji Zhiwen 20th-century Chinese Evangelical Protestant leader, evangelist, revivalist and philanthropist". http://bdcconline.net/en/stories/andrew-gih [accessed 3 September 2018].

Lian Xi. 2004. "The Search for Chinese Christianity in the Republican Period (1912–1949)". *Modern Asian Studies* 38, 4: 851–98.

________. 2010. *Redeemed by Fire: The Rise of Popular Christianity in Modern China*. New Haven and London: Yale University Press.

Lim Boon Keng [Wen Ching]. 1901. *The Chinese Crisis from Within*. London: Grant Richards.

Lim, Jason. 2004. "Assumptions and Evidence: The Case of Philip Robinson (1830–1886)". *Brethren Archivists and Historians Network Review* [*BAHNR*] 3: 18–47.

________. 2006. "The Early Years of a New Assembly: Bethesda Gospel Hall, Singapore, 1864–1914". In *The Growth of the Brethren Movement: National and International Experiences Essays in Honor of Harold H. Rowdon*, ed. Neil T.R. Dickson and Tim Grass, pp. 145–53. Eugene, Oregon: Wipf & Stock.

Lim, Timothy T.N. 2015. "Pentecostalism in Singapore and Malaysia: Past, Present and Future". In *Global Renewal Christianity: Spirit-Empowered Movements, Past, Present, and Future*, Vol. 1: Asia and Oceania, ed. Vinson Synan, Amos Yong, and J. Kwabena Asamoah-Gyadu, pp. 126–35. Lake Mary, Florida: Charisma House.

Lin Wei-ping. 2008. "Conceptualizing Gods Through Statues: A Study of Personification and Localization in Taiwan". *Comparative Studies in Society and History* 50, 2 (April 2008): 454–77.

Lincoln, Waldo. 1902. *Genealogy of the Waldo Family: A Record of Descendants of Cornelius Waldo of Ipswich Mass. From 1647 to 1900*. Worcester, MA: Press of Charles Hamilton.

Lineham, Peter J. 1982. "Tongues Must Cease: The Brethren and the Charismatic Movement in New Zealand". *Christian Brethren Review* 96 (December 1982). Biblicalstudies.org.uk [accessed 22 June 2016].

________. 2006. "Brethren Revivalism: A Second Look at New Zealand". In *The Growth of the Brethren Movement: National and International Experiences,* ed. Neil T.R. Dickson and Tim Grass, pp. 154–75. Eugene, Oregon: Wipf & Stock.

Links of Help with Other Lands. 1911–35. Edited by T. Mortimore Sparks. Glasgow: Pickering & Inglis.

Liu Wennan 2013. "Redefining the Moral and Legal Roles of the State in Everyday Life: The New Life Movement in China in the Mid-1930s". *Cross-Currents: East Asian History and Culture Review* 2, 2 (November): 335–65.

Logan, James Richardson. 1857. *Government Records Inquiry into the Chinese Grievances at Penang*. Supplement to the *Singapore Free Press*. 10 December 1857.

London Missionary Society. 1824. "The Case of John Smith One of the Missionaries at Demerara, As Given by the Directors of the London Missionary Society with some Prefatory Remarks". Pamphlet. Newcastle: J. Clark.

Lovett, Richard. 1899. *The History of the London Missionary Society 1795–1895*. Two vols. London: Henry Frowde.

Lovitt, Lucy. 1904. *A Brief Memoir of Lucy Elizabeth Lovitt by Her Two Sisters*. Edinburgh.

Lozada, Eriberto P., Jr. 2001. *God Aboveground: Catholic Church, Postsocialist State, and Transnational Processes in a Chinese Village*. Stanford: Stanford University Press.

Lu Xun. 1936. 故事新編 (*Gushi Xinbian, Old Tales Retold*). 2nd ed. Peking: Foreign Languages Press, 1972.

Lumsdaine, David H., ed. 2009. *Evangelical Christianity and Democracy in Asia*. Oxford: Oxford University Press.

Lutz, Jessie. 1985. "Karl F.A. Gutzlaff: Missionary Entrepreneur". In *Christianity in China: Early Protestant Missionary Writings*, ed. Suzanne Wilson Barnett and John King Fairbank, pp. 61–87. Published by The Committee on American-East Asian Relations of the Department of History and the Council on East Asian Studies/ Harvard University. Cambridge: Harvard University Press.

________. 2008. *Opening China: Karl F.A. Gutzlaff and Sino-Western Relations, 1827–1852*. Grand Rapids, Michigan: WM. B Eerdmans Publishing Co.

Lutz, Jessie G. and Rolland Ray Lutz. 1998. *Hakka Chinese Confront Protestant Christianity, 1850–1900 With the Autobiographies of Eight Hakka Christians and Commentary*. Armonk, New York: M.E. Sharpe.

MacDonald, William. 1973a. *Christ Loved the Church*. Rev. ed. Kansas City: Walterick Publishers.

________. 1973b. *Revelation: Visions of Judgment and Glory*. Rev. ed. Dubuque: Emmaus Correspondence School.

________. n.d. "William MacDonald Personal Information". Online Library of Brethren Writers. http://www.plymouthbrethren.org/user/6 [accessed 21 June 2018].

Mahan, Alfred Thayer. 1918. *The Influence of Sea Power upon History 1660–1783*. 12th ed. Boston: Little, Brown and Co.

Mahoney, Ralph. 1998. "World MAP Bible Teaching: The Great Crisis in World Evangelism". *WMAP Digest* (October).

Marchant, L.R. 1966. *A Guide to the Archives and Records of Protestant Christian Missions from the British Isles to China, 1796–1914*. Nedlands: University of Western Australia Press.

Marks, Henry Freeman. 1953. *Reminiscences: The Call to Serve the Lord in Malaya and Subsequent Years of Service from 1900–1952*. Privately printed booklet. Vancouver, B.C.

Martin, David. 2002. *Pentecostalism: The World Their Parish*. Oxford and Malden, MA: Blackwell Publishers.

Mauss, Marcel. 1909 [2003]. *On Prayer*, ed. W.S.F. Pickering. Translated by Susan Leslie. New York: Durkheim Press/Berghahn Books.

________. 1925 [1967]. *The Gift: Forms and Functions of Exchange in Archaic Societies*. Translated by Ian Cunnison, and with an Introduction by E.E. Evans-Pritchard. New York: W.W. Norton and Company.

Maxwell, Ian Douglas. 1991. "Civilization or Christianity? The Scottish Debate on Mission Methods, 1750–1835". In *Christian Missions and the Enlightenment*, ed. Brian Stanley, pp. 123–40. Grand Rapids: William B. Eerdmans Publishing Co. and Richmond, Surrey: Curzon Press Ltd.

May, Thomas Erskine. 1863 [1912]. *The Constitutional History of England: Since the Accession of George the Third*. Vol. 2, British Law: Consitutional Law. London: Longmans, Green & Co.

Mazur, Mary G. 2007. "Discontinuous Continuity: The Beginnings of a New Synthesis of 'General History' in 20th-Century China". In *The Politics of Historical Production in Late Qing and Republican China*, ed. Tze-ki Hon and Robert Culp, pp. 109–42. Leiden: Brill.

Medhurst, Walter Henry. 1832. *A Dictionary of the Hok-këèn dialect of the Chinese language, according to the reading and colloquial idioms: containing about 12,000 characters. Accompanied by a short statistical account of Hok-këèn*. Batavia: East India Company Press.

Meyer, Birgit. 1994. "Beyond Syncretism: Translation and Diabolization in the Appropriation of Protestantism in Africa". In *Syncretism/Anti-syncretism: The Politics of Religious Synthesis*, ed. Charles Stewart and Rosalind Shaw, pp. 45–68. London: Routledge.

Midgley, Clare. 2007. *Feminism and Empire: Women Activists in Imperial Britain, 1790–1865*. London and New York: Routledge.

Mission Chapel (Farquhar Street, Penang). 1890–1920. *Marriage Register Book*. Penang.

Mission Chapel (Farquhar Street, Penang) and Burmah Road Gospel Hall. 1920–57. *Marriage Register Book*. Penang.

Missionary Echo, The. 1872–84. Bath: Echoes of Service.

Missionary Reporter, The. 1853–61. Edited by James Van Sommer. London.

Morgan, George E. 1909. *"A Veteran in Revival" R.C. Morgan: His Life and Times*. New York: Gospel Publishing House.

Moore, Sally Falk. 1987. "Explaining the Present: Theoretical Dilemmas in Processual Ethnography". *American Ethnologist* 14, 4: 727–36.

________. 1994. "The Ethnography of the Present and the Analysis of Process". In *Assessing Cultural Anthropology*, ed. Robert Borofsky, pp. 362–76. New York: McGraw-Hill.

Morrison, Eliza. 1839. *Memoirs of the Life and Labours of Robert Morrison*. Vol. II. London: Longman, Orme, Brown and Longmans.

Müller, George. 1837–86. *Narrative of the Lord's Dealings with George Müller*, Parts I–VI (1837, 1841, 1845, 1856, 186?, 1886).

________. 1840. *Narrative of the Lord's Dealings with George Müller*, written by himself, First Part, 5th ed. London: J. Nisbet & Co, 1855.

________. 1861. *The Life of Trust being a Narrative of the Lord's Dealings with George Müller*. Edited and condensed by Rev. H. Lincoln Wayland. Boston: Gould and Lincoln.

________. 1984. *The Autobiography of George Müller*. New Kensington: Whitaker House.

Murray, Rev. W. 1921. "Religious Singapore". In *One Hundred Years of Singapore*, vol. II, ed. Walter Makepeace, Gilbert E. Brook, and Roland St. J. Braddell, pp. 235–77. Reprint. Singapore: Oxford University Press, 1991.

National Council of Churches of Singapore 1998. *A Guide to Churches and Christian Organisations in Singapore 1999–2000*. Singapore: National Council of Churches of Singapore.

________. 2003. *A Guide to Churches and Christian Organizations in Singapore*. Singapore.

Nee, Watchman. 1938. 工作的再思 *(Gongzuo de Zai Si, Rethinking our Work [The Normal Christian Church Life*]). Shanghai: Gospel Book Room.

________. 1939. *Concerning our Missions*. London: Witness & Testimony Publishing.

________. 1957. *The Normal Christian Life*. Preface by Angus I. Kinnear. Bombay: Gospel Literature Service.

________. 1982 [1939]. *The Church and The Work*. 3 vols. Rev. ed. New York: Christian Fellowship Publishers, Inc.

________. 1993a. *The Collected Works of Watchman Nee Set 2 Vol. 25: Collection of Newsletters (1)*. Anaheim, CA: The Living Stream Ministry.

________. 1993b. *The Collected Works of Watchman Nee Set 2 Vol. 26: Collection of Newsletters (2) & Watchman Nee's Testimony.* Anaheim, CA: The Living Stream Ministry.

________. 1993c. *The Collected Works of Watchman Nee Set 2 Middle Period (1934–1942), vol. 31: The Open Door (1),* issues 1–8. Anaheim, CA: The Living Stream Ministry.

________. 1993d. *The Collected Works of Watchman Nee Set 2 Middle Period (1934–1942), vol. 32: The Open Door (2),* issues 9–19. Anaheim, CA: The Living Stream Ministry.

Neill, Stephen. 1985. *A History of Christianity in India, 1707–1858.* Cambridge: Cambridge University Press.

________. 1986. *A History of Christian Missions.* 2nd ed., revised by Owen Chadwick. Reprint. London: Penguin Books, 1990.

News at a Glance. 1949. "Pastor Wilson Wang at First Church, Minneapolis". *Evangelical Beacon* 18, 22: 6. Evangelical Free Church of America.

Nida, Eugene. 1954. *Customs and Cultures: Anthropology for Christian Missions.* New York: Harper and Brothers.

Nienkirchen, Charles W. 2010. *A.B. Simpson and the Pentecostal Movement: A Study in Continuity, Crisis, and Change.* Eugene, Oregon: Wipf & Stock.

Noll, Mark A. 2001. *American Evangelical Christianity: An Introduction.* Oxford: Blackwell Publisher.

Northcott, Michael S. 1992. "Two Hundred Years of Anglican Mission". In *Christianity in Malaysia: A Denominational History,* ed. Robert Hunt, Lee Kam Hing, and John Roxborogh, pp. 34–74. Petaling Jaya: Pelanduk Publications.

Oberman, Heiko. 1979. "Preface" to *True Christianity,* by Johann Arndt. Translation and Introduction by Peter Erb, pp. xi–xvii. New York: Paulist Press.

Obituary. 1837. "Joseph Tarn". *The Evangelical Magazine and Missionary Chronicle,* Vol. XV, New Series, May 1837, pp. 212–7. London: Thomas Ward.

________. 1845. "A Sketch of the Life and Labours of the Rev. T. Beighton, Twenty-six years a Missionary to the Heathen". In *The Evangelical Magazine and Missionary Chronicle,* Vol. XXIII, New Series, March 1845, pp. 113–22 and April 1845, pp. 169–75. London: Thomas Ward.

________. 1868. "Rev. William Burns, China". *The Free Church of Scotland Monthly Record* (1 August 1868): 184.

________. 1884. "John Eliot Howard". Reprinted from the *Chemist and Druggist of London. Pharmaceutical Record: A Semi-Monthly Journal of Pharmacy, Chemistry, Materia Medica, and the Allied Sciences* 4, 2 (15 January 1884): 46.

Opper, Marc. 2018. "Revolution Defeated: The Collapse of the Chinese Soviet Republic". *Twentieth-Century China* 43, 1 (January 2018): 45–66.

Orr, James Edwin. 1955. *The Second Evangelical Awakening*. London: Marshall, Morgan & Scott.

________. 1964. *The Second Evangelical Awakening: An Account of the Second Worldwide Evangelical Revival Beginning in the Mid-nineteenth Century*, Rev. ed. London: Marshall, Morgan & Scott.

Orsler, M. n.d. *History of the Province Wellesley Mission Institution*. Penang: Georgetown Printers Ltd.

Osteen, Joel. 1978. *Rivers of Living Waters*. Humble, Texas: John Osteen Publications.

O'Sullivan, Leona. 1984. "The London Missionary Society: A Written Record of Missionaries and Printing Presses in the Straits Settlements, 1815–1847". *Journal of the Malaysian Branch of the Royal Asiatic Society* 57, 2 (247): 61–104.

OED Online/Oxford English Dictionary. 2018. Oxford: Oxford University Press.

Pew Forum. 2011. "Global Christianity: A Report on the Size and Distribution of the World's Christian Population". http://www.pewforum.org/2011/12/19/global-christianity-movements-and-denominations/ [accessed 7 February 2015].

Phang Swee Lan. 1981. *Reminiscences: Taiping Gospel Hall 1880–1980*. Taiping: Taiping Gospel Hall.

Pickering, Henry. 1918. *Chief Men Among the Brethren*. Reprint. Neptune, NJ: Loizeaux Brothers, Inc., 1996.

Pierson, Arthur T. 1899. *George Müller of Bristol and His Witness to a Prayer-Hearing God*. New York: The Baker and Taylor Company.

________, ed. 1909. *The Missionary Review of the World*, Vol. XXII, New Series (January–December 1909). New York: Funk & Wagnalls Co.

Piggin, Stuart. 1994. "The History of Revivals in Australia". In *Re-Visioning Australian Colonial Christianity: New Essays in the Australian Christian Experience 1788–1900*, ed. Mark Hutchinson and Edmund Campion. Studies in Australian Christianity Vol. 1. Sydney: Centre for the Study of Australian Christianity.

Pigott, C.A. 1903. *Steadfast Unto Death or Martyed for China: Memorials of Thomas Wellesley and Jessie Pigott*. London: The Religious Tract Society.

Pinson, Koppel S. 1934. *Pietism as a Factor in the Rise of German Nationalism*. New York: Columbia University Press.

Pitcher, Philip Wilson. 1893. *Fifty Years in Amoy or, a History of the Amoy Mission, China*. Board of Publication of the Reformed Church in America.

Porter, Andrew. 2004. *Religion versus Empire? British Protestant Missionaries and Overseas Expansion, 1700–1914*. Manchester and New York: Manchester University Press.

Porteus, Beilby, Lord Bishop of London. 1801. "A Summary of the Principal Evidences for the Truth, And Divine Origin, of the Christian Revelation". 3rd ed. New York: Isaac Collins.

Pousson, Edward K. 1992. *Spreading the Flame: Charismatic Churches and Missions Today*. Grand Rapids: Zondervan Publishing House.

Prime, Edward Dorr Griffin. 1874. *Around the World: Sketches of Travel Through Many Lands and Over Many Seas.* New York: Harper & Bros.

Purcell, Victor. 1948. *The Chinese in Malaya.* Reprint. Kuala Lumpur: Oxford University Press, 1967.

Putten, Jan Van Der. 2006. "Abdullah Munsyi and the Missionaries". *Bijdragen tot de Taal-, Land- en Volkenkunde* 162-4 (2006): 407–40.

Ramerini, Marco. 1998. "The Dutch Burghers of Sri Lanka. Dutch Ceylon". http://www.colonialvoyage.com/dutch-burghers-sri-lanka-dutch-ceylon/ [accessed 7 February 2015].

Reid, Rev. William. 1876. *Plymouth Brethrenism Unveiled and Refuted.* Edinburgh: William Oliphant & Co.

The Revival: A Record of Events [published Thursday] and a Summary of Events [published Saturday] Connected with the Present Revival of Religion. 1859–70. London: Morgan and Chase.

Rhenius, Charles Theophilus Ewald. 1834. "A Review of a Work Entitled the Church; Her Daughters and Handmaidens, Her Pastors and People, &c". Tinevelly. Reprinted in 1835. London: J. Harvey.

Rhenius, Johann. 1841. *Memoir of the Rev. C.T.E. Rhenius comprising Extracts from his Journal and Correspondence, with Details of Missionary Proceedings in South India.* London: James Nisbet and Co.

Richard, Timothy. 1916. *Forty-Five Years in China: Reminiscences.* New York: Frederick A. Stokes Co.

Robbins, Joel. 2004. *Becoming Sinners: Christianity and Moral Torment in a Papua New Guinea Society.* Berkeley: University of California Press.

Robert, Dana L. 2000. "Shifting Southward: Global Christianity Since 1945". *International Bulletin of Missionary Research* (April 2000): 50–8.

________, ed. 2008. *Converting Colonialism: Visions and Realities in Mission History, 1706–1914.* Grand Rapids, Michigan/Cambridge: William B. Eerdmans Publishing Company.

Roberts, Dana. 2005. *Secrets of Watchman Nee.* Orlando: Bridge-Logos.

Roberts, Kyle. 2006. "Locating Popular Religion in the Evangelical Tract: The Roots and Routes of The Dairyman's Daughter". *Early American Studies* 4, 1 (Spring 2006): 233–70.

Rogers, Mark. 2013. "End Times Innovator: Paul Rader and Evangelical Missions". *International Bulletin of Missionary Research* 37, 1 (January): 17–24.

Roland, Joan G. 2017. *The Jewish Communities of India: Identity in a Colonial Era.* 2nd ed. New York: Routledge.

Ross, Elizabeth A. 1980. “Victorian Medicine in Penang”. *Malaysia in History* 23: 84–90.

Rowdon, Harold H. 1967. *The Origins of the Brethren 1825–1850*. London: Pickering & Inglis.

________. 1989. “Into All the World: Papers on World Mission Today”. *Christian Brethren Review* No. 40. Exeter: The Paternoster Press.

Roxborogh, John. 1992. “The Roman Catholic Church”. In *Christianity in Malaysia: A Denominational History*, ed. Robert Hunt, Lee Kam Hing, and John Roxborogh, pp. 1–33. Petaling Jaya: Pelanduk Publications.

Rubinstein, Murray A. 1994. “The New Testament Church and the Taiwanese Protestant Community”. In *The Other Taiwan: 1945 to the Present*, ed. Murray Rubinstein, pp. 445–73. Armonk, New York: M.E. Sharpe Press.

________. 1996a. *The Origins of the Anglo-American Missionary Enterprise in China, 1807–1840*. Lanham, MC and London: The Scarecrow Press.

________. 1996b. “Holy Spirit Taiwan: Pentecostal and Charismatic Christianity in the Republic of China”. In *Christianity in China from the Eighteenth Century to the Present*, ed. Daniel H. Bays, pp. 353–66. Stanford: Stanford University Press.

Ryrie, Charles C. 1953. *The Basis of the Premillennial Faith*. Neptune: Loizeaux Brothers.

________. 1996. “Dispensationalism”. In *Dictionary of Premillennial Theology*, ed. Mal Couch, pp. 93–8. Grand Rapids: Kregel Publications.

Sahlins, Marshall. 1981. *Historical Metaphors and Mythical Realities: Structure in the Early History of the Sandwich Islands Kingdom*. Ann Arbor: University of Michigan Press.

________. 1985. *Islands of History*. Chicago: University of Chicago Press.

Sanneh, Lamin. 2005. “Introduction: The Changing Face of Christianity: The Cultural Impetus of a World Religion”. In *The Changing Face of Christianity: Africa, the West, and the World*, ed. Lamin Sanneh and Joel A. Carpenter, pp. 3–18. Oxford: Oxford University Press.

________. 2008. *Disciples of All Nations: Pillars of World Christianity*. Oxford: Oxford University Press.

Sapir, Edward. 1924. “Culture, Genuine and Spurious”. *The American Journal of Sociology* 29, 4 (January 1924): 401–29.

Sawatsky, Rodney J. 2006. “Evangelical and Fundamentalist Movements”. Canadian Encyclopedia. http://www.thecanadianencyclopedia.ca/en/article/evangelical-and-fundamentalist-movements/ [accessed 20 May 2018].

Scott, David W. 2016. *Mission as Globalization: Methodists in Southeast Asia at the Turn of the Twentieth Century*. Lanham: Lexington Books.

Scott, Hew, 1925. “Cookney (Q.S.) Alexander Grant”. *Fasti Ecclesiae Scoticanae: Vol. V Synods of Fife, and of Angus and Mearns*, p. 458. New ed. Edinburgh: Oliver and

Boyd. http://www.archive.org/stream/fastiecclesiaesc05scot#page/458/mode/1up [accessed 9 August 2018].

Scott, P.G. 1972. "Richard Cope Morgan, Religious Periodicals, and the Pontifex Factor". *Victorian Periodicals Newsletter* No. 16 [Vol. 5, No. 2] (June 1972): 1–14.

Scriptural Knowledge Institution (SKI) [George Müller]. 1860. *Brief Narrative of Facts relative to The New Orphan Homes of Ashley Down Bristol and the Other Objects of the Scriptural Knowledge Institution for Home and Abroad*. 21st report (26 May 1859–26 May 1860). London: James Nisbet and Co.

________. 1862. 23rd report (26 May 1861–26 May 1862).

________. 1863. 24th report (26 May 1862–26 May 1863).

________. 1864. 25th report (26 May 1863–26 May 1864).

________. 1867. 28th report (26 May 1866–26 May 1867).

________. 1869. 30th report (26 May 1868–26 May 1869).

________. 1870. 31st report (26 May 1869–26 May 1870).

________. 1871. 32nd report (26 May 1870–26 May 1871).

________. 1872. 33rd report (26 May 1871–26 May 1872).

________. 1873. 34th report (26 May 1872–26 May 1873).

________. 1905. 66th report (26 May 1904–26 May 1903).

Seow Yin Kheam, Eugene. 萧寅谦 1997. 追本朔源：新加坡福音堂(弟兄会)华文教会的源及展 (*Tracing to the Source: The Origin and Development of the Chinese Church of the Evangelical Church of Singapore [the Brethren]*). Singapore: The Singapore Gospel Halls Hokkien Speaking Assembly. 新加坡：宏茂桥福音堂 (Singapore: Ang Mo Kio Gospel Hall).

Seton, Rosemary. 2013. *Western Daughters in Eastern Lands: British Missionary Women in Asia*. Santa Barbara, CA: Praeger.

Sharrock, Roger. 1948. "Spiritual Autobiography in the Pilgrim's Progress". *Review of English Studies* 24 (April 1948): 102–20.

圣经报 *Shengjing Bao*. 1918, 1936–41, 1947–51, 1954. Reprint, 2006. 北京：全国图书馆文献缩微复制中心 Beijing: Quanguo Tushuguan Wenxian Suowei Fuzhi Zhongxin (National Library Document Microcopy Center).

Shih, Toong Siong. 2004. *The Foochows of Sitiawan: A Historical Perspective*. Sitiawan, Perak: Persatuan Kutien Daerah Manjung.

Short, Arthur Rendle. n.d. *A Modern Experiment in Apostolic Missions*. Bristol: W.H. Harris.

Simmel, George. 1950. *The Sociology of George Simmel*. Translated, edited, and with an Introduction by Kurt H. Wolff. New York: Free Press.

Sims, A., ed. n.d. *George Mueller Man of Faith*. Singapore: The Navigators [reprinted by permission of Zondervan Publishing House].

Singapore Free Press. 1960. "Made Toothpaste—Now Camera Importers". 3 June 1960: 8.

Sinitiere, Phillip Luke. 2015. *Salvation with a Smile: Joel Osteen, Lakewood Church, and American Christianity*. New York: New York University Press.

SKI, see Scriptural Knowledge Institution.

Sng, Bobby E.K. 2003. *In His Good Time: The Story of the Church in Singapore, 1819–2002*. 3rd ed. Singapore: Bible Society of Singapore and Graduates' Christian Fellowship.

Society for Promoting Female Education in China, India, and the East (London) [Female Education Society or FES]. 1847. *History of the Society for Promoting Female Education in the East: Established in the Year 1834*, with a preface by Baptist Wriothesley Noel. London: E. Suter.

Spence, Jonathan D. 1996. *God's Chinese Son: The Taiping Heavenly Kingdom of Hong Xiuquan*. New York: W.W. Norton & Company.

Stanley, Brian. 1991. "Christianity and Civilization in English Evangelical Mission Thought, 1792–1857". In *Christian Missions and the Enlightenment*, ed. Brian Stanley, pp. 169–97. Grand Rapids: William B. Eerdmans Publishing Co. and Richmond, Surrey: Curzon Press Ltd.

________. 2018. *Christianity in the Twentieth Century: A World History*. Princeton: Princeton University Press.

Singapore Department of Statistics. 2011. *Census of Population 2010 Statistical Release 1 Demographic Characteristics, Education, Language and Religion*. Singapore.

Stoeffler, F. Ernest. 1973. *German Pietism during the Eighteenth Century*. Leiden: E.J. Brill.

Stoler, Ann Laura. 1985. *Capitalism and Confrontation in Sumatra's Plantation Belt, 1870–1979*. Ann Arbor: University of Michigan Press.

Stunt, Timothy C.F. 1967. "James Van Sommer, An Undenominational Christian and Man of Prayer". *Christian Brethren Research Fellowship Journal* 16 (August 1967): 2–8.

________. 2000. *From Awakening to Secession: Radical Evangelicals in Switzerland and Britain, 1815–35*. Edinburgh: T&T Clark.

________. 2014. "Brethren and the Armed Services". In *Culture, Spirituality, and the Brethren*, ed. Neil T.R. Dickson and T.J. Marinello, pp. 79–100. Troon, Ayrshire: BAHN (Brethren Archivists and Historians Network).

________. 2015. *The Elusive Quest of the Spiritual Malcontent: Some Early Nineteenth Century Ecclesiastical Mavericks*. Eugene, Oregon: Wipp & Stock.

Stunt, W.T., A. Pulleng, G.P. Simmons, D.K. Boak, and S.F. Warren. 1972. *Turning the World Upside Down: A Century of Missionary Endeavor*. Bath: Echoes of Service.

Summerton, Neil. 2003. "George Müller and the Scriptural Knowledge Institution". Unpublished paper.

________. 2016. "George Müller and the Promotion of Mission". In *The Brethren and Mission: Essays in Honour of Timothy C.F. Stunt,* ed. Neil T.R. Dickson and T.J. Marinello, pp. 77–105. Glasgow: Brethren Archivists and Historians Network.

Summerton, Pauline. 2000. "Cholmeley Evangelical Church, Highgate, London, 1884–1994: A History From a Personal Perspective". *Brethren Archivists and Historians Network Review* 2 (2000): 3–12.

Sunquist, Scott W. 1995. "Dyer, Samuel". In *The Blackwell Dictionary of Evangelical Biography, 1730–1860*, Vol. II, ed. Donald M. Lewis, p. 338. London: Blackwell Reference.

Talib, Sayyidah. 1991. *My Times are in his Hands: A Biography of Dr. Benjamin Chew*. Singapore: Singapore Youth for Christ.

Tambiah, Stanley J. 1973. "The Persistence and Transformation of Tradition in Southeast Asia, With Special Reference to Thailand". *Daedelus* 102, 1: 55–84.

Tan, Charles K.H. 1980. "The Teaching of Witness Lee and the Local Church (The Church in Singapore) Evaluated". BA research paper. Singapore Bible College.

Tan Jin Huat. 2011. "Pentecostals and Charismatics in Malaysia and Singapore". In *Asian and Pentecostal: The Charismatic Face of Christianity in Asia*, 2nd ed., ed. Allan Anderson and Edmonton Tang, pp. 227–47. Eugene, Oregon: Wipf and Stock.

Tan, Karen. 2018. "Jim and Ernest Chew: Bound by Brotherhood, Bible, and Billy Graham". Salt & Light (22 September 2018). https://saltandlight.sg/relationships/jim-and-ernest-chew-bound-by-brotherhood-bible-and-billy-graham/ [accessed 9 November 2018].

Tatford, Frederick A. 1984. *That the World May Know Volume 5: The Mysterious Far East*. With an appendix by T. Carson. Bath: Echoes Publications.

Tatham, C. Ernest. 1976. *Let the Tide Come In!* Lake Mary, Florida: Creation House.

Taylor, Dr and Mrs Howard. 1911. *Hudson Taylor in Early Years: The Growth of a Soul.* Reprint. OMF: Littleton, Co., 1998.

Taylor, Hudson. 1986. *J. Hudson Taylor: The Autobiography of a Man Who Brought the Gospel to China*. Previously published under the title *A Retrospect*, 1894. Minneapolis: Bethany House Publishers, 1894.

Teh Phai Lian [T.P. Jean] (Mandarin: Zheng Peiran 鄭沛然). 1948. "這個人" 的福音 ("Zhege Ren" de Fuyin, The Gospel of "This Man"). 聖經報 (*Shengjing Bao*) N.S. 2, 2: 1–4.

________. [Cheng Pei Jan]. 1950. "勸人受恩歸道" (*Quanren Shou'en Guidao*, Exhortation to accept God's Grace). 聖經報 (*Shengjing Bao*) N.S. 4, 6.

________. 1954. "出埃及記裏的福音" (*Qu'ai Jiji li de Fuyin*, The Good News in the Book of Exodus). 聖經報 (*Shengjing Bao*), No. 3: 11–22.

________. [T.P. Lian]. 1957. "約韓三章十六節" (*Yuehan Sanzhang Shiliu Jie*, The Gospel of John Chapter 3 verse 16). 聖經報 (*Shengjing Bao*) 11, 6: 11–22.

________. 1958 [1961]. 故事新講 (*Gushi Xinjiang, A New Explanation of Old Stories*). 滨城：福音堂 (Penang: Gospel Hall).

________. 1962. 故事新講 (*Gushi Xinjiang, A New Explanation of Old Stories*). Vol. 5. Hong Kong: Christian Literature Service (聖文社)。

________. 1964a. 真道辯正：駁"評今日的方言運動"之謬論 (*Zhen Dao Biang Zheng: Bo "Ping Jin Ri de Fangyan Yundong" zhi Miu Lun, Justifying the Truth: A Refutation of* [Wu Enpu's] "Critique of Today's Charismatic Movement"). 滨城：滨城教会 (Penang: Church of Penang).

________. 1964b. 放言灵祷我所经历的 (*Fangyan Lingdao: Wosuo Jinglide, Praying in the Spirit, in Tongues: What I have Experienced*). Penang [Photocopy].

________. 1965. 奶蜜火焰 (*Naimi Huoyan, Milk and Honey, Flames of Fire*). Penang: Church of Penang.

________. n.d. 奶蜜火焰 (*Naimi Huoyan, Milk and Honey, Flames of Fire*). Rev. ed. [Photocopy].

________. 1976a. 生命與能力 (*Shengming yu Nengli, Life and Power*). Mandarin transcription of 1975 Hokkien audiotape, interpreted and recorded by Albert Tan (陈兆旺). Penang: Church of Penang.

________. 1976b. *Life and Power*. English translation of 1975 Hokkien audiotape, interpreted and recorded by Alberta Tan. Penang: Church of Penang.

________. 1980a. *Ancient Chinese Stories with a Modern Message* (Vols. I & II). Translated by Goh Guan Eng. Penang: Tithes Dental and Photo Supply Ltd.

________. 1980b. *Ancient Chinese Stories with a Modern Message* (Vols. III & VI). Translated by Goh Guan Eng.

Teh Phai Lian and Yeoh Kiam Hiong, eds. 1950–63. *Daolu, Zhenli, Shengming* 道路, 真理, 生命 (Way, Truth, and Life). Penang: Burmah Road Gospel Hall.

Thompson, Phyllis. 1960. *Faith by Hearing: The Story of Gospel Recordings*. Los Angeles: Gospel Recordings Incorporated.

Thompson, Roger R. 2007. "Reporting the Taiyuan Massacre: Culture and Politics in the China war of 1900". In *The Boxers, China, and the World*, ed. Robert Bickers and R.G. Tiedemann, pp. 65–92. Lanham, MD: Rowman & Littlefield Publishers.

Tiedemann, R.G. 2008. "Indigenous Agency, Religious Protectorates, and Chinese Interests: The Expansion of Christianity in Nineteenth-Century China". In *Converting Colonialism: Visions and Realities in Mission History, 1706–1914*, ed. Dana Robert, pp. 206–41. Grand Rapids, Michigan/Cambridge: William B. Eerdmans Publishing Company.

________. 2009. *Reference Guide to Christian Missionary Societies in China: From the Sixteenth to the Twentieth Century*. 2nd ed. Armonk, NY: M.E. Sharpe.

________, ed. 2010. *Handbook of Christianity in China*. Leiden: Brill NV.

Toda, Kenji. 2012. "Anti-Opium Movement, Chinese Nationalism and Straits Chinese in the Early Twentieth Century". *Malaysian Journal of Chinese Studies* 1 (2012): 85–100.

Tolstoy, Leo. 1899 [1999]. *Resurrection.* Translated by Louise Maude, Introduction and Notes by Richard F. Gustafson. Oxford: Oxford University Press.

Tong Suit Chee. 2014. *The Brethren Story: 150 Years of History in Singapore.* Singapore: Brethren Networking Fellowship.

Tow, Timothy. 1985. *John Sung My Teacher.* Singapore: Christian Life Publishers.

________. 1993. *Born Again in the Singapore Pentecost.* Singapore: Christian Life Publishers.

________. 1994. *William C. Burns: Grandfather of Bible-Presbyterians.* Singapore: Christian Life Publishers.

Tozer, A.W. 1948. *Let My People Go: The Life of Robert A Jaffray.* Camp Hill, Pennsylvania: Wing Spread Publishers.

Trocki, Carl A. 1990. *Opium and Empire: Chinese Society in Colonial Singapore, 1800–1910.* Ithaca: Cornell University Press.

Tseng, Timothy. 2004–06. "Protestantism in Twentieth-Century Chinese America: The Impact of Transnationalism on the Chinese Diaspora". *The Journal of American-East Asian Relations* 13, Special Vol., *Christianity as an Issue in the History of U.S.-China Relations*: 121–48.

Turnbull, C.M. 2009. *A History of Modern Singapore, 1819–2005.* Singapore: NUS Press.

Turner, W.G. 1944. *John Nelson Darby.* London: C.A. Hammond.

Ung, K.C. 2005. "Know our Roots and Know our Role Models". www.berita-bethel-ung.com/anniversary/Know%20Our%20Roots.doc [accessed 13 October 2018].

Vaters, Karl. 2014. "Every Revival has its own Soundtrack (New Music, Part 1)". http://newsmallchurch.com/new-music-2/ [accessed 31 March 2017].

Veer, Peter van der. 2001. *Imperial Encounters: Religion and Modernity in India and Britain.* Princeton: Princeton University Press.

________. 2014. *The Modern Spirit of Asia: The Spiritual and the Secular in China and India.* Princeton: Princeton University Press.

Ven, Hans van den. 2003. *War and Nationalism in China, 1925–1945.* London: RoutledgeCurzon.

Wacker, Grant. 2001. *Heaven Below: Early Pentecostals and American Culture.* Cambridge: Harvard University Press.

Wagner, C. Peter. 1995. *Praying Through the 100 Gateway Cities of the 10 – 40 Window.* Seattle: YWAM.

Walker, E.A. 1899. *Sophia Cooke; or, Forty-two Years' Work in Singapore.* London: Elliot Stock.

Walker, Kirsty. 2014. "Intimate Interactions: Eurasian Family Histories in Colonial Penang". In *Sites of Asian Interacction: Ideas, Networks and Mobility*, ed. Timothy Norman Harper and Sunil S. Amrith, pp. 79–104. Cambridge: Cambridge University Press.

Walls, Andrew F. 2002. "Eusebius Tries Again: The Task of Reconceiving and Re-visioning the Study of Christian History". In *Enlarging the Story: Perspectives on Writing World Christian History*, ed. Wilbert R. Shenk, pp. 1–21. Maryknoll: Orbis Books.

Wang, Leland (王载 Wang Zai). n.d. "No Bible No Breakfast". http://www.joyfulheart.com/maturity/no-bible-no-breakfast.htm [accessed 27 May 2018].

Wang, Wilson (王峙 Wang Zhi). 1949a. 患难日神的搭救 (*Huannan Ri Shende Dajiu*, God's Deliverance in the Day of Trouble). 聖經報 *Shengjing Bao* (*Bible Magazine*) Pt. 1 NS Vol. 3, No. 2: 80–90.

________. 1949b. 患难日神的搭救 (*Huannan Ri Shende Dajiu*, God's Deliverance in the Day of Trouble). 聖經報 *Shengjing Bao* (*Bible Magazine*) Pt. 2 NS Vol. 3, No. 4: 80–93.

________. 1949c. 神的搭救 (*Shende Dajiu, God's Deliverance in the Day of Trouble*). In English and Chinese. Lexington, Massachusetts.

________. 1956. 台講恩救 (*Taijiang Enjiu, Salvation Sermons*). Hong Kong: The Alliance Press.

Ward, W.R. 2004. "Evangelical Identity in the Eighteenth Century". In *Christianity Reborn: The Global Expansion of Evangelicalism in the Twentieth Century*, ed. Donald M. Lewis, pp. 11–30. Grand Rapids and Cambridge, UK: William B. Eerdmans Publishing Company.

Wardin, Albert W. 2013. *On the Edge: Baptists and Other Free Church Evangelicals in Tsarist Russia*. Eugene, Oregon: Wipf and Stock.

Warne, Frederick G. 1934. *George Müller The Man of Faith and the Work Established by Him*. London: Pickering and Inglis.

Watt, James G. 1981. "Battle for America". *Full Gospel Business Men's Voice* 31, 10: 2–7, 28.

Wee, Dr Peter H.L. 1997. *Woman's Head Covering & the Glory of GOD*. 2nd ed. Singapore: Eudokia Book Room.

Wee, Samuel T.W. 1996. *Robinson and Bethesda*. Singapore: Bethesda Hall (Ang Mo Kio).

________. 2014. *Simply Gathered in the Malayan Peninsula*. Singapore: Ho Printing.

________. 2015. *Losing Sight: A Review of One Hundred and Fifty Years of Assembly Testimony in Singapore*. Singapore: Ho Printing.

West, Gerald T. 2016. *From Friends to Brethren: The Howards of Tottenham—Quakers, Brethren, and Evangelicals*, ed. Tim Grass. Troon, Ayrshire: Brethren Archivists and Historians Network.

White, Chris. 2017. *Sacred Webs: The Social Lives and Networks of Minnan Protestants, 1840s–1920s*. Leiden: Koninklijke Brill.

White, E. Aldersey. 1932. *A Woman Pioneer in China. The Life of Mary Ann Aldersey*. London: Livingston Press.

Whitehouse, John Owen. 1896. "No. 395 Lechler, John Michael". *London Missionary Society: A Register of Missionaries Deputations Etc. From 1796 to 1896*, 120. London: London Missionary Society.

Whittaker, Thomas E.I. 2016. "Providence, Prophecy, and Prosperity: Rethinking the 'Romantic' Premillennialism of the 1920s through the Faith Principle of Anthony Norris Groves". In *The Brethren and Mission: Essays in Honour of Timothy C.F. Stunt*, ed. Neil T.R. Dickson and T.J. Marinello, pp. 23–48. Glasgow: Brethren Archivists and Historians Network.

Williams, William Plumbridge, compiler. 1856. *The Acts of the Legislative Council of India, relating to the Madras Presidency, from 1848 to 1855*. Madras: The Church of Scotland Mission press.

Williamson, Rev. G.R. 1848. *Memoir of the Rev. David Abeel, D.D. Late Missionary to China*. New York: Robert Carter.

Willard, W. Wyeth. 1950. *Fire on the Prairie: The Story of Wheaton College*. Wheaton: Van Campen Press.

Wilson, Elisabeth. 2003. "Your Citizenship is in Heaven: Brethren Attitudes to Authority and Government". *Brethren Archivists and Historians Network Review* 2: 75–90.

Wilson, Renate. 1998. "Philanthropy in 18th-Century Central Europe: Evangelical Reform and Commerce". *Voluntas: International Journal of Voluntary and Nonprofit Organizations* 9, 1: 81–102.

________. 2000. *Pious Traders in Medicine: A German Pharmaceutical Network in Eighteenth-Century North America*. University Park: The Pennsylvania State University Press.

A Witness and a Testimony. 1923–71. Guildford and London: Billing and Sons.

Wittfogel, Karl A. 1951. "The Influence of Leninism-Stalinism on China". *Annals of the American Academy of Political and Social Science* Vol. 277, *Report on China* (September 1951): 22–34.

Wong, Hoover. 2000. "Wang, Leland Wang (1898–1975)". In *Evangelical Dictionary of World Missions*, ed. A. Scott Moreau, p. 1005. Grand Rapids, Michigan: Baker Books.

Wong, James. 2002. "The Life Ministry of Canon James Wong (Parts 1 & 2): A Prequel to the CHC Story". In *Harvest Times Bimonthly Magazine* 16 (January/February) & 17 (March/June).

Woodbridge, David. 2016. "'Finding that more in accordance with what they saw in the Word' Watchman Nee and the Brethren in China". *The Brethren and Mission:*

Essays in Honour of Timothy C. F. Stunt, ed. Neil T.R. Dickson and T.J. Marinello, pp. 301–13. Glasgow: Brethren Archivists and Historians Network.

________. 2019. *Missionary Primitivism and Chinese Modernity: The Brethren in Twentieth-Century China*. Leiden: Brill.

Woods, Grace W. 1927. *The Half Can Never Be Told*. World Wide Revival Prayer Movement.

Wu Enpu (Elisha Wu) 吳恩溥. 1964. 評今日的方言運動 (*Ping Jinr de Fangyan Yundong, A Critique of Today's Charismatic Movement*), Pts. I & 2. Hong Kong: Shengwenshe. 香港： 聖文社.

________. 1981. 辨别圣灵与邪灵 (*Bianbie Shengling yu Xieling, Distinguishing the Holy Spirit from Evil Spirits*). 香港：聖文社 (Hong Kong: Shengwenshe). Taibei: Xiaoyuan Shufang Zhongjin. 台北：校園書房中心. https://wellsofgrace.com/messages/wueb/spirit/index.htm [accessed 1 September 2018].

Xinyang Duben, Good News Reader (信仰讀本). N.d. Singapore.

Yu, Moses Lee-Kung. 2000. Acknowledgements in "Aspects of the Emergence of the Chinese Church from the Missionary Movement, 1900–1949". PhD thesis in Theology, University of South Africa.

Zetzsche, Jost Oliver. 1999. *The Bible in China: The History of the Union Version or The Culmination of Protestant Missionary Bible Translation in China*. Sankt Augustin, Germany: Monumenta Serica Monograph Series XLV.

Zhang Xiantao. 2007. *The Origins of the Modern Chinese Press: The Influence of the Protestant Missionary Press in Late Qing China*. London and New York: Routledge.

Zheng Peiran. See Teh Phai Lian.

Zheng Yangwen. 2017. *Sinicizing Christianity*. Leiden: Brill.

Index

Page numbers in *italics* refer to illustrations and maps.